Essay Essentials
WITH READINGS

THIRD EDITION

Essay Essentials

WITH READINGS

THIRD EDITION

SARAH NORTON & BRIAN GREEN

THOMSON

NELSON

Australia   Canada   Mexico   Singapore   Spain   United Kingdom   United States

THOMSON
NELSON

**Essay Essentials with Readings,
Third Edition**

Sarah Norton and
Brian Green

Editorial Director and Publisher:
Evelyn Veitch

Acquisitions Editor:
Anne Williams

Marketing Manager:
Cara Yarzab

Developmental Editor:
Klaus Unger

Senior Developmental Editor:
Mike Thompson

Production Editor:
Natalia Denesiuk

Senior Production Coordinator:
Hedy Sellers

Copy Editor:
Joan Rawlin

Creative Director:
Angela Cluer

Proofreader:
Emily Ferguson

Interior Design:
Sonya V. Thursby,
Opus House Incorporated

Interior Design Modifications:
Gabriel Sierra

Cover Design:
Ken Phipps

Cover Image:
© Vinnie Amesse/Photonica

Compositor:
Susan Calverley

Indexer:
Jin Tan

Printer:
Webcom

**National Library of Canada
Cataloguing in Publication Data**

Norton, Sarah, 1941–
  Essay essentials with readings /
Sarah Norton, Brian Green.—3rd ed.

Includes bibliographical references
and index.
ISBN 0-17-622454-8

1. Essay—Authorship. 2. Report
writing. 3. English language—
Rhetoric. 4. College readers.
I. Green, Brian. II. Title.

PE1471.N69 2002   808'.042
C2002-905029-4

Preface: To the Instructor

Essay Essentials with Readings, Third Edition, is designed for Canadian college students who are learning to write for academic and professional purposes. The book has been substantially revised to include a new chapter on style and usage, an expanded section on research and documentation, a streamlined workbook, and 16 new essays, 8 of them by student writers. Chosen for their value as good prose models as well as for their appeal to a broad spectrum of student interests, these essays represent a variety of styles in the middle range of the language register. We have avoided the extremes of stiffly formal and slangy popular style and selected pieces that demonstrate the levels of language that are appropriate for most academic, technical, business, and public writing.

Essay Essentials with Readings is divided into six parts. The first three sections explain, exemplify, and provide practice in planning, drafting, revising, and editing.[1] Because most people learn better and with more satisfaction in concert with other learners, many of the exercises are interactive. Some involve the whole class, but most are designed to be done in pairs or groups. These exercises begin with a discussion to clarify the assignment and motivate students, proceed to a writing task, and conclude with a peer review to enhance and reinforce learning. A primary goal of this book is to show students that effective writing necessarily involves revising and editing. To this end, we have incorporated these phases of the writing process in various ways throughout the book.

Part Four, Patterns of Development, offers explanations and examples of the traditional rhetorical modes. The emphasis in this section is on exposition, the kind of writing students will be required to produce both in college and on the job. Part Four begins with description and narration, strategies that are often required in expository writing, and concludes with a new treatment of argumentation. Each chapter contains a selection of readings to illustrate the mode or pattern under discussion and concludes with a longer, more complex essay that employs a combination of writing strategies. The questions following each essay are designed to promote understanding of the essay's structure and development as well as to provoke thinking and discussion.

---

[1]Note that answers to exercises marked with an asterisk are provided in Appendix A. Answers to other exercises are available on our Web site.

Part Five, The Research Paper, has been revised to include a fuller discussion of the responsible use of electronic source materials and their documentation. In response to users' requests, we have rewritten the chapter on incorporating source information into research papers. For essays on non-literary topics, we encourage students to rely more on summary and paraphrase and less on direct quotation. Part Five concludes with two model research papers, one on a topic of general interest and the other a critical analysis of a literary work. Purchasing *Essay Essentials* gives students access to InfoTrac®, a database that catalogues more than 600 periodicals and journals. Having an online library of easy-to-search reliable sources at their fingertips will facilitate students' learning in all of their courses as well as their mastery of the research and documentation skills covered in Part Five.

Part Six, the workbook section of the text, reviews the basics of syntax, grammar, punctuation, and spelling. We assume that many students will be working through this unit on their own, and answers to most of the exercises are provided in the back of the book. The four sections of this unit can be covered in any order, but the chapters within each section are interdependent and should be studied sequentially, since competency in later chapters often depends on mastery of previous ones.

Inside the front cover is a Guide to Revision. We encourage students to use the Guide as a checklist with which to revise and edit their work. Instructors can duplicate the guide, attach a copy to each student's paper, and mark ✔or ✘ beside each point to identify the paper's strengths and weaknesses. This strategy provides students with specific feedback in a consistent format; it also saves hours of marking time.

New to this edition is a Web site designed to support both teachers and learners (**http://www.essayessentials3e.nelson.com**). Students who need more practice than is included in the text will find additional exercises and self-scoring practice tests on the Web site. The site also provides information that could not conveniently be included in the text itself. For example, details of APA format and documentation complement the MLA-based instruction and examples given in Chapter 22; an overview of logical reasoning and common logical fallacies supplement the introduction to argumentation in Chapter 19. There are also definitions and examples of the parts of speech and common sentence patterns, links to reference sites, a write-in "Ask the Authors" feature, and much more. The instructors' site includes a teaching manual; interactive exercises; suggested answers for most of the questions in Parts One through Five; answers to the chapter Mastery Tests in Part Six; PowerPoint slides and transparency masters; *The Essentials Test Manual* (a comprehensive bank of multiple-choice diagnostic and pre- and post-tests); reading and reference links; and a writers' forum:

a direct link to the authors for comments, criticisms, questions, and dialogue on the text, on teaching, or on writing problems.

Nelson provides another resource to make teaching and managing your course even easier. With MyCourse 2.0 instructors can create their own Web site without any prior knowledge of programming or html. Provided free of charge upon adoption of any Thomson Learning title, MyCourse allows you to post a syllabus, create quizzes, and manage your gradebook in one easy-to-use platform. For more information about this customizable solution and how it can make teaching your class easier, visit **http://mycourse.thomsonlearning.com** or contact your Nelson sales representative for more information.

Acknowledgments

Much of the new material in this edition is attributable to the efforts of colleagues and friends across Canada. We wish, first, to record our special thanks to Paul Allen, Jess Friedland, Danny Irvine, Rita Klein-Geltink, Bernie Kowalewski, and Shandi Mitchell, whose work we are proud to introduce in this edition, and to Deborah Bowen (Redeemer University College), Paul Hutchinson (Niagara College), and Susan Lieberman (Grant MacEwan College), who suggested these new student contributors. In addition to identifying errors and oversights, our reviewers offered helpful comments and suggestions: Janine Falck, Mount Royal College; Sherry Finney, University College of Cape Breton; Tom Gwin, Red Deer College; Christine Kirchner, Camosun College; Paul Hutchinson, Niagara College; Melanie A. Rubens, Seneca College; and Susan Wilson, Camosun College. We are indebted to Sue Bartlett (Niagara College) and Nell Waldman (Centennial College) for their help in updating the book's information on research and documentation skills. We thank Centennial College for permission to reproduce portions of the *Revised Style Sheet* in Part Five and on the Web site. Carmen Gindi (Fanshawe College) and Chris Petty (Red River College) contributed suggestions and examples for the argumentation chapter. Kendra Brown's patient assistance with the detailed revisions to Part Six enabled us to meet, just barely, our deadline. And finally, we wish to thank Valerie Grabove, who created many of the interactive exercises that help students learn to write if not with ease, at least with some enjoyment.

Sarah Norton
Brian Green

Contents

PART SIX A Review of the Basics

Introduction: Why, What, and How to Learn to Write

Few people enjoy writing; after all, it's hard work. Writing is a complex process, a learned skill that requires patience, concentration, and persistence. Unlike most of the skills you acquire in a career program, however, writing is not job-specific. The skills you learn from this book will be useful to you not only in all your college courses, but also in every job you hold throughout your working life. If you have graduated from college or university, your prospective employer will assume that you are able to communicate in writing frequently, correctly, and in a manner that will do credit to the company. The higher you climb on the organizational ladder, the more you will write and the more complex your writing tasks will become. Furthermore, evaluations of your performance in any job will be based at least in part on your communication skills.

Essay Essentials will teach you to write essays of various kinds. The word "essay" comes from the French *essayer*, to try or attempt. An essay is an attempt to communicate information, opinion, or emotion. In the context of a college or university, an essay is an exercise that gives students an opportunity to explore and explain their own and others' thoughts about a subject. In the larger world, essays appear in newspapers and magazines as editorials, reviews, opinion pieces, and commentaries on news and public affairs.

If at times the essay form seems a little artificial, or unrelated to the kinds of writing you expect to do in your profession, remember that thinking, organizing, and researching are basic to all practical writing tasks. In this book, you will learn to find and organize thoughts, to develop ideas in coherent paragraphs, and to express yourself clearly, correctly, and concisely. Once you've mastered these basics, you can develop any job-specific writing styles that may be required of you. If you can write well-organized, convincing, and error-free essays of five or more paragraphs, you will have no difficulty adapting your skills to business or technical reports, instructions, proposals, memoranda, sales presentations, commercial scripts, or legal briefs.

There can be little doubt that literacy is in decline. People do not write as often or as well as they once did. But this fact does not make the ability to write less important; in fact, it means that those who can write competently are in high demand. You can learn to write well if you are willing to work at it. We have designed this text to enable you to master the theory of good writing and to practise it successfully. Because it is more fun and more efficient to learn with others than it is to struggle alone, we have included many group-based exercises. To make the process less onerous, we have also introduced a few humorous essays, and, in Part Six, as many entertaining exercises as we could think of. If you purposefully choose to learn how to write and you follow the guidelines in this book, you will produce effective essays in college and creditable communications in your career.

THE WEB SITE

In addition to the material in this book, you will find useful information and helpful exercises on our Web site. Go to **www.essayessentials3e. nelson.com**, click on "Students' Site" and enter your password to find the menu of options available to you. Under "More Information" you will find helpful supplements to the book, and under "More Practice" you will find additional exercises for the chapters in Part Six. The answers to these exercises are marked automatically, so you will know instantly whether or not you have understood the material. Also on the Web site are practice tests, reference links, an "Ask the Authors" button that allows you to send us any questions you may have about *Essay Essentials* or about your writing, and a "Mailbag" where we post (anonymously) questions and answers that may be helpful to other readers. Purchase of this book also entitles you to free access to InfoTrac®, an easy-to-use online library of source materials you can use for your research in this and other courses. You will learn more about InfoTrac® and other databases in Chapter 20.

WHAT THE SYMBOLS MEAN

When this symbol appears in the margin beside an exercise, it means the exercise is designed to be done by two or more students working together. Carefully read the directions that introduce the exercise to find out how many students should participate and what task is to be performed. Often you are instructed to begin work in a pair or group, then to work individually on a writing task, and finally to regroup and review your writing with your partner(s).

This symbol means "note this." We've used it to highlight writing tips, helpful hints, hard-to-remember points, and information that you should apply whenever you write, not just when you are dealing with the specific principle covered in the paragraph marked by the icon.

When an exercise in the workbook is marked with this icon, it means the activity is a mastery test—an exercise designed to check your level of understanding of the principles covered in the chapter you have just completed. The answers to these exercises are not in the back of the book; your instructor will provide them.

GO TO WEB

EXERCISE

When this symbol appears in the text, it means that you will find on the *Essay Essentials* Web site information or exercises to supplement the chapter you are working on. Once you've logged on to the Web site, click on the button that says "More Practice," then click on "Web Exercises." The information and exercises are listed by chapter, so to get to the exercises for the apostrophe, for example, click on Chapter 41 in the list, then go to the numbered exercises identified for you below the icon.

THE PROCESS OF WRITING

Writing is a three-step process consisting of
1. planning or prewriting
2. drafting
3. revising and editing

This book explains and illustrates two approaches to the process of writing: top-down and bottom-up. The **top-down approach** assumes that you know what you have to say before you begin to write. You identify your subject and main points, draft your thesis statement (the statement that orients your readers to the content of the paper), and plan your topic sentences (those sentences that identify the content of each paragraph). Research papers, business reports, and essay questions on exams are examples of writing that requires a "top-down" approach.

The **bottom-up approach** is useful when you do not know ahead of time what you want to say. You discover your meaning through the act of writing. With this approach, you rely on prewriting strategies such as brainstorming and freewriting to "get into" the process of writing.

You will probably need to use both approaches. Sometimes you will discover your subject through writing; at other times, using "top-down" strategies will help you to express clearly what you already know. You should experiment with both approaches so that you can comfortably use whichever is more appropriate for a particular writing task.

WHAT YOUR READERS EXPECT

Whichever approach you use, your goal is to make your finished essay easy for your readers to read and understand. To achieve that goal, you must meet your readers' expectations.

Readers have five unconscious expectations when they begin to read a piece of extended prose. They expect to find

- paragraphs
- a sentence (usually the first) in each paragraph that identifies the topic
- unified paragraphs, each of which explores a single topic
- connections (transitions) within and between paragraphs
- a preview (in the introduction) of the content and organization of the paper

Keep in mind that readers want to obtain information quickly and easily, without backtracking. They rely on the writer—you—to make efficient reading possible.

Your readers will read more easily and remember more of what they read if you include a thesis statement to introduce them to the content and organization of the piece, and if you begin each paragraph with a topic sentence. If you do not organize and develop your paper and its paragraphs in a clearly identifiable way, readers will impose their own organization on the paper. The result will be longer reading time, or difficulty in understanding and remembering the content, or, worse, the assumption that a paragraph or even the whole paper has a meaning other than the one you intended. You can help your readers to read efficiently if you follow the old adage: "Tell them what you're going to tell them; tell them; then tell them what you've told them."

HOW TO BEGIN

We have all listened to people who talk on and on in conversation and never seem to get to the point. Perhaps these speakers have no point to make or are hoping one will turn up as they speak. For their unfortunate listeners, the experience is both tiresome and frustrating. Readers react similarly to poor writing. An essay—or any other form of written communication—that has no point and that rambles on will turn them off.

How can you avoid boring, confusing, or annoying your readers? To begin with, you need to have something to say and a reason for saying it. Very few people can write an essay straight through from start to finish without spending a considerable amount of time thinking and planning. Some prewriting will help you to develop the structure more easily; freewriting and brainstorming (Chapter 3 will explain these) are useful to stimulate thinking.

Once you've determined what it is you want to say, you need to arrange your main points in the most effective order possible. If you organize your ideas carefully, you won't ramble. Writing an essay is like building a house. If you have a clear plan or blueprint, you can construct the house without the frustration of having to tear down misplaced walls or convert windows to doors. You are less likely to need to double back or even to start all over again from the beginning. A good plan saves time.

As a general rule, the more time you spend on prewriting and planning, the less time you'll need to spend on drafting and revising. Careful planning will enable you to produce papers that your readers will find clear and understandable.

THE PARTS OF AN ESSAY

An essay, like most other forms of oral and written communication, has a beginning, a middle, and an end. The most basic form is the five-paragraph essay, which we outline and illustrate below. Will you be writing five-paragraph essays in your other courses or on the job? Probably not. You will, however, be required to write other highly structured forms of prose: research papers, memoranda, minutes, proposals, and reports are just a few examples. The five-paragraph essay is the shortest, simplest format that teaches you everything you need to know about writing nonfiction prose. Think of it not as a straitjacket that stifles your creativity, but rather as a pattern to follow while you develop the skills and abilities you need to build other, more complex prose structures.

The beginning, or **introduction**, tells your reader the point, the purpose, and the scope of your essay. If your introduction is well crafted, its **thesis statement** will identify the main points you will discuss in the paragraphs that follow.

The middle, or **body**, of an essay consists of paragraphs that discuss in detail the points that have been identified in the introduction. In a short essay, each paragraph develops a separate main point. Each paragraph should contain three essential components:

- a **topic sentence**, which identifies the point of the paragraph
- development, or **support**, of the topic sentence. Supporting sentences provide the detailed information the reader needs in order to understand the point.
- a **concluding sentence** that either brings the discussion of the topic to a close or provides a transition to the next paragraph

The end, or **conclusion**, of an essay is a brief final paragraph. Unless your essay is very short, you summarize the main points to reinforce them for the reader, then say goodbye with a statement that will give your readers something to think about after they have finished reading your essay.

Bertrand Russell's "What I Have Lived For" is a good example of a well-structured essay. The introduction contains a clear thesis statement. Each paragraph of the body consists of a clearly identifiable topic sentence, development sufficient to explain it, and a concluding sentence. The conclusion is brief, pointed, and memorable.

WHAT I HAVE LIVED FOR
Bertrand Russell

INTRODUCTION
Thesis statement

Three passions, simple but overwhelmingly strong, have governed my life: the longing for love, the search for knowledge, and unbearable pity for the suffering of mankind. These passions, like great winds, have blown me hither and thither, in a wayward course, over a deep ocean of anguish, reaching to the very verge of despair.

BODY
Topic sentence

Support

Concluding sentence

I have sought love, first, because it brings ecstasy—ecstasy so great that I would often have sacrificed all the rest of life for a few hours of this joy. I have sought it, next, because it relieves loneliness—that terrible loneliness in which one shivering consciousness looks over the rim of the world into the cold unfathomable lifeless abyss. I have sought it, finally, because in the union of love I have seen, in a mystic miniature, the prefiguring vision of the heaven that saints and poets have imagined. This is what I sought, and though it might seem too good for human life, this is what—at last—I have found.

Topic sentence

Support

Concluding sentence

With equal passion I have sought knowledge. I have wished to understand the hearts of men. I have wished to know why the stars shine. And I have tried to apprehend the Pythagorean power by which number holds sway above the flux. A little of this, but not much, I have achieved.

Topic sentence

Support

Concluding sentence

CONCLUSION

Love and knowledge, so far as they were possible, led upward toward the heavens. But always pity brought me back to earth. Echoes of cries of pain reverberate in my heart. Children in famine, victims tortured by oppressors, helpless old people a hated burden to their sons, and the whole world of loneliness, poverty, and pain make a mockery of what human life should be. I long to alleviate the evil, but I cannot, and I too suffer.

This has been my life. I have found it worth living, and would gladly live it again if the chance were offered me.

Russell, Bertrand. "What I Have Lived For." Prologue. *The Autobiography of Bertrand Russell.* By Russell. Boston: Little, Brown, 1967. 3–4.

PART 1

Planning

1

Your Audience and You

Before you begin to write anything—an essay, a report, an e-mail message, or a set of instructions—you must have something to write about (your subject) and someone to write for (your audience). Writing is communication, and for communication to take place, you (the writer) must be able to make your ideas or message clear to your readers.

Addressing Your Readers

Keep your audience in mind as you plan, draft, and revise your paper. How old are they? What is their level of education? Profession? Income? What is their cultural background? Gender? Does it matter? While you must be careful to avoid generalizing or stereotyping, the answers to these questions do influence most people's views, and you would be wise to consider them before you begin to write.

It may help if you think of every piece of writing as if it were a letter.

Before you begin to plan an essay, write at the top of the page the specific audience for whom your message is intended.

Naturally, your instructor is going to be reading your early (and your late) assignments, but, for your first draft, you should write at the top of the page the name of someone other than your instructor whom you might expect to be interested in your subject. Be creative: your high school principal, a recent immigrant, a union official, a member of the Liberal Party, a religious leader, the CEO of a polluting company, someone receiving social assistance income. Keeping this reader in mind will help you to plan, develop, and write your assignment in a tone and style appropriate to your message.

Spend a little time thinking about your subject in relation to your audience. Consider carefully the following three questions when you are deciding what to include in your essay.

1. What does my reader know about my subject?
2. What is my reader's attitude toward my subject?
3. What are my reader's needs in regard to my subject?

READERS' KNOWLEDGE

The first question will help you choose the kind and amount of information you include. Are you writing for someone who knows little about your subject, or for someone with fairly detailed knowledge? Do you have to cover all the basics, or can you take it for granted your reader is familiar with them? You don't want to bore your audience by telling them things they already know. On the other hand, if you fail to provide information they need in order to understand your message, you'll turn them off or lose them entirely.

READERS' ATTITUDES

The second question helps you decide how to approach your subject. Will your audience be sympathetic to what you have to say? If so, you will aim to reinforce their agreement. You will probably state your opinion up front, to show you're on their side. If, however, you think they may be hostile to what you have to say, you might lessen their resistance by providing reasons and support for your ideas before revealing your point of view. Gentle persuasion is usually more effective than confrontation in writing, as it is in life.

READERS' NEEDS

The third question helps you to decide whether to persuade or instruct, to compare or classify, to describe or analyze. Which approach will give your audience the information they need about your subject? The answers to this question will determine whether your remarks should be fairly general or quite specific. Is it your intention to add to or reinforce your readers' general knowledge, or is your information to be applied in specific situations?

Reflecting Yourself

Once you are clear about who your readers are, what they know, and what they need to know, you should spend a little time considering your role in the communication process. Any time you speak or write, you present yourself in a particular way to your audience. We all play a variety of roles. We choose a role, often unconsciously, that we hope will suit the expectations of the people we are communicating with. These roles are not false or hypocritical; they are simply facets of our personality that we try to match to the needs of each situation. Choosing and maintaining an appropriate role is essential in successful communication.

Each day, for example, you meet a variety of people. Some of them you know well—parents, siblings, friends, classmates, teachers, co-workers, supervisors. Others you know only casually—the cashier in the restaurant, the police officer at the radar trap, the enumerator for the upcoming election, the checkout person in the grocery store. With each of these people, whether the contact is casual or intense, you consciously or unconsciously adjust your language in order to communicate. If you speak to your spouse as you might to your dog, you'll be sleeping on the couch. If you speak to a salesperson as you would to a love interest, you'll get arrested.

Consider the following three questions when you are deciding what role would be most appropriate in a particular communication situation.

1. What is my purpose in writing?
2. What is my attitude toward my subject?
3. What are my readers' expectations of me in this communication?

YOUR PURPOSE

The most common purposes of writing are to inform, to persuade, and to entertain. Your purpose will depend largely on the needs and expectations of your readers. It will influence your choice of supporting details to develop your points and will affect your tone. How you say something often has more impact on your audience than what you say.

YOUR ATTITUDE

The second question requires you to clarify your attitude to the subject of your paper. This involves more than simply asking, "Am I for or against it?" You should consider how strongly you feel about the subject because your attitude will influence your tone as well as the kinds of evidence you present. You should also think about how personal you want to be in presenting your ideas, or how balanced and objective you wish (or are able) to be. To help you answer these questions, consider how closely your attitude toward the subject aligns with your audience's attitude. If your views coincide, then a fairly informal approach may be appropriate; if they differ, then an impersonal, objective approach is preferable.

YOUR ROLE

The third question requires you to think about what role your audience is likely to expect of you. If you write as an authority, will you be credible? If you write as a peer or friend, will you be effective? What are your readers likely to expect from someone in your position writing to them on this subject? Taking the time to think about your readers' expectations will help you to make appropriate choices with respect to the point of view you take, the examples and support you provide for your ideas, and the level of language you use.

You should know that many colleges and universities expect students to write academic papers in an impersonal, non-conversational style. Formal papers use third person pronouns (*he, she, one, they*). Informal, personal writing with first and second person pronouns (*I* and *you*) may not be acceptable. (For an explanation of "person," see page 478.) Check with your instructor to find out what policy applies at your school and follow it.

Levels of Language

There are many **levels of language** in spoken English. They range from almost unintelligible mutters and groans, through slang and colloquialisms, right up to the formal English used in the law courts and on ceremonial occasions. A parallel range is possible in written English: from graffiti up to the formal report.

The key to finding the appropriate level for your message is to consider not only the subject but also the receiver. Sometimes compromises must be made, as when you send one message to a wide variety of receivers. In general, you aim at the highest level of receiver and trust that the others will understand. Thus, wedding invitations, even those to the bridegroom's buddies, are usually stylized and formal.

No one has to tell you what level of language to use when you communicate with your friends; that level has been established over many years.

In other circumstances, however, it may not be clear what level you should be using. At such times, you need to consider your reader's preference. If your sociology teacher wants you to write papers in a formal style, and you want to get good marks, you will have to write formally. Likewise, because employers generally favour formal letters of application over casual ones, if you want to get a job, you will have to write your letter in a formal style. A more relaxed and personal style may be appropriate for a talk given to your class. Most of what you read and write falls somewhere between these two extremes. Business writing, for example, usually employs what is called general level standard written English.

There are no hard-and-fast divisions of language; the three levels often overlap. To help you choose the style most appropriate for your message and audience, we have outlined the basic characteristics of informal, general, and formal language in the table below.

	Informal	General	Formal
Vocabulary and Style	Casual, everyday; usually concrete; some slang, colloquial expressions, contractions. Written in 1st and 2nd persons.	The language of educated persons; nonspecialized; balance of abstract and concrete; readily understood. Can use 1st, 2nd, and 3rd persons.	Often abstract, technical, or specialized; no contractions or colloquialisms. Written in 3rd person.
Sentence and Paragraph Structure	Sentences short, simple; some sentence fragments; paragraphs short.	Complete sentences of varying length; paragraphs vary, but are often fairly short.	All sentences complete; sentences usually long, complex; paragraphs fully developed, often at length.
Tone	Conversational, casual; sounds like ordinary speech.	Varies to suit message and purpose of writer.	Impersonal, serious, often instructional.
Typical Uses	Personal letters, some fiction, some newspapers, much advertising.	Most of what we read: newspapers, magazines, novels, business correspondence.	Academic writing, some textbooks, scientific reports, some journal articles, legal documents.

No one level is "better" than another. Each has its place and function. Your message, your audience, and your purpose in writing are what should determine which level you choose.

Read the following selections and consider each writer's purpose, the audience for whom the message is intended, and why the writer's level of language is appropriate to the readers, the subject, and the purpose.

INFORMAL

I love baseball the way some people love candy, but even I don't understand all the rules. I'd like to tell you about a rule that I do understand but, from what I've seen and heard at the ball park, not many other people have figured out. That's the balk rule.

The reason for the rule is so that a runner at first base can't be tricked unfairly by the pitcher. Let's say you've made it to first base. Your next goal is to get to second base. OK, I'm the pitcher and I've got two jobs. First, I've got to try to get the next batter out, and second, I've got to make sure you don't get to second base. Without the balk rule, I could wind up and make all the motions as if I were going to throw a pitch and then, at the last second, whip the ball over to the first baseman. Bingo! You're out because you've taken a lead away from the base toward second to get a head start. If I were allowed to do this, you'd never take a lead away from the base, would you? You'd stick right on the bag and wait until there was a safe hit before taking off for second. That would take a lot of the exciting plays out of the game. Plays like steals, advancing to third on a single, and the hit-and-run would be out the window.

The only way to keep a balance between your being able to make it to second and my being able to get you out is to make sure I can't trick you like that. The balk rule says that I have to come to a complete stop before throwing the ball. After that pause, I have to throw to the plate or to first base, but I must move clearly one way or the other. In other words, I can't make a motion toward the plate, even with my knee or foot, and then throw to first. This protects you from being fooled by me and allows you to take a reasonable lead.

Who is the intended audience? These paragraphs are intended for general readers, but not people who are seeking a definitive and legal description of the baseball rule. The writer assumes some knowledge of and interest in the subject, but not much expertise.

What is the writer's role? The writer is seeking to inform readers, but not by coming across as a teacher or an expert. This sort of information is discussed among friends. One can imagine the writer and the audience sharing a relaxed and informal conversation about their favourite game.

Why is the level of language appropriate? The use of contractions and colloquialisms ("out the window," "OK," "taking off") and especially the use of the first and second persons ("I"—the pitcher—and "you"—the baserunner) clearly mark this as an informal and friendly communication. Short sentences and many instances of conversation style ("a lot," "your being able to make it to second") add to the informal tone.

GENERAL

A good business letter is one that gets results. The best way to get results is to develop a letter that, in its appearance, style, and content, conveys information efficiently. To perform this function, a business letter should be concise, clear, and courteous.

The business letter must be concise. Little introduction or preliminary chat is necessary. Get to the point, make the point, and leave it. It's safe to assume that your letter is being read by a busy person with all kinds of paper to deal with. Such a person does not want to spend much time on a newsy letter about your ski trip or medical problem. Hone and refine your message until the words and sentences you have used are precise. This takes time for revision and rereading but is a necessary part of writing a good letter. A short business letter that makes its point quickly has much more impact on a reader than a long-winded, rambling exercise in creative writing. This does not mean that there is no place for style or even, on occasion, humour in the business letter. While it conveys a message in its contents, the letter also provides the reader with an impression of you, its author: the medium is part of the message.

The business letter must be clear. You should have a firm idea of what you want to say, and you should let the reader know it. Use the structure of the letter—paragraphs, topic sentences, introduction, and conclusion—to guide the reader point by point from your introduction, through your reasoning, to your conclusion. Paragraph often to break up the page and reinforce the organization of the letter. Use an accepted business-letter format: there are several, and they can be found in any book of business English. Reread what you have written from the point of view of someone who is seeing it for the first time, and be sure that all explanations are adequate and all necessary information is provided (including reference numbers, dates, and other identification). A clear message, clearly delivered, is the essence of business communication.

The business letter must be courteous. Sarcasm and insults are ineffective and can often work against you. If you're sure you're right, point that out as politely as possible, explain why you are right, and outline what the reader is expected to do about it. Always put yourself in the place of the person to whom you are writing. What sort of letter would you respond to? How effective would sarcasm and threats be in making you fulfil a request? Another form of courtesy is taking care in your writing and typing of the business letter. Grammatical and spelling errors (even if you call them keying errors) tell a reader that you don't think enough of him or her to be careful. Such mistakes can lower the reader's opinion of you. There are excuses for ignorance; there are no excuses for sloppiness.

The business letter is your custom-made representative. It speaks for you and is a permanent record of your message. It can pay big dividends on the time you invest in giving it a concise message, a clear structure, and a courteous tone.

Who is the intended audience? Readers of this essay will be seeking specific information about business-letter style. They will, therefore, have some knowledge about the subject and a high-school graduate level reading and writing ability.

What is the writer's role? The author is providing information from an expert point of view, but in a friendly way. The use of humour and casual language makes the instruction easy to take. A persuasive element in the essay makes it warmer and gentler than straightforward instruction would be.

Why is the level of language appropriate? There are a few contractions and no slang, both of which are common in informal writing, but the vocabulary and writing style are easily understood by general readers. The use of the second person and direct address ("If you're sure you're right, point that out as politely as possible . . .") adds to the personal nature of the language. Questions addressed to the readers in order to assist persuasion also make the tone more conversational than formal, without ever becoming colloquial. This message is designed to appeal to the widest possible audience.

FORMAL

No human activity is without risk. While some people dwell morbidly on the dangers of life and others blithely ignore them, sensible people seek a middle ground between these two extremes. Those who understand and manage risk are more likely than their fearful or heedless cousins to survive, even enjoy, life's uncertainties.

Most people do not understand risk. Ignorance and fear lead some to worry unnecessarily and others to put themselves in danger's way. The prospect of a camping trip, for example, often triggers anxiety about bears, despite the fact that the chances of being attacked by a bear are far lower than those of being killed by lightning. Indeed, by far the most dangerous part of any wilderness adventure is the drive to get there. Another reason people fail to understand risk is fear of the unknown. Irrationally, humans fear the unfamiliar but accept and ignore commonplace dangers. The chance of drowning in a bathtub is one in 650 000, about the same as the chance of being struck by lightning. But the former is never considered a danger, while the latter often causes irrational terror, especially during spectacular storms. Bears and lightning are exotic but rarely life-threatening; traffic and bathing are commonplace but sometimes treacherous. A realistic understanding of the risks involved in events and activities is the key to being able to manage them.

Risk management is a term most often applied to investment. Knowing their individual willingness and ability to take risks, wise investors make purchases that are consistent with their level of tolerance. The same principle may be applied to everyday life: understanding the risk involved enables people to make appropriate decisions about activities they wish to engage in. The incidence of cigarette smoking, especially among young people, demonstrates that risk management is not widely practised: one in three smokers will die prematurely of tobacco-related illness. Admittedly, it is not possible to live a risk-free life; just getting up each day exposes one to more hazards than staying in bed. But it is possible to choose behaviours that are less dangerous than others, and that choice is critical when high risk factors are present. Anyone who chooses to drink heavily and then operate a snowmobile or power boat, for example, has a 30 to 50 percent chance of being involved in an accident.

On the other hand, risk management does not mean wasting one's life away worrying about personal safety. Part of the excitement of living is taking on challenges and pushing limits, but common sense calls for meeting challenges wisely. Sensible people do not cross the line between adventure and foolhardiness. Going into bear country is an adventure; leaving food lying around the campsite or taking a snack into the tent is foolhardy at best and suicidal at worst. Everyone must engage at least occasionally in potentially harmful behaviours, but wise people manage the risk to minimize the danger. The most dangerous activity most people do regularly is to drive or ride in a car, an act that claims far more lives per occurrence each year than bungee jumping, sky diving, or downhill skiing. Driving aggressively, at high speed, in an unfit vehicle, or without a seatbelt are all behaviours that demonstrably increase the chance of accident and death. It is only sensible to minimize the risks involved in necessary or enjoyable but potentially hazardous activities.

How someone handles the risks of everyday life says much about that person. One who heedlessly ignores risk and participates in dangerous activities while engaging in unsafe practices is a fool. On the other hand, one who sees danger around every corner and cautiously scrutinizes every opportunity in an effort to avoid risk is a coward. As in most of life's choices, the middle ground is best: those who understand risk and learn to manage it stand the best chance of living long and interesting lives.

Who is the intended audience? The readers of this passage are literate and well read. They are likely to be people in an early or middle stage of their career who enjoy the sorts of recreation activities mentioned in the article.

What is the writer's role? The writer's purpose is to reinforce the readers' understanding of the role risk plays in their lives. The writer does not present himself as a distant expert addressing those who are less well informed; rather, his role is that of a knowledgeable peer—someone who also enjoys the activities he uses as examples to support his argument.

Why is the level of language appropriate? The vocabulary is fairly sophisticated but not technical; it is appropriate for the content. There are no contractions or colloquialisms, no first or second person pronouns. The writer addresses his readers as if they were peers, perhaps colleagues in a profession, but not close friends. The frequent use of parallel structure contributes to the formality of the piece and lends weight and seriousness to the subject. The argument is logical and clearly organized; each main point is supported with factual and statistical detail. The style and tone are appropriate for an article in a professional magazine.

Exercise 1.1*

Read the excerpts below and discuss the intended audience, the author's role, and the appropriateness of the language.

1. Until quite recently, respectable women did not wear make-up. Colour on the face suggested passion, and passion was what they were supposed to avoid. Shortly after the First World War, lipstick was referred to as only being appropriate "to repair the ravages of time and disease on the complexion of coquettes." They were probably the only ones to put up with it, too, as it was then little more than a greasy rouge containing crushed and dried insect corpses for colouring, beeswax for stiffness, and olive oil to help it flow—this latter having the unfortunate tendency to go rancid several hours after use. The New York Board of Health considered banning lipstick in 1924, not because of what it might do to the women who wore it, but because of worry that it might poison the men who kissed the women who wore it.

Bodanis, David. *The Secret House: 24 Hours in the Strange and Unexpected World in Which We Spend Our Days and Nights.* New York: Simon & Schuster, 1986. 45–47.

Who is the intended audience? _____

_____

_____

_____

_____

What is the writer's role? _____

_____

_____

_____

_____

Why is the level of language appropriate? _____

_____

_____

_____

_____

2.   The "inletting" or "butt mortise" plane is designed to cut precise mortises for butt hinges, lock fronts, and strike plates, or to repair jambs, doors, furniture, and millwork, wherever the ability to do inletting is important. The plane has a completely open throat so that you can watch what you are doing. The 3/4" wide cutter is set at a 40 degree pitch for general work. This can be increased to 70 degrees (plus or minus) for difficult grain simply by inserting the blade bevel-up. For inletting, such as hinges, you set the blade extension at the hinge leaf thickness, score the outline and plane to depth, using overlapping strokes for a smooth bottom. The same technique would be used for a veneer repair on solid wood.

_____

Lee Valley Catalogue. Tenth Anniversary Issue, 1987–88. 23.

Who is the intended audience? _____

_____

_____

_____

What is the writer's role? _____

_____

_____

_____

_____

Why is the level of language appropriate? _____

_____

_____

_____

_____

3.   Doing business with the Chinese is an enterprise fraught with peril for the unwary Western business person. While in the West most business is ultimately conducted face to face between the principals, negotiations seldom if ever achieve this intimacy in the Orient. It is common for gatherings of ten or more to take part in the early stages of agenda-setting and prioritizing, and the hapless Westerner who has not engaged the services of a Chinese guide will have to sort out the Party overseers from the ineffectual hangers-on and try to hone in on the power brokers who often remain in the background to assess and evaluate before making themselves known. Often the early stages of business relationships are conducted in the very formal atmosphere of banquets, with hierarchical seating arrangements and ritual toasts. Coping with the exotic atmosphere, the oblique method of negotiation, the recondite formality, and the unidentifiable food is a formidable challenge: one that should be undertaken without assistance by only the most intrepid and experienced of Western entrepreneurs.

Czereczovich, Katlin. "Business Abroad." *Canadian Women Entrepreneurs* Spring 2002: 91.

Who is the intended audience? _____

_____

_____

_____

_____

What is the writer's role? _____

_____

_____

_____

_____

Why is the level of language appropriate? _____

_____

_____

_____

_____

4.   A parent quickly learns that no matter how much money you have, you
        will never be able to buy your kids everything they want. You can take a
        second mortgage on your house and buy what you think is the entire
        Snoopy line: Snoopy pajamas, Snoopy underpants, Snoopy linen, Snoopy
        shoelaces, Snoopy cologne, and Snoopy soap, but you will never have it all.
        And if Snoopy doesn't send you to the poorhouse, Calvin Klein will direct
        the trip. Calvin is the slick operator who sells your kids things for eighty-
        five dollars that cost seven at Sears. He has created millions of tiny snobs,
        children who look disdainfully at you and say, "Nothing from Sears."
        However, Dad-Can-I fought back: I got some Calvin Klein labels and sewed
        them into Sears undershorts for my high fashion junkies.

        _____

        Cosby, Bill. *Fatherhood*. New York: Doubleday, 1994. 41–42.

Who is the intended audience?   _____

_____

_____

_____

_____

What is the writer's role?   _____

_____

_____

_____

_____

Why is the level of language appropriate?   _____

_____

_____

_____

_____

5.   The conclusion of *Jane Eyre* has Jane and Rochester married at last. Jane
        no longer needs to compromise herself in order to be with him, and his

first wife is not the only obstacle that has been removed. The man who insisted that she abandon her conscience to live in sin has changed significantly. Rochester now complements Jane as never before. His mutilation has been referred to as a "symbolic castration" by Richard Chase (qtd. in Gilbert and Gubar 368), but it is his spirit rather than his masculinity that seems to have been honed. Rochester has been humbled, and the taste of humility has taught him wisdom. He is able to admit to Jane, "I did wrong: I would have sullied my innocent flower—breathed guilt on its purity" (Brontë 495; ch. 37). During their first engagement, Jane was unsure and often uncomfortable about her place in Rochester's life. In her description of their marriage, however, she says that "we are precisely suited in character—perfect concord is the result" (Brontë 500; ch. 38). Such a perfect fit is only made possible by Rochester's movement away from his earlier extreme. He has become a close match for Jane on every level, and therefore becomes her ideal mate.

Friedland, Jess. "The Evolution of Moral Balance in Charlotte Brontë's *Jane Eyre.*"

Who is the intended audience? _____

_____

_____

_____

_____

What is the writer's role? _____

_____

_____

_____

_____

Why is the level of language appropriate? _____

_____

_____

_____

_____

Exercise 1.2

As a class, select one of the five paragraphs found on pages 18–22. First, be sure you all agree on the intended audience and purpose of the paragraph. Your objective is to "translate" the paragraph for a different audience. The purpose of your revision will be the same as that of the original, but the language and tone will be adapted to suit the audience for whom the new message is intended.

Next, in groups of three, choose an audience for your revision from the following list. (Each group must select a different audience.)

elementary school children	very hip, very cool Grade 12 students
your family	your English instructor
a close friend	*Globe and Mail* readers
an elderly relative	your college newspaper

Once all groups have completed their translations, compare the results by reading the newly translated paragraphs aloud. Try to guess who each other's intended audience is. How do you know? How does the language work to meet the needs of the new audience?

Now let's try an exercise in **role playing**—communicating effectively with an audience by adjusting your role (and your level of language) to suit your purpose, your message, and your audience.

Exercise 1.3

Imagine, in each of the following situations, that you must deal with three different audiences face to face. Before you begin, analyze each audience in terms of knowledge, attitudes, and needs; then clarify the purpose of your message, your attitude toward your subject, and your audience's expectations of you.

1. You prepared your company's sales presentation in PowerPoint and stored it on the hard drive of your notebook computer. On your way to a meeting with clients in Detroit, your notebook was handled very roughly by the customs inspectors at the airport, who tried to pry open the casing. When you got to the sales meeting, your computer would not open PowerPoint.

You made the sales presentation as well as you could, but the clients were not impressed, and your company did not get the contract. Explain these circumstances to

- your supervisor in the sales department
- the U.S. Customs complaint bureau
- a representative of the computer company, which claims its notebook computers are practically indestructible

2. At 8:30 this morning, you got a phone call from your friend Jaron, who was calling from a police station. He had been arrested because, according to the arresting officer, he had 37 unpaid parking tickets outstanding. He claims he's innocent; he's never had a parking ticket. He has called to ask you to come down and bail him out. If you do so, you will be late, probably very late, for work. Jaron refuses to call his parents for help. Tell this story to

- your parents
- your boss
- Jaron's parents

3. You recently bought a pair of silk pants from Bottom Drawers Pants Company. They ripped in the crotch the first time you bent over. You were dancing enthusiastically with a very attractive partner and were deeply embarrassed. Before you could recover your composure, the owner of the club asked you to leave immediately. Tell your story to

- Bottom Drawers
- the owner of the club
- your dancing partner

4. After only three weeks at your new job, you felt you had to tell someone about the thievery that was going on in the workplace. Employees were routinely taking home office supplies, sales samples, and even tools and equipment. After speaking to your union steward and your manager, you were laid off without any explanation or warning, and as a probational employee you have no protection. Explain your situation to

- the president of your union
- a longtime employee of the company who doesn't know why you were let go
- an employment counsellor

5. You are short of money—so short you can't even buy gas for your car. If you can't get gas money, you will be late for work, and your boss is annoyed because you've been late twice this week already. Ask for money from

- your parents
- a friend
- someone who owes you money

6. Turn one of the 15 role-playing situations above into a written assignment.

When you have a clear fix on your intended reader and on your own purpose and role in writing, it's time to turn to the first step in the actual writing of your essay: choosing a suitable subject for your paper.

2

Selecting a Subject

Approximately one-third of the time you devote to producing an essay should be spent on the planning stage. (The remainder is devoted to drafting and revising.) If you take the time to analyze your audience, find a good subject, and identify interesting main points to make about that subject, you will find that the mechanics of writing will fall into place much more easily than if you try to sweat your way through the paper the night before it's due. After you have considered your readers' background, needs, and expectations, the next step is to choose a satisfactory subject to write about.

Even when you are assigned a topic for an essay, you need to examine it, focus it, and consider different ways of approaching it. Depending on your knowledge of the topic and the readers you are writing for, the range of specific subjects for any broad topic is almost endless. For example, given the broad topic "Research sources," here are some of the approaches you might choose from.

Can you trust Internet sources?
Interviewing to develop original source material
Books: still the best "random access device"
Journal indexes: an underused source of mountains of material
How to do an effective Internet search

Your first task, then, is to choose a satisfactory subject, one that satisfies the basic principles of the **4-S test**:

A satisfactory subject is significant, single, specific, and supportable.

If it passes the 4-S test, your subject is the basis of a good essay.

MAKE YOUR SUBJECT SIGNIFICANT

Your subject must be meaningful both to you and to your readers. The subject you choose must be worthy of the time and attention you expect your readers to give to your paper. Can you imagine an essay on "How to buy movie tickets" or "Why I hate pants with button flies," for example, as being significant for most readers?

Exercise 2.1*

From the list below, choose those subjects that would be significant to a typical reader. Revise the others to make them significant, if possible. If not, suggest another, related subject that is significant. When you have finished this exercise, compare your answers with those provided on page 483.

1. Tips for travelling with small children
2. Using the reference library
3. Page-turning techniques
4. The perfect vacation spot
5. How to use the number pad on a calculator
6. Television is a threat to Canadian independence
7. Why you should write on one side of the page only

MAKE YOUR SUBJECT SINGLE

Don't try to crowd too much into one paper. Naturally, different assignments in school and projects on the job will have varying requirements of length and scope, but be careful that your subject is not actually two or three related subjects masquerading as one. If you attempt to write about a multiple subject, your readers will get a superficial and possibly confusing overview instead of the interesting and satisfying detail they expect to find in a well-planned paper. A subject such as "The problem of league expansion in hockey and other sports" includes too much to be dealt with satisfactorily in one essay. You'd need to write a book to give your readers new and significant information on such a broad topic. In an essay, you and your readers will both benefit if you try something like "The problems of league expansion in the NHL" or "Why Halifax can't get an NHL franchise."

Exercise 2.2*

From the following list, choose the subjects that are single and could be satisfactorily explored in a short essay. Revise the others to make them single.

1. Causes of unemployment in British Columbia and Saskatchewan
2. Pub night at different colleges

3. How to change a tire and adjust the timing
4. The importance of accuracy in newspaper and television reporting
5. Methods of preventing the spread of STDs
6. Causes of injury in industry and professional sports
7. Nursing and engineering: rewarding careers

MAKE YOUR SUBJECT SPECIFIC

Given a choice between a broad, general topic and a narrow, specific one, always choose the specific one. Again, assignments and projects will vary in length and scope, but remember that your readers want to be both informed and interested in what you have to say. Most readers find concrete, specific details more interesting than broad generalizations.

It would be difficult to say anything very detailed about a huge subject such as "The roles of women in history," for example. But with some research, you could write an interesting paper on "The roles of women in medieval England" or "Famous female pilots." You can narrow a broad subject and make it more specific by applying one or more *limiting factors* to it. Try thinking of your subject in terms of a specific *kind*, *time*, *place*, *number*, or *person* associated with it. By applying this technique to the last potential subject above, you might come up with "Amelia Earhart's last flight."

Exercise 2.3*

In the list below, identify the subjects that are specific and could be explained satisfactorily in a short essay. Revise the others to make them specific by applying one or more of the limiting factors to each one.

1. Summer employment opportunities in B.C.'s fishing industry
2. Modern heroes
3. How to enjoy winter weather
4. The effects of government cutbacks on low-income families
5. The problems of urban living
6. How to repair your home appliances
7. Binge drinking among college women

MAKE YOUR SUBJECT SUPPORTABLE

You must know something about your subject (preferably more than your readers know), or you must be able to find out about it. Remember, your

readers want information that is new, interesting, and thought-provoking—
not obvious observations familiar to everyone. You must be able to include
specific examples, facts, figures, quotations, anecdotes, or other *supporting details*.
Supporting information can be gathered from your own experience, from the
experience of other people, or from both. If you don't know enough about
your topic to write anything but the obvious, be prepared to do some research.

Exercise 2.4*

From the subjects given below, choose those that are clearly supportable in a
short essay. Revise the others to make them supportable.

1. My career as a student
2. Movie review: *Shrek*
3. Canadian corporate mergers in the year 2000
4. The Chinese secret service
5. Space travel in the year 2100
6. Art through the ages
7. The hazards of working in a fast-food outlet

Exercise 2.5*

Together with a partner, discuss the acceptability of the potential subjects listed
below. Indicate with check marks (✔) whether each subject below passes the
4-S test by being *sig*nificant, *si*ngle, *sp*ecific, and *sup*portable. Revise each
unsatisfactory subject (fewer than four check marks) to make it a satisfactory
subject for a short essay.

The 4-S Test

Subject	sig	si	sp	sup	Revision
1. Computers	___	___	___	___	_____
					_____
2. Insomnia and other stress-related disorders	___	___	___	___	_____
					_____
3. The Arctic 200 years from now	___	___	___	___	_____
					_____

Subject	*sig*	*si*	*sp*	*sup*	Revision
4. Dressing for an interview	——	——	——	——	———————
5. Architecture	——	——	——	——	———————

GO TO WEB

EXERCISE 2.1

Exercise 2.6

Write down three subjects that you think pass the 4-S test. Take your time—this task is not as easy as it sounds. When you've finished, exchange papers with another student and carefully check each other's work.

Now that you've learned how to select an appropriate subject, it's time to move on to the next stage: identifying solid main points to support that subject.

3

Managing the Main Points

While you were selecting subjects and testing them against the four principles presented in Chapter 2, you were thinking about some of the things you might say about each. **Main points** are the two or three or four most important things you have to say about your subject. Selecting them carefully is a vitally important part of the writing process.

Generating Main Points: The Bottom-Up Approach

If you are feeling intimidated by your task and unsure about how to present your subject, some prewriting activities can be helpful. Writers use several methods to stimulate thinking and prepare for a productive first draft. Two techniques are especially effective: freewriting and brainstorming. Either will get your creative juices flowing; we recommend that you try both to see which works best for you in particular situations. Understand that these techniques are used when you already have the necessary material in your head. Either you are writing from personal experience or you've done some research. (You'll learn about research in Part Five.) Freewriting and brainstorming are designed to get your ideas on the page in any order, shape, or form. Don't worry about making a mess. You can clean it up later.

FREEWRITING

Freewriting does what its name implies. It sets you free to write without worrying about any of the possible writing errors you might make that block the flow of your ideas. We are not suggesting that you abandon attention to grammar, spelling, word choice, and so on, forever. Just forget about them for a while, until you get some ideas down on the page. Here's how to go about freewriting.

1. Put your watch and a pad of paper on your desk. If you can type faster than you can write, open a new document on your computer. (Some writers find it helpful to turn the monitor off.) Write your subject at the top of the page or tape it to the top of your computer monitor. Ideally, your subject will have passed the 4-S test, but if you're really stuck, you can begin with just a word or a phrase.

2. Make a note of the time and start writing. Don't stop until you have written for three, five, or even ten minutes straight. Write anything that comes to mind, even if it seems boring or silly. If you get stuck for words, write your subject or even the last phrase you've written over and over until something new comes to mind. (Don't worry, it will!)

3. Write as quickly as you can. Don't pause to analyze or evaluate your ideas, and don't scratch out or delete anything. This technique is designed to get thoughts into words as quickly as possible without self-consciousness.

4. When the time is up, stop and stretch. Then read over what you've written. Underline anything that is related to your subject. Much of your freewriting will be irrelevant nonsense that you can delete. But what you have underlined will be useful in the next step—identifying the main points you will focus on to explain your subject.

5. Turn the phrases, fragments, and sentences you have underlined into clear, understandable points. If you don't end up with at least ten points, continue freewriting for another few minutes and see what new ideas you can discover.

6. On a separate piece of paper, list the points you have identified. Study the possible relationships among these points and cluster them under two or three headings. These are your main points. Now you can move on to the next step: testing each main point to see be sure it is satisfactory for your essay.

Here is an example of the freewriting technique. The assigned topic, for a course in law enforcement fundamentals, was "Crime and Punishment." Victor Chen was interested in the difference between crime as it is portrayed in the media and the reality of Canada's justice system. After doing some research and finding statistics that he thought might be useful, he drafted the following on his computer in 15 minutes.

What's really happening in our system in terms of crime and punishment is really different from what we see in the media. Look at TV crime shows. It used to be that all the courtroom shows were about defense lawyers trying to prove their clients innocence. The prosecutors were the bad guys doing everything they could to put the defense attorney's client in jail or worse. There has been a big shift in the last five years or so and now we seem to have developed a taste for law and order. Now it's the prosecutors who are the good guys and the defense attorneys are trying to prevent their sleazy clients from escaping justice. The sad thing is that we form opinions about what goes on in real court rooms based on stories like these. Almost all of the courtroom dramas on TV are American, and what goes on in American courtrooms is different from Canada's court procedures, so we are definitely not very aware of how our justice system really works.

To prove this, look at the study that was done by Roberts and Doob. They took a group of people and gave them the newspaper articles about a trial. When they had read the stories, they were asked about the trial. Most of them thought the criminal had gotten a sentence that was too light and only 15% thought the sentence was too tough. Then they took another group and gave them the court documents and transcripts of what actually went on in the trial. This group was reversed, more than half of them thought the sentence was too tough. Less than 20% agreed with the majority in the other group that the criminal should have got a longer sentence. This shows that we are getting a distorted impression of reality when we read about violent crime in the papers or on TV. It's like we're living in two worlds, the imaginary media one and the real one we don't know about. Also the news distorts violence. Reading the papers or watching TV, you'd think there was an epidemic of crime and that our streets are unsafe and murder was a common occurrence. This is so they can sell more papers and attract more viewers. In fact crime rates are falling. About half the crime reported in the news is violent while violent crime is actually less than 12% of cases that are reported. Murders are less than 1% of violent crimes but they are 25% of crime stories. If all you did was read the papers and watch TV you'd think that violence and murder were very common but actually they are quite rare. It's easy to see how we get the idea that violence in our society is a real problem. So its really important that the people who make the laws don't rely on the media, because it is very distorted information.

After completing this freewriting exercise, Victor underlined all the points that he considered significant, supportable, and related to the subject. He quickly realized that the paper was going to be too long, and that one of his points was based on personal observation rather than provable facts. He

crossed out everything related to television shows and then rearranged the
other information into a rough outline of an essay with two main points.

Intro: the reality of the justice system and the media accounts of it are two
different things. Take two examples: violence and court proceedings.

1. Crime
   • murders in reality vs. murders in the media
   • violent crime in reality vs. violent crime in the media
2. Courts—the Roberts and Doob study
   • opinions of group that read newspaper accounts of a trial
   • opinions of group that read court documents of a trial

Conclusion: lawmakers need to base decisions on reality and not on the
media or public opinion.

Working from this rough outline, the writer developed a first draft. In
reading it over, he noted where he needed to add more support to make the
contrast clearer and more emphatic. After two more revisions and a careful
edit, Victor submitted "Justice and Journalism," which you will find on
pages 199–200.

Exercise 3.1

Choose a subject, or work with an assigned subject. Generate some ideas using
the freewriting method.

BRAINSTORMING

In **brainstorming**, you write down a list of every idea you can think of
about a specific subject. You can brainstorm alone, with a partner, or—best
of all—in a group. If you run out of ideas too quickly, then try the age-old
journalists' technique: ask the questions Who? What? Why? When?
Where? and How? about your subject. Here's how to proceed. (The first
three steps below assume you are working with a partner or in a small
group. You can also do them by yourself, but you'll have less fun.)

1. Write your topic at the top of the page. Again, you will save time if
   you've checked your subject against the 4-S test. Decide how much
   time you will spend on this exercise: three, five, or more minutes. As in
   freewriting, working against the clock can bring surprising results.
2. Write down in short form—words or phrases—every idea you can think
   of that is even vaguely related to your subject. Choose the fastest writer
   in your group to be the recorder. Work quickly. Don't slow yourselves

down by worrying about grammar or repetition. Many of the points won't be usable in the final list; worry about that later.

3. When the time is up, relax for a minute, then go over the list carefully. Underline the points that seem most clearly related to your subject and scratch out any duplicates or any ideas that are vague, trivial, or irrelevant. If you don't end up with at least three or four points that are meaningful to you, brainstorm again for a few minutes using the six journalists' questions to generate more ideas.

4. Working alone now, take your three or four most significant points and rephrase them in clear sentences on a new sheet of paper. Now you're ready to move on to the next step: testing your main points to ensure that they are suitable for use in your essay.

The following example demonstrates how brainstorming can be used to overcome the most frustrating inertia. The subject was "The value of a college writing course." As you might expect, the class groaned when the subject was assigned, but one group's quick brainstorming produced some unique and interesting approaches to the topic. The time limit given for this exercise was four minutes. After brainstorming, at least one student was convinced that her career opportunities would improve if she learned how to communicate better.

The Value of a College Writing Course

- have to take it
- should like it but I don't
- writing is important
- speaking's easier than writing
- bosses will hire you if you can write
- you can get a job
- letter of application
- have to write on the job
- have to write to the boss, other departments
- have to write to customers
- embarrassed about my writing
- people don't respect a poor writer
- writing helps you think
- writing helps you read better
- have to write reports
- need to know how to write a good report
- have to prepare slides for presentations
- need to write to get promoted

This list contains several significant points along with some irrelevant and trivial ones, which the group deleted. Then they talked about possible relationships among the remaining items on the list.

At this point, each student began working alone. After one student had underlined the points she felt were most important, she noticed that two points were closely related. She combined these into one idea. Here is her list of revised points.

College English is useful because
- it improves writing and thinking skills
- you will get hired
- you will communicate better on the job
- you will get promoted

Now it's your turn. Try your hand at the following exercise.

Exercise 3.2

Working with two or three other students, choose a subject, or work with an assigned subject. Brainstorm for five minutes. Then, working independently, underline the three or four ideas you like best. If you don't have enough points, repeat the exercise. When each of you has at least three points, compare your results. If you have all selected the same points, you are finished. If your lists of points are different, what do you think might account for the differences?

Generating Main Points:
The Top-Down Approach

Another way to find out what you have to say about a subject is to ask specific questions of it. Questioning lets you "walk around" your subject, looking at it from different angles, taking it apart and putting it back together again. Each question is a probe that enables you to dig below the surface and find out what you know. The top-down approach is more structured than the strategies we have discussed so far, but it has the advantage of producing clear main points with few or no off-topic responses. It also identifies for you the kinds of development you can use in your essay.

Questioning your subject works best if you know it well or have done some research, but are not sure how to approach it. Any subject can be approached in a number of ways. The needs of your audience and your purpose in writing should determine the approach you choose.

Here's how to use the questioning technique to generate ideas:

1. Once again, begin by writing your proposed subject at the top of the page, or tape it to your monitor.
2. Now apply the twelve questions listed below, one at a time, to your subject to see which ones "fit" best. That is, find the questions that call up in your mind answers that could be used as points to develop your subject. As you go down the list, you will probably find more than one question that you can think up answers for. Do not stop with the first question that produces answers. The purpose of this idea-generating technique is to discover the *best* approach for your target audience and writing purpose.
3. Go through the entire list and record your answers to any questions that apply to your subject. Ignore the questions that make no sense in relation to the subject.
4. Finally, study the questions that produced answers and choose the one that generated the ideas that are closest to what your reader needs to know and what you want to say.

Ready? The questions listed in the column on the left lead to the kinds of essay development listed in the column on the right. Don't worry about these now. We'll discuss them in detail in Part Four.

The Answers to This Question	**Produce This Kind of Paper**
1. What does your subject *look, feel, sound, smell,* and/or *taste* like?	*Description*
2. How did your subject *happen*?	*Narration*
3. How is your subject *made* or *done*? 4. How does your subject work?	*Process*
5. What are the main *kinds* of your subject? 6. What are the component *parts* of your subject? 7. What are the significant *features, characteristics,* or *functions* of your subject?	*Classification/ Division*
8. What are the *causes* of your subject? 9. What are the *effects* or *consequences* of your subject?	*Cause/Effect*
10. What are the *similarities* and/or *differences* between your subject and *X*?	*Comparison/ Contrast*
11. What are the main *advantages/disadvantages* of your subject? 12. What are the reasons *in favour of/against* your subject?	*Argument/ Persuasion*

By applying these questions to your subject, you will find at least one question to which you can give answers appropriate to your purpose. Your answers will be the main points of your essay. As an example, we've chosen the subject "Great rock bands." The subject passes the 4-S test: it is single, specific, supportable, and (we think) significant to our readers. Now let's apply the questions to see which one yields the best answers.

1. What does a great rock band look, feel, and sound like?
   We could describe how one band looks and sounds, but every band sounds different, and we can't describe them all.
2. How did a great rock band happen?
   We could tell how one particular band came about, but that wouldn't be very enlightening about great rock bands in general.
3. How is a great rock band made?
   Some ideas come to mind, but because great bands usually just "happen" rather than being deliberately put together, the answers to the question are not going to be supportable with much detail.
4. How does a great rock band work?
   They all work differently, so we would have to answer the question separately for each band. No way.
5. What are the main kinds or types of great rock bands?
   This question presents possibilities. We could answer this one by discussing heavy-metal bands, personality bands, dance bands, post-punk anarcho-machinist bands, and many more. We can put a check mark beside this question as the best possibility so far.
6. What are the main parts of a great rock band?
   This question produces answers (drums, keyboards, strings, vocalists), but because great bands and terrible bands can have the same kinds of instruments and performers, it won't provide any useful information.
7. What are the significant features or characteristics of a great rock band?
   Bingo. Another check mark. We can begin to answer this question because, although bands are all different, we have some clear ideas about what characteristics make a *great* band: performance, determination, appeal, and adaptability, to name a few. But let's try the rest of the questions just to be sure there isn't a better one.
8. What are the causes of a great rock band?
   This question doesn't produce any usable answers.
9. What are the effects of a great rock band?
   We could say something about a great band's effects on its fans, but nothing very specific. Let's move on.
10. What are the similarities and/or differences between great rock bands and . . . what? lousy rock bands? great marching bands? great single performers? We can't think of a comparison that would be significant for our readers.

11. What are the advantages (or disadvantages) of a great rock band?
    Doesn't make sense.
12. What are the reasons in favour of (or against) great rock bands?
    Doesn't make sense.

We found two questions that work for our subject. Now we can choose the question we have more to say about, or the one that is more appropriate to our intended audience and writing purpose, and begin developing the answers that will become our main points.

We chose question 7 and found three answers that would serve as good main points: "The main characteristics of a great rock band are popular appeal, exciting stage performance, and ability to adapt." (To see how the essay worked out, turn to "Rock of Ages" on page 184.)

Generating main points is not a difficult process, but it can be time-consuming. Don't rush; take the necessary time. This is a crucial stage in the writing process. To sharpen your skills, look at the sample subjects given below, the questions that might be applied to them, and the main points that could result. Study these samples until you're sure you understand how to find suitable main points for any subject. As you read each subject and main points, think about the essay that might result.

Subject	Selected Question	Main Points
Hockey violence	What are the reasons in favour of violence in hockey?	• releases aggression • keeps players alert • attracts fans
Law enforcement officers	What are the main functions of law enforcement officers?	• preventing crime • apprehending criminals • enforcing the law • acting as role models
Job interviews	How do you make a negative impression in a job interview?	• be late • be inappropriately dressed • be ignorant about the company • complain about former employers
Essay topics	What are the characteristics of a satisfactory essay topic?	• single • significant • specific • supportable

Exercise 3.3

Working in pairs, apply the questions on page 37 to each of the subjects listed below. Select the question that produces the answers you both like best, and list three or four of these answers as main points.

Subject	Selected Question	Main Points
1. Procrastination		•
		•
		•
		•
2. Voice mail		•
		•
		•
		•
3. Horror movies		•
		•
		•
		•
4. Business dress codes		•
		•
		•
		•
5. Ice cream		•
		•
		•
		•

In pairs, choose two subjects that you think would be suitable for short essays. Be sure all are significant, single, specific, and supportable. For each subject, list at least three good main points. Use the questions on page 37 to help you to identify main points. When you've finished, exchange your ideas with another team, critique each other's main points, and make suggestions.

Subject   _____

Selected Question   _____

Main Points   •

                        •

                        •

Subject   _____

Selected Question   _____

Main Points   •

                        •

                        •

Testing Your Main Points

Now that you've practised identifying main points using freewriting, brainstorming, and the questioning approach, the next step is to examine the points you've come up with to make sure each is going to work as a major component in your essay. Some may be too minor to bother with; some may overlap in meaning; some may even be unrelated to your subject. Here's how to test your main points to be sure they are satisfactory. Whether you've arrived at your main points through freewriting, brainstorming, or questioning, the test is the same.

Main points must be
significant, distinct, and relevant.

ARE YOUR MAIN POINTS SIGNIFICANT?

Each main point should be worth writing and reading about. If you can't write at least one interesting and informative paragraph about a point, it is probably not significant enough to bother with. To waste your readers' time with trivial matters gains you only irritated readers. In the following example, one of the main points does not have the same "weight" or importance as the others. It should be eliminated or replaced.

Reasons for attending college
- to learn career skills
- to improve one's general knowledge of the world
- to enjoy the social life
- to participate in student government

ARE YOUR MAIN POINTS DISTINCT?

Each of the main points you choose must be different from all the others; there must be no overlap in meaning. Check to be sure you haven't given two different labels to what is really only one aspect of your subject. Eliminate or replace any main points that duplicate other points or that can easily be covered under another point. Here's an example of a list that contains a redundant main point.

Advantages of cycling
- improves fitness
- stimulates enjoyment of surroundings
- keeps one in shape
- doesn't damage the environment

ARE YOUR MAIN POINTS RELEVANT?

The main points you choose must be clearly and directly related to your subject. They all must be aspects of that subject and must add to the development of your readers' information on the subject. In this example, the third main point listed is inappropriate because it does not relate to the stated topic. It must be eliminated.

The miseries of winter
- numbing cold
- layers of uncomfortable clothes
- Christmas presents
- dangerous driving conditions

Exercise 3.5*

At least one main point in each item below is unsatisfactory. Identify each faulty point and explain why it should be deleted. When you have finished, check your answers on page 484.

1. Business communication devices
   - telephone
   - e-mail
   - fax
   - mail
   - cell

2. Advantages of locating a business outside the city
   - cheaper cost of living
   - calmer pace
   - distance from suppliers and markets
   - government subsidies and tax benefits

3. Kinds of television commercials
   - boring
   - clever
   - misleading
   - puzzling
   - repetitive

4. Causes of college failure
   - lack of preparation in high school
   - procrastination
   - poor study habits
   - irregular attendance

5. How to choose a place to live
   - determine your needs
   - determine your budget
   - find a reliable real estate agent
   - seek expert advice

6. Reasons for high staff turnover
   - salary lower than industry standard
   - no chance for advancement
   - uncomfortable work environment
   - competitors offer better pay

Organizing Your Main Points

After you've identified the main points for your essay and checked to make sure they are satisfactory, your final step in the planning process is to list them in order. (This list of points is sometimes called a plan of development or a path statement.)

Careful thinking at this stage can make a big difference in your readers' understanding of your essay. Main points are like menu items on a Web site: the more logically they are arranged, the easier it is to navigate your way through them.

> There are four ways to order your main points: chronological, climactic, logical, and random.

CHRONOLOGICAL ORDER

When you present your points in order of time from first to last, you are using **chronological order**. You will find it most appropriate in process essays, but it can be used in other essays as well. Here are two examples.

Subject	Main Points
The process of writing a paper	• select an appropriate subject • list and edit the main points • write a thesis statement • write an outline for the paper • write a first draft • revise, edit, and proofread
The evolution of a relationship	• meeting • attraction • discovery • intimacy • disillusionment

CLIMACTIC ORDER

Persuasion most often uses a climactic arrangement, but climactic order is also common in papers based on examples, comparison or contrast, and classification or division. In **climactic order**, you save your strongest or most convincing point for last (the climax of your argument). You lead off your essay with your second-strongest point, and arrange your other points in between, as in this example.

Subject	Main Points
Advantages of a college education	• development of skills • friendships and contacts with compatible people • higher income potential for life • discovery of one's own potential

LOGICAL ORDER

Cause-and-effect essays, or any writing in which one point must be explained before the next point can be understood, use **logical order**. The points you are making have a logical progression, and you cannot take them out of order without confusing your readers. Consider the following sequence.

Subject	Main Points
Main causes of youth crime	• lack of opportunity or motivation for work • lack of recreational facilities • boredom • quest for "kicks"

The logical links here are clear: because of unemployment, recreational facilities are needed. Because of both unemployment and inadequate recreational facilities, boredom and the quest for "kicks" become problems. Readers must grasp each point before the next can be explained and understood.

RANDOM ORDER

On the rare occasions when your points can be explained in any order without affecting your readers' understanding, you can use **random order**. A random arrangement is possible only if all your main points are of equal significance and if they are not linked together logically or chronologically. In this example, all three points have equal weight.

Subject	Main Points
The garbage disposal crisis	• disposal sites are hard to find • cartage costs are high • new technologies are not yet fully developed

Exercise 3.6*

Choose the type of order—chronological, climactic, logical, or random—you think is most appropriate for each of the following subjects. Arrange the main points in that order by numbering them.

Subject	Order	Main Points
1. How to impress a client	_____	_____ firm handshake _____ friendly closing _____ well prepared sales presentation _____ knowledge of client's needs _____ appropriate business attire
2. How to handle tax preparation	_____	_____ do your own _____ don't bother to file a return _____ go to a franchise tax preparation company _____ hire an accountant
3. Reasons for listening to the CBC	_____	_____ it offers informative programs _____ your taxes are paying for it _____ it provides a sense of Canadian unity
4. Methods of quitting smoking	_____	_____ nicotine patch _____ cold turkey _____ gradual withdrawal
5. Causes of dissatisfaction with employment	_____	_____ incompetent or unfriendly supervisor _____ incompatible co-workers _____ inappropriate pay for skills and effort _____ unfulfilling work assignments

GO TO WEB

EXERCISE 3.1

Exercise 3.7

Now go back to the subjects and main points that you developed in Exercise 3.4. First, reconsider your main points: are they all significant, distinct, and related to the subject? Next, put the main points in the order that is most appropriate for the subject to which they belong.

When you've finished this task, exchange papers with another student and check each other's work. Can your partner identify the order of points you have chosen? Does he or she agree with your choice?

In this chapter, you've learned how to identify main points, how to test them for suitability, and how to arrange them in the most appropriate order. You're ready now to go on to the next step: writing the thesis statement—probably the most important sentence in your paper.

4

Writing the Thesis Statement

The key to clear organization in any paper is a thesis statement near the beginning that announces the paper's subject and scope. The thesis statement not only helps a reader to see how you are going to approach the subject, but also serves to keep you, the writer, on track.

A **thesis statement** is one or more sentences that clearly and concisely indicate the subject of your paper, the main points you will discuss, and the order in which you will discuss them.

In business communication, technical writing, and some academic writing (e.g., research papers and dissertations) it is important to indicate the subject and scope of your paper at the outset. Readers expect this sort of preview.[1]

The number of sentences in a thesis statement depends on what the subject is, how best to phrase it, how many points there are, and how complex they are. A thesis statement in a short paper is usually a single sentence at the end of the first paragraph, but in a lengthy paper on complicated issues, it might be several sentences or even a paragraph long. Occasionally (in a technical description, for example), a writer will choose a short thesis and omit the main points from the thesis statement.

To write a thesis statement, join your subject to the main points you have selected and arranged into an appropriate sequence. Here is a simple formula for constructing a thesis statement:

---

[1]In less formal writing, such as newspaper or magazine articles and informal essays—including some of the essays in this book—a thesis statement is unnecessary.

S	**consists of**	**1, 2, 3 . . . etc.**
(subject)	(link)	(main points)

These three elements can be combined in various ways. For example:

The most prolific producers of unnecessary jargon are politicians, sports writers, advertising copy writers, and educators.

Because the United States influences Canada's foreign policy, dominates its culture, and controls its economy, Canada is little more than an American satellite.

Fad diets are not the quick and easy fix to weight problems that they may appear to be. On the contrary, they are often costly, ineffective, and even dangerous.

Two cheers for democracy: one because it admits variety, and two because it permits criticism. (E. M. Forster)

Once you have mastered the basic formula, you can experiment with creative ways of expressing a thesis statement. Just be sure that it is appropriate in form, language, and tone to the kind of paper you are writing. The thesis statements in the exercise below are examples of the range of possibilities you can explore: they range from short to long, formal to informal, and serious to flippant.

Exercise 4.1*

In each of the following thesis statements, underline the subject with a double line and the main points with a single line. When you have finished all seven, compare your answers with those on pages 484–85.

1. Students who try to combine a full-time job with a full-time program face problems at school, at work, and at home.
2. To be successful in a broadcasting career, you must be talented, motivated, and hardworking.
3. The ideal notebook computer for business applications is reliable, lightweight, powerful, and flexible.
4. Establishing a local area network would increase efficiency and flexibility in the office.
5. The chairperson's job calls for a responsible and sensitive person, someone who is knowledgeable about company policy, sensitive to personnel issues, and a creative problem solver. It wouldn't hurt if he or she could also walk on water.

6. The business traveller can learn much from the turtle. Carry everything you need with you. Move slowly but with purpose and consistency. Keep your head down until you are sure you know what's going on.

7. Large energy producers and some provincial governments say we cannot afford to live up to the terms of the Kyoto accord, which seeks to reduce the production of greenhouse gases. But can we afford not to comply with this international agreement? Can we afford to compromise the health of Canadians by continuing to pollute? Can we afford to risk the effects of global warming on our environment? Can we afford to fall behind the rest of the world in research and development leading to a solution to the problem of greenhouse gases?

Now try your hand at analyzing the introductory paragraphs in the exercise below.

Exercise 4.2

Each of the five introductions below contains a thesis statement. Working in groups of three or four, identify the thesis statement in each paragraph.

1. What does an interviewer look for in a new job applicant? Good credentials, good preparation, good grooming, and good communication skills are essential features for anyone who wants a job. No interviewer would seriously consider an applicant who comes to an interview without the required educational background and work experience, without information about the job and the company, without appropriate clothing, and without the ability to present ideas clearly in the interview.

2. In the traditional manufacturing sectors, sales growth has stagnated in Canada over the past five years. Our products and services have secured as large a market share as we can expect, and we can anticipate further decline over the next ten years as a result of increased competition. For these reasons, we have undertaken a study to determine where our best expansion opportunities lie. The following report outlines growth opportunities in three emerging markets: Croatia, Hungary, and Slovenia.

3. Suddenly a man steps into the road in front of me. He's wearing a uniform and he's waving his hand for me to pull over to the side. My heart pounds and my pores prickle with anxiety. I feel guilty, but I don't know what I've done wrong—maybe speeding ten kilometres over the limit, but no more. Anyone who has been caught in a radar trap knows this momentary feeling of panic, guilt, and resentment. We fear that the police officer will be brusque and blaming, but we are often surprised. There are as many kinds of police officers as there are people. Four kinds, however, dominate the profession: the confident veteran, the arrogant authoritarian, the cocky novice, and the friendly professional. As I roll down my window, I wonder which kind of police officer has stopped me.

4. After a hard day's work, do you relax with two or three stiff drinks? Do you enjoy a few beers while watching a game on TV? Do you believe mixed drinks make a party more fun? Do you cool off with gin fizzes on a hot afternoon? If you answered "Yes" to most of these questions, you are probably abusing alcohol. The line between excessive social drinking and a serious addictive habit is a blurry one. Most alcoholics don't know they are hooked until they try to stop drinking. What are the signs that a drinker is no longer drinking for pleasure only? If a person "needs" a drink, or drinks alone, or can fall asleep only after a few drinks, or can find enjoyment only when drinking, that person is probably in trouble.

5. Ours is a transient society. Most of us travel more kilometres in a year than our grandparents travelled in a lifetime. We move from one city to another, one province to another, and one country to another. In the course of moving, we inhabit many homes. The family home of the past might have been inhabited by several generations, consecutively or concurrently. Today's average Canadians will probably have ten or more addresses during their adult lives. Our restlessness is particularly hard on the children in our migrating families: they have to leave familiar surroundings and friends, and they must adjust to a new environment, new habits, and sometimes a new language. These children pay a heavy price for the mobility of modern impermanence.

Phrasing Your Statement of Subject

Your statement of subject should be as clear and concise as you can make it. It must not be boring, however. Beginning writers often fall into the trap of stating the obvious: "In this paper, I am going to discuss . . ." or "The subject of this memo is . . . ." Your readers *know* it's your paper; you needn't hit them over the head by pointing out your authorship or the fact that the paper contains your ideas. Here are three examples of faulty subject statements and their revisions.

Poor	Better
In this essay, I am going to discuss violence in hockey.	Violence in hockey is misunderstood by the non-playing public.
This paper is about Canada's multiculturalism policy.	Canada's multiculturalism policy is neither practical nor desirable.
I am going to examine the three most common causes of small-business failure.	Three common errors lie behind the large number of failures in small-business enterprises.

Phrasing the Main Points

When you combine your statement of subject with your main points to form your thesis statement, be sure that all your main points are phrased in the same way, in grammatically parallel form. If point 1 is a single word, then points 2, 3, and so on must also be single words. If point 1 is a phrase, then all the points following it must be phrases. If point 1 is a clause or a sentence, then the succeeding points must also be in clause or sentence form.

The following sentence contains a main point that is not parallel with the others.

Of the many qualities that combine to make a good nurse the three most important are strength, intelligence, and she must be compassionate.

Rewritten to be grammatically parallel, this statement might read as follows:

Of the many qualities that combine to make a good nurse the three most important are strength, intelligence, and compassion.

Or, the sentence could be rewritten this way:

Of the many qualities that combine to make a good nurse the three most important are that she or he be strong, intelligent, and compassionate.

If you have trouble with grammatical parallelism, turn to Chapter 28 before you try the exercise below.

Exercise 4.3

In each of the following lists, one point is not parallel with the others. Rephrase the incorrect item so that all are in grammatically parallel form.

1. Our employees are
    a. motivated
    b. good training
    c. knowledgeable
2. Our doctor is
    a. full of medical knowledge
    b. competent
    c. caring

3. I've noticed that my friends are increasingly
   a. concerned about smoking
   b. interested in fitness
   c. environmental awareness
4. To upgrade our educational system, we need
   a. more effective teacher training
   b. better liaison between levels of education
   c. students must be motivated to learn
5. An investment strategy must be
   a. based on current information
   b. appropriately diversified
   c. the client has to be tolerant of the degree of risk

Exercise 4.4

Work in pairs to develop two thesis statements for potential essays. Phrase the two thesis statements so that one has a poor statement of subject and the other lacks parallelism. Switch these creations with another team and identify the problems. Then correct the sentences.

Exercise 4.5

Working with a partner, combine each of the following subjects with its main points to form a clear thesis statement that is expressed in grammatically parallel form.

1. Causes of stress
   - change of employment
   - financial problems
   - death of family member

Thesis statement: _____

_____

_____

_____

_____

2. Steps in finding a job
   - conduct an Internet job search
   - prepare a letter of application
   - perform well in the interview

Thesis statement: _____

_____

_____

_____

3. Methods of   • nicotine patches
   quitting smoking   • acupuncture
                          • hypnosis
                          • withdrawing gradually

Thesis statement: _____

_____

_____

_____

4. Evolution of a recession   • unemployment causes general
                                 economic slowdown
                               • consumer buying decreases, resulting
                                 in inflation
                               • inflation causes fear and further
                                 decrease in consumer demand

Thesis statement: _____

_____

_____

_____

_____

Exercise 4.6*

Working independently, combine each of the following subjects with its main points to form a grammatically parallel thesis statement.

1. Comparison between   • food
   McDonald's and   • atmosphere
   Burger King (or any other • service
   two fast-food restaurants) • price

Thesis statement: _____

_____

_____

_____

_____

2. Effects of urban   • traffic jams
   overcrowding   • too much air pollution
                             • high rate of homelessness
                             • violence on the streets

   Thesis statement: _____

   _____

   _____

   _____

   _____

3. Characteristics of a   • adequate capital
   successful small business • marketable product
                              • personnel that are dedicated
                              • workable business plan

   Thesis statement: _____

   _____

   _____

   _____

   _____

Exercise 4.7

In groups of three or four, share the thesis statements you developed for Exercise 4.6 and discuss your decisions. As a group, revise each statement until you are all satisfied they meet all the criteria for satisfactory thesis statements.

You have now covered all the steps leading to the construction of a good thesis statement. The exercises above have given you practice in the skills you need to phrase subjects and main points correctly and effectively. It's now time for you to write your own "live" example.

Exercise 4.8 will walk you through the process of developing a thesis statement for a subject of your own choice. As you fill in the blanks in Exercise 4.8, you will be reviewing the contents of the first four chapters and testing your mastery of the writing skills they presented.

Exercise 4.8

1. Select a subject.

   _____

   _____

2. Test whether your subject is significant, single, specific, and support-able.

3. Using either a bottom-up or a top-down approach to generate ideas, identify three to five main points in support of your subject.

   _____

   _____

   _____

   _____

   _____

4. Test whether your main points are all significant, distinct, and clearly related to your subject.

5. Arrange your main points in the order that is most likely to guarantee your readers' understanding of your subject: chronological, climactic, logical, or random.

   _____

   _____

   _____

   _____

   _____

6. Now rewrite your main points so that they are grammatically parallel: all single words, all phrases, or all clauses.

   _____

   _____

_____

_____

_____

7. Combine your statement of subject with your main points to produce your thesis statement.

_____

_____

_____

_____

_____

The seven points listed in Exercise 4.8 summarize the steps to follow in planning an essay. Keep this outline handy and refer to it when you start your next paper or research report.

5

Drafting the Outline

Writing a paper is like building a house: you save much time and frustration if you start with a plan. No builder can work from a vague description of what the customer wants. Builders need a detailed blueprint that shows the structural components, measurements, and layout. This doesn't mean that the client can't change his or her mind, but the time to make major changes is at the planning stage—on the blueprint—not on the finished building.

Writers can't create papers out of thin air, either. For anything longer than about 250 words, writers need a detailed plan or outline to guide them as they begin to build words into sentences, sentences into paragraphs, and paragraphs into the final product, whether it's a term paper, a research report, a business plan, or a market analysis. Wise writers treat an outline as tentative, not something chiseled in stone. As you draft your paper, you may discover new ideas or a new arrangement of information that better suits your purpose. If so, change your thesis statement and outline to accommodate it. (It's a good idea to make these changes in pencil or in a new file because you may decide at the end of the draft that these new ideas weren't so great after all.)

All buildings share some basic structural features—a foundation, supporting walls, and a roof—but the buildings themselves can range from one-room cottages to palatial mansions. So it is with writing. As we have seen, all written messages consist of an introduction, a body, and a conclusion, but each of these may vary from one to several paragraphs in length, and from simple to sophisticated in style. The model format on the next page is an outline for a basic five-paragraph essay. Once you've mastered this basic structure, you can modify, expand, and develop it to suit any of the kinds of writing you'll be called upon to do.

Outline Format

Title _____

INTRODUCTION _____

Attention-getter* _____

_____

_____

Thesis statement <u>Subject consists of 1, 2, and 3.</u> _____

BODY <u>Topic sentence introducing main point 1 goes here.</u>

Support for first main point
- _____
- _____
- _____
- _____

<u>Concluding (or transition) sentence goes here.</u>

<u>Topic sentence introducing main point 2 goes here.</u>

Support for second main point
- _____
- _____
- _____
- _____

<u>Concluding (or transition) sentence goes here.</u>

<u>Topic sentence introducing main point 3 goes here.</u>

Support for third main point
- _____
- _____
- _____
- _____

<u>Concluding (or transition) sentence goes here.</u>

CONCLUSION

Summary
- _____
- _____
- _____

Memorable statement*
- _____
- _____ .

---

*Terms marked with an asterisk are explained and illustrated in Chapter 10.

The outline below follows the format on the previous page. You'll find your first draft much easier to write if you prepare an outline before you begin. The final version of "Ready, Willing . . . and Employable" appears after the outline.

Essay title	Ready, Willing . . . and Employable
Attention-getter	What are employers looking for today?
Thesis statement	Employers are looking for a new breed of employee: one who has knowledge, flexibility, and the right attitude.
1. Topic sentence	Knowledge is still first on the list.
Support for first main point	• colleges offer a broad range of programs to meet employers' needs • graduates must know current trends as well as theory • some employers test for knowledge • some rely on college's reputation plus recommendations of professors and recruiters
2. Topic sentence	Adaptability is essential for a prospective employee.
Support for second main point	• today's jobs require multi-tasking • flexible workers are more cost effective and better problem solvers • flexible workers can adapt to change • students need to broaden their education and learn a variety of skills
3. Topic sentence	Employers complain about graduates' poor attitude.
Support for third main point	• graduates lack the ability to take direction, use team skills, communicate well, and motivate themselves • similar problems show up in class —chronic lateness —lack of cooperation —laziness • students need to correct these attitude problems on their own
Summary of main points	Students must be ready, able, and willing to work.
Memorable statement	With these skills, a good résumé, and professional contacts, graduates can enter the workforce with confidence.

READY, WILLING . . . AND EMPLOYABLE

What are employers looking for in today's job market? Several recent surveys point to a subtle shift in the requirements of businesses looking to hire college and university graduates. Only a few years ago, knowledge was the prerequisite to employment in most industries. Employers needed workers with the highly specialized skills of an emerging high-tech workplace. Now many of those skills are taken for granted, and other characteristics have become increasingly important. Employers are seeking a new breed of employee: one who has the knowledge required to do the job, the flexibility to adapt, and—most important—the attitude to succeed.

Attention-getter

Thesis statement

Knowledge of how to do the job is, understandably, still first on the shopping list that employers bring to job fairs. Colleges across the country have responded to marketplace requirements with an array of programs designed to prepare students to meet the needs of industries from broadcasting to photonics, from micro-electronics to wine-making. Graduates are expected to have up-to-the-minute information on current trends in their fields, as well as solid grounding in the theory and practice of their specialty. Some employers test applicants for this knowledge; others rely on the reputation of the institution, the recommendation of professors with whom they have professional connections, and the insights of recruiters. As valuable as knowledge is to the employer, however, an employee's flexibility is quickly becoming just as important.

Topic sentence

Support for first main point

Concluding statement (transition)

"Multi-tasking" is a buzz word often used to describe the ability to move quickly and easily between projects and work environments, bringing a wide range of skills to bear on a variety of situations. Adaptability is an essential characteristic of any prospective employee. Workers who can use their expertise simultaneously on several different tasks within a project are valuable not only because they are more cost-effective than several single-task specialists, but also because they tend to see projects holistically and are better problem solvers as a result. In addition, flexible workers are those who most quickly and easily adapt to changes in technology or work practice, and such changes are a way of life in today's work environment. Students must prepare themselves to be flexible workers by broadening their education and by learning as many skills as possible. Unlike their parents, workers in the current generation have little hope of finding a job that will require only one skill set over the course of a career. Adaptability is a critical skill, but even when combined with knowledge, it is not enough to ensure employability. Increasingly, attitude is the determining factor in who gets hired (and promoted!).

Topic sentence

Support for second main point

Concluding statement

Transition

Employers continually complain to colleges and universities that students on placement and graduates in their first position fail to impress, not from lack of knowledge, skill, or preparation, but from a broad range of inadequacies best summed up as "poor attitude." Among the faults cited under this broad heading are inability to take direction, failure to work well with colleagues,

Topic sentence

*Support for
third main
point*

inability to communicate effectively, and lack of enthusiasm and initiative. How can such problems be corrected before graduates reach the workplace? Colleges do not offer courses in attitude adjustment, but perhaps they should. Most of these problems have surfaced in classes long before graduation. Students who are chronically late, frequently unco-operative, constantly complaining, or visibly lazy are those who, with all the skills and ability in the world, will not succeed in any job worth having. Even highly motivated and ambitious graduates have sometimes had difficulty adjusting to entry level positions when they find themselves working under the supervision of others who they feel are less talented or skilled. It is up to students themselves to correct their attitudinal deficiencies. They need to pay attention to the criticisms of teachers, classmates, even family members, and make an honest evaluation of consistently noticed faults. Only when such attitude faults have been identified and acknowledged can they be corrected, and only when they have been corrected will the student be an asset to an employer.

*Concluding
statement*

*Summary
and
Memorable
statement*

As graduation draws near, most students view their coming transformation into workers with eagerness liberally mixed with anxiety. Statistics tell us that most college and university graduates find employment in their fields within a year of graduation. Armed with this encouraging information together with a good résumé, professional contacts, and the knowledge, flexibility, and attitude to succeed, graduates can face employers and the workplace with confidence.

Now it's your turn to develop your outlining skills.

Exercise 5.1

Read "Of Men and Machines" (pages 188–89) and "Lightweight Lit." (pages 210–11). Identify in each essay the sentences that correspond to the major structural items in the outline formats that follow. If you're working through the textbook in order, you may not have studied some of the terms mentioned, but you should be able to make a good guess at identifying the attention-getter and the memorable statement. To make your task easier, the sentences in each essay have been numbered.

OF MEN AND MACHINES

INTRODUCTION

Attention-getter   Sentence(s)   _____

Thesis statement   Sentence(s)   _____

BODY PARAGRAPH #1

Topic sentence   Sentence(s)   _____

Support for first main point   Sentence(s)   _____

Conclusion/Transition   Sentence(s)   _____

BODY PARAGRAPH #2

Topic sentence   Sentence(s)   _____

Support for second main point Sentence(s)   _____

Conclusion/Transition   Sentence(s)   _____

BODY PARAGRAPH #3

Topic sentence   Sentence(s)   _____

Support for third main point   Sentence(s)   _____

Conclusion/Transition   Sentence(s)   _____

CONCLUSION

Summary/Reinforcement   Sentence(s)   _____

Memorable statement   Sentence(s)   _____

LIGHTWEIGHT LIT.

INTRODUCTION

Attention-getter   Sentence(s)   _____

Thesis statement   Sentence(s)   _____

BODY PARAGRAPH #1

Topic sentence   Sentence(s)   _____

Support for first main point   Sentence(s)   _____

Conclusion/Transition   Sentence(s)   _____

BODY PARAGRAPH #2

Topic sentence   Sentence(s)   _____

Support for second main point   Sentence(s)   _____

Conclusion/Transition   Sentence(s)   _____

BODY PARAGRAPH #3

Topic sentence   Sentence(s)   _____

Support for third main point   Sentence(s)   _____

Conclusion/Transition   Sentence(s)   _____

CONCLUSION

Summary/Reinforcement   Sentence(s)   _____

Memorable statement   Sentence(s)   _____

PART 2

Drafting

6

Understanding Paragraph Form and Function

What Does a Paragraph Look Like?

Essays are divided into paragraphs. **Paragraphs** are sentence groups that are separated from each other in their physical presentation and in their content. They usually have an indentation at the beginning (on a typed page, the first word begins five spaces in from the left margin) and some white space at the end (the last line is left blank following the paragraph's last word). Between the indentation and the final period comes the paragraph: a group of sentences that explains a single idea or topic.

If you were to draw a blueprint for a single paragraph, it would look like this:

A sentence that introduces the **topic** (or main idea) of the paragraph goes here.

Three or more sentences that specifically support or explain the topic go in here.

A sentence that concludes your explanation of the topic (or provides a transition to the next paragraph) goes here.

How Does a Paragraph Function?

Readers expect a paragraph to present a unit of thought or a single, developed idea. The white space at the beginning and end of each paragraph defines your thought units and also serves two other functions. First, it provides a visual cue that makes your writing "reader friendly." Imagine if the page you are now reading were one continuous block of printing: no headings, no indentations, no paragraphs. The page would look so intimidatingly difficult to read that few readers would even attempt it. Second, paragraphs divide your writing into linked but separate sections, helping both you and your readers to stay on track, always conscious of where you are in the development of the subject that is the focus of your essay. Without paragraphs, ideas would blur and blend one into another. Readers would find it difficult to identify them, let alone follow the organization and development of the writer's thoughts.

Paragraph indentations are like commercial breaks in a situation comedy. Mentally review a sitcom: the story will have a beginning, a middle, and an end, and these will be separated by commercials. Since about eight minutes of each half-hour show is reserved for commercials, writers have developed a format that divides any script neatly into segments. The opening scene presents the characters and reveals the story problem for the episode. After a commercial break, the problem intensifies. Another commercial interrupts just before the crisis or climax of the show. The final commercial precedes a brief ending that solves the problem, puts everything back together, and leaves you laughing so you'll tune in to the next week's show.

The paragraphs in a paper work much the same way. The white space before and after the paragraphs sets them apart as separate "action" sequences. In a typical essay, an introductory paragraph is followed by paragraphs that add details and depth to the ideas set out in the introduction. A concluding paragraph brings all the ideas together again and leaves the readers with a complete understanding of the writer's thinking.

Readers can tell a great deal about your thinking just by glancing at your page. A number of short paragraphs indicates a series of ideas, briefly (and perhaps superficially) explained. Long paragraphs—half a page or longer— suggest complex ideas that require explanation and details; they signal serious thought.

As a general rule, you explore one major idea or main point in each paragraph. When you have finished exploring one topic and wish to move on to another, you signal this shift to your readers by beginning a new paragraph.

How Long Should a Paragraph Be?

The answer to this question depends on the topic, your readers' familiarity with it, and your purpose in writing. If your topic is complex, your readers' knowledge is limited, and your purpose is to persuade readers who do not share your point of view, then you'll probably need a fairly long paragraph to accomplish your goal. On the other hand, if you're writing about a fairly common idea that your readers can be expected to be familiar with, and your purpose is simply to share your understanding of that topic with your readers, you may be able to accomplish your task in a few sentences.

Exercise 6.1

Work in groups of five or six. Each group will take one of the paragraphs below to read and analyze by answering the following questions. Share your analysis with the class.

- What is the topic of the paragraph, stated in a short phrase?
- How much knowledge of the topic does the writer assume the readers have?
- What is the writer's purpose in this paragraph?

1. Violence as a way of achieving racial justice is both impractical and immoral. It is impractical because it is a descending spiral ending in destruction for all. The old law of an eye for an eye leaves everybody blind. It is immoral because it seeks to humiliate the opponent rather than win his understanding; it seeks to annihilate rather than to convert. Violence is immoral because it thrives on hatred rather than love. It destroys community and makes brotherhood impossible. It leaves society in monologue rather than dialogue. Violence ends by defeating itself. It creates bitterness in the survivors and brutality in the destroyers. A voice echoes through time saying to every potential Peter, "Put up your sword." History is cluttered with the wreckage of nations that failed to follow this command.

King, Martin Luther, Jr. "Three Types of Resistance to Oppression." *Stride Toward Freedom*. New York: Harper & Row, 1958. 215.

2. Take William Lyon Mackenzie King, our prime minister through the war and, so it seemed, for all time until Pierre Trudeau came along and seemed to be prime minister for all time. King held power longer than any other Western politician in this century. How did such a pudgy, mundane little man do it? The truth is, he did it deliberately. He was shrewd and self-effacing, and he told his friends that he made every speech as boring as possible because then no one would ever remember what he said and hold

it against him. Twenty-two years in power, droning on and on over the airwaves, and meanwhile, he was as crazy as a loon.

Callaghan, Barry. "Canadian Wry." *Canadian Content.* Ed. Sarah Norton and Nell Waldman. 2nd ed. Toronto: Harcourt, 1992. 92.

3.   *Vinaya* means humility; it is the complete surrendering of the self on the part of the *shishya* [the disciple] to the *guru.* The ideal disciple feels love, adoration, reverence, and even fear toward his *guru,* and he accepts equally praise or scoldings. Talent, sincerity, and the willingness to practise faithfully are essential qualities of the serious student. The *guru,* as the giver in this relationship, seems to be all-powerful. Often, he may be unreasonable, harsh, or haughty, though the ideal *guru* is none of these. Ideally, he should respond to the efforts of the disciple and love him almost as his own child. In India, a Hindu child, from his earliest years, is taught to feel humble toward anyone older than he or superior in any way. From the simplest gesture of the *namaskar,* or greeting (putting the hands palm to palm in front of the forehead and bowing), or the *pranam* (a respectful greeting consisting of touching the greeted person's feet, then one's own eyes and forehead with the hands held palm to palm) to the practice of *vinaya* or humility tempered with a feeling of love and worship, the Hindu devotee's vanity and pretension are worn away.

Shankar, Ravi. "Studying Music in India." *My Music, My Life.* Delhi: Vikas Publications, 1968. 11–12.

4.   When I found [the snakeskin], it was whole and tied in a knot. Now there have been stories told, even by reputable scientists, of snakes that have deliberately tied themselves in a knot to prevent larger snakes from trying to swallow them—but I couldn't imagine any way that throwing itself into a half hitch would help a snake trying to escape its skin. Still, ever cautious, I figured that one of the neighborhood boys could possibly have tied it in a knot in the fall, for some whimsical boyish reason, and left it there, where it dried and gathered dust. So I carried the skin along thoughtlessly as I walked, snagging it sure enough on a low branch and ripping it in two. . . . I saw that thick ice still lay on the quarry pond and that the skunk cabbage was already out in the clearings, and then I came home and looked at the skin and its knot.

Dillard, Annie. *Pilgrim at Tinker Creek.* New York: Harper's Magazine Press, 1974. 73.

5.   Third, there needs to be a thorough revision of the maximum-penalty structure to remove the incongruities that riddle the current Criminal Code. Should forgery or certain kinds of fraud really have the same maximum penalty as sexual assault with a weapon? The maximum penalties are also much too high; most were created many decades ago, when our perceptions of the seriousness of various crimes differed from those today.

The maximum penalty for breaking and entering is life imprisonment, for example, but in practice the average sentence is well under one year. This is called "bite and bark" sentencing; the system barks more loudly than it bites, and creates false expectations among the public.

Roberts, Julian V. "Three Steps to Make the Punishment Fit the Crime." *Globe and Mail* 7 Dec. 1993: A25.

Exercise 6.2

Write a short paragraph (five to seven sentences) that demonstrates your understanding of paragraph form and function. Choose any topic you like. When you have finished, exchange papers with another student and check each other's paragraph for

- Form: Is there a clear introduction to and conclusion of the topic?
- Function: Is the paragraph sufficiently developed for the reader to understand the topic clearly? The reader should have no questions left unanswered.

7

Crafting the Topic Sentence

The **topic sentence** in each paragraph is the sentence that clearly identifies what the paragraph is about—its main idea. The topic sentence focuses the paragraph, helps to unify it, and keeps you and your readers on track. In professional writing, the topic sentence is not always the first sentence of the paragraph. Sometimes it is more effective to announce the topic in the second, third, or even the last sentence. But professional writers, through years of practice, have earned the right to break the rules. Beginning writers should remember this: *most readers assume that the first sentence of a paragraph identifies the topic of that paragraph.* If your first sentence doesn't do this, then your readers may go through your paragraph assuming the topic is something other than what you intended. Miscommunication frustrates readers and wastes their time. To be absolutely clear, identify your topic up front.

A good topic sentence does three things:

1. It introduces the topic of the paragraph.
2. It makes a point about the topic.
3. It makes a statement that is neither too broad nor too narrow.

Readers appreciate writers who get to the point quickly, make the point clearly, and support or explain it adequately. They also appreciate writers who can make their points in an interesting way. Take the time to write topic sentences that are something more than straightforward, flat announcements of your main idea. Compare the following pairs of topic sentences.

Weak	Strong
I am going to explain why I love "trash."	I'm ashamed to confess my secret vice, but because we're friends, I can tell you: I love "trash."
This paragraph is about violence.	Violence as a way of achieving social justice is both impractical and immoral (Martin Luther King, Jr.).

A good way to introduce the topic so that it is both interesting and effective is to make a point about it. You save your readers' time and eliminate the risk of confusion if you make clear at the outset your idea about or your attitude toward your topic. Consider these examples.

Weak	Strong
Many people around the world enjoy music.	Nothing bridges gaps between cultures like music.
Canadians are different from Americans.	Canadians should be thankful for their differences from Americans.

Finally, the topic you choose must be "the right size"—neither so broad that you cannot support it adequately in a single paragraph, nor so narrow that it doesn't require support. The 4-S test that you used to determine whether a subject was suitable for a paper can also be applied to potential paragraph topics. If your topic is single, significant, specific, and supportable, it should form the basis for a solid paragraph. Take a look at these topic sentences.

Weak	Strong
The legal system in Canada discriminates against men. (too broad)	Single fathers who seek custody of their children are often treated unfairly in family court.
My children won't eat peas, broccoli, or spinach. (too narrow)	Getting young children to eat a balanced diet is not an easy challenge.
Cars should be banned from city streets. (too broad)	Cars should be banned from the downtown core from 7:00 a.m. to 7:00 p.m.

Exercise 7.1*

Read through each of the following paragraphs, then underline the topic sentence.

1.   The third consideration is perhaps the most important. Canada makes no economic sense. There may be excellent reasons for Canada's existence historically, socially, culturally, and even geographically, but the lines of trade and commerce flow north–south. If a government's chief concern is the economy, that government will naturally draw the country closer and closer to the United States, cinching in those belts of commerce that bind Canada to her southern partner. Only governments whose major goals are cultural or social will loosen the longitudinal ties and seek east–west bonds.

2.   Tobacco was first used by North American Aboriginal peoples, who introduced it, along with potatoes and pumpkins, to the early European settlers. The Native peoples used tobacco in religious ceremonies; only later did it come to be used for pleasure. The traders and explorers who brought it back to their compatriots in Europe must have had a difficult time getting the sophisticated nobles of England and France to put burning leaves into their mouths and inhale the smoke. Bob Newhart, back in his standup comic days, did a very funny routine on this theme in which Sir Walter Raleigh tries to explain the pleasures of smoking to some sceptical financial backers whose ship he has just filled with tobacco leaves to be imported to Europe.

3.   Seen by scanning electron microscope, our taste buds look as huge as volcanoes on Mars, while those of a shark are beautiful mounds of pastel-colored tissue paper—until we remember what they're used for. In reality, taste buds are exceedingly small. Adults have about 10,000, grouped by theme (salt, sour, sweet, bitter), at various sites in the mouth. Inside each one, about fifty taste cells busily relay information to a neuron, which will alert the brain. Not much tasting happens in the center of the tongue, but there are also incidental taste buds on the palate, pharynx, and tonsils, which cling like bats to the damp, slimy walls of a cave. Rabbits have 17,000 taste buds, parrots only about 400, and cows 25,000. What are they tasting? Maybe a cow needs that many to enjoy a relentless diet of grass.

Ackerman, Diane. *A Natural History of the Senses.* New York: Vintage-Random House, 1991. 138.

4.   Scholarly explanations of humor fall into three major categories. According to superiority theories, we laugh at the henpecked husband and the woman hit with a banana cream pie because the misfortunes of others make us feel better about our own lot. The 17th century philosopher Thomas Hobbes, for example, described laughter as a result of the "sudden glory" of increased self-esteem at the expense of others. Incongruity theories . . . stress the cognitive jolt of bringing together

unrelated ideas. Thus the infant who chuckles when Mommy eats the baby food is savoring the incongruity of a grown woman making a fool of herself. Finally, tension-relief theories attribute our laughter to a sudden release from strain. Freud argued that our jokes, like our dreams, allow pent-up sexual and aggressive images to suddenly leap into consciousness, albeit in a disguised form.

"What's So Funny?" *Psychology Today* June 1978: 101.

5.   "Why do you want it?" This should be the first question a good computer salesperson asks a prospective customer. With the huge variety of computers now on the market, the determining factor in a purchase should be the job the machine will be expected to do. While a network card, premium audio system, and 3-D video display are great for watching movies, a user who wants a basic wordprocessor would be throwing away money to buy them. Home users and small businesses often get carried away with the desire for gigantic memory capacity, lightning speed, and high resolution capability, but these are advertising gimmicks rather than useful purchases for most small users. On the other hand, it can be a costly error for a buyer to underestimate long-term computer needs and buy a machine that must be upgraded or replaced in a year.

Now compare your answers with ours on page 485.

GO TO WEB

EXERCISE 7.1

Exercise 7.2

Each of the following thesis statements contains a subject and main points. Working with a partner or in a small group, develop the main points of each thesis statement into effective topic sentences.

1. Volunteering is a valuable addition to a college education because it provides work experience, develops professional contacts, and enhances self-esteem.
2. Unemployment, poverty, and loneliness are factors that may lead to depression.
3. Canadians emigrate to other countries for three main reasons: a warmer climate, better job opportunities, and new cultural experiences.

Exercise 7.3

For each of the thesis statements below, develop the main points into effective topic sentences. Make sure each topic sentence you write introduces the topic clearly, makes a point about the topic, and is neither too broad nor too narrow.

1. The driver who caused your accident last weekend was probably one of four types: a road hog, a tailgater, a speed demon, or a Sunday driver.
2. There are three types of supervisor in this world: the good, the bad, and mine.
3. The thought of moving to the country is attractive to many city dwellers because of the slower pace, the healthier environment, and the closer-knit communities.

8

Developing the Topic

Once you've written your topic sentence, the next step is to develop it. An adequately developed paragraph gives enough supporting information to make the topic completely clear to the readers. Unless you are writing from a detailed outline listing all the supporting material you need, it's time to focus once again on your intended audience. Put yourself in your readers' place. How much information do your readers already have about your topic? Are they inclined to agree or disagree with you? What do your readers need to know to understand your point clearly? There are seven ways to develop a topic. Not all will be appropriate in every case, and some will be more effective than others. Let your topic and your audience guide you in choosing the most appropriate kind(s) of development.

1. **Tell a story.** Everyone loves to read a story if it's relevant and well told. An anecdote can be an effective way to help your readers not only understand your idea but also remember it. Below are two examples that illustrate the use of narration to develop a topic.

I first experienced culture shock when I travelled to Egypt. I was walking down the main street on the day of my arrival when it suddenly struck me that the crowds on the street were stepping aside to make way for me. It was 1990, and my height, blond hair, and blue eyes were so unusual to the Egyptians that I was an object of intense curiosity. The staring and pointing followed me everywhere. Finally, unable to cope any longer with being constantly on display, I took refuge in the Canadian Embassy and spent a couple of hours quietly leafing through back issues of *Maclean's* magazine.

Imagine that two accountants do similar jobs for similar companies. One day they make the same discovery: with almost no chance of getting caught, they can embezzle a large sum from their employers. They can both use the money to pay off debts or buy a new car. The first accountant right away says to himself, "It's wrong to steal," and never considers the matter again. But the second accountant is torn. She, too, knows that stealing is wrong, but she's tempted and at first decides to go ahead. Then she decides she won't, and then that she will. Finally, after weeks of agonizing, she decides not to embezzle. Who is the morally better person?

Hurka, Thomas. "Should Morality Be a Struggle? Ancient vs. Modern Ideas about Ethics." *Principles: Short Essays about Ethics.* Toronto: Harcourt Brace, 1994. 83.

Exercise 8.1

Using a story to develop your topic, write a paragraph on one of following, or choose a topic of your own.

1. An adventure in retail
2. The day I became an adult
3. The customer is not always right
4. How not to treat employees
5. My most embarrassing (frightening, amusing, unlucky) experience

2. **Define your topic.** A definition paragraph explains and clarifies the meaning of a word or idea. Use the definition paragraph to explain a term that may be unfamiliar to your readers. (Write your own definition, please. Quoting from a dictionary is an overused and boring way to start a paragraph.) Below are definitions of terms that two writers wanted to be certain their readers understood.

Culture shock is the inability to understand or cope with experiences one has never encountered before. It commonly affects travellers who journey to lands whose climate, food, language, and customs are alien to the traveller. In addition to confusion and anxiety, culture shock may even produce physical symptoms: chills, fever, trembling, and faintness.

Whereas the flood is a single bulb, strip lighting is a series of lamps set in a rectangular trough. It can be used for general illumination, but its primary functions are to blend the acting areas, illuminate shadows, and, with the use of colour, provide tone for settings and costumes. Strips can be hung as footlights, as border lights, or as special-purpose lights to illuminate backings for windows or doors.

You should include a definition, too, if you're using a familiar term in an unusual way. Here Martin Luther King defines what he means by "the length of life":

Now let us notice first the length of life. I have said this is the dimension of life in which the individual is concerned with developing his inner powers. It is that dimension of life in which the individual pursues personal ends and ambitions. This is perhaps the selfish dimension of life, and there is such a thing as moral and rational self-interest. If one is not concerned about himself he cannot be totally concerned about other selves.

King, Martin Luther, Jr. "The Dimensions of a Complete Life." *The Measure of a Man.* 1959. Philadelphia: Pilgrim Press, 1969.

Exercise 8.2

Choose one of the following topics (or select one of your own) and write a paragraph in which you develop the topic by defining it.

1. Burn-out
2. A good boss (employee, customer, colleague)
3. An extrovert (introvert)
4. A great artist (musician, actor, writer, etc.)
5. A bad habit

3. **Use examples.** Giving examples is probably the most common method of developing an idea and supporting a statement. Readers can become confused or suspicious when they read unsupported statements of "fact," opinion, or ideas. One of the best ways to support your topic is by providing clear, relevant examples.

A number of examples may be necessary to develop a point, as in this paragraph.

All sports may be reduced to a few basic skills, which, if learned properly at the outset and drilled until they are instinctive, lead to success. Tennis is no exception; however, few people seem willing to spend the time needed to master the basics. Having been shown the proper grip and swing for a forehand, backhand, and serve, my students seem to feel they can qualify for Wimbledon. The basics are not learned that easily. Many tennis schools are now using a system first developed in Spain that is very successful in establishing the correct stroke in new players: for the first month of lessons, they aren't allowed to use a tennis ball. For that first month, correct positioning, proper swing, footwork, and technique are drilled without any of the distractions of keeping score, winning or losing, or chasing errant balls. That's how important the basics are to winning tennis.

Sometimes, as in the paragraph below, a short narrative example is enough to allow your readers to see clearly what you mean.

Culture shock can affect anyone, even a person who never leaves home. My grandfather was perfectly content to be an accountant until he retired, and was confident that his company would need his services for the foreseeable future. Computers were "silly toys" and modern business practices just "jargon" and "a new fad." When he was laid off four years before his retirement, he went into shock. It wasn't just the layoff; it was the speed of change— the idea that he was stranded in a new and unfamiliar culture for which he was unprepared, and in which he had no useful role.

Exercise 8.3

Using examples to develop your topic, write a paragraph on one of following, or choose a topic of your own.

1. Parents and privacy
2. The Internet
3. Childless by choice
4. Adjusting to life away from home
5. The incompetence (incomprehensibility) of men (women)

4. **Use a quotation or paraphrase.** Occasionally you will find that someone else—an expert in a particular field, a well-known author, or a respected public figure—has said what you want to say better than you could ever hope to say it. Relevant and authoritative quotations, as long as they are kept short and are not used too frequently, are useful in developing your topic. Two sources of quotations on practically any subject are *John Robert Colombo's Famous Last Words: Great Canadian Quotations* (Vancouver: Douglas & McIntyre, 2000) and *Bartlett's Familiar Quotations* (http://www.columbia.edu/acis/bartleby/bartlett). In the paragraph below, Martin Luther King uses a famous quotation to sum up and emphasize his point that we humans are responsible for each other.

As long as there is poverty in the world, I can never be rich, even if I have a billion dollars. As long as diseases are rampant and millions of people in this world cannot expect to live more than twenty-eight or thirty years, I can never be totally healthy even if I just got a good check-up at Mayo Clinic. I can never be what I ought to be until you are what you ought to be. This is the way our world is made. No individual or nation can stand out boasting of being independent. We are interdependent. So John Donne placed it in graphic terms when he affirmed, "No man is an island entire of itself. Every man is a piece of the continent, a part of the main." Then he goes on to say, "Any man's death diminishes me because I am involved in mankind, and therefore never send to know for whom the bell tolls; it tolls for thee." When we discover this, we master the second dimension of life. (King, "Dimensions" 48–49)

A paraphrase is a statement, in your own words, of someone else's idea. Don't forget to indicate whose idea you are paraphrasing, the way King does here.

Some years ago a learned rabbi, the late Joshua Liebman, wrote a book entitled *Peace of Mind*. He has a chapter in the book entitled "Love Thyself Properly." In this chapter he says in substance that it is impossible to love other selves adequately unless you love your own self properly. Many people have been plunged into the abyss of emotional fatalism because they did not love themselves properly. So every individual has a responsibility to be concerned about himself enough to discover what he is made for. After he discovers his calling he should set out to do it with all of the strength and power in his being. . . . (King, "Dimensions" 38)

Exercise 8.4

Choose one of the following topics (or select one of your own) and write a paragraph in which you develop the topic by using quotations and/or paraphrase.

1. The most inspiring (uninspiring) teacher you have known
2. Everything I know I learned from my mother
3. A favourite book (movie, Web site)
4. The wisdom of children
5. Father knows (does not know) best

5. **Use a comparison.** A comparison shows similarities between things; it shows how two different things are alike in a particular way or ways. If you

have a difficult or abstract topic to explain, try comparing it to something that is familiar to your readers, as this writer does.

Being left on your own in a foreign land is a bit like being forced to play a card game when you're the only one who doesn't know the rules. As the stakes get higher and the other players' excitement and enjoyment increase, you get correspondingly more frustrated and miserable. Finally, in desperation, you want to throw your cards on the table, absorb your losses, and go home.

In this next paragraph, the writer uses an **analogy**—an extended comparison—between a date and a car to make the point both clear and interesting.

The economy-model date features cramped conditions and a lack of power. The econo-date thinks that his personality can make up for the fact that you never go anywhere except for walks and never do anything that costs money. He tends to be shy, quiet, and about as much fun as an oil leak. It's not just that he doesn't have money to spend; it's that he doesn't use any imagination or creativity to compensate for his lack of cash.

Exercise 8.5

Choose one of the following topics (or select one of your own) and write a paragraph in which you develop the topic by using comparison.

1. The modern workplace
2. E-mail
3. Two consumer products
4. Type A (Type B) personalities
5. Engineering (or computer science, arts, or nursing) students

6. **Explain steps or stages in a process.** Sometimes the most effective way to develop the main idea of your paragraph is by explaining how something is done—that is, by relating the series of steps involved. Make sure you break the process down into its component parts and detail the steps logically and precisely.

In 1983, a Harvard Medical School team led by Dr. Howard Green found a revolutionary way to repair burned skin. Here is how it is done. Doctors cut up a small patch of skin donated by a patient, treat it with enzymes, then spread it thinly onto a culture medium. After only ten days, colonies of skin cells begin linking up into sheets, which can then be chopped up and used to make further sheets. In twenty-four days, enough skin will be produced to cover an entire human body. About ten days later, the gauze is removed, and the skin soon grows into a surface much smoother and more natural-looking than the rough one a normal skin-graft usually leaves.

Ackerman, Diane. *A Natural History of the Senses.* New York: Vintage-Random House, 1990. 69–70.

In writing a process paragraph, you need to pay particular attention to transitions, which are discussed in the next chapter, or you'll leave your readers gasping in the dust as you gallop through your explanation. The paragraph below illustrates a simple yet effective use of transitions.

The second step to flunking with style, disdaining your studies, is easy to master. They're probably B-O-R-I-N-G anyway. First, don't buy your books until close to midterm and keep them in their original condition; don't open, read, or note anything in them. Better yet, don't buy your texts at all. Second, never attempt to take notes in class. Third, stop going to class completely, but have lots of creative excuses for missed assignments: "My friend's aunt died"; "My gerbil's in a coma"; "My boyfriend was in another car wreck"; "My dog ate the lab report"; "I've got mono." You can bet your teachers will be really amused by these old stand-bys. By now, you are well on your way to disaster.

Waldman, Nell. "Flunking with Style." *Canadian Content.* Ed. Sarah Norton and Nell Waldman. 2nd ed. Toronto: Harcourt, 1992. 113.

Exercise 8.6

Choose one of the following topics (or select one of your own) and write a paragraph in which you develop the topic by describing the series of steps or stages involved in the process.

1. Career planning
2. Buying a used car
3. Understanding women (men)
4. Writing a business report
5. Getting out of debt

7. **Provide specific details.** Concrete, specific, descriptive details can be an effective way to develop your main idea. In some paragraphs, numerical facts or statistics are essential to make your argument convincing or to back up your opinion. (Just make sure that your facts are 100 percent correct!)

In the paragraph below, the writer uses specific details to support a comparison of two automobiles.

Performance of the two cars was very close, especially when you consider the tiny difference at the speeds involved. However, I was able to get the 'Vette from 0 to 100 kph in exactly six seconds, while the Porsche took more than half a second longer. In cornering, the Porsche was marginally superior, but the Corvette was the clear winner in braking. From 100 km/h it came to a complete stop in 68 m; the Porsche went almost 2 m farther before stopping.

In this next paragraph, notice how Pierre Berton appeals to our senses in his description of the mixture he uses to season his famous baked beans.

When it [the seasoned liquid] tastes pungent and hot (remember that the pungency will be cut by the beans), stir in a large quantity of molasses. Most people don't use enough molasses, and yet this is the essence of all good baked bean dishes. For there comes a critical moment when the sweetness of the molasses is wedded to the sharpness of the vegetables and herbs, and it is this subtle flavour, baked indelibly into the beans and mingling with the pork fat, that brings a sparkle to the eyes.

Berton, Pierre. "Baked Beans." *Canadian Content*. Ed. Sarah Norton and Nell Waldman. 2nd ed. Toronto: Harcourt, 1992. 114.

Exercise 8.7

Using specific details to develop your topic, write a paragraph on one of following, or choose a topic of your own.

1. A Web page
2. A migraine headache
3. The myth of the shorter work week
4. The best team in hockey (baseball, football, lacrosse)
5. Money can't buy happiness

In writing your own paragraphs, you will often need to use more than one method of development to explain your point. The seven methods described in this chapter can be used in any combination you choose.

How Do You End a Paragraph?

A paragraph, like a door, should close firmly, with a "click." Do not assume that the reader will know by the blank space after your discussion that you've come to the end of your paragraph. A good paragraph doesn't just end, it closes. Even though you're tempted to just stop writing, don't.

Finish your paragraph with a statement that serves either as a **clincher**—an unmistakable and appropriate conclusion—or a **transition** to the new idea that will be developed in the next paragraph.

Exercise 8.8

Turn back to the paragraphs in Exercise 6.1 (pages 69–71). Reread each one and decide whether it ends with a clincher or a transition sentence.

Exercise 8.9

To stretch your imagination and improve your mastery of the kinds of support you can choose from to develop a topic, write a short paragraph on one of the following topics, using two or more methods of development.

1. Getting along with co-workers
2. Performance appraisal
3. Training a new employee

9

Keeping Your Readers with You

As you write, keep in mind that you want to make it as easy as possible for your readers to follow you through your essay. Unity, coherence, and tone can make the difference between a paper that confuses or annoys your readers and one that enlightens and pleases them.

Unity

Unity means "oneness." The contents of a paragraph must relate to a single main idea. All supporting sentences in the paragraph must clearly and directly relate to the topic sentence of that paragraph. A paragraph is said to be unified when it contains nothing that does not contribute to its main idea.

Achieving unity requires care. You want to develop the points that you have set out to make, not other points that may occur to you as you are writing. The time to set down whatever happens to come to mind is in the prewriting stage, not the paragraph development stage. Any material that does not clearly support the topic sentence should be deleted or moved to another paragraph in the essay—assuming, of course, that it is directly relevant there.

Take a look at the following paragraph. It contains several sentences that spoil the unity of the paragraph because they do not clearly relate to the topic.

(1) I knew I wanted to return to school, but did I want to be a full-time or a part-time student? (2) The major consideration was, not surprisingly, money. (3) If I chose to go to college full time, then I would have to give up my full-time job. (4) The resulting loss of income would reduce my buying power to zero. (5) Even the tuition fees would be beyond my reach. (6) Also, my choice of program

would be a difficult decision, because I still wasn't sure which career path to follow. (7) My other option was part-time education. (8) If I kept my full-time job, I could at least pay for food, rent, and a modest amount of clothing. (9) Also, I could afford the tuition fees. (10) Going to school part time costs less per year because the expenditure is spread over a longer period of time than it is in the full-time program. (11) Therefore, I chose to educate myself part time, through continuing education courses. (12) While working, I could learn new skills in my spare time. (13) My career choice would still be in doubt, but I would have a longer time in which to make up my mind. (14) Money is scarce for a full-time, self-supporting student, but as a part-time student I could have the best of both worlds: a steady income and a college education.

Draw a line through the sentences that do not logically and directly support the topic of the paragraph: the writer's decision whether to be a full-time or part-time student.

The sentences that you should have crossed out because they do not belong in this paragraph and detract from its unity are 6, 12, and 13.

Exercise 9.1*

The paragraphs below contain some irrelevant sentences that disrupt unity. Read each paragraph through and then, with a partner, find and cross out the sentences that don't belong.

1. (1) A good pizza consists of a combination of succulent ingredients. (2) First, you prepare the foundation, the crust, which may be thick or thin, depending on your preference. (3) I like my crusts thick and chewy. (4) The crust is spread with a layer of basil- and oregano-flavoured tomato sauce. (5) Next, a rich smorgasbord of toppings—pepperoni, mushrooms, green peppers, bacon, anchovies—should be scattered over the tomato sauce. (6) *Smorgasbord* is a Swedish word meaning a buffet meal; *pizza* is Italian in origin. (7) Last of all, a double-thick blanket of grated mozzarella cheese should be spread over all. (8) Pizza is simple to make—all you need is dough, tomato sauce, vegetables, sausage, herbs, and cheese—but the combination has an unbeatable taste.

2. (1) Keeping a job is not easy in a tight market in which well-educated job-seekers are plentiful. (2) Here are a couple of hints you will find helpful in maintaining your "employed" status. (3) First, you should not only apply your specialized knowledge on the job every day, but also continually update it by taking seminars and evening courses to enhance your skills. (4) Doing your job effectively is difficult without becoming burned out. (5) Second, good communication—with the public, your fellow workers, and your supervisor—is perhaps the most important factor in keeping you on the payroll. (6) Upgrading your education and improving your communication skills are your best defences against the pink slip.

3.　　(1) Comedies are my favourite way to relax. (2) Horror films terrify me, and adventures become tedious after the tenth chase, but comedies entertain and refresh me after a long shift at work. (3) Woody Allen pictures, especially the early farces, help me to take my mind off the stress of the day. (4) For example, *Bananas*, a satire about American politics in the 1960s, is more relaxing for me than a double martini. (5) It's also less fattening, and I've been trying to give up drinking. (6) *Sleeper*, a futuristic spoof, has me laughing, on average, twice a minute. (7) Perhaps my favourite, however, is *Annie Hall*. (8) After viewing it, I am so weak with laughter that I can go to sleep within minutes. (9) Now that all of Allen's comedies are available on video, I never need to feel tense and worn out for longer than it takes to insert a cassette.

4.　　(1) My department's job is to produce reports. (2) We research and prepare year-end reports, stockholders' reports, reports on the competition, on the customers, on the suppliers, and on just about everything else. (3) We think of ourselves as creative rather than technical writers because there is no future in our company for anyone who is critical or who dares to tell the truth if truth isn't what the senior managers want to hear. (4) Instead of fixing the problem, they punish the person who tells them what's wrong; that is, they "shoot the messenger." (5) I believe this saying originated in ancient days, long before there were guns, so presumably the original idea was "knife the messenger" or "behead the messenger." (6) If employees understand this management practice, however, they can protect themselves. (7) For example, our department has developed three rules to help us produce reports that are guaranteed a favourable reception. (8) First, teamwork is essential; without it, you have no one else to blame. (9) Second, when you don't know what you're doing, do it neatly. (10) Third, if at first you don't succeed, destroy all evidence that you ever tried. (11) With these rules to guide us, our department has survived three new managers in the past two and a half years.

5.　　(1) The office manager who demands that all employees not only arrive on time but actually get in early to demonstrate their enthusiasm and drive is actually damaging productivity. (2) Such a manager is, of course, always in the office at least an hour early herself, and because she attributes her success to this habit, she demands it of others. (3) Not everyone is suited to an early start. (4) Individual biorhythms vary widely, and some employees may be better suited to demonstrating their keenness by staying late at night. (5) The old adage "The early bird gets the worm" is based on some truth, but there are many exceptions. (6) Besides, what office worker wants a worm, anyway? (7) For that matter, there are lots of other sayings and aphorisms that can apply just as readily to the situation. (8) If your manager cites this tired old phrase as her justification for demanding unreasonably early hours, you may want to point out that another saying is equally true: "The second mouse gets the cheese."

Choose one of the topic sentences below and develop it into a paragraph. Include one or two sentences that do not relate directly to the topic, but try to incorporate them into the paragraph so they are not obvious. Exchange paragraphs with a partner and read his or her paragraph carefully, crossing out the sentences that do not belong. Rewrite the paragraph to improve its unity, and then return the paragraph to its original author.

1. Co-operative education gives students a head start in the workplace.
2. Lotteries exploit the gullibility of those who want to get rich quickly.
3. Volunteer work can lead to good career opportunities.
4. Since September 11, 2001, flying has become a nightmare.
5. An office romance is a dangerous self-indulgence.

Coherence

Coherence means "sticking together." The sentences within each paragraph need to stick together, or cohere, as do the paragraphs within an essay. If your sentences and paragraphs are not coherent, your reader will have great difficulty trying to fit together your bits of information to make sense of the whole. Sorting out sentences as if they were pieces of a puzzle is not the reader's job. It is the writer's responsibility to put the pieces together to form a complete and clear picture.

Coherence is achieved in two ways. First, you need to arrange the sentences in each paragraph according to an organizational principle. Remember the ways that you ordered the essay paragraphs in Chapter 3, "Managing the Main Points"? You should arrange your development within paragraphs in the same ways: chronological, climactic, logical, or, infrequently, random order. (Turn to pages 44–46 to review these.)

Second, you achieve coherence by providing **transitions**, or connections between one idea and the next within a paragraph, and between one paragraph and the next within an essay. Why are transitions needed? Read the paragraph below and you'll see clearly that something is missing. The paragraph has adequate development, but no transitions.

We were bored one day. We didn't know what to do. It was Friday. We thought about going to the library. No one really wanted to do schoolwork. We went to the mall. For a short time we window-shopped. We discussed what to do. It was agreed that we would drive to the American side of the border. We would do our shopping. It was a short drive. We went to a discount mall. The bargains were great. We spent much more money than we intended to. We went home. We discovered that with the American exchange, prices were better at home. We should have gone to the library.

Not very easy to read, is it? Readers are jerked abruptly from point to point until, battered and bruised, they finally reach the end. This kind of writing is unfair to readers. It makes them do too much of the work. The ideas may all be there, but the readers have to figure out for themselves how the ideas fit together. After a couple of paragraphs like the one above, even the most patient readers can become annoyed.

Now read the same paragraph, rewritten with transitions.

Last Friday we were so bored we didn't know what to do. We thought about going to the library, but no one really wanted to study, so we went to the mall and window-shopped for a while. After a long discussion about what to do next, we agreed to drive to the American side of the border for some serious shopping. A short drive later, we arrived at a discount mall, where the bargains were so great that we spent much more money than we had intended. Finally, we returned home, where we discovered that, with the American exchange, prices were better at home after all. We should have gone to the library.

Here the readers are gently guided from one point to the next. By the time they reach the conclusion, they know not only what ideas the writer had in mind, but also how the ideas fit together to form a unit. The transitions make the reader's job easy and rewarding.

You can choose from an array of strategies to improve the coherence of your writing. There are five techniques to master. Be sure to use a variety of these techniques every time you write. Nothing improves the polish of your prose more than the use of coherence strategies.

1. **Repetition.** Repetition focuses the reader's attention on an idea and creates a thread of meaning that runs through a paragraph or a paper, tying the whole thing together. Don't overdo it, though.

2. **Synonyms.** Frequent repetition of a key word can become monotonous after a while. You can keep the reader focused on the idea by using synonyms, different words that convey the same meaning.

3. **Pronoun references.** Another way of maintaining the focus but varying the wording is to use appropriate pronouns to refer to a key noun. (This technique involves pronoun–antecedent agreement, a topic covered in Chapter 32.)

4. **Parallel structure.** Phrasing your sentences in parallel form helps to maintain focus, reinforces the unity of your thoughts, and adds emphasis.

Parallelism adds "punch" to your writing. (More punch is served in Chapter 28.)

5. **Transitional words and phrases.** Transitional words and phrases show the relationships between points in a paragraph as well as between paragraphs in an essay. They act like tape, sticking together the elements of a paragraph or a paper so your reader does not fall between the cracks. Use them the way you use turn signals on a car: to tell the person following you where you're going.

Here are some transitional phrases that will help make your writing read smoothly.

Transitional Function	Words/Phrases Used
1. **To show a time relationship between points**	• first, second, third • now, simultaneously, concurrently, at this point, while • before, to begin, previously • after, following this, then, later, next • finally, last, subsequently • during, meanwhile, presently, from time to time, sometimes
2. **To add an idea or example to the previous point**	• and, in addition, also, furthermore, besides, moreover, for the same reason • another, similarly, equally important, likewise • for example, for instance, in fact
3. **To show contrast between points**	• although, nevertheless, on the other hand, whereas • but, however, instead, nonetheless • in contrast, on the contrary, in spite of, despite
4. **To show a cause-and-effect relationship between points**	• since, because, thus, therefore, hence • as a result, consequently, accordingly
5. **To emphasize or repeat a significant point**	• in fact, indeed, certainly, undoubtedly • in other words, as I have said, that is to say
6. **To summarize or conclude**	• in brief, on the whole, in summary, in short • therefore, as a result, last, finally

The paragraph below is an excellent example of the use of transitional devices to achieve coherence. As you read, pay particular attention to the writer's use of repetition and parallelism.

While the Internet can be a useful tool for some businesses, studies have shown that in most workplaces it is a time-wasting drain on resources. As a result of one such study, Deloitte and Touche have issued a report pointing out the "five G's": risks of allowing employees unsupervised Internet activity during business hours. A company risks Giving, handing trade or business secrets over to the competition or the general public. A company risks Gawking, time-wasting employee fascination with particular sites, including pornography. A company risks Gambling, an increasingly common and potentially addictive lure for surfers. A company risks Goofing off, the pointless surfing of sites that are unrelated to the task at hand. A company risks Grabbing, the downloading of virus-infected material and copyrighted software. To counter the five G's, Deloitte and Touche recommend that companies establish clear policy on Internet use.

Owner Manager Advisor newsletter. *Globe and Mail* 25 Jan. 1998: B15.

Exercise 9.3*

Working with a partner, identify the transitional words and phrases that create coherence in each of the sentence groups below.

1. The spruce budworm threatens B.C.'s forests, killing trees that have resisted all other predators. Therefore, governments at both the local and provincial levels have begun a controlled burn program.
2. The two women spent the whole day tramping from car dealer to car dealer. Finally, they found a used Toyota they could live with, but the price was higher than they had hoped to pay.
3. There are many jokes about cats. Unfortunately, however, in most of them the cat is either very unhappy or dead.
4. There are those who think Quebec would thrive as a separate state. On the other hand, some feel that its economic viability depends on a close relationship with the rest of Canada.
5. Although we fear the size and power of our big banks, we must admit that they serve us well when compared with the banking institutions of other countries. For example, Canadian banks are second only to Japanese banks, and ahead of those in the United States and Germany, in the number of automated tellers per person they provide. In addition, they lead all three of these countries in the number of full-service branches per capita.

Exercise 9.4

In each of the following sentences, supply transitional words or phrases that help the meaning become clearer and make the sentence more coherent. When you've finished, exchange exercises with another student and check each other's answers. If you disagree with any of your partner's choices, explain why.

1. My first impression of my supervisor was that he was aloof and arrogant; _____, I discovered I was wrong. He was painfully shy.

2. Many best-sellers have become pathetic movies, now long forgotten. _____ many poor novels have been turned into movie classics, such as *Gone with the Wind*, that last forever.

3. Many sports were discovered by accident. _____, one day at Rugby school in the 1830s, an English schoolboy, during a game of rugby, threw the ball overhand down the field. Football (as we call it in North America) was born.

4. Architecture in the twentieth century has become more streamlined, geometrical, and uniform. _____, it has become monotonous.

5. The fountain of youth was rumoured to be in the swamps of Florida, _____ Ponce de Leon spent most of his last years looking for it.

Exercise 9.5*

Read the paragraphs below and identify the transitional strategies that contribute to coherence. Both paragraphs contain examples of all five techniques listed on pages 90–91.

1.   Finally, developing the proper attitude is the true key to winning tennis. I define winning tennis as playing the game to the best of your ability, hitting the ball as well as you know you can, and enjoying the feeling of practised expertise. Winning tennis has nothing to do with beating an opponent. Naturally, if you play winning tennis by learning the basics, practising sufficiently, and concentrating, you'll win many matches, but that is the reward of playing well, not the reason for playing well. People who swear and throw their racquets when they lose are very useful; they are the most satisfying players to trounce. But I don't understand why they play a game that causes them such pain. Tennis players who enjoy the feel

of a well hit ball and the satisfaction of a long, skilfully played rally are winners, regardless of the score.

2.   Travel abroad offers you the best education you can get. For one thing, travel is a course in communication skills. In order to function in a foreign language, you must practise every aspect of the communication process from body language to pronunciation. In fact, just making yourself understood is a lesson in creativity, a seminar in sign language, and a lab in communication theory. Another educational aspect of travel is the history, geography, and culture that you learn about almost unconsciously. Everywhere you go, you encounter memorable evidence of historic events you may dimly recall from school, and you are continually confronted by the practical realities of geography as you try to find your way around. As for culture, no book or course of study could provide you with the understanding and appreciation of another society that living in it can. A third way in which travel educates is through teaching you about yourself. Your ability—or inability—to cope with unfamiliar customs, with language difficulties, and with the inevitable problems of finding transportation and accommodation will tell you more than you might want to know about yourself. Without the safety net of family and friends, perhaps without even the security of knowing where you'll spend the night, you develop self-reliance or you go home. Either way, you learn valuable lessons. While you may not get a diploma from Travel U., you'll learn more about the world, about people, and about yourself than you will in any classroom.

Now compare your answers to ours on pages 485–86.

Exercise 9.6

Now consider the ways coherence strategies can be used to promote the smooth flow of ideas throughout an essay. Identify the transitional techniques used in the essay on risk-taking, which appears on pages 16–17.

Exercise 9.7

In pairs, rewrite the unified paragraphs you developed in Exercise 9.2, removing all the transitional words and phrases. Exchange the result with another team and rewrite each other's paragraphs to restore transitions. Share and discuss your results with the other pair.

Tone

As you write each paragraph of your paper, try to be conscious of your tone. **Tone** is a word used to describe the writer's attitude toward his or her subject and readers. Your tone is determined partly by the level of language you choose. Informal diction lends itself to warm, personal, or comic writing. Formal diction is appropriate for serious, solemn discussions. General level language can be used to express a multitude of tones: sympathetic, ironic, humorous, angry, or neutral. In addition to the words you use, the examples, quotations, and any other supporting materials you choose to help explain your main points all contribute to your tone. Once you've decided on the tone you want to use, stick with it. Your language and content should be consistent. An obituary is no place for a joke.

Be aware that when you are trying to explain something you feel strongly about, you may be tempted to be highly emotional in your discussion. If you allow yourself to "get emotional," chances are that you will not be convincing. What will be communicated is the strength of your feelings, not the depth of your understanding or the validity of your opinion. To be clear and credible, you need to channel your enthusiasm (or your anger) into presenting your points in a reasonable way.

Two suggestions may help you to find and maintain the right tone. First, never insult your readers, even unintentionally. Avoid phrases such as "any fool can see," "no sane person could believe," and "it is obvious that. . . ." Remember that what is "obvious" to you isn't necessarily obvious to someone who has a limited understanding of the subject or who disagrees with your opinion. Don't "talk down" to your readers as though they were children or simpletons. Don't use sarcasm, and avoid profanity.

Second, don't apologize for your interpretation of your subject. Have confidence in yourself: you've thought long and hard about the subject, you've found good supporting material to help explain it, and you believe in its significance. Present your subject in a positive manner. If you hang back, using phrases such as "I may be wrong, but . . ." or "I tend to feel that . . . ," your readers won't be inclined to give your points the consideration they deserve. Keep your readers in mind as your write, and your writing will be both clear and convincing.

Exercise 9.8*

Rewrite the following paragraph, adding transitions where necessary and correcting any lapses in tone.

I'm no expert—in fact, I really don't know anything about it—but it seems to me that anyone who enjoys watching baseball is a masochist. I may be wrong (I usually am), but it's a very dull game, don't you think? About every third pitch the batter swings. The fielders do nothing. There are about 15 hits in a three-hour game. The players actually do something for approximately $7\frac{1}{2}$

minutes of an entire afternoon. Home runs are dull. One man trots around the bases. The other players stand and watch. An awful lot of people seem to like baseball People who like baseball are probably boring people.

Exercise 9.9

Write a reply to this attack on baseball. Remember to keep your tone consistent, and use at least three different coherence strategies in your paragraph.

Exercise 9.10

Revise the following paragraph, adding transitions and moderating its tone.

The armed forces of most nations are trained to be psychopaths. Canada's military personnel face a greater challenge: they need to be schizophrenics. The boot-camp training that recruits undergo, together with instruction in combat and weaponry, produces efficient and remorseless killers—psychopaths. The role of Canada's armed forces over the past 50 years has been to keep the peace. When the Nobel Peace Prize was awarded to the United Nations peacekeeping forces, Canada, as the only nation to have participated in every mission, considered the prize largely hers. Canada's elite forces played a traditional military role as hunters and killers in Afghanistan. Is Canada's military adequately trained for these two contradictory roles? Our country needs highly trained units of efficient psychopaths. The majority of armed forces personnel need training in mediation, conflict resolution, cultural sensitivity, basic medical treatment, and infrastructure repair. This is a hard concept for fans of the military to get through their thick skulls: soldiers trained to prevent violence. Peacekeeping is still the Canadian military's primary function. Canada's armed forces have two roles. Both must be prepared for.

10

Writing Introductions and Conclusions

All of the concepts you've studied so far can be applied to any paragraph. Two paragraphs, however—the first and the last—serve special purposes and need extra care. All too often, the introduction and the conclusion of a paper are dull or clumsy and detract from its effectiveness. But they needn't be dull or clumsy. Here's how to write good ones.

The Introductory Paragraph

The introduction is worth special attention because that's where your readers either sit up and take notice of your paper or sigh and pitch it into the wastebasket.

When we first discussed the concept of dividing a paper into paragraphs, we used the analogy of the TV sitcom, which is separated into distinct parts by commercials. The first section of the sitcom functions in ways the other parts don't. First, it attracts the viewers with a particularly funny moment, a captivating situation, or an intriguing problem. Second, it sets the plot in motion or gets the action started. The introductory paragraph has a similar role in your paper.

There are two parts to an introductory paragraph:
1. an attention-getter
2. a thesis statement

Getting and Holding Your Readers' Attention

Your readers must be attracted to your writing or there's no point in putting your pen to paper or fingers to keyboard. The attention-getter must be appropriate to the content of your essay and to your intended readers. If your audience is known for a solemn approach to life and your topic is serious (environmental ethics, for instance, or antidiscrimination policies in the workplace), then there is no point in leading off with a pun or joke, no matter how witty. Such an opening would be inappropriate and probably offensive to your readers.

Your attention-getter does not have to be a single sentence; in fact, good ones are often several sentences long. Your readers will be committing varying amounts of personal time to reading your writing. You owe it to them to make your opening sentences clear, interesting, and creative.

An effective attention-getter should be followed by an equally effective thesis statement, one that slides smoothly and easily into place. Your readers should be aware only of a unified paragraph, not of two separate parts in your introduction.

Below are eight different kinds of openings you can choose from to get your readers' attention and lead up to your thesis statement. In each of the example paragraphs, note how the attention-getter and the thesis statement are solidly linked to form a unified whole. To demonstrate that you can take many different approaches to a subject, depending on your purpose and your audience, we have used the same subject—physical fitness—in all of the introductions.

1. **Spell out the significance of your subject.** If your subject's significance can catch your readers' interest, they will want to know more about it, especially if it is a subject that affects them directly.

More and more young people are dying of heart disease. Despite the statistics that say most people in our society are living longer thanks to advances in medicine and surgery, the figures can be misleading. It is a fact that people in their thirties and forties are dying from coronary problems that once threatened people in their fifties and sixties. What has caused this change? Certainly, the increase in stress, the fatigue of overwork, the rise in obesity, and the decline in physical activity are all contributing factors. To combat the risk of cardiovascular disease, we need physical activity. Regular exercise can forestall the ravages of heart disease and promote longevity.

2. **Begin with a well-phrased quotation.** You might choose a famous statement, a popular slogan, or a common saying. Use a quotation when it sums up your point of view more succinctly and effectively than your own words could. As a rule, you should identify the source of the quotation.

"Who can be bothered?" "I'm much too busy." "I get all the exercise I need at the office." We've all heard excuses like these, excuses for avoiding regular exercise. Modern life, with its distractions and conveniences, tends to make people sedentary and lazy, but the human organism cannot tolerate inactivity and stress indefinitely. Eventually, it begins to break down. Those who want to keep in shape for the challenges of modern life should consider the benefits of working out a few times a week. Regular exercise can rejuvenate the body, refresh the mind, and improve self-confidence.

3. **Use a startling statement.** Sometimes a surprising remark (not an insult or a false exaggeration) is effective in getting readers' attention. A little-known or striking fact will have the same effect.

After the age of thirty, the average North American puts on ten to twenty kilograms of fat. Presumably, the cause for this startling increase in avoirdupois is a combination of metabolic changes, decreased physical activity, and hundreds of kilos of junk food ingested since childhood. It's difficult to stop the spread of middle-aged corpulence, but experts tell us we *can* resist the rise in flab by reducing our caloric intake and increasing our physical activity. Regular exercise can rejuvenate the body, refresh the mind, and improve self-confidence.

4. **Ask a question or two.** Questions are often an effective way to encourage interest because your readers will find themselves thinking of answers. Some questions are rhetorical; that is, they will not have specific answers. Others might be answered in your essay.

Have you been feeling sluggish and exhausted lately? Has your blood pressure increased along with your waistline in the past few years? Are you stalled in front of the television set every night with potato chips and a beer? If so, you are probably suffering from a common middle-aged ailment called *flabitis*. This malady strikes most people over thirty: they put on weight, have trouble concentrating, tire easily, and prefer watching sports to participating in them. Fortunately, there is a cure for flabitis: a three-times-weekly dose of exercise. With regular exercise, you can rejuvenate your body, refresh your mind, and improve your self-confidence.

5. **Begin with a generalization related to your subject.** Generalizations can be useful for suggesting the context and scope of your subject. They must, however, be narrowed down carefully to a focused thesis statement.

Until the twentieth century, physical exercise was part of the normal workday. Our ancestors were farmers, pioneers, sailors, and so on. Few of our parents, however, made their living by ploughing the land or chopping down trees. Since the early 1900s, the trend in work has been away from physical exertion and toward automation. Today's generation uses technology to reduce physical activity even further: they pick up the phone, ride the elevator, and take the car to the corner store. Modern inactivity has negative consequences that only physical exercise can counter. To sustain good health, sharpen your mental edge, and have fun, you should take up aerobics or sports and use your body in the way it was intended—actively.

6. **Challenge a common opinion.** Perhaps your readers have also doubted a popular belief. Your thesis statement can assert that an opinion is false, and the body of your paper can contain evidence to support your opposing view.

Physical activity is for kids. Adults don't have time to hit a baseball or run around a field chasing after one, or to do aerobics and lift weights in a gym. They have to earn a living, raise families, and save money for retirement. They can leave exercise to their children. I firmly believed this until one morning when, late for work, I ran after a bus. My heart pounded; my lungs gasped; my head swam. It had been some years since my last stint of exercise, and I realized I wouldn't be around to do my job, support my family, or enjoy retirement unless I got into the habit of doing something physical to maintain my health. Regular exercise can rejuvenate the body, refresh the mind, and broaden one's interests.

7. **Begin with a definition.** A definition is a good way to begin if you are introducing a key term that you suspect may be unfamiliar to your readers. If the subject of your essay depends on a personal meaning of a term that most people understand in a different way, a definition is essential.

Myocardial infarction: the very term is frightening. It occurs when a person's muscles slacken from disuse, the veins clog up with sticky fats, and the heart has to work too hard to sustain even minor exertion such as raking leaves or shovelling snow. The muscles of the heart become strained to exhaustion or balloon outward because the veins cannot pass blood quickly enough. In plain English, a myocardial infarction is a heart attack. If the victim is lucky enough to survive, physicians prescribe a regimen of less stress, low fat intake, and regular exercise.

8. Describe an interesting incident or tell an anecdote related to your subject. Readers like stories; keep yours short and to the point by narrating only the highlights. The incident or anecdote you select might be a story from the media, an event involving family or friends, or a personal experience.

> Last year, I got a free invitation in the mail to a fitness club. I responded, out of curiosity, but I needed to be convinced. After all, I was thirty-five, had grown a little paunch, and was a bit short of breath on the stairs; ten years had passed since I had last played sports. My first workout was a nightmare. My joints ached, my muscles throbbed, and my head spun. I was in worse shape than I thought. After a few weeks, those symptoms disappeared, and I began to enjoy myself. My paunch vanished and my muscles toned up. My capacity for concentration increased. Also, I met some new people who have become friends. Obviously, ten years is too long between workouts, given that exercise not only rejuvenates the body and refreshes the mind but also improves one's social life.

Exercise 10.1

In groups of five, consider five movies you have all seen within the past year. How did each of these movies begin so that the audience was "locked in"? How do these movie "grabbers" relate to the kinds of attention-getters you have just read?

Exercise 10.2

Each of the following paragraphs is the introductory paragraph of an essay. Work in pairs and, using the strategy given in parentheses, write an appropriate attention-getter for each paragraph.

1. (significance of subject) _____

_____

TV commercials that portray unrealistic and unattainable lifestyles should be banned. Although I do not support censorship, I believe there is sufficient evidence of the damage done by these advertisements to justify eliminating them in the name of public interest. The objectionable commercials promote sexual stereotyping, set up unrealistic and dangerous expectations, and encourage irresponsible consumerism.

2. (quotation) _____

_____

Every sport has its strange expressions, just as every sport has its devoted fans, its famous teams, and its legendary heroes. A sport that gets very little attention in Canada but is very popular in many parts of the world, especially Commonwealth countries, is cricket. Like the sports that millions of Canadians follow enthusiastically, cricket is an exciting and fascinating game once you become familiar with its rules and style. In fact, it compares very favourably with baseball in skill, pace, and strategy.

3. (startling statement) _____

_____

Canadian roads are overrun by drivers who are a danger to themselves, their passengers, and others on the road. Inept drivers demonstrate their inadequacies in so many ways that it would be impossible to list them all in one short paper. Nevertheless, bad drivers can be broadly categorized as traumatized turtles, careening cowboys, and daydreaming dodos.

4. (question) _____

_____

Arranged marriages are a very important part of my culture. When my family moved to Canada, we left behind many of the traditions and customs that were as natural to us as breathing. However, my parents retained their right to choose a wife for me, even though they are aware that this custom is at odds with the Canadian way of life. Although their decision was at first difficult to accept, I believe there are good reasons that an arranged marriage may be best for me. The decision will be made by mature people in a thoughtful manner, uninfluenced by the enthusiasms of youth; the decision will be made by people who have at heart the best interests of our family, the bride's family, and me; and the decision will be made in accordance with a centuries-old tradition that has proven its success generation after generation.

5. (generalization) _____

_____

My first project manager was the sort of person that nightmares are made of. It's been a year since she was finally transferred to another department, but I still shudder when I recall our six months together. Denise was rude, bossy, and, worst of all, thoughtless.

6. (opinion you challenge) _____

_____

The evidence strongly suggests that overexposure to the sun can cause several forms of cancer at worst and premature aging at best. We can't completely avoid the sun's rays, but there are several measures we can take to prevent the damage that normal outdoor activity might cause. To enjoy the summer without fear, use an effective sun block, cover sensitive skin completely, and limit your time in the sun.

7. (definition) _____

_____

The choice of corrective lenses is an individual matter, but many people go through a tough decision-making process when confronting the issue. In deciding whether contact lenses or eyeglasses are more suitable, one should examine factors such as comfort, convenience, and appearance.

8. (anecdote or incident) _____

_____

Black flies are just one of the pests that make life less than comfortable in Canada during the spring, but they tend to be the most irritating. No method of combatting the pests is foolproof, but there are several methods that can be employed, either singly or together, to repel most of them. The campaign against the black fly begins with protective clothing, follows up with an effective repellent, and goes over the top with the secret weapon: garlic.

Exercise 10.3

With the class divided into five teams, consider the following essay topics. Each team will take one of the topics and develop the first sentence of an introductory paragraph for it. The sentence will then be passed in sequence to the next group, who will add a sentence to the paragraph. Continue this exercise until each paragraph contains both an attention-getter and a thesis statement. When each team gets back the paragraph it initiated, they will revise and polish the paragraph, identify the kind of attention-getter that has been developed, and underline the thesis statement. Share the results with the rest of the class. (Keep these paragraphs; you will need them later.)

1. Why I want to be a _____ (fill in your career choice)
2. Why I chose _____ (fill in your school)

3. How not to treat a co-worker
4. My favourite restaurant
5. The trouble with customers

The Concluding Paragraph

Like the introduction, the conclusion of your paper has a special form. Think back to your favourite television sitcom. The last section of the show wraps up the plot, explains any details that might still be unresolved, and leaves you with a satisfying sense that all is well, at least until next week. A concluding paragraph works in a similar way.

The last paragraph of your paper has two similar special functions.
1. It summarizes or reinforces the main points of your paper.
2. It ends with an appropriate memorable statement.

Your **summary statement** should be as concise as you can make it, and must be phrased in such a way that it does not repeat word-for-word the portion of your thesis statement that identifies the main points. (Note that a summary is not needed in a very short essay.)

A **memorable statement** is a sentence designed to leave your readers feeling satisfied with your essay and perhaps taking away with them something for further thought. Never end without a clincher. Don't just quit writing when your main points are covered, or you'll leave your readers hanging, wondering what to make of it all.

Six strategies you can choose from in writing a memorable statement are described below. Each of the strategies is illustrated by a sample concluding paragraph. Identify the summary and the memorable statement in each conclusion.

1. **End with a relevant or thought-provoking quotation.** You can use this type of ending in two ways: repeat an earlier quotation but give it a new meaning, or place your subject in a larger context by supplying a new quotation from a recognized authority in the field.

Since I began lifting weights every second day, I have lowered my blood pressure, improved my productivity at work, and made some new friends at the fitness club. I will never be Arnold Schwarzenegger, but that isn't my goal. My muscles are pleasantly sore after a good workout, but as Arnold says, "No pain, no gain." As long as the pain is so little and the gain is so great, I will continue to enjoy my regular workouts.

2. **Offer a solution to a problem discussed in your paper.** You can plan an organization for your paper that will allow you to resolve a problem or neutralize negative consequences in your conclusion.

I've got the best intentions in the world. I know that exercise benefits me physically, mentally, and emotionally—but I still don't have the time. I didn't, that is, until last month, when I was home from work for a week because I sprained my ankle while walking the dog. That never would have happened if I had been in shape. Since then, I have forced myself to manage my time to allow for a fitness program. Four hours of exercise a week is not a very big investment of time compared with four days of lying on the couch with a painfully swollen foot.

3. **End with one or more relevant or thought-provoking questions.** The advantage of clinching with a question is that readers tend automatically to mull over a question: questions stimulate thought. Before they know it, readers will begin to formulate answers to your question—and that activity will make them remember your points. One caution, however: be sure your question relates directly to your subject.

My life has improved considerably since I took up jogging three times a week: I enjoy better health, less brain-fog, and more confidence. And I'm inspired to continue jogging by the fact that coronary disease runs in my family. My father and grandfather both suffered heart attacks in their fifties. If they had done regular exercise, could they have reduced their chances of coronaries? Would they still be alive today?

4. **Point out the value or significance of your subject to your readers.** If you emphasize your subject matter at the end of your paper, you can stamp its importance on your readers' memory.

Regular exercise is the best way to stay in shape, be sharp, and feel strong; it is the best way to reduce the risk of arthritis, arterial decay, and heart dysfunction. In a country where the most common cause of mortality is coronary collapse, everyone needs to consider the value of consistent exercise. It is a small daily inconvenience that pays large and long-term rewards.

5. **Make a connection to a statement made in your introduction.** This strategy provides your readers with a sense of closure. They will recall your earlier statement and feel satisfied that the loose ends have been tied.

Having exercised now for six months, I can run for the bus without losing my breath, sweating profusely, or feeling dizzy. My body is in better trim; my endurance and confidence on the job have grown. After a lapse of twenty years, I have even taken up the bicycle again: I go riding along local bike trails with friends. And now, when my children are playing baseball in the yard, I don't think, "Baseball is for kids." I'm first at the plate. Batter up!

6. **End with a suggestion for change or a prediction about the future.** Your suggestion for change will influence your readers if they have been persuaded by your arguments. Your predictions of events that might occur should not be misleading or exaggerated, or your readers will be sceptical. Make predictions that are possible and plausible.

If those of us who still prefer junk food, overwork, and television don't shape up, then the incidence of coronary disease will continue to rise. Moderate exercise will benefit body, mind, and spirit. If we follow common sense and change our habits of self-pollution and self-destruction, all of us can lead long, active, and healthy lives.

Exercise 10.4

Each of the following is the concluding paragraph of an essay. Working in pairs, underline the summary statement and write a memorable conclusion. See if you can use a different kind in each paragraph.

1. Both games are enjoyable for spectators and create real enthusiasm among fans. High schools that have chosen soccer have seen no reduction in school spirit or fan support. For educational institutions to make the switch from football is really a "no-lose" proposition because soccer provides dramatic advantages in reducing player injury, increasing player fitness, and shaving thousands of dollars from school expenses.

    _____

    _____

    _____

    _____

2. Opinion about the two shows is pretty evenly divided, but is certainly passionate. Late-night television viewers either love them or hate them. In truth, there are more similarities than differences between the two shows because both rely on humour and celebrity guests to attract viewers. Those who favour Letterman love his zany humour, irreverent style, and the constant surprises he

springs. Leno appeals to those who enjoy more topical humour and like hearing from his impressive guest list. My own preference is for Letterman, but there are millions of North Americans who disagree.

_____

_____

_____

_____

3.   Although the causes of dropout among first-year students are as individual as the students themselves, the effects are easier to categorize. Conflict with parents and others whose expectations have not been met comes first, followed by a loss of self-esteem. The determination to succeed despite this unfair setback is common, but statistics show that low-paying, dead-end jobs are the norm for the college dropout. The situation is much worse, of course, for those who don't complete high school.

_____

_____

_____

_____

4.   Great parties seldom just happen; they are the products of careful thought and planning. If a truly great party should occur spontaneously, then chance has brought the right ingredients together, just as chance can sometimes result in high marks on multiple-choice tests. The right people, brought together in the right place, for the right reason, will produce a memorable event every time.

_____

_____

_____

_____

5.   Drinking and driving must be stopped. To stop it will require substantial commitment from all levels of government, both in terms of money and in terms of political will. The penalties for driving while under the influence of alcohol must be increased, and more money must be spent for education and publicity. But, more than these measures, it will take the individual will of every Canadian to make the promise not to drive after drinking. Nothing will bring my sister back, but there are lots of other sisters out there—and brothers and mothers and fathers—who can be saved.

_____

_____

_____

_____

Exercise 10.5

With the class divided into the same five teams as in Exercise 10.3, write concluding paragraphs to complement the introductions you developed in that exercise. Here's how to proceed. Begin by reviewing the introductory paragraph you developed for Exercise 10.3. Now write the first sentence of a concluding paragraph for this same topic. Pass your sentence, together with your introductory paragraph, along to the next group, who will write a second sentence for the conclusion. Continue this process until the conclusion is complete and contains both a summary or reinforcement and a memorable statement. Return the paragraph to the group that initiated it for revising and polishing. Share the results with the rest of the class.

11

Choosing the Right Words

In this chapter we will examine language that is appropriate—and inappropriate—in academic and professional communication. In the workplace, we know that our supervisors, clients, co-workers, and customers all expect us to wear appropriate clothing. They also expect a certain level and style of language from us. Like the clothing we choose, the language we use tells the people with whom we come into contact what we're like and helps to influence how they respond to us. Cut-off jeans and a torn T-shirt convey an image; the same image is conveyed by the phrase "I should of helped out, but I didn't do nothing." While both might be acceptable in some circumstances, they are not appropriate in the kind of jobs college graduates are seeking. Just as there are many inappropriate styles of dress, there are several inappropriate types of language. Among the most serious offenders are clichés, jargon, slang, pretentious writing, sexist language, wordiness, and what we call "abusages."

Clichés

A **cliché** is an expression that has been used so often it has lost its impact, if not its meaning.

> We are sick and tired of the tried and true approach to office management and are seeking a breath of fresh air.

Sick and tired, tried and true, and *breath of fresh air* are clichés. Readers know what these phrases are supposed to mean, but they have been used so often, they no longer communicate effectively. Cliché-filled writing will not only bore readers, it will also affect their impression of your entire message: "There's nothing new here. It's all been said before."

Spoken English is full of clichés. In the rush to express an idea, we often take the easy way and use ready-made expressions to put our thoughts into words. There is less excuse to use clichés in writing. Writers have time to think through what they want to say. They also have the opportunity to revise and edit. Writers are expected to communicate with more care, more precision, and more originality than speakers.

Clichés are easy to recognize if you are a native speaker. When you can read the first few words of an expression and automatically fill in the rest, the phrase is a cliché: free as a _____; a pain in the _____; last but not_____; it goes without _____. It is difficult to get rid of *all* clichés in your writing, but you can be aware of them and use them as seldom as possible. The solution to a cliché problem involves time and thought. Think carefully about what you want to say; then say it in your own words, not everyone else's.

As you read through Exercise 11.1, notice how hard it is to form a mental picture of what the sentences mean and how hard it is to remember what you've read—even when you've just read it!

Exercise 11.1

Rewrite these sentences, expressing the ideas in your own words. When you're finished, exchange papers with another student and compare your results.

1. The boardroom was so quiet you could hear a pin drop.
2. It was raining cats and dogs, but we slept like a log through the storm.
3. When you are playing poker, you should keep your cool; otherwise, you could lose your shirt.
4. The CEO could not find a way to stay afloat, so she threw in the towel.
5. I burned the midnight oil and managed to finish the assignment at the crack of dawn.
6. Is this concept a flash in the pan or an idea whose time has come?
7. The crisis we face is the result of cutting corners instead of pulling out all the stops.
8. She stopped dead in her tracks. Lying on the floor was her son, crying his eyes out.
9. Your proposal is as good as they come; however, until the deal is signed, sealed, and delivered, we had better not count our chickens.
10. Despite the fact that I worked night after night until the wee hours, I didn't get a bonus this year. As a result, I am sadder but wiser.

Slang and Jargon

Dressing for an office job in baggy denims with a neon Hawaiian shirt and boarder boots is the clothing parallel of slang. **Slang** is "street talk": non-standard language that indicates a close, informal relationship among those who speak it. It is used by people who share a culture or lifestyle or who want to appear to share a culture or lifestyle. Slang serves to reinforce membership in subgroups that can be as large as a generation or as small as a city block. It is highly colourful, non-technical language that has the primary purpose of indicating to the listener that the speaker is part of the group; communicating meaning is secondary. Slang is also very short-lived and, except for one or two expressions that might enter mainstream communication, goes out of fashion very quickly.

When written, slang limits and can even block your communication with your readers. If they do not share your subgroup, they are unlikely to understand what you are talking about. Because it dates so quickly, slang can distract readers from what the writer is saying. What would you think of a writer who used expressions such as *Right on, man*; *Groovy!* or *Far out!* in a text?

Unless you are quoting someone who has used slang, avoid it in professional and academic writing. If you are uncertain of the status of a word, check the dictionary. The notation *sl.* or *slang* appears after words that are slang or have a slang meaning. (Some words, such as *neat*, *chick*, and *hammered*, have both a general meaning and a slang meaning.) Taking the time to choose language appropriate to standard written English increases your chances of successful communication and shows courtesy to your readers.

Exercise 11.2

Write a list of ten slang words that are in current use in your peer group. "Translate" them into words or phrases that could be appropriately used in writing. Here are some examples to get you started.

whack   ill   freak   cool   fly   hang

Jargon is similar to slang because it, too, is the private language of a subgroup; however, whereas the subgroups for slang are formed by culture or lifestyle, the subgroups who speak jargon are formed by profession or trade. The jargon of some professions is so highly technical and specialized it amounts almost to a private language.

Although jargon is useful, even necessary, in the context of some jobs, it is inappropriate in most writing because it does not communicate to a general reader. As a writer, you need to be sensitive to your audience and their ability to understand quickly, clearly, and easily everything you write. Our vocabulary and even the content of our writing is influenced by our experiences and the contexts within which we work and live. Consider this example:

A group of people witness a car accident. What each person sees, and how he or she describes it, is determined to a large extent by the language each one normally uses. A doctor or nurse would see and describe contusions, lacerations, and hemorrhages. A lawyer would think it terms of civil liabilities and criminal negligence. A mechanic would see crushed fenders, bent axles, and damaged chassis. A psychologist would be concerned about stress reactions, trauma, and guilt. You or I might see and describe the pain and injury caused by a driver's error in judgement or lapse of skill.

Miller, D. E. *The Book of Jargon*. New York: Collier, 1981. 26.

The existence of jargon is not the problem; the inappropriate use of jargon is the problem. It limits your audience to those who share your specialized vocabulary and limits or destroys your ability to reach a wider audience. The cure for jargon is simple: be considerate of your readers. Unless they share your technical background, use non-specialized language.

Exercise 11.3

Working in small groups, write down as many examples of technical jargon as you can for each of the following occupations.

1. police officer (e.g., perpetrator, murder two)
2. nurse (e.g., bug, elopement risk)
3. car enthusiast (e.g., shift throw, stance)
4. financial analyst (e.g., beauty contest, fallen angel)
5. film maker (e.g., sync sound, M.O.S.)

Choose five technical terms from your own career field and write a general-level equivalent for each one.

Pretentious Writing

Some writers try so hard to impress their readers that they forget that the purpose of all writing is to communicate. Writing marked by chains of abstract, multi-syllable words and long, complicated sentences is **preten-**

tious. Sometimes called "gobbledygook," pretentious language has sound but no meaning:

> Thus, the meaningful verbalization of conceptual improvisation at the interpersonal interface is contraindicated by frustrations arising from idiosyncratic linguistic actualization, in terms of vocabulary, so that the verbalized formulations of the initiating consciousness actuate latent rejection mechanisms.

Who knows what this means? More important, who cares? Few readers would have the patience to go through this passage, dictionary in hand, trying to translate its tortured prose into plain English.

One symptom of pretentious writing is the use of "buzz words." These are words and phrases that have become popular because they reflect the latest academic or psychological fad. They are often nouns with *-ize* added to them to make them into verbs; e.g., *utilize, verbalize, conceptualize*. What's wrong with saying "use" or "say" or "think"?

Writers who are unsure of their subject matter sometimes try to impress their readers with pretentious prose. Every teacher knows this; so do most managers. Unfortunately, instead of impressing readers, pretentious language causes readers to lose respect for the writer. If you really want to get your message across, write plainly and clearly in language your readers can understand.

Exercise 11.4*

Rewrite the following sentences, expressing the ideas in a way that allows the reader to grasp your meaning clearly, easily, and quickly. Then compare your answers to our suggestions on pages 486–87.

1. We were forced to utilize the moisture-removing apparatus in our motorized personal conveyance when precipitate liquid impacted our windshield.
2. The chronologically less advanced generation sometimes achieves a communication deficit with authority figures and parental units.
3. The witness was ethically disoriented truthwise, when she claimed that her interface with the accused resulted in his verbalization of an admission of guilt.
4. The parameters of our study vis-à-vis the totality of research in the field demonstrate that surveywise our validity is on a par with that of other instruments.
5. The cancellation of IMF funds to the Pacific rim countries could lead to negative distortion of mutual interrelationships between developed and developing nations.

Sexist Language

Any writing that distracts your readers from your meaning is weak writing. Whether the distraction is caused by grammatical errors, spelling mistakes, slang, or the use of sexist language, your readers' concentration on your message is broken, and communication fails. **Sexist** (or gender-biased) **language** includes the use of words that signify gender (e.g., *waitress, sculptress, actress*) and the use of the pronouns *he, his, him* to refer to singular antecedents such as *everybody, anyone, no one*. Some readers object to terms that draw attention to gender differences, such as *man and wife* or *host and hostess*, preferring instead gender-neutral, inclusive terms such as *married couple* and *hosts*.

It is easy to dismiss non-sexist writing as "politically correct," but the language we use is a powerful force that influences the way we think. If we consistently refer to a *chairman* or *businessman*, we are perpetuating the idea that only men qualify for these positions. Far from being a politically correct fad, the use of inclusive or neutral words is both accurate and evenhanded.

Even liberal, unbiased writers can find sexism creeping into their writing unless they are conscious of the problem and careful to avoid it. Here are three tips to help you steer clear of sexist writing.

- Avoid using the word *woman* as an adjective. There is an implied condescension to phrases such as *woman athlete* and *woman writer* and *woman engineer*.
- Be conscious of the dangers of stereotyping. Physical descriptions of women are appropriate only where you would offer a similar description if the subject were a man. Just as some men can be excellent cooks, some women can be ruthless, power-hungry executives. It is possible for men to be scatterbrained and gossipy, while women can be decisive, tough, even violent.
- When making pronouns agree with singular antecedents, be careful that your pronouns do not imply bias. For example, "A teacher who discovers plagiarism must report it to *his* supervisor." Either use masculine and feminine pronouns interchangeably, or switch to a plural noun and avoid the problem: "Teachers who discover plagiarism must report it to their supervisors."

Exercise 11.5*

Correct the use of sexist and gender-biased language in the following sentences. Exchange papers with a partner and compare revisions. When you think you have found and identified all the instances of "loaded" words, turn to page 487 to compare your answers with our suggestions.

1. The well-known female producer, Elaine May, often regrets that she cannot go out in public without attracting the attention of fans and photographers.
2. Amy King, an attractive, blonde mother of two, first joined the company as a saleswoman; ten years later, she was promoted to president.
3. A businessman sitting in the first class cabin rang for the stewardess, a friendly gal who quickly arrived to assist him.
4. The list of ingredients on food packages contains information that may be important to the housewife, especially if she is the mother of young children.
5. The typical working man with a wife and two children is often hard-pressed to find time for recreation with his bride and the kids.

Wordiness

Just as some people tend to overdress, wearing clothing and jewelry that is inappropriately formal for the occasion, some writers tend to overwrite. This writing fault is **wordiness**; sometimes it is called "fill" or "padding." Like pretentious language, wordiness is the result of trying to impress a reader with words instead of meaning. Sometimes wordiness results from failing to revise carefully. In the edit stage of writing, you should be looking for the best words to express your meaning. Wordy expressions and awkward phrasing often come to mind when you are struggling to express an idea, and they often make their way into a first draft. There is no reason for them to survive a careful edit and make it to the second draft, however.

Here's an example of what can happen when a writer tries to impress with complicating sounding phrases:

> In my personal opinion, the government of this country of ours needs an additional amount of meaningful input from the people of Canada.

This wordy sentence could be nicely condensed into "In my opinion, our government now needs to hear more from the people." The writer has chosen impressive sounding phrases (*meaningful input, this country of ours*) and has slipped in unnecessary and meaningless words that should have been caught during editing (*personal opinion, an additional amount*). The result is a sentence that is so hard to read that it isn't worth the effort to decipher.

As you can see from the above example, one of the symptoms of wordiness is redundancy, or saying the same thing twice. Another is using several words where one would do:

We continued on into the living room, where a magnificent wool carpet, deep blue in colour, was complemented by pale genuine leather furniture and a remarkably unique Oriental Chinese wall hanging.

Continued on, blue in colour, genuine leather, remarkably unique, and *Oriental Chinese* are examples of the kind of phrasing that weak writers use in the mistaken impression that wordy expressions add authority or weight to their message.

The following list contains some of the worst offenders collected from student writing, corporate memoranda, form letters, and advertisements.

Wordy	Concise
a large number of	many
absolutely nothing/everything/ complete	nothing/everything/ complete/perfect
actual (*or* true) fact	fact
almost always	usually
at that point in time	then
at the present time	now
consensus of opinion	consensus
continue on	continue
could possibly (*or* may possibly, might possibly)	could (*or* may, might)
crisis (*or* emergency) situation	crisis (*or* emergency)
due to the fact that	because
end result	result
equally as good	as good
few and far between	rare
final conclusion	conclusion
for the reason that	because
free gift	gift
I myself (*or* you yourself, *etc.*)	I (*or* you, *etc.*)
I personally think/feel	I think/feel
in actual fact	in fact
in every instance	always
in my opinion, I think	I think
in the near future	soon
in today's society/in this day and age	now (*or* today)
is able to	can
many different kinds	many kinds
mutual agreement/cooperation	agreement/cooperation
my personal opinion	my opinion
no other alternative	no alternative

Wordy	Concise
personal friend	friend
real, genuine leather (*or* real antique, etc.)	leather (*or* antique, *etc.*)
red in colour (*or* large in size, *etc.*)	red (*or* large, *etc.*)
repeat again	repeat
return back	return (*or* go back)
really, very	*These words add nothing to your meaning. Leave them out.*
8:00 a.m. in the morning	8:00 a.m.
solid fact	fact
such as, for example	such as
take active steps	take steps
totally destroyed	destroyed
truly remarkable	remarkable
very (most, quite, almost, rather) unique	unique

To avoid wordiness, eliminate clichés, repetition, redundancy, and unnecessary jargon from your writing.

Exercise 11.6*

Revise these sentences to make them as concise as possible.

1. I myself personally feel that there is absolutely no basis in fact for the idea that UFOs exist.
2. Getting up at 5 a.m. in the morning and repeating the exact same daily routine every day for three weeks wore me out and exhausted me.
3. It has come to my attention that our competitor's products, though not equally as good as ours are, are nevertheless, at this point in time, selling better than those which we produce.
4. In my opinion, I believe that my essay is equally as good as Jill's and deserves equally as good a mark, which it would have got if it weren't for the actual fact that the professor hates me.
5. There is absolutely nothing at the present time to suggest that this almost unique set of circumstances will ever again be repeated in the foreseeable future, so we can proceed ahead with real and genuine confidence.
6. My sister and I share quite a few physical characteristics in common, such as, for example, exactly identical curly hair and a quite unique eye colour: green.

7. In my view, I feel that an English course that teaches the basic funda-mentals is an essential prerequisite before a person can succeed in col-lege, the business world, and the community at large.

8. "As a new beginning teacher," we told our English instructor, "you should try to understand the utter impossibility of gaining and holding the respect of us students so long as you are so completely and totally devoted to insisting that we follow grammar rules and regulations that totally inhibit the creativity in our writing."

9. I myself believe that, in all probability, this trend can be turned right around if we return back to basic fundamentals in our design process and introduce a few new innovations in our manufacturing process.

10. Due to the fact that the law, not to mention our company's policy, rules, and regulations, absolutely prohibits any mention of race, age, sex, religion, or marital status in official documents such as personnel documents, we have made sure that all such descriptors are entirely eliminated from our files, resulting in the fact that all our personnel documents are now almost virtually identical.

Abusages

While all the writing faults discussed in this chapter will distract readers from the meaning of a message, there are some words and expressions that stand out so glaringly that they cause readers to lose respect for the writer. We call these misused, ungrammatical, or non-standard expressions "abusages." Usage errors occur when bad speech habits spill over into writing. Using them makes the writer appear ignorant to anyone who knows anything about the English language. **Abusages** are never correct, even in speech; however, we hear them so often that they begin to sound right. They aren't, and you need to be aware of the ones that are most likely to appear in your writing. The following list includes some of the worst examples, but you should add to it any that your instructor points out in your own writing.

Read the examples listed in the left-hand column and mark the expres-sions that sound all right to you. Then memorize the standard English equivalent beside each one. These are the expressions you need to watch for when you edit your writing.

allready	A common misspelling of *already*.
alot	There is no such word. Use *much* or *many*.
	(*A lot* is acceptable in informal usage.)

anyways (anywheres)	There is no *s* on these words.
between you and I	A commonly misused expression for *between you and me.*
can't hardly **couldn't hardly**	Use *can hardly* or *could hardly.*
could of (would of, should of)	The helping verb needed is *have*, not *of.* Write *could have, would have, should have.*
didn't do nothing	All double negatives ("couldn't see nothing," "couldn't get nowhere," "wouldn't talk to nobody") are wrong. Write *didn't do anything, couldn't see anything, couldn't get anywhere, wouldn't talk to anyone.*
for free	Use *free* or *at no cost.*
in regards to	Use *in* (or *with*) regard to.
irregardless	There is no such word. *Regardless* is the word you want.
media **used as singular**	The word *media* is plural. The singular is *medium.* Newspapers and television are mass *media.* Radio is an electronic *medium.*
most all	Use *most* or *almost all.*
off of	Use *off* alone: "I fell *off* the wagon."
prejudice **used as an adjective**	It is wrong to write "She is *prejudice* against blondes." Use *prejudiced.*
prejudism	There is no such word. Use *prejudice.* "A judge should show no *prejudice* to either side."
real **used as an adverb**	"Real good," "real bad," and "real nice" are wrong. You could use *really* or *very*, but such filler words add nothing to your meaning.
reason is because	Use *the reason is that*: "The reason is that my printer blew up."
suppose to	This expression, like "*use to*," is non-standard. Use *supposed to* and *used to.*

themself	Also "theirself," "ourselfs," "yourselfs," and "themselfs." These are all non-standard words. The plural of *self* is *selves: themselves, ourselves,* and so on. Don't use "theirselves"; it's another non-standard word.
try and	Use *try to.*
youse	There is no such word. *You* is the singular and plural form of the pronoun. This word is often heard in restaurants: "Are youse ready to order?" and labels the server as a speaker of non-standard English.

Exercise 11.7*

Correct the following sentences where necessary. Suggested answers are on pages 487–88.

1. Irregardless of what you think, the problem between her and I has nothing to do with you.
2. If you want to be in the office pool, I need $5.00 off of you today because there will be no spots left by tomorrow.
3. Because they didn't finish the job theirself the way they should of, we will have to work real late to get it done.
4. I didn't feel like seeing nobody, so I went home, turned on the TV, and didn't do nothing for the rest of the night.
5. This use to be a real good place to work, but now we are suppose to work a full shift every day, or a penalty is deducted off of our pay.
6. Alot of young people today fight against prejudism not only in society but also within themselfs.
7. I'm suppose to ask youse if the reason for the delay is because there has been another bomb threat.
8. It's unresponsible of us to blame television or any other media for causing violence.
9. Television is partly responsible, however, for the fact that alot of ungrammatical expressions sound alright to us.
10. Between you and I, the reason I didn't speak to no one about Elmo's cheating is because he would of broke my arm.

PART 3

Revising

12

The Three Steps to Revision

No one can write in a single draft a paper that is perfectly organized and developed, let alone one that is free of errors in sentence structure, grammar, spelling, and punctuation. The purpose of the first draft is to get down on paper something you can work with until you're satisfied it will meet your reader's needs and expectations. Planning and drafting should take about half the time you devote to writing a paper. The other half should be devoted to revision.

Revision is the process of refining your writing until it says what you want it to say in a way that enables your readers to understand your message and to receive it favourably. These two goals, clear understanding and favourable reception, constitute good communication. You can accomplish these goals only if you keep your readers in mind as you revise. Because it reflects the contents of the writer's mind, a first draft often seems all right to the writer. But in order to transfer an idea as clearly as possible from the mind of the writer to the mind of the reader, revision is necessary. The idea needs to be reshaped and refined until it is as clear to your reader as it is to you. By revising from your reader's point of view, you can avoid misunderstandings before they happen.

What Is Revision?

Revision means "re-seeing." It does *not* mean recopying. The aim of revision is to improve your writing's organization, accuracy, and style. Revising is a three-stage process. Each step requires that you read through your entire essay, painful though this may be. The goal of your first reading is to ensure that your reader's information needs are met. In your second reading, you focus on structure. Your third reading concentrates on correctness. Here are the steps to follow in revising a paper.

1. Improve the whole paper by revising its content and organization.
2. Refine paragraph and sentence structure, and correct any errors in grammar.
3. Edit and proofread to catch errors in word choice, spelling, and punctuation.

Inexperienced writers often skip the first two stages and concentrate on the third, thinking they will save time. This is a mistake. In fact, they waste time—both theirs and their readers'—because the result is writing that doesn't communicate clearly and won't make a positive impression.

The best way to begin revising is to do nothing to your first draft for a day or two. Let as much time as possible pass between completing your first draft and rereading it. Ten minutes, or even half a day, is not enough. The danger in rereading too soon is that you're likely to "read" what you think you've written—what exists only in your head, not on the paper. But if, like many writers, you haven't allowed enough time for this cooling-off period, don't despair. There are two other things you can do to help you get some distance from your draft. If your first draft is handwritten, type it out. Reading your essay in a different form helps you to "re-see" its content. Alternatively, read your paper aloud and try to hear it from the point of view of your reader. Listen to how your explanation unfolds, and mark every place you find something unclear, irrelevant, inadequately developed, or out of order.

Step 1
Revise Content and Organization

As you reread your paper, keep in mind the three possible kinds of changes you can make at this stage:

1. **You can rearrange information**.   This is the kind of revision that is most often needed but least often done. Consider the order in which you've arranged your paragraphs. From your reader's point of view, is this the most effective order in which to present your ideas?

2. **You can add information.** Adding new main ideas or more development is often necessary to make your message interesting and convincing as well as clear. It's a good idea to ask a friend to read your draft and identify what needs to be expanded or clarified. (Be sure to return the favour. You can learn a great deal by critiquing other people's writing.)

3. **You can delete information.** Now is the time to cut out anything that is repetitious, insignificant, or irrelevant to your subject and reader.

Your outline is the best place to begin checking the adequacy and organization of your information. Keep it beside you and change it as your revise your essay. Nothing you've written should be considered sacred or carved in stone. In most cases, your paper will only be improved by rearranging, adding, and subtracting ideas.

The thesis statement is your contract with your readers, so it should be the guiding principle of your paper. It should contain nothing that is not developed in the body of the essay, and there should be nothing in the essay that is not directly related to your thesis statement. When you find a mismatch between the thesis statement and the paper, change one or the other or both until the two agree. With a good word processor, moving blocks of text around is as easy as shuffling a deck of cards.

If you are not already using a word processing program, now is the time to begin. Before starting to revise, change the computer's settings to meet the format requirements of your paper: set the spacing, margins, font style and size, etc. (See Chapter 23 for instructions and examples.) Most people find it easier to revise from a paper copy, so print out your draft double- or triple-spaced. Read it through carefully, making notes for changes in the margins or in the spaces between the lines; then go back to the computer to make the changes.

Remember to save your work frequently. It takes only a split second to click on the Save icon, but that split second could save you hours—even days—in the event of a computer disaster. Learn to save your work in a systematic and easy-to-find filing system. Calling a paper "draft" or "essay" will cause frustration later when you want to reopen the file to revise it but can't remember the name of the file you were working on. Give each file a distinctive name (or name and number), and save each draft separately just in case you want to go back and use material from a previous version of your document.

Use the checklist that follows to guide you as you review your paper's form and content.

CONTENT AND ORGANIZATION CHECKLIST

ACCURACY

Is everything you have said accurate?

- Is your information consistent with your own experience and observations or with what you have discovered through research?
- Are all your facts and evidence up to date?

COMPLETENESS

Have you included enough main ideas and development to explain your subject and convince your reader? Remember that "enough" means from the reader's point of view, not the writer's.

SUBJECT

Is your subject

- significant? Does it avoid the trivial or the obvious?
- single? Does it avoid double or combined subjects?
- specific? Is it focused and precise?
- supportable? Have you provided enough evidence to make your meaning clear?

MAIN POINTS

Are your main points

- significant? Have you deleted any unimportant ones?
- distinct? Are they all different from one another, or is there an overlap in content?
- relevant? Do all points relate directly to your subject?
- arranged in the most appropriate order? Again, "appropriate" means from the reader's perspective. Choose chronological, climactic, logical, or random order, depending on which is most likely to help the reader make sense of your information.

INTRODUCTION

Does your introduction

- catch the reader's attention and make him or her want to read on?
- contain a clearly identifiable thesis statement?
- identify the main points that your paper will explain?

CONCLUSION

Does your conclusion

- contain a summary or reinforcement of your main points, rephrased to avoid word-for-word repetition?

- contain a statement that effectively clinches your argument and leaves the reader with something to think about?

TONE

Is your tone consistent, reasonable, courteous, and confident throughout your essay?

When you have changed your draft to satisfy these questions, you have completed the first step in the revision process: you have covered the "large issues" of content and organization.

Exercise 12.1

The following passage is the first draft of a paragraph. When the student had finished it, he was quite pleased with his work. He thought he had explained his points effectively and that a reader would have no difficulty in understanding his argument. Read it through, see what you think, and answer the questions that follow. Discuss questions 1 to 4 with a partner or in a small group.

Why did I do it? This was one of those times you think something is really going to be exciting and fun, but you don't think it through to the consequences. Once I got the idea, I just got carried away and couldn't stop. I wish I had had better sense and it probably would have helped if I hadn't been drunk. If I had thought about the possible consequences, my friends would still be speaking to me and I wouldn't have to pay for the damage. I guess it could of been worse, I mean the police could have been called and instead of just paying for the repairs I could of been charged and maybe even a criminal record. My advice is to always think carefully before doing something that could get out of hand, even if it seems like a lot of fun at the time.

1. Does this writer have a clear idea of who his readers are? How can you tell?
2. What is the writer's purpose in the paragraph?
3. What is the topic of the paragraph? Is it clearly stated?
4. What event or incident underlies the lesson the writer learned? Do you know? Do you need to know?
5. Rewrite the paragraph, using an incident from your own experience to support the point. Don't worry about the errors in grammar and sentence structure; just be sure the content of your paragraph is unmistakably clear and well organized from a reader's perspective.

Exercise 12.2

In teams of three or four, write the first draft of a paragraph. Write your team name at the top. Exchange papers with another team and revise the paragraph by adding information. Pass the paper on to another team and revise again, this time by deleting, clarifying, or rearranging information. Exchange papers one last time, and revise again, concentrating on making the paragraph appeal to a specific audience. Return the paper to the original authors. Discuss your revised paragraph, using the questions in Exercise 12.1 as a guide.

Step 2
Revise Paragraphs and Sentences

The second step in revising is to examine your paragraph and sentence structure, grammar, language, and tone. You scrutinize the structure of each paragraph and review its content for unity and coherence. You check each sentence to ensure that it is correctly constructed and that your sentences are varied in length and complexity. Readers appreciate variety almost as much as they do clarity. If all your sentences are the same length, you'll put your reader to sleep. This is also the time to make sure your level of language is appropriate: not too casual or too formal, not too simple or too technical for your audience. Don't worry at this stage about spelling and punctuation errors. These will be corrected at step three.

Inexperienced writers often move too quickly between ideas without fully explaining each point. This happens because, as the writer, you are familiar with the subject matter and can fill in any gaps in the information you've provided. The poor reader, however, is left behind, unable to follow your explanations without more information. Be alert for this tendency in your writing, and, as you revise, use your word processor to insert additional sentences that will bridge the gap between your knowledge and that of your readers.

Sometimes you can make your argument easier to follow by changing the order of ideas. Your word processor's cut-and-paste function makes it easy to move sentences around within a paragraph as well as to move paragraphs around within a paper. As you reread your draft, think about the placement of each point and consider whether changing the sequence of your sentences might make the ideas flow more smoothly. Try it. If the change doesn't work, you can always undo it. A good working knowledge of the functions of your word processor will speed your work. You should know how to select, delete, cut, copy, and paste text, and how to find and replace words or phrases. If you don't already know these functions, learn them now.

Allow at least a day between your first revision and your second. Enough time must elapse for you to see your essay as if for the first time. This time, read your draft aloud, and use the list of questions below to guide you through the second stage.

PARAGRAPH AND SENTENCE CHECKLIST

PARAGRAPHS

1. Does your paper begin with an introduction that
   - is appropriate to your subject and your audience?
   - contains a clear, comprehensive, and grammatically parallel thesis statement?
2. Does each paragraph contain an identifiable topic sentence?
   - Is the topic sentence the first or second sentence of each paragraph? If not, should it be moved?
3. Do the supporting sentences of each paragraph
   - relate clearly and directly to the topic?
   - present one or more kinds of development appropriate to the main idea?
4. Is each paragraph unified?
   - Do all sentences relate clearly and directly to the topic sentence?
   - Is each sentence in the best position relative to other sentences?
5. Is each paragraph coherent?
   - Does each sentence flow smoothly into the next?
   - Have you used transitions to signal the relationship between sentences? Between paragraphs?
6. Does each paragraph end with a clincher or a transition to the next paragraph?
7. Does the conclusion of your paper include
   - a statement that summarizes or reinforces your main points (and avoids a word-for-word repetition of your thesis statement)?
   - a memorable statement that is appropriate to your purpose and to your intended audience?

SENTENCE STRUCTURE

1. Is each sentence correct and clear?
   - Are there any fragments or run-ons?
   - Are there any misplaced or dangling modifiers?
   - Are all lists (whether words, phrases, or clauses) expressed in parallel form?
2. Are your sentences varied in length? Could some be combined to improve the clarity and impact of your thoughts?

GRAMMAR

1. Have you used verbs correctly?
   - Are all verbs in the correct form?
   - Do all verbs agree with their subjects?
   - Are all verbs in the correct tense?
   - Are there any confusing shifts in verb tense within a paragraph?
   - Are all verbs in the active voice unless there is a specific reason for using the passive?
2. Have you used pronouns correctly?
   - Are all pronouns in the correct form?
   - Do all pronouns agree with their antecedents?
   - Have vague pronoun references been eliminated?
   - Are there any confusing shifts in number or person within a paragraph?

LANGUAGE

1. Is your level of language
   - appropriate to your subject and to your readers?
   - consistent? Are there any lapses into colloquial or inappropriate technical language?
2. Is your tone reasonable, courteous, and consistent throughout your paper?
3. Have you used words accurately, to communicate meaning rather than to impress?
   - Have you eliminated clichés, slang, jargon, and sexist language?
   - Have you cut out all unnecessary words?
   - Have you corrected any "abusages"?

When you have answered these questions satisfactorily, it is time to move on to the third and final step in the revision process.

Exercise 12.3

Read the following paragraph and consider it in terms of the questions you should ask in the second stage of revising a paper. Identify all the errors you find, and then exchange papers with another student and check each other's work.

To begin with, let's get rid of the tea bag with a string on it. This stupid American invention is the worst thing to happen to tea since the Boston Tea Party. Real tea is brewed from the leaves themselves. Which can be purchased in any good supermarket or in specialty shops. You need a kettle and a china or clay teapot. Fill the kettle with cold water. Put it on to boil. When boiling, pour some into the teapot and swirl it around. This warms the pot. An essential step in making good tea. I don't know why, but I do know that tea made in an unwarmed pot is not as good as tea made in a warmed one. Coffee doesn't need a warmed pot, but I don't really care for coffee, so I probably couldn't taste the difference anyway. Empty the water from the teapot. Put in one teaspoon of tea leaves for each cup you are serving. Add one more teaspoon of tea leaves. Take the teapot to the boiling kettle, this ensures that the water is still boiling rapidly when you put it into the pot. Pour over the tea leaves as much boiling water as is needed for the number of cups you are making. Wait five minutes. This is called steeping. Pour the tea into cups. Some people drink it with milk. Fussy tea drinkers insist that the milk must go into the cup before the tea is poured. Some like sugar. Some take both. A few people enjoy it with a slice or a squeeze of lemon. However you take your tea, it will taste better if you follow these simple steps.

Step 3
Edit and Proofread

By now, you're probably so tired of refining your paper that you may be tempted to skip **editing**—correcting errors in word choice, spelling, and punctuation—and **proofreading**—correcting errors in typing or writing. These tasks are essential if you want your paper to make a positive impression. Faulty diction, misspellings, incorrect punctuation, and messiness don't always create misunderstandings, but they may cause the reader to form a poor opinion of you and your work.

Word processors offer several features to help make editing easier, but these tools are effective only in the hands of a diligent and thoughtful user. Most writers will change spelling errors that are highlighted by a spell check program, but many do not take the next step: checking a document for homonyms, words that sound alike but are spelled differently. Others will consult the program's thesaurus when they need a word and then randomly choose a word from the list, or—even worse—pick a big word they've never seen before, hoping that it will impress the reader. Here are some suggestions about how to use editing tools responsibly.

Spellcheckers cannot identify words that have been misused. If you use *affect* instead of *effect*, no software program will point out your error. Remember, too, that spellings acceptable to American spell checkers are not standard in the Canadian environment. The words *labour* and *humour* and *centre* will be flagged as errors if the program is set to recognize US spellings. By all means, rely on your word processor to catch typing errors and misspelled words, but remember that it is not a substitute for careful reading and editing in the final draft.

An electronic thesaurus is a helpful tool, enabling a quick onscreen scan of synonyms for a word you have overused or for one that isn't quite "right." To be useful, however, a thesaurus must be used with care. Inexperienced writers often don't take the time to find precisely the right words to convey their meaning. Part of good revision is being critical of what you have written and finding better ways of expressing what you mean. As you edit your work, pause at any word that doesn't sound quite right or doesn't say exactly what you intend. Use the thesaurus to find a word that does a better job, but do not choose a word you are not sure of. If you are unfamiliar with the word, look it up in your dictionary. Then decide if it is appropriate in your sentence. Never use a word whose meaning you don't know!

Most grammar checkers will check for passive-voice verbs; they will question—but not correct—your use of apostrophes; they will sometimes catch errors in subject-verb agreement; and they will even assess the readability of your writing. But do not make the mistake of thinking that they will do all, or even most, of your editing for you. Useful as they are, they cannot replace a human editor. Here's an example of what we mean. The following sentences passed without comment through one of the most sophisticated grammar checkers on the market:

> The audience rose to their feet and it applauded, madly until the cast whom they so well deserved returned to the stage to take an other curtain call. They would if I had of been their in addition threw money onto the stage.

Everything you write is judged by readers on three counts: what you say, how you say it, and how you present it. All three factors are important in getting the response you want. Whether you're writing a résumé, a love letter, or an interoffice memo, your message will be judged on appearance and style as well as on content.

Here are the questions to ask yourself when you are editing.

EDITING CHECKLIST

WORDS

Usage

Have you used words to "mean" rather than to "impress"?

- Have you eliminated any clichés, slang, jargon, and pretentious or sexist language?
- Have you cut out any unnecessary words?
- Have you corrected any "abusages"?

Spelling

Are all words spelled correctly?

- Have you double checked any sound-alikes or look-alikes?
- Have you used capital letters where they are needed?
- Have you used apostrophes correctly for possessives and omitted them from plurals?
- If any words had to be hyphenated, are the hyphens in the right place?

PUNCTUATION

Within Sentences

- Have you eliminated any unnecessary commas and included commas where needed? (Refer to the five comma rules explained in Chapter 33 as you consider this question.)
- Have you used colons and semicolons where appropriate?
- Are all quotations appropriately marked?
- Have you used parentheses and dashes only where appropriate?

Beginnings and Endings

- Does each sentence begin with a capital letter?
- Do all questions—and only questions—end with a question mark?
- Are all quotation marks correctly placed?

Exercise 12.4*

Read the following sentences carefully and edit them to correct any errors in usage, spelling, and punctuation. Then compare your answers to our suggestions on page 488. (Our thanks to *Fortune* magazine for collecting these howlers from real résumés and cover letters.)

1. I demand a salary commiserate with my qualifications and extensive experience.

2. I have lurnt Microsoft Word and Excel computor and spreadsheet progroms.

3. I received a plague for being salesperson of the year.

4. Reason for leaving last job; maturity leave.

5. You will want me to be Head Honcho in no time.

6. I am a perfectionist and rarely if if ever forget details.

7. Marital status: single. Unmarried. Unengaged. Uninvolved. No commitments.

8. In my previous job I became completely paranoid, trusting completely no one and absolutely nothing.

9. As indicted, I have over five years of analyzing investments.

10. I was responsible for ruining the entire operation for a Western chain store.

TIPS FOR EFFECTIVE PROOFREADING

By the time you have finished editing, you will have gone over your paper so many times you may have practically memorized it. When you are very familiar with a piece of writing, it's hard to spot the small mistakes that may have crept in as you produced your final copy. Here are some tips to help you find those tiny, elusive errors.

1. Read through your essay line by line, using a ruler to guide you.
2. If you've been keeping a list of your most frequent errors in this course, scan your essay for the mistakes you are most likely to make.
3. Use the "Quick Revision Guide" on the inside front cover of this book to make a final check of all aspects of your paper.

Your "last" draft may need further revision after your proofreading review. If so, take the time to rewrite the paper so that the version you hand in is clean and easy to read. One last word of advice:

Don't forget to keep a copy for your files!

Exercise 12.5*

The following paragraph has passed through the first two revision stages; it now needs editing. Working in pairs and using the editing checklist on page 133 as your guide, find and correct the 15 errors in spelling, word choice, and punctuation. Then exchange papers with another team and circle any edits that were missed.

In comparing cross-country and downhill skiing, I consider four factors. On everyone, cross country came out ahead. First, Nordic (cross-country) skiing is way less expensive, both for the equipment and for a days enjoyment of the activity. Second it is alot more convient. Unless you happen to live on a ski hill, you have to drive miles to a slope for Alpine sking, whereas cross-country can be done anywheres. Third cross-country skiing is better exercise since you are working steadily instead of stanidng around three quaters of the time, waiting for a lift to the top of a hill. Finaly, you can have more fun exploring new country, away from the crowds. You can enjoy the scenery, and there is no danger of running into other people or being run into by hotdogers or snowborders. Yes, I'll take cross-country over downhill skiing every time.

GO TO WEB

EXERCISE 12.1

Exercise 12.6*

Is the following essay ready for submission? Go over it carefully, correcting any errors. Then get together with another student and compare your proofreading skills. (There are 20 errors in this exercise.)

According to a recent survey in Maclean's magazine, only 43% of Canadians are satisfied with their jobs. What can you do to ensure that you will not be one of the 57% who are unhappy with the work they do. There are three questions to consider when seeking employment that will provide satisfaction as well as a paycheque.

First are you suited to the kind of work you are applying for. If you enjoy the outdoors, for example, and like to be active, your not going to be happy with a nine to five office job, no matter how much it pays.

Second is the job based in a location compatible with your prefered lifestyle. No matter how much you like your work, if you go home every night to an enviorment you are miserable in, it will not be long before you start transfering your disatisfaction to your job. If you like the amenities and conviences of the city, you probably will not enjoy working in a small town. If, on the other hand, you prefer the quiet and security of small town life, you may find the city a stressful place in which to live.

Finally, is it one that you want to work for. Do you need the security of generous benifits, a good pension plan, and incentives to stay and grow with one company? Or are you an ambitous person who is looking for variety, quick advancement, and a high salary. If so, you may have to forego security in favour of commissions or cash incentives and be willing to move as quickly and as often as opportunities occur. Some carful self-analysis now, before you start out on your career path, will help you chose a direction that will put you in the 43% minority of satisfied Canadian workers.

Exercise 12.7

This exercise will serve as a review of the three stages of the revision process. Below is a first draft of an essay. Applying all the principles you have learned in Chapter 12, revise this essay to make it a model of good communication: complete, correct, concise, and courteous. When you have finished, exchange papers with another student and compare your results. What errors did you miss? If this assignment were worth 20 percent of your final grade, would you hand it in now, or would you revise it again?

We are having a garbage crisis. There is so much waste being produced in North America, we no longer have any idea of were to put it. Toronto's garbage problem is so great that they are talking of trucking it hundreds of kilometers North of the City and putting it into abandonned mine shafts near Kirkland lake. But how long will that last? We must act now, and we must act as individuals. We cannot wait for the Government to save us from this crisis. It is us who make the garbage, it must be us who solves the problem. In very practical, down to earth, concrete terms, here are some things we can do to reduce, recycle, and reuse.

First we must reduce the amount of garbage we produce. We can do this be refusing to buy products that are over packaged, like fast food that comes in styrafoam containers and chocolates that have a paper wrapping, a box, lining paper, a plastic tray for the candies, and foil wrap around each chocolate. By not purchasing such wasteful items, we say to the manufacturer, Either reduce the packing in your product or lose business to your competition. We can also be less wastful in our own habits by carpooling, for example, or by using cloth diapers or biodegradable disposables.

We must recycle everything we can instead of sending it to the dump. Old cloths can be sent to the Salvation Army, the Scott mission, or other charitable organizations. As can furniture, appliances, books, and most other household items. There are dozens of ways to make useful items from packaging that would otherwise be thrown away, such as bird feeders from plastic jugs, braided rugs from old rags, and fire logs from newspapers. We don't need to consume as much as we do, and it won't hurt us to use things longer instead of buying new items before the old ones are completely worn out. Many companies now manufacture products from recycled goods, and we should be on the lookout for their products to support their efforts and to reduce the waste that is dumped into landfills.

Third, we can reuse most things. Composting vegetable garbage is a good way to put waste to valuable use. Or we can offer the things we no longer want to others through lawn sales and flea markets.

This is an absolute necessity. If we do not stop producing so much waste, we will inevitibly destroy our own enviornment. Unlike most efforts to improve things, the move to recycle, reuse, and reduce has one other advantage: it doesn't cost any money. In fact, it can save every household that practices it hundreds of dollars a year.

PART 4

Patterns of Development

Introduction

College papers, like most professional writing, fall into three broad categories:

1. descriptive and narrative writing
2. expository writing
3. persuasive writing

These categories are not separate and distinct. In general-interest, business, and technical prose, they often overlap. (In fact, one could argue that *all* writing is persuasive, because all writing attempts to convince readers that the information presented is reasonable and true.) It is useful, however, to consider the three categories one at a time and to learn the techniques involved in each separately before you attempt to combine them in an essay or report.

All effective writing depends to some extent on *description* and *narration*, the subjects of the next two chapters. Whether you are describing the exact layout of a retail space you're designing or narrating your experiences at a professional conference, you'll find these techniques useful again and again. *Expository* writing includes *process analysis, classification and division, cause and effect,* and *comparison and contrast.* These patterns of development are often required in on-the-job writing: Why is a component manufactured by one supplier better than the one made by another? Explain to a new employee how to perform a complex procedure. Why did sales decline in the last quarter? We look at the techniques involved in effective exposition in Chapters 13 to 18. Chapter 19 focuses on *persuasive* writing, which has a wide variety of applications—from a letter of application to a proposal to increase efficiency by introducing flextime, from sales letters to budget requests.

Each chapter begins with a definition of a kind of essay, together with an outline of its practical applications. Next, we offer tips on how to write that kind of essay and present four or five short examples, followed by questions designed to help you understand their structure and technique. The last selection in each chapter is a longer piece illustrating the kind of writing that is the focus of the chapter in combination with other writing strategies.

13

Description

Description covers many writing applications in academic and professional contexts. Architecture, interior design, biology, botany, anthropology, archaeology, engineering, criminology, and the health sciences are just some of the fields in which practitioners must be skilled in writing precise, concrete descriptions. A description is a verbal picture of an object, a scene, a person, or an event. In all descriptive writing, the objective is to provide readers with a picture of what it was like to be there.

By learning to write good description, you will become better at all kinds of writing. Making your readers see what you have seen, even in your imagination, is the essence of communication.

Tips on Writing Description

1. Engage all the senses, if possible: sight, sound, smell, touch, and taste.
2. Describe precisely, using words that create specific images. Don't say that something is "beautiful" or "impressive" or "wonderful" without telling your readers specifically how the object or event exhibited those qualities.
3. Select words with care. Never use a general word where a more specific, descriptive one could be used.

Example: The man walked toward the figure standing in the shadows.

Examples with specific words replacing general ones:
The *detective crept* toward the *suspect lurking* in the shadows.
The *old man hobbled* toward the *puppy cowering* in the shadows.
Dirty Harry bounded toward the *villain crouching* in the shadows.

4. Choose a viewpoint for your description. As the describer, take a position and describe what you see from that spot. Tell what is visible from left to right or from far to near, or "walk" your readers around an object or along a defined pathway, but don't confuse them by changing your viewing point unnecessarily.

Read the following descriptive papers and answer the questions that follow each essay.

DIAMONDS ARE FOREVER

Brian Green

1   Montreal's "Big O" and Toronto's SkyDome are wonderful places for loyal subjects to pay homage to baseball's royalty. We can watch the game in air-conditioned comfort, fearing neither rain nor cold, just as though we were at home viewing the proceedings on TV. Whereas modern stadiums are fittingly lavish for highly paid major-leaguers to perform their feats, baseball for most Canadians has a much different atmosphere. Many of us have in common the sights, sounds, smells, and "feel" of the dirt diamonds, grass outfields, wooden bleachers, and hometown crowds of small-time baseball.

2   Where I grew up, baseball meant the hometown Star Cleaners in their white uniforms with red trim. The infield of our diamond was hard red clay, raked over and loosened prior to game time so that by the middle innings the players were covered in fine rust; latecomers could tell what inning it was by the degree of colour in the uniforms. A fastball would explode in the catcher's mitt in a satisfying cloud of dust, and a slide at second would sometimes be obscured from the bleacher crowd. In the early part of the season, the outfield grass was always bright green and as lush as a cemetery lawn. As the dry weather of August approached, however, brown patches would appear, until, by playoff time, the outfield was straw brown relieved by the odd green patch.

3   The newly mown outfield grass and, especially, the perfume of fried onions from the Lions Club snack bar behind the stands remain the most vivid scents of summer, and the thwack! of ball hitting leather the most exciting sound. The yelling of the hometown fans stirred excitement, and the hilarious jibes of the local wit in the back row of the bleachers brought comic relief, but the sounds on the field were what we were all there for. The smack of the bat on a well-hit ball, the umpire's guttural exclamations, the grunt of a player's effort, cries of encouragement from the players' benches: all these blended together in a happy symphony. But the slap of the ball into the leather of the first-baseman's glove, that breathless moment when so much is at stake—that's the sound that I crouched in the front row of the bleachers to hear.

4   Individual great plays still raise the hair on the back of my head when I recall them: "Moose" Christie catching a line drive in his bare, pitching hand; the reserve player/coach (his name now forgotten) who came off the bench in the sixteenth inning to hit a game-winning triple; my fifth-grade teacher, "Squirt" Dunsmore, striking out the side in the ninth inning; the entire, delirious game on a sunny Sunday when the Star Cleaners won the provincial championship. I love the Expos and adore the Blue Jays, and I live and die with them all season long. But somehow, their game is plastic, artificial, and remote beside the baseball being played on dirt diamonds by men and women who play for the love of it.

1. Sight, sound, smell, and touch are the senses engaged in this essay. Identify specific words the author has used to appeal to each of these senses.
   Sight: _____
   _____
   Sound: _____
   _____
   Smell: _____
   _____
   Touch: _____
   _____

2. From what viewpoint does the author describe his subject?
3. This essay has elements of comparison/contrast. How do they add to the description?
4. In the introduction, the author begins with a brief description of other places before shifting to the real theme of the essay. Is this an effective way to start? Why?
5. Draft an outline for the essay, listing the main and supporting points.

THE WHITE DARKNESS
Wade Davis

1   The challenge of travel is to find a way to isolate and understand the germ of a people, to measure and absorb the spirit of place. In Haiti one begins in Port-au-Prince. The capital lies prostrate across a low, hot, tropical plain at the head of a bay flanked on both sides by soaring mountains. Behind these mountains rise others, creating an illusion of space that absorbs Haiti's multitudes and softens the country's harshest statistic: a land mass of only ten thousand square miles inhabited by 6 million people. Port-au-Prince is a sprawling muddle of a city, on first encounter a carnival of civic chaos. A waterfront shantytown damp with laundry. Half-finished public monuments. Streets lined

with *flamboyant* and the stench of fish and sweat, excrement and ash. Dazzling government buildings and a presidential palace so white that it doesn't seem real. There are the cries and moans of the marketplace, the din of untuned engines, the reek of diesel fumes. It presents all the squalor and all the grace of any Caribbean capital.

2   Yet as you drive through the city for the first time, down by the docks perhaps, where the shanties face the gleaming cruise ships and men with legs like anvils haul carts loaded with bloody hides, notice something else. The people on the street don't walk, they flow, exuding pride. Physically, they are beautiful. They seem gay, jaunty, carefree. Washed clean by the afternoon rain, the entire city has a rakish charm. But there is more. In a land of material scarcity, the people adorn their lives with their imagination—discarded Coke cans become suitcases or trumpets, rubber tires are turned into shoes, buses transformed into kaleidoscopic *tap-taps*, moving exhibits of vibrant, naive art. And it isn't just how things appear, it is something in the air, something electric— a raw elemental energy not to be found elsewhere in the Americas. What you have found is the lens of Africa focused upon the New World.

Davis, Wade. "The White Darkness." *Shadows in the Sun: Essays on the Spirit of Place.* Edmonton: Lone Pine, 1992. 50–51.

1. The author begins this piece by announcing its purpose in a subtle thesis statement. In the paragraphs that follow, find specific descriptive details that develop the "measure" and the "spirit" of Haiti.
2. What overall impression of Haiti does Davis convey? List at least five negative details and five positive details that contribute to this impression. What single sentence best sums up the paradoxical nature of this island?
3. Which of the physical senses does Daivs appeal to in this verbal picture of Haiti? Give examples for each.
4. The first paragraph contains a number of sentence fragments. How do these fragments help contribute to the dominant impression the writer wishes to communicate?
5. What does the last sentence mean? Why is it an effective conclusion?

A NATIONAL BILLBOARD
Witold Rybczynski

1   An embassy is unique among building types. It is culturally and legally foreign, even though it may be a familiar part of the city. It is usually forbidding—not altogether private, nor yet really public; indeed, most people never go inside an embassy, and when they do, it is likely to be that of another

country, not their own. The first Canadian embassy that I visited was in New Delhi. I was not sure what to expect. Once through the front door, I felt immediately at home. Not only the familiar accents of the embassy staff but the furnishings—the desks and chairs, the pictures on the wall, even the staplers—were recognizably Canadian. The building itself made little impression; it was merely one more official edifice along embassy row, distinguished only by its maple-leaf flag and its Canadian diffidence.

2   On the other hand, visitors to the Canadian embassy in Washington, DC, cannot help noticing the architecture. Officially opened in 1989, this is an unusual design, an unusual embassy, . . . and, not the least, unusual for a building representing Canada.

3   The . . . embassy is, indeed, a very beautiful building. The walls, of cream-and-grey-streaked stone, are lovely; so are the hanging roses, azaleas, and hawthorn blossoms that cover the stepped-back façade inside the courtyard. The materials are assembled with great attention to detail. There are satisfactions for the ear as well as for the eye: a sheet of water spills over to sheathe the base of the rotunda and gurgles mysteriously into a gap beside the sidewalk. There is also the pleasure of movement—up a wide stair, between columns, and under the building—and of shifting views.

4   The twelve pillars of the rotunda are intended to symbolize the ten provinces and the two territories of Canada. As if anticipating Canadian expansion or subdivision, the circle is not quite closed—space is left for one or two more pillars. Oddly, the provincial pillars don't stand on solid ground but emerge from water, like islands. Is this a sly comment on the state of Canadian federalism? The rotunda is dwarfed by a row of six mammoth fluted columns inside the court. Here the symbolism is less clear. Do these represent the federal government? If so, why are these columns headless? And why do they support nothing more substantial than a giant planter?

5   The difficulty with the game that [architect] Erickson is playing is that it raises precisely such questions. The results demonstrate not so much the limits of his talent as the limits of the modernist approach, at which he is usually so adept. As a beautiful abstract sculpture, the building is a success; as a postmodern symbolic architectural statement, it sends ambiguous messages.

6   The interiors, by contrast, are strictly in the modernist idiom, which is to say cool, metallic, and, to my mind, uncongenial. There is a handsome semi-circular staircase, but the lobby is rather too splendid. It makes the casually attired staff and Bermuda-shorted visitors look out of place. The offices—and an embassy is really an office building—are unremarkable, except for the ambassador's suite, which is a concoction of puffy decor and cream-coloured leather furniture. I cannot image that it will be too long before they are replaced by dark wood panelling and sensible Georgian wing chairs.

7   As one approaches from the streets and climbs the stair leading to the court and the main entrance, which is marked by an unprepossessing,

pyramid-roofed pavilion, the sequence is so smooth, so skilfully orchestrated, that one never notices the absence of a fence or gate, or of a barrier of any kind. When I visited, people were strolling around the court, children were throwing coins into the fountain, and two tourists were testing the acoustics of the rotunda dome. There were no members of the Protective Service (a uniformed division of the U.S. Secret Service) accosting loitering photographers, no security guards on view. As everyone knows, the land on which an embassy is built is extraterritorial, in this case a piece of Canada; here is a piece of Canada that is open even to the most casual passerby.

8   This unrestricted access is partially continued inside; there are a public art gallery and a library, also open to the public. The decision to make a large part of the embassy in effect a public place is a truly unusual one and required a range of security devices: strategically located checkpoints, zoned access, much bulletproof glass, and, I assume, a battery of hidden electronics. Whatever the cost of such gadgetry—and a spokesman for the Department of External Affairs would provide no figures, although he assured me that it was "not inexpensive"—it was well worth it. Such openness makes this embassy, as far as I know, unique, and both the client and the architect deserve much credit for the achievement.

Rybczynski, Witold. "A National Billboard." *Looking Around: A Journey through Architecture.* New York: HarperCollins, 1992. 167–72.

1. The first two paragraphs comprise the introduction of this essay. The attention-getter contains a generalization about embassies and a short example of "usual" embassies. Sketch an outline of the rest of the piece, beginning with its thesis statement in paragraph 2. Which paragraphs develop the first main point? The second? Why is the third main point not developed separately from the others?

2. For what audience is this piece intended? Does the use of architectural jargon make it difficult for a layperson (a general reader) to understand? If you think this is so, identify two or three examples of jargon that you, as a layperson, were not familiar with.

3. After reading this essay, do you have a clear picture of the Canadian embassy in Washington? Assuming the author's purpose was to enable you to picture the building's public space, could the description have been made more effective? What additional details would you need before you could draw a rough sketch of the exterior and the interior of the building?

4. Rybczynski mentions symbolism as part of his description. What architectural and design features in the Canadian embassy might be considered symbolic, and what do you think these features might symbolize?

MY POLISH GRANDMOTHER
Bernie Kowalewski

1   I remember vividly that special day my sister and I met our Polish grandmother: it was 1960, at the start of a cold, wintry fall. I was seven and my sister was nine. The previous week had been an agony of anticipation; we had heard much about our paternal grandmother from both Father and Mother, but their stories tended to differ. In fact, this long-expected visit had been the subject of many incomprehensible arguments between our parents. We could not have imagined the effect she was to have on us.

2   That morning, we were to stay downstairs in our rooms until eight o'clock and have our faces washed, our hair combed, and be dressed in clean and tidy clothes. When we met "grand" mother, we were not to speak unless spoken to and we were not to stare, because Granny had arrived late the previous night and would be tired.

3   Precisely on the hour, we were rushing up the stairs, only to screech to a stop at the landing, arrested by the sight of a strange coat in the closet. Could this be Granny's coat? My sister reached over to grasp the furred cuff. "It's so soft!" she whispered as she buried her nose into the shiny black fur. The rest of the coat was covered in small tight coils of gray fur. I was afraid to touch this odd-looking overcoat smelling of lavender, moth-balls, and dust, but I pictured my grandmother wearing it, thick collar high up around her head, perhaps sliding swiftly through a snowstorm in a troika like Dr. Zhivago. For effect, I added vicious, salivating wolves in pursuit. A loud voice interrupted my reverie; behind the door into the kitchen, we could hear Father's machine-gun-like Polish ricocheting through the house from the living room. By pressing our ears to the door, we could hear my mother and another lady speaking. This woman spoke Polish in a softer, flatter way than we had ever heard before. Knowing we could not just go in, we glumly sat on the stairs waiting for our absence to be noticed. Shortly, my mother's smiling face appeared in the doorway: "Come in for breakfast," she whispered with a wink, "It's your favorite, pancakes and jam!"

4   After breakfast, we were shooed into the living room where my father and grandmother sat stiffly opposite one another in separate armchairs. We were introduced. To my bewilderment, I was called "Bennek," my sister was "Baboush," and we could address my grandmother as "Babchka." While this was happening, "Babchka" smiled sparingly and bowed her head like the Queen Mother, her white-gloved hands clutching a teacup. In spite of that smile, she looked hard and grumpy. This did not look like a woman I would call "Granny," even in Polish!

5   Through a fog of disappointment, I saw father motioning to us to approach Grandmother. Setting her cup down, she opened her arms wide to

embrace us, but an awkward moment passed before we reacted. She squeezed us tightly against her huge bosom for an eternity, and I couldn't help squirming, fighting for air. We both fell back when she released us, so anxious were we to escape. Turning in embarrassment toward Mom, I saw she was smiling and pointing to a couch across the room from where Grandmother sat.

6   We then sat quietly as my father spoke rapidly in Polish, gesturing energetically in our direction as he leaned toward my grandmother. I understood little Polish, but I knew what he was saying; we had heard "the lecture" repeated many times before to my mother: Canadian kids were poorly educated, showed little or no respect toward their elders, weren't required to wear uniforms to school, and generally were poor role models for us miserably mannered excuses of children. His words echoed distantly in my head. A barely audible procession of words marched softly across my mind: "Sit still, don't stare, don't speak unless spoken to, sit still, don't stare . . ." like an endlessly looping prompt tape.

7   I caught myself staring at my grandmother, at her drab, faded-purple dress buttoned up to her chin; her gleaming, black, lace-up boots; her pulled-back, wiry gray hair; and her tiny, dark eyes framed by a constant frown. She looked ancient, fat, white, and doughy. A cane leaned by her side. This was not the granny I had imagined. Angry with my father and pierced by a deep feeling of loss, I lowered my eyes miserably.

8   "Come, let's get ready for a walk! The sun is shining for the first time in a week!" Mom said cheerfully. Gratefully, we let her take us away to get prepared for an outing. That day, we were to be dressed like proper European children: matching navy blazers and white button-up shirts, a longish skirt for my sister, and dress shorts for me. I had to wear my hand-made Belgian school shoes. Ugly and heavy, they were built to last for generations and featured half-inch layered leather soles, triple-stiched cowhide uppers, and a stainless steel foot plate. "Cop shoes," my classmates called them, and "Frenchie feet." (The teasers were soon silenced when they felt the pain of my well-placed kicks to their legs and backsides.) Nevertheless, wearing those shoes was yet another characteristic that set me apart as "that weird Frenchie kid."

9   The ensuing day seemed endless: a very slow walk in the park (having to stay several steps behind our waddling "Babchka"), a welcome but skimpy lunch, and long tours of various Canadian "department stores." The prospect of another week with Grandmother seemed more than discouraging; it was unimaginable! Little did we know that the evening to come was to change our lives, and our concepts of ourselves, forever.

10   Eventually suppertime came, and a stiff and formal affair it was. However, we did get a sip or four of rich, dark, Burgundy wine. Feeling dizzy and giggly and stupidly cheerful, my sister and I finally settled down properly on the couch after several fiery looks from Mom. We would have to listen to non-

stop, undecipherable Polish yakking without wiggling or hitting each other (our favorite pastimes). "Blah, bla blaaah, blab blaw, bla bla blah": I felt like Charlie Brown having to listen to his teacher just before being let out of school for summer holidays. Suddenly we caught some words in French. What was that?! Did we know the "Our Father" in Polish? Sweat spread on my brow as I looked to my mother to save us. Years ago it seemed, we had had to memorize what was to us only meaningless gibberish. We were told it was the "Our Father" in Polish, but we really had no way of knowing if it was in Japanese or German instead. No, my mother was saying, she and "Kostec" (my Father, Sir to us) had decided to wait awhile before teaching us Polish, as we were already having enough trouble at school with English. My father's stern, angry face turned red, his five o'clock shadow almost seeming to disappear; this was his only concession of embarrassment. He bit his tongue and remained silent.

11   A long moment passed, and then we heard a low moan from my grand-mother as she pushed herself up on her cane. She swayed slowly toward my sister and me, pulled up the untouchable antique chair (Mom's pride and joy), and sat down heavily upon it, puffing noisily. The chair, of course, complained loudly. I had a mental image of my mother pulling out her hair. No one had ever sat on this chair in living memory, but amazingly, it held solid, bravely silent from then on. Babchka proceeded to painfully loosen her tightly laced boots. She then slumped back in the chair as if she had removed from her girdle the broomstick that normally held her upright. She began speaking to us kids, who were by this time recoiling back into the cushions, in perfect but heavily accented French. I stole a glance at my sister, and she turned slightly towards me, scrunching her nose. I knew what she meant. I had tried to ignore the smell of Grandmother's tired old feet, swelling from their release from the laces, feeling that if I acknowledged the odor, I might lose my respect for this mysterious and long-anticipated grandmother. I watched as her tight, thin lips moved, fascinated by how little they needed to open for her to speak. The monotone drone began to hypnotize me; all I was aware of was the slowly developing droplet of clear fluid at the end of her nose. Abruptly, it fell.

12   Tears! My ears, my eyes, indeed, all of my senses snapped to attention. My gaze flew to her eyes; unattended tears were flowing from them down into the creases of her cheeks, hanging momentarily suspended from the drought-cracked chin before falling to join a growing stain on her silk shirt. Impossible—this was a woman who could only smile stiffly and nod her head when every one else was laughing uncontrollably.

13   I began to catch snippets of a story: a night-time escape from Russia into Poland; a desperate, exhausting train ride with her terrified little girl and screaming baby boy; men with guns and sabres and huge mustaches (the good guys); hairy, dirty, wild-eyed men with antique rifles and pitchforks (the bad guys); shots and blood and all-consuming fear. My sister and I sat upright like a couple of pieces of angle iron set in cement, paralyzed by the richly

descriptive words pouring out of Babchka without a trace of inflection or audible emotion. And yet the stain on her shirt was ever growing. She spoke of my grandfather, sent to Siberia to die a ten-year death, finally returning years after she had remarried, dying and racked with tuberculosis, hoping to see and hold his children, only to be forced to observe them playing from a distance, oblivious of him, untouchable, lest he, leper-like, contaminate them with a loving embrace. Slowly, humbly, I understood.

14 The deeply etched frown, the hardened, forbidding face, these had been sculpted by years of tragedy and deprivation such as I could not really comprehend. When she had finished, I felt as if all the blood had left my face. I felt old, a different person. I saw through blurry eyes that Mom was cradling my sister. My sister, older than me, invincible, had collapsed, weak and shaking, onto the floor. I looked up to see Granny holding her hands toward me, and robot-like, I fell into her arms. I cried a long time, holding my Babchka, unwilling to let go.

15 I would never be the same. A moment of lost innocence, of insight into human suffering and victories filled with loss; this newfound empathy would be part of me from then on. My separation from my classmates grew even larger. I could bear their petty cruelties a little better, but now I would tolerate their lack of understanding even less. The opening of this window into time began the slow opening of other windows into my family history. I could now really believe the many stories my parents were telling me because I had touched the reality of my grandmother's being.

16 Those stories became my friends when I needed strength, my identity when others tried to steal it, and my pride when I had done nothing to be proud of. Years later, I look back on this encounter as my first step toward manhood, and my first step toward wisdom.

Kowalewski, Bernie. "My Polish Grandmother." *Confluence*. Edmonton: Grant MacEwan College, 2001. 39–43.

1. Identify the senses the author appeals to in paragraphs 3 and 11. Which paragraph in the essay do you think engages the reader's senses most powerfully?
2. Underline the descriptive details that convey the author's disappointment when he first glimpses his grandmother (paragraph 7).
3. Twice the author uses foreshadowing to prepare us for a dramatic event. Identify these two "previews" and the purpose they serve.
4. Although the subject of this essay is the author's grandmother, we learn incidentally about other members of the family. In your own words, describe the author's father and mother. What clues to their personalities does the author provide?
5. This piece is written from a child's point of view. What details reinforce the fact that the narrator is seven years old?

Exercise 13.1

In pairs, brainstorm at least ten characteristics for any one of the persons listed below. Then, individually, write a paragraph about this person that incorporates at least seven of the characteristics you've identified by brainstorming. Share the results with your partner.

a petty criminal   a grandparent
a fitness instructor   your favourite comedian
your girlfriend/boyfriend, past or present   your present boss
a small child   a homeless person
an accident victim   a cafeteria or restaurant
                                                    employee

Exercise 13.2

1. In pairs, identify a famous person, hero, or historical figure whom you and your partner know something about and are interested in.
2. Imagine that your person has recently been invited to write a description of a special place he or she recently visited. This piece will be posted on the famous person's Web site to be read by fans.
3. After you have finished your description, share it with another pair. Discuss how the writing is affected by the author's role, the intended audience, the subject, and the purpose of the piece.

Exercise 13.3

In pairs, select a site or a building that pertains to your career. Then, working alone, write a paragraph describing the physical appearance of the site or building. When you have finished, exchange papers with your partner and critique each other's description. What similarities do you find in your two paragraphs? What differences? What accounts for these similarities and differences?

Exercise 13.4

To the paragraph you wrote in 13.3, add a paragraph describing the sounds, smells, and feelings (if any) you might experience if you were at the site or in the building you are describing. Again, share the results with your partner and discuss the similarities and differences between the details each of you chose to include.

Exercise 13.5

1. Write a paragraph describing a well-known contemporary figure. Do not discuss your choice of topic with your partner or name the person in your paragraph. The purpose of your description is to make the person come alive for your reader. Specific details (including mannerisms, possessions, unique characteristics, activities) will bring the character to life more than abstract descriptions of his or her personality, and a detailed physical description will help to convey a clear picture.

2. When you have completed your description, exchange papers with another student and see if you can identify each other's subject. If you cannot, what additional details do you need to know?

14

Narration

Narration is the kind of writing you do when you want to tell your readers how something happened. The ability to write good narration is required in any career that draws on personal interviews in its practice or research. Social work, education, health sciences, and criminology are just a few examples. Your purpose in telling a story may be to illustrate a point or to persuade, but all good narrative papers follow a basic pattern. The introduction presents a thesis or an overall theme for the story. The story then unfolds, usually in chronological order, with sufficient detail and description that your readers can experience the events along with you. The conclusion brings the story to a satisfying end and reinforces its point.

Like description, narration is seldom found in its "pure" form in academic or professional writing. It is usually used in combination with other kinds of development. For example, explaining a process (how something works or is done) is a special kind of narration; explaining a cause–effect relationship frequently involves narration, as does arguing a position. Almost everything you write will include at least some description and narration; that is why we are dealing with these two forms first. Because they are specific rather than general, narration and description add interest to whatever kind of writing you do. They enable readers to *see* and *feel* what you are saying, and they make your ideas easier to understand and remember.

Tips on Writing Narration

1. The story you tell must have a clear purpose; it must have a point. Good narration tells who did what to whom, where, when, and how. It also states or clearly implies why the event or incident is significant.

Remember: the subject of your essay is the point you are making, not the story you are telling.

2. Draft an outline of your story and then fill in descriptive details. Outlining will help you to arrange your events in chronological order and to group the events appropriately. Begin each paragraph after a natural break in the narrative. Be sure to use transitions to ensure the coherence of your narrative. (See pages 90–91.)

3. Make sure that your opening paragraph introduces the scene and major characters fully enough that your readers are not confused. In your closing paragraph, draw the events of the story together to leave your readers with a feeling of satisfactory closure.

4. Dialogue is a common device in narration, but use it sparingly. Traditionally, each piece of dialogue is given a separate paragraph, so it takes up a lot of space. Paraphrase and summary are more efficient but less vivid.

5. Don't use so much description that events are drawn out beyond their natural length; you may make your readers impatient.

6. Don't try to include too many events in a short narrative.

Read the four narrations that follow and answer the questions after each one.

THE INCOMPLETE ANGLER

Brian Green

1   While visiting a kind and well-meaning friend in Sarnia, I revealed myself to be an avid, if not very expert, sports fisherman. My friend confessed that he found fishing slightly less enthralling than watching algae grow in his swimming pool, but he had a pal who was a fishing fanatic. A phone call later, I was to be the special guest of "Ol' Jack" on an all-day fishing expedition to the Thames River the very next day. It has taken me four years to recover sufficiently from this adventure to tell you about it.

2   On the fateful day, Ol' Jack picked me up at 5:30 a.m. in his monstrous blue four-wheel-drive truck. Attached to the trailer hitch on the bed was a 14-foot aluminum tub with an outboard motor of adequate horsepower to push the *Queen Mary*. In the back of the truck about 20 fishing rods lay tangled together in a heap, together with assorted tackle boxes, coolers, paddles, and hip waders. Surmounting this mess of miscellaneous gear was a green fishing net that could comfortably have held Moby Dick. I was beginning to get a picture of the kind of fisherman Ol' Jack was.

3   I credit a tough constitution and my battered fishing hat for my survival during our trip to the river. Even with the protection of the hat, by the time

we pulled up at the dock I was nursing a scalp wound and two goose eggs on my skull from being tossed around the cab. Jack hurled the mound of fishing paraphernalia into the back, launched the boat, and we were off; no one was going to beat us to the "good spots." As we tore up the river, leaving a four-foot wake on either side, Jack pulled out a vodka bottle filled with an evil-looking red liquid. After taking a long swig, he handed me the bottle. "Bloody Mary," he said. "Just the thing to start the day." Gingerly, I sniffed the contents and took a tiny taste. Jack laughed as I recoiled and spat the stuff over the side. "Didn't have any tomato juice," he howled, "so I just dropped a little ketchup in the vodka!"

4   For the rest of the day, we thrashed up and down the river, dragging various strange devices behind us in a futile attempt to attract a fish. While Jack stood tall in the cockpit, handling throttle, wheel, fishing rod, and bottle, I huddled miserably in the stern, hoping I would not be recognized by any of the canoeists or fishermen we were swamping in our wake and sending scurrying for shore with our erratic trolling. Jack waved jauntily at the shaken fists and obscene gestures directed our way and tipped his baseball hat to those who favoured us with shouted curses.

5   Noon found me trying to decide whether sunburn, hunger, and exhaust fumes from the leaky outboard motor would end my misery before the inevitable collision and death by drowning or lynch mob. I favoured whichever end would be quicker. By midafternoon Jack had decided we weren't using the right lures, so we swept up to several anchored boats to find out what was working. These manoeuvres added seasickness to my list of woes. When anyone admitted to having caught a fish, Jack offered to buy the successful lure on the spot. However, even with these measures, he failed to entice any fish into attaching themselves to our lines. By suppertime, even Jack was ready to admit defeat and head for the dock. I was beyond caring.

6   Back in Sarnia, Jack dropped me at my friend's house and roared off with the promise to pick me up the next morning at 4:30. I staggered into the house and, when the trembling stopped, told the story of the day's fun on the river. Later, as I was helped up the stairs for a hot bath and long night's sleep, I begged my friend to call Jack with the news that I had come down with a potentially fatal attack of presbyopia and would be unable to join him in the morning. I haven't killed, caught, or eaten a fish since.

1. The narration in this essay begins with the first sentence. There is no general introduction, but the thesis is clearly implied in the first paragraph. State the thesis of the essay in a short sentence.

   _____

   _____

2. Who are the author's intended readers?

3. The author shows himself as the victim of this humorous escapade. What is his role? What is his purpose?
4. This story is entertaining, but is there any lesson or moral point underlying the narrative? What did the author learn from his experience?

BABA AND ME
Shandi Mitchell

1 In 1922, my father, at the age of two, came to Canada with his parents and five brothers and sisters from the Ukraine. They landed at Pier 21 in Halifax and headed west to homestead in northern Alberta. They lived in a sod and log house and suffered the prejudice of the times and the poverty of a barren existence. Forty years later, I was born into a lower-middle-class Canadian existence.

2 In that short span, the Ukrainian culture had been lost to me. My Baba (grandmother) never learned to speak English and I knew no Ukrainian. She was as much a stranger to me as were her customs, foods, thoughts, and life. As a child, I was frightened of her.

3 I knew nothing of her past and none of her secrets. No one spoke of my grandfather. I remember the family visiting a weed-infested lot set aside from the main cemetery. It wasn't until many years later that I was told he had killed himself.

4 It was then 1938: the prairies were choking on dust and Baba was newly widowed, with six children to support. In the next town over, Old Man Kurik's wife had died in childbirth. And so began Baba's next marriage. The old man used the kids as field hands and boxing bags, excepting his own son, whom he schooled to become a "gentleman." Then World War II exploded. One by one all of Baba's children left for the cities. They ran from the wheat fields and their rich, decaying earth.

5 They ran to the plastic, shiny chrome worlds filled with starched sailors and armed forces personnel. They ran to heroes' deaths and cowards' retreats. They fell in love and became "Canadians" or "Americans." They changed their names and became Marshalls, Smiths, and Longs. They traveled the world and sent postcards back home to Baba. She saved the exotic images in a cookie tin under her bed. Eventually, even Baba and Old Man Kurik moved to town. Baba became a grandmother and was asked not to speak Ukrainian around her grandchildren.

6 Baba wrote letters in Ukrainian to the old country, but they remained unanswered. Undaunted by political barriers, she continued to save her pennies, quarters, and nickels for her visit home. She didn't believe that she wouldn't be let in. Her children shushed her when she spoke of her Communist brother. It was as if the world grew up around Baba. Then one day, she found herself

a widow again. That morning, she opened every window and door in the house and breathed deeply. It was January.

7   My Baba got old in the seventies. Sometimes, she babysat my brother and me. My parents would drop us off for the weekend. I hated going there. She didn't speak any English, and I blocked out her Ukrainian. She dressed funny, she cooked funny, and she smelled of garlic. She tried to teach me about Ukrainian things. I didn't want to know. My friends were outside playing, the first McDonald's in town was opening down the street, and the Bay City Rollers had a new record. . . . I had better things to do than hang around with Baba. Back then, I didn't know the word "ashamed."

8   Baba didn't need English in the town where she lived. There were Ukrainian newspapers, TV and radio stations, stores, neighbours, churches and all the essentials in this weed of a town poking up out of nowhere in northern Alberta. The town of 1600 was divided neatly into French in the north, Ukrainians in the south, Assiniboine in the east, English in the center, and everyone else crammed into the west. It was in Baba's town that I first learned about poverty, alcoholism, domestic abuse, and racism.

9   When the old man next door died, his house was boarded up, and it became a popular place to sniff glue and drink aftershave. The neighbours pretended not to see. In the safety of daylight, we kids would venture in and gather up the few bottles amongst the cans and then cash them in at the confectionery for nickel candy. Once, we thought we'd found a dead body, but he had only passed out. Baba tended her garden, seemingly oblivious to the world next door, and kept on planning her trip home to the old country.

10   When the neighbourhood began to gentrify with condos and supermarkets and it was decided that Baba's best friend, Mrs. Westavich, couldn't keep her chickens anymore, Baba rallied to help her and used her precious savings in the process. When the two old women lost their battle, they took the chickens out to the front yard. Baba swung the axe while Mrs. Westavich held the birds down. They chopped their heads off one by one and let the birds' bodies flail and flop over the manicured lawns.

11   When the family decided it was best for Baba to go into a Home, there was no one left to fight for her. The first place was called Sunnyvale. The kids pulled her out from there when they found that she hadn't been bathed in a month and was covered in bed sores; also, her bank account was unaccountably low. Baba liked the new place better. She had a window box there, and grew tomatoes. I went to visit her, once. I called out, "Hi Baba!" and twenty wizened babas turned expectantly to me.

12   I hear Baba's house rents cheap now. The garden is filled with three cars up on blocks. I don't know what happened to her belongings. Her body is buried in Edmonton. I think the family felt it was a greater tribute to be buried in a city lot.

13   So here I sit in front of my computer with cell phone in hand and a cof-feemaker brewing, and wonder about my grandmother. I have only one black and white photograph of her. She is squat and round, with huge breasts. She wears a cotton shift dress. Her nylon stockings are bunched at her ankles. A babushka covers her head. She stands shyly beside a shiny late-model 1950s car. Next to her is my mother, with dark glasses, over-sized sun hat, and wasp waist, posed very much like Greta Garbo. I stand at the edge of the frame, a skinny kid looking as if I'm about to run.

Mitchell, Shandi. "Baba and Me." *Confluence*. Edmonton: Grant MacEwan College, 2001. 53–55.

1. What is the author's purpose in this essay, other than chronicling the life of her grandmother? State in one sentence what you think the purpose or "lesson" of the story is. How did the story affect you?
2. Identify the separate events of this story. In what order are they arranged? In point form, write an outline of the narrative.
3. What transitional techniques does the author use to link paragraphs 1 and 2? 4 and 5? 7 and 8?
4. The concluding paragraph is a description of a photograph. What do the specific details tell you about the people in the photograph: the grandmother, the mother, and the author as a child? What does the author imply about the relationship between these people?
5. Compare this short essay with Bernie Kowalewski's much longer "My Polish Grandmother" (pages 147–50). What similarities do you find? What differences (besides the obvious one of length). Which piece do you prefer? Why?

THE TRAIN RIDE

Therese Y. Siemers

1   Willow River, B.C., a hamlet so small it isn't even on most road maps, is located about 20 miles from Prince George in the heart of huge, wild forests. Twenty years ago, life was simpler and slower-paced, and a car was almost a luxury. . . . Consequently, trains were still a central part of life in Willow River, and a train ride was an exciting treat for a five-year-old boy. People still took pride in their work, [found] time for the little things in life, and [showed] an interest in others' feelings.

2   . . . I can still picture the day I set out for the doctor's appointment, hur-rying my two freshly scrubbed small sons, Benny and Dougie, over the path, through the stiff wire fence, to the tiny CNR way station. Catching the train was a risky adventure, and it was important to arrive before the only passenger-freight train whistled by at noon.

3   Nattily attired in their cowboy boots and matching shirts, heads topped with cowboy hats, shoulders squared, the boys led the way. As a special treat, they were allowed to bring their own considerable earnings which they had amassed selling pop bottles. Each had the huge sum of *one whole dollar*. Dougie entrusted his savings to my care, but Benny proudly patted the back pocket that contained his fortune in a brand-new plastic wallet.

4   The boys soon got restless waiting for the train and began exploring their surroundings. Through the deserted station's rooms, over the path, under the pilings, and over the railings they climbed to pass the time. Finally, the train arrived. [Nothing can compare to the excitement of a small boy rushing] to the edge of the elevated platform, holding a red flag to signal that huge, smoking monster diesel to a screeching, chugging, whistling stop. Holding onto the railing, the boys were assisted up the steel steps by the conductor. We made our way up the long, narrow aisle to a seat. Slowly, the train started chugging on its way, and soon the conductor ambled down the aisle to collect [the fares]. As I dug into my purse for my wallet, Benny, not realizing that children under six travelled free, reached for his back pocket, proudly telling the conductor, "I have a dollar. I can pay for my own ticket!" To his dismay, he couldn't find the wallet. It was gone!

5   Slowly it sank in: the realization that he had no more wallet, no more money. He was going into town, and he couldn't get a treat. Bravely, Benny tried to make the best of it. He sighed, "Oh well, we can find it when we get back." Unhappily, I had to remind him that many other children played around the train station and that his wallet was unidentified. By the time we returned on the midnight train, there would be little hope of retrieving his wallet. I was trying to console my little boy when suddenly, . . . the train whistled, screeched, lurched and came to a grinding halt.

6   Everybody looked around, wondering why we had stopped. Then the train started to back up. Benny looked around with mounting interest. Realization dawned. Could it be possible? Was this mile-long freight train returning to the station? Dared he hope? Would the train back up as far as Willow River station? Was this just for him? The suspense was unbearable as the trees sped by. After what seemed an interminable time, the train slowed its backward journey and crept to a halt. The door of the very car we were in stopped directly in front of the station.

7   Wordlessly, the same conductor who had collected the fares strolled unhurriedly down the aisle. He reached the door, turned, and slowly descended the steps, still without saying a word. Excitedly, Benny crept up to the door. He watched, beaming. Sure enough, the conductor was looking around the station. And there it was, the little white wallet with the Indian chief on the front, just a few steps from where Benny had boarded the train. Slowly, deliberately, and with no hint of emotion, the conductor bent down . . . and picked up the wallet. He climbed back on board and silently returned the [prize] to Benny.

Still no emotion crossed his face as he received a big hug from the ecstatic little boy.

8   Silently, this anonymous stranger, a conductor who had a job to do, who was responsible for keeping this passenger-freight train on schedule, made his way down the aisle: back to work, no more time for delays. But yes, something was there as he made his way down the aisle: just a hint, a ghost of a grin; the satisfaction of a job well done . . . and the immeasurable reward of a little boy's gratitude.

Siemers, Therese Y. "The Train Ride." *Contest: Essays by Canadian Students.* Ed. Murray McArthur. 3rd ed. Toronto: Harcourt, 1998. 54–56.

1. Most narratives do not contain a fully developed thesis statement. (To be successful, a narration must involve suspense. If the reader knows at the outset what the ending will be, why would he or she bother reading on?) What about this piece? Identify the thesis statement and explain why the piece would (or would not) be less effective without it.

2. Siemers' essay is a story about a single incident. Is the effect of the piece limited to the reader's response to that single incident, or does the essay have a wider application? What point is Siemers making in this story?

3. Good films are based on strong narratives. Do the visual images in this story allow you to picture the scene and the action? Identify as many images as you can that would translate effectively to a film treatment of this story.

4. The story of the train ride ends in paragraph 7. What is the function of the last paragraph? Would the essay be equally effective if the author had not included paragraph 8? Why?

GROWING UP NATIVE

Carol Geddes

1   I remember it was cold. We were walking through a swamp near our home in the Yukon bush. Maybe it was fall and moose-hunting season. I don't know. I think I was about four years old at the time. The muskeg was too springy to walk on, so people were taking turns carrying me—passing me from one set of arms to another. The details about where we were are vague, but the memory of those arms and the feeling of acceptance I had is one of the most vivid memories of my childhood. It didn't matter who was carrying me—there was security in every pair of arms. That response to children is typical of the native community. It's the first thing I think of when I cast my mind back to the Yukon bush, where I was born and lived with my family.

2   I was six years old when we moved out of the bush, first to Teslin, where I had a hint of the problems native people face, then to Whitehorse, where there was unimaginable racism. Eventually I moved to Ottawa and Montreal, where I further discovered that to grow up native in Canada is to feel the sting of humiliation and the boot of discrimination. But it is also to experience the enviable security of an extended family and to learn to appreciate the richness of the heritage and traditions of a culture most North Americans have never been lucky enough to know. As a film-maker, I have tried to explore these contradictions, and our triumph over them, for the half-million aboriginals who are part of the tide of swelling independence of the First Nations today.

3   But I'm getting ahead of myself. If I'm to tell the story of what it's like to grow up native in northern Canada, I have to go back to the bush where I was born, because there's more to my story than the hurtful stereotyping that depicts Indian people as drunken welfare cases. Our area was known as 12-mile (it was 12 miles from another tiny village). There were about 40 people living there—including 25 kids, eight of them my brothers and sisters—in a sort of family compound. Each family had its own timber plank house for sleeping, and there was one large common kitchen area with gravel on the ground and a tent frame over it. Everybody would go there and cook meals together. In summer, my grandmother always had a smudge fire going to smoke fish and tan moose hides. I can remember the cosy warmth of the fire, the smell of good food, and always having someone to talk to. We kids had built-in playmates and would spend hours running in the bush, picking berries, building rafts on the lake and playing in abandoned mink cages.

4   One of the people in my village tells a story about the day the old lifestyle began to change. he had been away hunting in the bush for about a month. On his way back, he heard a strange sound coming from far away. He ran up the crest of a hill, looked over the top of it and saw a bulldozer. He had never seen or heard of such a thing before and he couldn't imagine what it was. We didn't have magazines or newspapers in our village, and the people didn't know that the Alaska Highway was being built as a defence against a presumed Japanese invasion during the Second World War. That was the beginning of the end of the Teslin Tlingit people's way of life. From that moment on, nothing turned back to the way it was. Although there were employment opportunities for my father and uncles, who were young men at the time, the speed and force with which the Alaska Highway rammed through the wilderness caused tremendous upheaval for Yukon native people.

5   It wasn't as though we'd never experienced change before. The Tlingit Nation, which I belong to, arrived in the Yukon from the Alaskan coast around the turn of the century. They were the middlemen and women between the Russian traders and the Yukon inland Indians. The Tlingit gained power and prestige by trading European products such as metal goods and cloth for the rich and varied furs so much in fashion in Europe. The Tlingit controlled Yukon

trading because they controlled the trading routes through the high mountain passes. When trading ceased to be an effective means of survival, my grandparents began raising wild mink in cages. Mink prices were really high before and during the war, but afterwards the prices went plunging down. So, although the mink pens were still there when I was a little girl, my father mainly worked on highway construction and hunted in the bush. The Yukon was then, and still is in some ways, in a transitional period—from living off the land to getting into a European wage-based economy.

6   As a young child, I didn't see the full extent of the upheaval. I remember a lot of togetherness, a lot of happiness while we lived in the bush. There's a very strong sense of family in the native community, and a fondness for children, especially young children. Even today, it's like a special form of entertainment if someone brings a baby to visit. That sense of family is the one thing that has survived all the incredible difficulties native people have had. Throughout a time of tremendous problems, the extended family system has somehow lasted, providing a strong circle for people to survive in. When parents were struggling with alcoholism or had to go away to find work, when one of the many epidemics swept through the community, or when a marriage broke up and one parent left, aunts, uncles, and grandparents would try to fill those roles. It's been very important to me in terms of emotional support to be able to rely on my extended family. There are still times when such support keeps me going.

7   Life was much simpler when we lived in the bush. Although we were poor and wore the same clothes all year, we were warm enough and had plenty to eat. But even as a youngster, I began to be aware of some of the problems we would face later on. Travelling missionaries would come and impose themselves on us, for example. They'd sit at our campfire and read the Bible to us and lecture us about how we had to live a Christian life. I remember being very frightened by stories we heard about parents sending their kids away to live with white people who didn't have any children. We thought those people were mean and that if we were bad, we'd be sent away too. Of course, that was when social workers were scooping up native children and adopting them out to white families in the south. The consequences were usually disastrous for the children who were taken away—alienation, alcoholism, and suicide, among other things. I knew some of those kids. The survivors are still struggling to recover.

8   The residential schools were another source of misery for the kids. Although I didn't have to go, my brothers and sisters were there. They told stories about having their hair cut off in case they were carrying head lice, and of being forced to do hard chores without enough food to eat. They were told that the Indian culture was evil, that Indian people were bad, that their only hope was to be Christian. They had to stand up and say things like "I've found

the Lord," when a teacher told them to speak. Sexual abuse was rampant in the residential school system.

9   By the time we moved to Whitehorse, I was excited about the idea of living in what I thought of as a big town. I'd had a taste of the outside world from books at school in Teslin (a town of 250 people), and I was tremendously curious about what life was like. I was hungry for experiences such as going to the circus. In fact, for a while, I was obsessed with stories and pictures about the circus, but then when I was 12 and saw my first one, I was put off by the condition and treatment of the animals.

10   Going to school in Whitehorse was a shock. The clash of native and white values was confusing and frightening. Let me tell you a story. The older boys in our community were already accomplished hunters and fishermen, but since they had to trap beaver in the spring and hunt moose in the fall, and go out trapping in the winter as well, they missed a lot of school. We were all in one classroom and some of my very large teenage cousins had to sit squeezed into little desks. These guys couldn't read very well. We girls had been in school all along, so, of course, we were better readers. One day the teacher was trying to get one of the older boys to read. She was typical of the teachers at that time, insensitive and ignorant of cultural complexities. In an increasingly loud voice, she kept commanding him to "Read it, read it." He couldn't. He sat there completely still, but I could see that he was breaking into a sweat. The teacher then said, "Look, she can read it," and she pointed to me, indicating that I should stand up and read. For a young child to try to show up an older boy is wrong and totally contrary to native cultural values, so I refused. She told me to stand up and I did. My hands were trembling as I held my reader. She yelled at me to read and when I didn't she smashed her pointing stick on the desk to frighten me. In terror, I wet my pants. As I stood there fighting my tears of shame, she said I was disgusting and sent me home. I remember feeling this tremendous confusion, on top of my humiliation. We were always told the white teachers knew best, and so we had to do whatever they said at school. And yet I had a really strong sense of receiving mixed messages about what I was supposed to do in the community and what I was supposed to do at school.

11   Pretty soon I hated school. Moving to a predominantly white high school was even worse. We weren't allowed to join anything the white kids started. We were the butt of jokes because of our secondhand clothes and moose meat sandwiches. We were constantly being rejected. The prevailing attitude was that Indians were stupid. When it was time to make course choices in class—between typing and science, for example—they didn't even ask the native kids, they just put us all in typing. You get a really bad image of yourself in a situation like that. I bought into it. I thought we were awful. The whole experience was terribly undermining. Once, my grandmother gave me

a pretty little pencil box. I walked into the classroom one day to find the word "squaw" carved on it. That night I burned it in the wood stove. I joined the tough crowd and by the time I was 15 years old, I was more likely to be leaning against the school smoking a cigarette than trying to join in. I was burned out from trying to join the system. The principal told my father there was no point in sending me back to school so, with a Grade 9 education, I started to work at a series of menial jobs.

12   Seven years later something happened to me that would change my life forever. I had moved to Ottawa with a man and was working as a waitress in a restaurant. One day, a friend invited me to her place for coffee. While I was there, she told me she was going to university in the fall and showed me her reading list. I'll never forget the minutes that followed. I was feeling vaguely envious of her and once again, inferior. I remember taking the paper in my hand, seeing the books on it and realizing, Oh, my God, I've read these books! It hit me like a thunderclap. I was stunned that books I had read were being read in university. University was for white kids, not native kids. We were too stupid, we didn't have the kind of mind it took to do those things. My eyes moved down the list, and my heart started beating faster and faster as I suddenly realized I could go to university, too!

13   My partner at the time was a loving supportive man who helped me in every way. I applied to the university immediately as a mature student but when I had to write Grade 9 on the application, I was sure they'd turn me down. They didn't. I graduated five years later, earning a Bachelor of Arts in English and philosophy (with distinction). . . .

14   Today, there's a glimmer of hope that more of us native people will overcome the obstacles that have tripped us up ever since we began sharing this land. Some say our cultures are going through a renaissance. Maybe that's true. Certainly there's a renewed interest in native dancing, acting, and singing, and in other cultural traditions. Even indigenous forms of government are becoming strong again. But we can't forget that the majority of native people live in urban areas and continue to suffer from alcohol and drug abuse and the plagues of a people who have lost their culture and have become lost themselves. And the welfare system is the insidious glue that holds together the machine of oppression of native people.

15   Too many non-native people have refused to try to understand the issues behind our land claims. They make complacent pronouncements such as "Go back to your bows and arrows and fish with spears if you want aboriginal rights. If not, give it up and assimilate into white Canadian culture." I don't agree with that. We need our culture, but there's no reason why we can't preserve it and have an automatic washing machine and a holiday in Mexico, as well.

16   The time has come for native people to make our own decisions. We need to have self-government. I have no illusions that it will be smooth sailing—there will be trial and error and further struggle. And if that means crawling before we can stand up and walk, so be it. We'll have to learn through experience.

17   While we're learning, we have a lot to teach and give to the world—a holistic philosophy, a way of living with the earth, not disposing of it. It is critical that we all learn from the elders that an individual is not more important than a forest; we know that we're here to live on and with the earth, not to subdue it.

18   The wheels are in motion for a revival, for change in the way native people are taking their place in Canada. I can see that we're equipped, we have the tools to do the work. We have an enormous number of smart, talented, moral Indian people. It's thrilling to be a part of this movement.

19   Someday, when I'm an elder, I'll tell the children the stories: about the bush, about the hard times, about the renaissance, and especially about the importance of knowing your place in your nation.

Geddes, Carol. "Growing Up Native." *Canadian Content.* Ed. Sarah Norton and Nell Waldman. 4th ed. Toronto: Harcourt, 2000. 41–46.

1. What is the author's purpose in this essay? Which paragraph most clearly states that purpose?
2. This narrative is filled with specific detail. Choose one paragraph and identify the details the author has included to help the reader form a vivid mental picture.
3. Look at paragraph 10. What does the anecdote in that paragraph tell you about the author? About her teacher? Find another anecdote in the essay that also illustrates the clash between two cultures.
4. A good narrative introduces the scene and major character(s) in the opening paragraph. Consider Geddes' first paragraph. Do you think it is effective? Why?
5. How does the concluding paragraph contribute to the unity of the piece?

Exercise 14.1

You hear narration every day when your friends, family, classmates, and teachers tell you about incidents that happened to them. Most of these are insignificant incidents that seemed important at the time but are soon forgotten. What makes a narrative memorable? What kinds of stories stick in your mind long after you have heard them? Why?

Exercise 14.2

Narration relies on the same principle as description in that it is a detailed account that appeals to the senses. However, effective narration goes a step further than description: it answers the question "What was it like to be there when this event happened?" Imagine yourself as a central figure in a career-related event. Write a paragraph that conveys to your readers some of the important details of the event and your thoughts as a participant. For example, you might choose to write about making a presentation for some prospective clients, dealing with a difficult customer, or trying to help a fellow employee solve a work-related problem.

Exercise 14.3

Using the same incident that you created in Exercise 14.2, write a third-person account of the event as a witness might have experienced it, perhaps as one of the clients in the first example, or as another customer overhearing the discussion in the second example.

Exercise 14.4

In good narration, the story told is often used as an example to illustrate a general theme. Briefly outline a story you might tell from personal experience to demonstrate one of the following themes, but do not name the theme.

frustration	the reward (or futility) of hard work
leadership	loss
panic	jealousy
peer pressure	obsession

Exercise 14.5

Using the outline you produced in Exercise 14.4, write a narrative paper. Remember that good stories are carefully planned and structured; poor ones are often the products of writers who begin at the top of the page and stumble downward until the story comes to an end. When you have completed your work, exchange papers with another student. Can you identify the point of each other's narrative—what theme the story is intended to illustrate? Discuss how each piece could be made more effective.

Exercise 14.6

Embarrassing incidents often make good narratives, both because most are entertaining and because listeners and readers can often learn a lesson from the embarrassing mistakes of others. Briefly rough out, in point form, a narrative of the most embarrassing experience you have ever had. Use third-person pronouns (he/she); that is, outline the story as if it had happened to someone else. This may make a good paper when you are assigned a narrative to write. It might also be good therapy!

Exercise 14.7

Narrate the plot of a movie that you enjoyed and remember clearly. Give important details, not just the simple facts of the story. Try to make the experience of reading your paper as vivid and interesting as viewing the movie itself. Find a partner who has not seen your movie and whose movie you have not seen. (This may take a few minutes.) Exchange papers and critique each other's work. Are there any holes in the narratives? Has the point or theme of each movie been made clear?

Exercise 14.8

Your life is full of experiences that you share with many others: your first day at school, your first day at work, your wedding day, a memorable vacation, and so on. However, no two of these experiences are the same; each person's is unique. Below is a list of "first" or "last" or "only" experiences. Only you can narrate how yours happened. Plan and develop one of these events into a full paper. Remember to focus on a limited length of time and give most attention to highlights.

a speeding ticket	my first speech
my first car purchase	my first time skiing (*or* another sport)
an equipment failure	moving day
the last day on a job	the day my childhood ended
my first day in college	my first business venture

15

Process

Like narration, **process** writing explains events that follow one another in time. There are two kinds of process writing: instruction and analysis. When you explain how to get from the Registrar's Office to the Resource Centre, how to make perfect pastry, how to start a wet motor, or any other "how to" topic, your purpose is to enable your readers to perform the process for themselves. Giving instructions or directions is often done in point form: think of a recipe, for example, or the instructions that come with a product that requires assembling. Instructions are usually written in the second person (*you*), and include commands (e.g., "Leave time to revise").

Process analysis, on the other hand, describes how something is done, or is made, or works. In explaining how the citizenship process works or how a specific food gets from the farm to the table; how snowflakes form or phosphorus kills lakes; how plants produce food or the stock market operates, you do not expect your readers to be able to reproduce the process. Your purpose is simply to inform them. Process analysis is usually written in the third person (e.g., "Wise writers leave plenty of time for revision") and often includes the passive voice ("When the paper has been edited, it is ready for submission"). The tone of your essay, and the amount and kind of detail you include, will vary depending on your audience and purpose.

Whether you are writing instructions or analysis, keep your language simple and clear. Remember that your readers probably do not share your expertise on the subject (if they did, you wouldn't be explaining it). If you use highly technical language or skip over steps that are obvious only to an expert, you will confuse or mislead your readers. Consider the following instructions:

To execute the cast, play out about 10 metres of fly line in front of you. Ensure that there is no slack in the line, and begin your back cast. As the rod tip reaches about one o'clock, stop the backward motion and begin a crisp forward motion, loading the rod. On the back cast, the line must straighten behind you, parallel to the ground, before the forward motion begins.

The quick forward thrust, stopping abruptly at about ten o'clock, will result in an aerodynamic loop that will travel the length of the fly line, straightening the line in front of you, and resulting in the perfect cast.

These directions break the process of fly casting down into chronologically arranged steps, but the writer has forgotten the most basic rule of good writing: remember the reader. Only someone who already knows what the writer is talking about would be able to follow these instructions. An effective process paper, whether instruction or analysis, takes into account the readers' familiarity—or lack of it—with the process, their experience, and their level of vocabulary. Finally, it communicates the steps of the process in a way that holds the readers' interest.

One of the most challenging aspects of process analysis is making sure that you have included all the necessary steps. Only an expert, someone who knows what the result should look like, can leave out a step or two, or combine steps, or take short-cuts. As you write, try to imagine yourself in the reader's position: someone with little or no experience who is reading the instructions or description for the first time.

Tips on Writing Process Papers

1. Plan carefully. Prepare an outline listing all the steps of the process. Include everything that your readers need to know, and use language they can understand. Now put the steps in chronological or logical order. (See pages 44 and 45 for definitions and examples.) Be prepared to revise your list several times before your steps are arranged correctly. Too much detail can be as confusing as too little, so if there are many small steps, group them into a number of more easily manageable stages.
2. Write the introduction. State your purpose, and include any background information or theory (for example, identify any necessary equipment).
3. Write a thesis statement that makes it clear what your readers are about to learn. If it is appropriate, include a preview of the major steps you will describe.

The steps involved in becoming a winning tennis player can be summed up in four words: basics, practice, concentration, and attitude.

Getting married is a process that involves fulfilling arcane legal requirements, enduring an official ceremony, and surviving the abuse of one's in-laws.

For the executive chef, creating a signature dish is a process that involves selecting fresh, local ingredients, preparing them to bring out the best of their flavours in combination, and presenting the finished product with imagination and flair. (Niagara Culinary Institute)

4. Develop each step in a paragraph. Be sure to use transitions both within paragraphs and between paragraphs. Transitions help your reader follow the sequence of the process; they also make your writing easier to read. Review the list of transition techniques on pages 90–91 before you begin your essay.

5. Avoid shifts in person. Inexperienced writers often start with the third person and then switch to *you* and give commands. If you focus on your purpose—either to instruct or to inform—as you write, you will be less likely to use pronouns inconsistently.

6. Write the conclusion. Sometimes a brief summary is useful, especially if the process is a complex one. Alternatively, you could end your paper with an evaluation of the results, or remind your readers of the importance or usefulness of the process.

7. When revising, put yourself in the position of someone who knows nothing about the process and see if you can follow the instructions or description with ease. Have you included all the steps or stages? Have you defined any technical terms? Better yet, ask someone who really is a novice to read your paper and try to follow your directions or understand your description.

In the four essays that follow, you will find examples of both kinds of process analysis. Read each selection and answer the questions that follow.

HOW TO PLAY WINNING TENNIS
Brian Green

1   As a tennis instructor for the past three summers, I have watched many people waste their money on hi-tech racquets, designer outfits, and professional lessons, and then complain loudly that in spite of all the expense they still can't play the game. Unfortunately for them, a decent backhand is one thing that money can't buy. No matter what level of player you are, though, or what level you wish to be, there are four steps to accomplishing the goal of winning tennis. They can be summed up in four words: basics, practice, concentration, and attitude.

2   All sports may be reduced to a few basic skills, which, if learned properly at the outset and drilled until they are instinctive, lead to success. Tennis is no

exception; however, few people seem willing to spend the time needed to master the basics. Having been shown the proper grip and swing for a fore-hand, backhand, and serve, my students seem to feel they can qualify for Wimbledon. The basics are not learned that easily. Many tennis schools are now using a system developed in Spain that helps new players establish the correct stroke. For the first month of lessons, they aren't allowed to use a tennis ball. For that first month, correct positioning, proper swing, footwork, and technique are drilled without any of the distractions of keeping score, winning or losing, or chasing errant balls. That's how important the basics are to winning tennis.

3   Having acquired the basics, a beginning player must now practise and practise and practise to remember and refine those important skills. It isn't very much fun sometimes to play against a ball machine that never swears or sweats and doesn't care whether you hit a winning return. Drills and exercises won't do much for your social life while your friends are on the next court playing "pat-a-ball" with a couple of good-looking novices. Those basic strokes that you must keep hitting correctly hundreds of times a day aren't as impressive as the sexy spins and tricky between-the-legs shots the club players are perfecting . . . but if you're going to play winning tennis, practice is vital. Your feet must move instinctively to get you to the ball properly positioned for an effective stroke; a smooth backhand must become automatic from everywhere on the court; a crisp forehand, hit with accuracy, must be as nat-ural as breathing.

4   When you're finally ready for competition, everything seems calculated to make you forget all you've learned. It requires enormous concentration to shut out distractions and continue to practise the basics that are essential to your game: watch the ball, keep your head down, turn 90 degrees from the path of the ball, keep your feet moving, and so on and so on. With an opponent opposite you, people watching, and your own self-esteem on the line, it's difficult to keep your mind from wandering. Tennis is about 50 per-cent mental effort. Successful players are those who are able to block out dis-tractions and concentrate on making the racquet meet the ball with precision.

5   Finally, developing the proper attitude is the key to winning tennis. I define winning tennis as playing the game to the best of your ability, hitting the ball as well as you know you can, and enjoying the feeling of practised expertise. Winning tennis has little to do with beating an opponent. Naturally, if you play winning tennis by learning the basics, practising sufficiently, and con-centrating, you'll win many matches, but that is the reward of playing well, not the reason for playing well. People who swear and throw their racquets when they lose are very useful; they are the most satisfying players to trounce. But I don't understand why they play a game that gives them such pain. Tennis players who enjoy the feel of a well-hit ball and the satisfaction of a long, skilfully played rally are winners, regardless of the score.

1. Describe typical readers the author may have been thinking of. Consider their interests and goals.
2. What is the role of the author?
3. What are the main points the author covers in explaining the steps of improving performance in the game? Roughly outline the main and supporting points of this essay.
4. What functions does the introductory paragraph serve in this essay?
5. Discuss the final paragraph as an effective conclusion to the essay.

FORGING: THE BLACK ART
Paul Allen

1   The art of shaping metal by forging is as old as civilization itself. Its significance to human progress is evident in the names we give to historical periods: the Bronze Age, the Iron Age. Forging is the working of metals by heating them until they are pliable, and then hammering or pressing them into shapes. The process can be used to produce objects ranging from giant propellers to tiny manicure scissors. Whether the end product weighs tonnes or grams, the procedure is the same: the metal to be forged must be prepared, processed, and finished.

2   The first step in the process is to identify precisely the material to be forged and to determine its weight and grade. The carbon content and the presence of any alloying elements, such as nickel or molybdenum, will determine the temperature and duration of the heating process. Once the calculations are complete, the metal can be heated. While it heats to forging temperature (1200°C), any tools that are required for shaping should be prepared. Punches are needed if rings are being forged; blocks of varying thicknesses are required if bars or shafts are being formed.

3   Forging begins when all the preparations have been completed and the material has reached forging temperature. The part is removed from the furnace and taken to the forging hammer or press. Hammer forging involves shaping the metal by a series of swift blows; press forging squeezes the metal into shape. Press forging is slower than hammer forging, but it can produce closer tolerances in shape and size.

4   Finishing is the final stage of the process. When a part has been forged, it must be inspected to ensure that it is precisely the right size and configuration. Inspection is crucial because if required tolerances are not met, the part may need to be forged again or scrapped. Manufacturers have good reasons for wanting to get the piece right the first time: the materials range from a few cents to $150 a kilogram, and labour costs are as high as $15 a minute. Once the forging has passed inspection, each piece is stamped with an identification

mark such as the customer's name and order number. The part can now be allowed to cool before any finishing or fine shaping. Materials that may crack if they lose heat too quickly require slow cooling in a specially prepared furnace.

5   Forging is not just "metal beating," as some have described it; it is a complex operation requiring highly skilled workers. Metalworking is sometimes called "the black art," and the descriptor is apt. There is something magical about the transformation of a cold lump of steel into parts for a jet engine, a submarine, or a nuclear generator. To produce a high-quality forged part requires considerable skill and careful judgment. Neglect or carelessness in preparing, processing, or finishing means the loss of time, effort, and money.

Reprinted by permission of the author.

1. What is the purpose of this essay? Is it intended to teach readers how to perform the process themselves? How do you know?
2. For what audience is this essay intended? How would the piece be different if the target readers were ten years old? Retired steelworkers?
3. What is the author's attitude toward his subject? What clues can you find that provide an indication of his feeling about forging?
4. Study the introductory and concluding paragraphs. Identify the attention-getter, the thesis statement, the summary, and the memorable statement. Are these clear? Effective? Why?

    How does the concluding paragraph contribute to the unity of the essay?
5. Not many readers are likely to be familiar with the process described in this essay. How has the author made his subject accessible to general readers?
6. An essay like this is often accompanied by photographs. Which points in the process would you like to see illustrated?

GETTING PANCAKE SAUCE FROM TREES
Geoffrey Rowan

1   Soon the sap will be running—which is not a comment on the base-stealing abilities of any specific Toronto Blue Jay. It's maple sap we're talking about, for maple-syrup season is upon us. For centuries, people have been tapping maple trees, drawing off sap, and boiling it down into sweet, sticky, amber syrup that's a perfect sauce for pancakes, French toast, and waffles. Making maple syrup can be extremely low-tech, requiring little more than a bucket, a pan, a wood fire, and, of course, a maple tree or two. Making lots of maple syrup takes a bit more technical sophistication.

2   First, something about the trees. Most maple syrup comes from the sugar or rock maple (*acer saccharum*), found only in North America, and the black maple (*acer nigrum*). It take a maple 20 to 80 years to grow to a tappable diameter of 25 centimetres. The sap, which is mostly water and about 2 to 4 percent maple syrup, is formed through the process of photosynthesis: the tree draws water from the ground and carbon dioxide from the air, and uses the energy of sunlight, absorbed through its leaves, to manufacture organic compounds, including sugar, from the water and carbon dioxide. In winter, the sap retreats to the tree's roots. When the temperature gets above freezing, the sap starts to rise. Maple-syrup producers say the optimum conditions for drawing sap are below-freezing nights and above-freezing days, which create a sort of pump action over the 4- to 6-week-long sap season. Worst is a warm spell, which produces a gush of sap for a few days and then nothing for the rest of the season. It can also give the sap a bad taste. Sap production varies greatly from tree to tree, but producers say they like to get 1 to 2.5 litres of syrup per tap. It takes about 40 litres of sap to make 1 litre of syrup.

3   Once a tappable tree has been identified, a tap—called a spile—is driven 3.5 centimetres into the tree. A spile is simply a small tube, tapered at one end. Some have a little hook hanging below the lip of the exposed end for hanging a bucket. But big syrup producers don't use buckets anymore. They run plastic tubing from trees to feeder lines to main lines and back to a collection centre, creating a bizarre cat's cradle in the woods. The problems with tube collection are deer, elk, and moose, which can pull tubing down as they wander among the trees, and squirrels, which chew holes in it. (Who knows why squirrels do anything?) Some producers arrange the lines so gravity will pull the sap through the tubes to storage tanks. Others use pumps to create a vacuum that draws the sap along the lines. Vacuum power can suck about 50 percent more sap out of a tree than gravity.

4   From a holding tank in the sugar house, the sap flows into an evaporator, which is basically a pan with a corrugated bottom. The ridges on the bottom create more surface area, making it more efficient to apply heat to boil away the water. The most sophisticated evaporators have automatic draw-off systems. Sensors monitor the density and temperature of the syrup and start the draw-off at the proper time. Less sophisticated systems rely on producers paying careful attention to their thermometers and density metres. Some large producers have introduced a step between the storage tank and the evaporator. They pump the sap through a reverse-osmosis unit, which contains a semi-permeable membrane that can remove up to 75 percent of the sap's water. Once in the evaporator, the sap is kept over the fire until enough water has boiled off to make it 66 percent sugar. At this point it has become maple syrup and is drained off, filtered through felt, and poured into hot bottles.

5   Then there are the really unsophisticated systems for small-scale hobbyists, systems that are closer to the time-honoured process involving buckets and

pans and hardwood fires than to the high-tech procedures today's producers employ. Maple-syrup kits are available that include spiles and an evaporator that will fit on a gas barbecue. All you need is a couple of productive, healthy maple trees. A word of caution: don't try to boil down your sap on the stove or in the oven unless you want a sticky, sugary coating over everything in the house.

Rowan, Geoffrey. "How They Get Pancake Sauce from Trees." *Globe and Mail* 15 Mar. 1994: A11.

1. What is the author's purpose in this article: to tell readers how to make maple syrup, or to tell readers how syrup is made?
2. Where in the article does Rowan clearly identify his subject? Why does he not also outline the major steps in the process?
3. What do you think of the author's attention-getter? Is it effective?
4. Outline the main points of the process Rowan describes. Are they arranged in logical order or in chronological order? Why did the author choose this arrangement?
5. What purpose does the second paragraph serve? Would the article be equally effective if this paragraph were omitted?
6. Consider the concluding paragraph: how does it bring the article to a satisfying close?

A TREE-PLANTING PRIMER

Danny Irvine

Tape # 1: Introduction

1   "Welcome to the wonderful world of tree-planting. You are about to embark on an adventure of awesome proportions, fending for yourself in the coniferous Klondike—the very heartland of Canada. Are you intimidated? Don't be. You can rest assured that any stories you may have heard about the grueling savagery of the tree-planting experience, about inhospitable land-scapes, maimed bodies, and inhuman exhaustion are wild exaggerations, nothing more than hallucinations of former planters who are suffering the residual effects of some obscure psychological trauma.

2   "The wilderness is a nurturing, healing place, and it is well known that physical labour can be a contemplative, therapeutic activity. You can see its effects in the euphoria of the planters at the end of the season. Nevertheless, you may still be a little apprehensive about the planting contract and may feel somewhat alien in your new environment, so far away from the familiar comfort of the city, with its paved roads and snowless summers, its docile elements and herbivorous wildlife. We encourage you to think of the North as your 'home away from home': the trees and rocks your walls and floors, the

darkening clouds your vaulted ceiling, the bears and wolves your friendly neighbours. What's more, you have this primer, which is designed to help you to survive and to profit from your silvicultural experience."

Tape # 2: Equipment

3   "By this time, you will have been given your tree-planting equipment. Your planting bags—three pouches of high-tensile nylon, suspended from a padded, ergonomic belt and adjustable shoulder straps—are the first order of business. You will wear this set of bags all day, every day, for the duration of the contract. They will be your uniform, the armor of the noble tree planter; they will adorn and distinguish you; they will soak up your sweat and bear your scent. Think of them as indispensable articles of clothing, a sort of 'second underwear,' which you put on as soon as you awake and without which you never leave home. Do not get caught without your planting bags. Since this second underwear will be weighted with more than 20 kg of trees, you will want to adjust the belt and shoulder straps to the position most closely approximating comfort. Ignore any uncomfortable chafing you may experience; this abrasion will soon become too familiar to be troublesome.

4   "The second piece of equipment: your shovel. Hold it in your hand. Grip it. Swing it. Can you feel the earth part before you? No? Swing it again. Hit something with it. This is no ordinary shovel; this is your livelihood. This is your weapon. This steel-spaded, wood-shafted, D-handled shovel is the instrument with which you will split the earth and subdue the forests. It will be your trusty machete when you encounter obstructive branches and brush. It will be your means of carving yourself bathroom facilities when you are miles from civilization. It will be your sure defense in the event of an encounter with squirrels, raccoons, or small, sickly black bears. For these reasons, it is important that you respect your shovel. Never let it out of your sight. Take care of it. Name it. Talk to it. It will be your best and only friend in the long days of solitude out on the clear-cut. At first, your shovel may feel awkward and heavy, but after several weeks of continuously gripping it, you will feel as if it were a fifth limb. You and your shovel will form such a bond that you will find it almost unbearably painful to unclench your grip at night."

Tape # 3: Getting Started

5   "Once you have familiarized yourself with your equipment, you are ready to plant. To begin, put your planting bags around your waist. If the belt slips, readjust it. If it continues to slip, duct-tape the straps together. If even duct tape fails to maintain a fit, the problem is probably faulty belt buckles. Find a fellow planter with undamaged bags and inconspicuously swap your bag for hers. Write your name on your new bag with a waterproof magic-marker and avoid that planter for a few days.

6   "Next, decide how many trees you are willing to carry in one trip, and load up your bags. This is not a casual decision. On the one hand, since you are being paid per tree, there is financial reward in carrying as many trees as you can squeeze into your bags. On the other hand, a heavy load will weigh and slow you down. You will tire quickly, and you will not be able to stop for a rest until your bags are fully unloaded. What's that? You don't plan on taking any breaks? That's the attitude! Heavy or light: you must find a middle road. Forestry is, after all, fundamentally a matter of balance: harvesting lumber without decimating the sustainable forests, planting new growth without destabilizing the ecosystem, working harder than a machine without destroying your body, keeping the bugs away without developing cancer from insect repellent.

7   "Once you have packed up your trees, scan the area and pick up any trees you may have inadvertently dropped. The forestry company has paid a good deal of money for these trees, and you will find that they get quite upset if they discover any lying on the ground. Throw any fallen trees into your bag, or, alternatively, onto the ground where another planter has been working.

8   "Packing up your trees, or 'bagging up,' as you will become conditioned to call it, can, admittedly, be a time-consuming procedure. Having to sit in one place to perform it can be particularly irritating if it happens to be raining or snowing; if it happens to be in the frigid early months or the scorching later months of the season; or if the blackflies, mosquitoes, horseflies, or deer-flies happen to be out. But never mind. Having packed up your bags, knowing precisely how many trees you are carrying, you are ready to go. What? You didn't keep track of how many you put in? Well, you'd better take them all out and count again.

9   "Once you have confirmed your count, take your shovel in your right or left hand, whichever is the stronger. This will be your 'shovel hand'; your weaker hand will be your 'bag hand.' Your bag hand is the hand that will pick up and plant each tree; that is why you have put the trees into the pouch on that same side. What? You didn't know this, and put the trees into the pouch on the side of your stronger hand? Well, you'd better take them all out and start again.

10   "Your bags strapped and loaded, your shovel firmly gripped, you are at long last ready to plant your first tree. Make your way to the piece of land, 'the block,' that has been allotted to you. The block may be a short, convenient distance from your tree depot. More often, however, you will have a long hike to get to the entrance to your land. You may be compensated if this travel time is unusually lengthy or particularly grueling. But don't count on it. Your employer is more likely to consider this trek an opportunity for you to explore the untamed wilderness and reflect on your contribution to the development of our country's sustainable resources."

Tape # 4: Planting a Tree

11   "Planting a tree is an art that requires control and precision and, for many individuals, takes years to learn. In Japan, for instance, bonsai-tree planters are chosen while they are still infants and taken to mountain pagodas, where they spend their youth in rigorous training under the tutelage of revered masters. Each day they spend hours in the forest, learning respect for the trees; they participate in disciplined physical exercises, developing scrupulous control of their bodies; and only after seven years of bare-handed labour in the stony Japanese soil are they permitted to handle a shovel.

12   "You, on the other hand, have the good fortune to live in a much less demanding culture. With this guide to help you, you can easily learn to plant a tree without years of arduous training. To be a successful tree planter, you need to learn two things. First, you must understand and accept the essential, organic, and spiritual union of body and land—a dynamic, beautiful marriage of arms, legs, back, and shovel with tree and soil. Second, you must learn to harness and relentlessly exploit this union for your own purposes.

13   "Begin by retrieving a tree from your bag with (you guessed it) your bag hand. At the same time, step forward with the corresponding leg, pinpoint the spot where you wish to plant a tree, and, with your shovel hand, raise your shovel.

14   "This is probably a good point at which to discuss generating and maintaining motivation and morale while out on the clear cut. As everyone knows, a certain degree of mental fortitude is helpful when you are repeatedly performing even the simplest of tasks. The oppressive, dark, and forbidding clouds that perpetually crowd the skies this far north may already have suggested to you that not every planting day will be a sunny outing in the woods. Some planters have even experienced moments of mild discouragement at their work.

15   "If ever you should feel a twinge of despair over your ability to fulfil the planting contract, to meet the quota of trees that you have set as a standard for yourself; if ever you are worried that you will not earn enough money to pay off your student debts and will have to sell the family heirlooms to pay your tuition; if you have been planting in a swamp for three weeks and have not spoken to another soul for days; if you notice the extremities of your body turning numb from the cold, from insect bites, or from the pesticides on the trees; if the zipper on your tent has torn and your boots have holes in them and your leg is broken and infected and your girlfriend or boyfriend has stopped writing letters and your mother has forgotten about you and rented out your room to a new son or daughter and you are on the verge of impaling yourself on your own planting shovel, do not be dismayed. Stop. Look about you at the miles of muddied and overturned land, at the endless expanse of barren clear cut, at the infinitely distant and uncompromising sky, and reflect on your relative insignificance. Remember that compared to the

immensity and mysterious purposefulness of the universe, your life and worries are inconsequential. Then, your mind cleared and reinvigorated, take a
deep breath, and get back to work.

16   "So, with your shovel aloft in your shovel hand, and with a tree in your
tree hand, take a second step forward—this time with your other leg, the
one that corresponds to your shovel hand. Bring down your shovel with a
swift, heavy stroke, stabbing the blade into the earth as deeply as possible.
If your shovel doesn't penetrate the surface, it is likely that you have struck
a rock or some sort of impervious sun-fired clay. Nevertheless, you must
plant a tree as close to this spot as you can. Move to the next nearest
planting spot. If the soil in this location visibly leeches water when you step
on it, it is too wet and will drown your tree. Move to the next closest location. If this one is within two metres of a tree that has somehow miraculously
survived the clear-cutting, bulldozing, and chemical spraying that has otherwise sterilized the land, keep moving. Eventually, you will find a patch of
acceptable soil, a sufficiently rotten stump, or a sizable pile of bear droppings in which to plant your tree.

17   "With your shovel plunged in the earth, take the third and final step, again
with the leg that corresponds to your bag hand. Twist the D-handle of your
shovel away from you in a wide outward arc, laying open a hole in the
ground, and, with the tree still in your bag hand, bend down over your
shovel. Poke the roots of the tree into the freshly dug hole and hold the
seedling in place while pulling your shovel from the soil. As you straighten
your back, slide your fingers up the length of the tree until they gently grip
the tip. Remember, the needles of the trees are laced with pesticides, so avoid
pricking your fingers. Once you are upright, close the hole by lightly
stomping on the ground immediately beside the tree. Finally, give the
seedling a small tug to ensure that it is snug in the soil.

18   "Congratulations! You have planted your first tree. Know that you are following in a great human tradition, one that began when agricultural man
first informed the flora and fauna of the world that he knew better than they
did how and where they should grow. Since then, humankind has been
proudly asserting its place in the natural world and now you, too, are a part
of this noble history. Your father and mother are every farmer who ever
pressed a seed into the soil, every gardener who ever ripped a weed from its
bed, every farm hand who ever forced a bit into a horse's mouth.

19   "All that stands between you and fortune are three easy steps, a swift
bend, and a few fluid motions with your shovel—repeated three or four thousand times a day. You have planted your standard. Eventually, one tree at a
time, you will own the North.

20   "Unless, of course, your tree is not within the two- or three-millimetre margin
of depth; unless it is leaning; unless it is crooked, or its roots are not straight;
unless it is less or more than the permitted distance from any other tree, natural

or planted; unless the tree is unhealthy, diseased, smothered by loose dirt or missing its tip; or if, as you filled the hole, it got stepped on, or . . . .

Reprinted by permission of the author.

1. What is a "primer"? Is this essay is a good example of a primer? Why? Find at least five examples of words you are unfamiliar with, and look up their definitions.
2. The author assumes the role of an expert providing instructions and advice to the reader, who is presumed to be a novice tree planter. Is this really an instructional process? Does the author really intend to teach readers how to succeed as tree planters? If not, what are his real purposes?
3. In an essay not intended to be taken seriously, the author uses sophisticated vocabulary and many long, convoluted, sentences. Why? What is the effect of the contrast between the stated subject—a simple process—and the formal, complex style in which the subject is explained?
4. List, in order, the steps in planting a tree. The author provides a great deal of detail about each step. In the "Tips," we suggest that too much detail is likely to overwhelm readers. Is that the case here? Why does the author include so much detail? What purpose does this descriptive detail serve, if not to explain how to plant a tree?
5. After 13 paragraphs of instruction that bring us to the point of actually planting a tree, the author suddenly breaks off and begins discussing how to maintain "motivation and morale while out on the clear cut." Why? What are the effects of this digression?
6. The first sentence in paragraph 15 is a monster run-on that goes on for 11 lines. The author stops punctuating the clauses about two-thirds of the way through the sentence. Why? How does the structure of the sentence reinforce its content?
7. Consider the author's concluding paragraphs. Identify the summary. There is no real conclusion to this essay; the last sentence just trails off into silence. Why? Given the author's purpose, is this ending effective?

Exercise 15.1

It is five years in the future, and you are internationally famous. A national news magazine wants a short biography highlighting how you got to where you are. Write a process analysis of your rise to fame.

Exercise 15.2

You have some expertise that is not shared by others. Although others may be able to do it, no one does it as well as you. Your skill may be making friends, serving customers, eating spaghetti, or designing Web pages. Choose an activity at which you excel and write a short process essay that describes how to do what you do so well.

Exercise 15.3

Write a process essay on one of the following topics. Review the tips on pages 169–70 before you begin.

How my family came to Canada
How to cope with stress
How to perform well in a job interview
How to get fired
How to get along in a language you don't speak
How to cure a hangover
How not to treat customers
How to get a bargain
How a biological process works (e.g., how skin heals, how the lungs function)
How a fuel cell works (or any other mechanical, chemical, or electronic device)

16

Classification
and Division

Classification and **division** are based on the natural human instincts for arranging and analyzing things. We group things that are alike into categories or classes, and we identify the component parts of something in order to understand them better. For example, college students might be classified into undergraduates and graduates. The undergraduate class might be divided into programs or majors such as engineering, nursing, arts and science, and so on. When you look at a menu in a restaurant, you note that the dishes offered are classified into categories such as appetizers, entrées, desserts, and beverages. And when you order your meal, it might be divided into courses: soup, salad, entrée, dessert.

The process of **definition** involves both classification and division. We define a concept (e.g., a good student) by identifying the features or characteristics that are shared by all members of the class to which it belongs: a good student is one who is hard-working, interested, and creative. Writing a classification paper requires grouping similar things together to identify them as belonging to one of several categories; writing a division paper requires examining one entity and breaking it down into constituent parts or features or characteristics. Here are some examples of classification and division topics:

Classification

Saturday a.m. TV
- cartoons
- sports shows
- interview programs

Division

Saturday a.m. TV
- informative
- infuriating
- infantile

Classification		**Division**	
Patients doctors hate to treat	• clingers • deniers • demanders	The ideal patient	• co-operative • knowledgeable • self-disciplined
Types of bad parents	• overprotective • uninterested • disengaged	A good parent	• kind • firm • consistent

Tips on Writing Classification and Division

1. The key to a good paper is choosing your main points carefully. Make sure that all points are of approximately equal weight and importance and that the points do not overlap.
2. If you have deliberately left out some aspects of the subject, briefly let your readers know this and why you have limited your discussion. Some topics are too complex to discuss exhaustively in a short paper. You are better off discussing a few representative points in detail than skimming over all the categories or components.
3. Your thesis statement should set out your subject and its main points, as in the following examples.

   Inanimate objects can be classified into three major categories—those that don't work, those that break down, and those that get lost.

   An appropriate wardrobe for work consists of outfits that are comfortable, easy to maintain, and, within limits, distinctive.

   Our softball team is made up of has-beens, might-have-beens, and never-weres.

The following five essays illustrate classification and division. In the first essay, the subject is defined by a description of its characteristics. The next three pieces show how subjects (here, steel products, methods of conflict resolution, and dates) can be classified into categories. The last essay analyzes the ingredients of a consumer product. Read the essays and then answer the questions that follow.

ROCK OF AGES
Brian Green

1   There are not many rock bands that can be defined as truly great. The history of rock is full of "one-hit wonders" and cult favourites, but very few groups have achieved both popular success and staying power. To be considered great, a rock band must have broad popular appeal, an exciting stage performance, and the ability to evolve with tastes and times.

2   Popularity is an important consideration in determining the greatness of a band, but because popular taste is so changeable, it can't be the only criterion. It takes great talent to produce lyrics and music, a style, and a personality that will keep a band in the public's favour for any length of time. Some bands manage to stay in business for years with a small, specialized following; others produce one platinum hit and are wildly popular for a few months before disappearing forever. But neither type of band qualifies for greatness.

3   Although popularity can be achieved with studio releases, a necessary ingredient in greatness is live performance. Studio bands can produce wonderful effects and a polished sound, but unless they can go on the road and demonstrate their abilities on stage, they will not be able to hold their audience beyond one or two albums. A stage performance need not be hi-tech or fantastically expensive to be successful; in fact, many groups who indulge in extravagant light shows and explosives to impress their fans are covering up for a lack of substance in the music. Great music well played, visually interesting performances, and appealing personalities are the characteristics of a great live performance.

4   Staying power is, in part, a product of popularity and performance, but versatility and adaptability are also needed if a band is going to have a long enough life span to qualify for greatness. Some bands that qualified under the other two criteria fell apart over personality differences, money, drugs, or music style before they could become truly great. Others didn't have the talent to change their style or adapt their themes as musical tastes evolved. Truly great bands possess the musical ability and the collective strength to shape and set style, rather than labour to catch up with what's popular.

5   Naturally, personal tastes will differ, but no one can deny that popular appeal, spectacular live performance, and versatility and adaptability are the factors that made the Beatles, the Stones, U2, and others like them the great bands of rock.

1. Describe the audience this writer had in mind when writing the essay. Include age, education, interests, musical knowledge, and any other details you can.
2. What are the essential characteristics of "greatness," according to this writer?

3. What other characteristics could have been used in writing an essay on this subject?
4. Write a one-sentence explanation of the function or purpose of each of the five paragraphs in "Rock of Ages."

BRANCHES OF STEEL
Paul Allen

1   The city of Sheffield, England, has long been associated with the manufacture of high-quality steel and steel products. A "Sheffield thwytel [knife]" was even mentioned by Chaucer back in the fourteenth century. Not nearly so well known as its name, however, is the fact that the city's wealth and fame were built on three main branches of the steel industry: carbon and alloy steels, cutlery, and edge tools.

2   The manufacture and processing of special and alloy steels constituted by far the largest sector of the steel trade. This branch of the industry can be traced back to 1743, when a clockmaker named Benjamin Huntsman invented crucible steel. Crucible steel was made by melting pieces of carbonized iron in a clay pot. The carbon content could be altered as the metal melted, allowing for a better quality finished product. Huntsman's process revolutionized what had been essentially a small-scale industry. Over the next 200 years, the manufacture of carbon and alloy steels grew at an astonishing rate. Many of the alloy steels still in use today were invented in Sheffield, including the most famous of them all: stainless steel. The surge in steel production affected other industries too, most notably the cutlery industry.

3   The manufacture of cutlery was the second largest of the steel trades in Sheffield. In common language, cutlery means knives and forks and spoons, but not in Sheffield; there, the term was largely reserved for knives. Later, the term "cutlery" came to include scissors and razors, which were first introduced in the eighteenth century, but knives of all shapes and sizes continued to dominate the industry. Knives had been manufactured in the Sheffield region for hundreds of years before the invention of crucible steel, and the finer grades of steel made available by the Huntsman method led to huge growth in the cutlery trades. The words "Made in Sheffield" could be seen stamped on knife blades the world over, giving Sheffield cutlery a reputation for quality that was without equal.

4   Knives were not the only steel product that could hold a cutting edge, and the production of hand tools grew rapidly along with the cutlery industry. The manufacture of saws, files, scythes, and woodworking tools employed large numbers of skilled workers. Some of the companies that grew to be giants in the steel-making sector began as small-scale tool manufacturers; in addition, many small- to medium-sized steel producers began making tools from their

own steel. A number of these smaller companies would eventually drop steel making and go on to become world renowned names in the edge tool industry; Spear and Jackson and Eclipse are just two examples. Tool manufacturing, although less well known than the alloy steel and cutlery industries, represents an important part of Sheffield's industrial legacy.

5   During the last thirty years, all three branches of the Sheffield steel trades have suffered from severe contraction. Many skilled tradesmen lost their jobs as a combination of cheap foreign imports, government policies, and technological advances made them redundant. At their height, the steel works, cutlery factories, and tool manufacturers employed over 100,000 people in the city. Today, the number is less than ten percent of that figure. The skills remain, however, and the name Sheffield continues to be synonymous with the manufacture of high quality steel, cutlery, and hand tools.

Reprinted by permission of the author.

1. Consider the first two sentences of this essay. What introductory strategies has the author used to get his readers' attention?
2. Identify three of the definitions the author has included to help readers understand a subject they probably know little or nothing about.
3. Referring to the list of transition techniques on pages 90–91, identify at least three different strategies the author has employed to unify his essay. Underline the sentences that act as transitions between paragraphs.
4. Is the conclusion of this essay effective? Why?

METHODS OF CONFLICT RESOLUTION
Eva Tihanyi

1   Imagine you are the supervisor of a call centre that employs a full-time staff of 40 telephone sales representatives. During the past few months, there has been an increase in employee requests for schedule changes in order to accommodate personal needs. These employees, of course, would prefer not to lose pay, so they want to make sure they work their regular number of weekly hours. Unfortunately, the growing number of schedule changes is having an adverse effect, creating confusion and inconvenience for you, the payroll department, and the employees in general. You, as the person in charge, recognize that you must deal with this situation quickly and fairly—before it escalates. There are four methods of conflict resolution to consider: deference, competition, compromise, or co-operation.

2   If the scheduling issue is not a major one, you might opt to defer; in other words, "let the other side win." Employees could continue to ask for schedule changes as they saw fit, and you would do your best to accommodate them and ignore the inconvenience. Maintaining employee morale would be more important than enforcing a smooth scheduling process.

3   If, on the other hand, you view the scheduling issue as so important that it must be resolved to the company's advantage, you will want to exercise your authority and insist on a no-change policy. Employees would be assigned to particular shifts, and if they wanted time off, they would have to take it without pay. There would be no re-scheduling. This is a competitive approach, one which ensures that you "win" while the other side "loses"—and one which also ensures that your relationship with the "losers" will be tarnished.

4   A more empathetic way of managing the situation would be to compromise. You could circulate a memo in which you laid out parameters, specific guidelines for how and when schedule changes could occur. This would allow some flexibility, but would at the same time limit the frequency and nature of schedule change requests. In this way, both you (i.e., the company) and the employees would "win"—partially. Both sides would get a part of what they wanted, but both would also lose a part. And so long as both sides were satisfied, this could be an effective solution.

5   Finally, if you're a supervisor who believes in the concept of mutual benefit, in the notion that it's possible for both sides to "win," you will choose the method of co-operation. You and the employees might brainstorm the scheduling issue together and in the process discover new ways in which it might be settled to the satisfaction of both sides—not compromise, but resolution. Because co-operation produces no "loser," it fosters an atmosphere of trust and respect; and, although certainly more time-consuming than the other three methods, it is generally the best way to encourage goodwill in the workplace.

6   Deference, competition, compromise, and co-operation are all viable ways of handling conflict. The one you choose will most likely depend on how significant the issue is, how much time you have to deal with it, to what extent you value employee morale, and what the word "winning" means to you.

Tihanyi, Eva. "Methods of Conflict Resolution." 1999.

1. What introductory strategy does the author use to set up her thesis? (See pages 98–101 for a review of eight different ways to introduce an essay.) A good introduction intrigues readers, involves them in the subject, and makes them want to read on. How does Tihanyi's introductory paragraph accomplish these goals?

2. Describe the audience this writer had in mind: approximate age, level of education, special interests, and any other details you can.

3. One of the reasons this essay is so easy to read is that the author has structured it very carefully. She outlines the problem in paragraph 1, then offers four different solutions to the problem, using a single pattern of development, in paragraphs 2 to 5. For each possible solution, she offers a definition, remarks on the practical effects of its implementation, and comments on how the implementation would affect company morale. Identify these three components in paragraphs 2, 3, 4, and 5.

4. Another reason this essay is easy to read is that the author has made skilful use of transitional devices. Turn to pages 90–91 to review the five transitional techniques that an author can employ. Which ones does Tihanyi employ in this essay? Identify one example of each technique.

5. In Chapter 10, you learned that a good conclusion should (a) summarize or reinforce the main points of the paper and (b) end with a memorable statement. Does Tihanyi's conclusion satisfy these criteria?

OF MEN AND MACHINES
Brian Green

1   (1) There has got to be a better way! (2) The North American system of mate selection by dating is so inefficient that I wonder why it works even as often as it does. (3) If we selected cars using the same methods we employ to choose a mate, few of us would bother driving. (4) Dates, like cars, have a few basic things in common: a body, an image, and (if you're lucky) insurance. (5) Beyond the basics, however, each model is so individual that making a selection becomes a matter of guesswork. (6) Nevertheless, for research purposes, we can classify cars and dates into these general types: the economy model, the standard North American model, and the exotic sports model.

2   (7) The economy-model date features cramped conditions and a lack of power. (8) The econo-date thinks that his personality can make up for the fact that you never go anywhere except for walks and never do anything that costs money. (9) He tends to be shy, quiet, and about as much fun as an oil leak. (10) It's not that he doesn't have lots of money to spend, it's that he doesn't use any imagination or creativity to compensate for his lack of cash. (11) The economy model's greatest ambition is someday to move up and compete with the standard North American model.

3   (12) The standard North American date is big on comfort and appearance, but short on quality. (13) He'll pay big money for an ordinary meal, then tip lavishly for poor service, thinking he's impressing you. (14) He is loud, confident, showy, and sure he is the best thing that could happen to you.

(15) Unfortunately, he can't carry on a conversation about anything but himself and, occasionally, sports. (16) Although he would never admit it, he secretly wants desperately to grow up to be an exotic sports type.

4   (17) The exotic, high-powered sports date is rich, sophisticated, gorgeous, and nasty. (18) If you should get a date with one of these creatures, you will be the envy of all your friends. (19) Unfortunately, he has cultivated his vanity like a fine art, and your value to him is purely ornamental. (20) Equality of the sexes is something he either doesn't understand or reserves for his equally wealthy and attractive friends. (21) My mother always reminded me that "beauty is only skin deep"; the exotic sports date is proof that she was right.

5   (22) If this sounds terribly pessimistic, I guess it is. (23) If only we could select mates as intelligently and carefully as we choose cars! (24) Of course, with my luck, I'd probably end up with something that has the power of an econo-model, the quality of the North American standard, and the repair bills of an exotic.

1. While planning "Of Men and Machines," the author had a particular audience in mind. Who was it?
2. Into what categories are dates classified in this essay?
3. "Of Men and Machines" uses the technique of analogy. It makes a statement about types of men by comparing them to types of cars. Is this analogy accurate? Is it effective?
4. The conclusion makes a serious point. What is it? Does it work?

PUCKER UP
David Bodanis

1   Until quite recently, respectable women did not wear make-up. Colour on the face suggested passion, and passion was what they were supposed to avoid. Shortly after the First World War, lipstick was referred to as only being appropriate "to repair the ravages of time and disease on the complexion of coquettes." They were probably the only ones to put up with it, too, as it was then little more than a greasy rouge, containing crushed and dried insect corpses for colouring, beeswax for stiffness, and olive oil to help it flow—this latter having the unfortunate tendency to go rancid several hours after use. The New York Board of Health considered banning lipstick in 1924, not because of what it might do to the women who wore it, but because of worry that it might poison the men who kissed the women who wore it.

2   For the liberated woman of today, the product has been transformed, rethought, entirely remade. Insect corpses have been expunged as a barbarity; beeswax and olive oil have been rejected too. What goes in tubes of lipstick today is only what the best of late 20th century cosmetic science can devise.

3   At the centre of the modern lipstick is acid. Nothing else will burn a colouring sufficiently deeply into the lips for it to stay. The acid starts out orange, then sizzles into the living skin cells and transforms into a deep red where it sticks to them. Everything else in lipstick is there just to get the acid into place.

4   First, it has to be spread. Perhaps at some time you've noticed children playing with softened food shortening, smearing it over their faces. Such shortening (hydrogenated vegetable oil, as in Crisco) spreads very well, and accordingly is one of the substances found mixed in with almost all lipsticks on the market. Soap smears well too, and so some of that is added as well.

5   Unfortunately, neither soap nor shortening are good at actually taking up the all-crucial acid that's needed to do the dyeing. Only one smearable substance will do this to any extent: castor oil. Good, cheap castor oil, used in varnishes and laxatives, is one of the largest ingredients by bulk in every lipstick, from the finest French marks on down. The acid soaks into the castor oil, the castor oil spreads on the lips with the soap and shortening, and so, through this intermediary, the acid is carried where it needs to go.

6   If lipstick could be sold in modified shortening jars or castor oil bottles, there would be no need for the next major ingredient. But the whims of the lip-conscious consumer do not allow for such ease of packaging; the mix has to be sold in another form. It must be transformed into a rigid, streamlined stick, and to do that nothing is better than heavy petroleum-based wax. Such wax can soak up the shortening, soap, and acid-impregnated castor oil, and it will still have enough stability in its micro-crystalline structure to stand up firm. It's what provides the "stick" in lipstick.

7   Of course, certain precautions have to be taken in combining all these substances. If the user ever got a sniff of what was in there (all that castor oil) there might be some problems in continuing consumer acceptance. So a perfume is poured in at the manufacturing stage before all the oils have cooled— when the future cosmetic is still what the engineers call a "molten lipstick mass." At the same time, food preservatives are poured in the mass, because apart from smelling rather strongly, the oil in there would go rancid . . . without some protection.

8   All that's lacking now is the glisten. Women who smear on lipstick expect to get some glisten for their troubles, and their wishes do not go unheeded. When the preservatives and perfume are pouring, something shiny, colourful, almost iridescent—and, happily enough, not even too expensive—is added. That something is fish scales. [They are] easily available from the leftovers of commercial fish packing stations. The scales are soaked in ammonia then bunged in with everything else.

9   Is that it then? Shortening, soap, castor oil, petroleum wax, perfume, food preservatives, and fish scales? Not entirely. There is still one thing missing: the colour. The orange acid that burns into the lips only turns red on contact. That

means another dye has to be added to the lipstick, a soothing and suggestive red one this time, so that what you see in the tube looks at least vaguely lip colour and not a horrifying orange-juice orange. Which means, if you think about it, that the red dye you see in the tube has only a little to do with the colour that's going to end up on your lips.

_____

Bodanis, David. *The Secret House: 24 Hours in the Strange and Unexpected World in Which We Spend Our Days and Nights.* New York: Simon & Schuster, 1986. 45–47.

1. This essay analyzes lipstick by dividing it into its component parts. Identify each ingredient and the paragraph(s) in which it is described.
2. Why did the author not reveal in the thesis statement the aspects of the topic that are described in the body paragraphs of the essay? What would the effect on the reader have been if the author had named all the ingredients up front?
3. Identify six or seven examples of the author's use of vivid descriptive details to help communicate key points. Bodanis uses words that are very different from those we are familiar with in advertisements that describe the same product. What effect does the author's diction have on the reader?
4. Identify two or three specific examples of the author's ironic humour. How would you describe the tone of this piece? Do you find the tone appealing or alienating? Why?
5. What was the author's purpose in writing this piece? Is there a serious intent behind the obvious fun he had in shocking his readers?

Exercise 16.1

This exercise is designed to improve your skill in identifying *unity* within classification or division. In each of the following thesis statements, cross out any point that doesn't belong.

1. A good teacher doesn't bark at the students, give last-minute assignments, study for a test the night before, or grade unfairly.
2. Computer applications commonly used in business environments include word processors, spread sheets, CD-ROMs, and data base managers.
3. A media person has four major tasks: to report news accurately, to entertain with social information, to collect a big salary, and to prevent government control of information.
4. Finding the right career depends on careful planning: getting all the education you can, continually monitoring your enthusiasms and interests, being flexible enough to shift focus as circumstances change, and having luck on your side.

5. The music I enjoy can be divided into five distinct categories: country, light rock, vocal, Celtic, and New Age.

6. Newspapers are my main source of information. At least twice a week I read the *Halifax Gazette*, *Le Devoir*, *The Globe and Mail*, and *People Weekly*.

7. It's not easy to work for a perfectionist. She wants perfect results, double the work in half the time, unpaid overtime, and memos for everything.

Exercise 16.2

Humans have a strong instinct to classify everything. List at least seven classifications to which you belong.

Exercise 16.3

To help explain what things are, we usually divide them into their constituent parts. For each of the following terms, list four or five characteristics that would help to define it. After discussion, agree on the best three.

- a good manager/team leader/coach
- a good résumé
- an ideal vacation
- a worthwhile college course
- a good excuse

Exercise 16.4

Select one of the terms you used in Exercise 16.3 and expand your list of characteristics into an essay.

Exercise 16.5

Think of an example of a test question on a recent exam that required you to classify or divide in order to explain, or make up a possible test question that would require a classification or division essay in response.

Exercise 16.6

Sports analogies are very common ("He can't get to first base," or "Just when she was making the right moves, she dropped the ball"). For each of the following subjects, give an analogy and an example that would help your readers' understanding in a classification or division essay.

Subject	Analogy	Example
Overwork	electronics	When the brain's circuits are overloaded, a fuse can blow, resulting in nervous breakdown.
Physical fitness	auto mechanics	_____ _____ _____
Marriage	travel	_____ _____ _____
Aging	_____	_____ _____ _____

Exercise 16.7

Focus each of the following general topics into a specific subject suited to a classification or division paper. For each, identify three types or categories; or three parts, characteristics, functions, or features.

Restaurants   Subject _____
                   • _____
                   • _____
                   • _____

Managers   Subject _____
                   • _____
                   • _____
                   • _____

Television   Subject _____
commercials   • _____
                   • _____
                   • _____

Drivers   Subject _____
                   • _____
                   • _____
                   • _____

Salespersons   Subject _____
                   • _____
                   • _____
                   • _____

Exercise 16.8

Here is an outline for an essay on the characteristics necessary for career success. The thesis statement and main points are provided. Working in pairs, fill in appropriate topic sentences and support. When you are both satisfied, turn your outlines into full essays and compare your results.

Career Success

Attention-getter
_____

_____

_____

Thesis statement
To be successful in your career, you must prepare adequately in college, work hard on the job, and communicate well with employers, colleagues, and the public.

1. Topic sentence:
(Preparation)
_____

_____

_____

Support
_____

_____

_____

2. Topic sentence:
(Hard work)
_____

_____

_____

Support
_____

_____

_____

3. Topic sentence:
(Communication)
_____

_____

Support
_____

_____

_____

_____

_____

_____

_____   *Summary*

_____

_____   *Memorable*
                                                    statement

_____

Exercise 16.9

Write an essay on one of the following subjects.

The main kinds, types, or categories of
- employees
- bicycles
- sports fans
- small businesses
- movies
- alternative medicine practitioners
- body piercing

The characteristics of
- an ideal job
- an ideal marriage
- a bad movie
- a successful interview
- a good employer
- a good Web page
- an average Canadian

The component parts of
- an oral presentation
- a citizenship review
- a love affair
- a winning hockey team
- a golf swing (or slap shot, or save, etc.)
- a business plan
- a religious service or ceremony

17

Comparison and Contrast

If you are focusing on the similarities between two things (or ideas or concepts or points of view), you are writing a **comparison**. If you are focusing on the differences, you are writing a **contrast**. Most people, however, use the term "comparison" to cover both (as in "comparison shopping"), and similarities *and* differences are often discussed together in a paper.

You can choose from two approaches when you are organizing a comparison. In the first option, you discuss one item fully and then turn to the other item. This approach is called the **block method** of organizing. The alternative option is to compare your two items **point by point**. For example, suppose you decided to compare Pierce Brosnan and Tom Cruise. You might identify the following three points:

- physical appearance
- acting technique
- on-camera heroics

Using the block method, you would first consider Brosnan in terms of these three points; then you would do the same for Cruise. You would need to outline only four paragraphs for your essay:

1. Introduction
2. Brosnan's physical appearance, acting technique, and on-camera heroics
3. Cruise's physical appearance, acting technique, and on-camera heroics
4. Conclusion

The block method works best in short papers, where the points of comparison are easy to understand and remember. As comparisons get more complex, your readers will be able to understand your points better if you present them point by point. You would then need to write an outline of five paragraphs for your essay:

1. Introduction
2. Physical appearance of Brosnan and Cruise
3. Acting technique of Brosnan and Cruise
4. On-camera heroics of Brosnan and Cruise
5. Conclusion

    The introductory paragraph in the comparison essay usually tells readers what two things are to be assessed and what criteria will be used to assess them. The concluding paragraph may (or may not) reveal a preference for one over the other.

Tips on Writing a Comparison or Contrast

1. Make sure that the two items you have chosen are appropriately paired; to make a satisfactory comparison, they must have something in common. Both might be baseball teams or world leaders; but to compare the Toronto Blue Jays and the Calgary Stampeders or to contrast Queen Elizabeth and your Aunt Agatha would be futile and meaningless.
2. Your main points must apply equally to both items. Reject main points that apply to one and have only limited application to the other. For example, in a comparison of digital and analog instruments, a category for dial configuration would be pointless.
3. Your thesis statement should clearly present the two items to be compared and the basis for their comparison. Consider these examples.

   Memos and letters differ not only in format but also in style and purpose.

   The major points of comparison in automobiles are performance, comfort, and economy, so I applied these factors to the two cars in the running for my dollars: the Saturn and the Protégé.

4. Use transitional words and phrases within and between paragraphs to provide coherence. (See page 91.)

    The following four examples demonstrate different approaches to writing comparisons and contrasts. After reading each essay, answer the questions that follow it.

THE CANADIAN CLIMATE
D'Arcy McHale

1   The student who comes to Canada from a tropical country is usually prepared for cold Canadian winters, a sharp contrast to our hot northern summers. What the student may not be prepared for is the fact that Canadian
personalities reflect the country's temperature range but are less extreme.
Canadian personalities fall into two categories: warm and cool. The two
groups share the Canadian traits of restraint and willingness to compromise,
but they are dissimilar in their attitudes both to their own country and to the
foreign student's country of origin.

2   Warm Canadians are, first of all, warm about Canada and will, at the first
sound of a foreign accent, describe with rapture the magnificence of the
country from the Maritimes to the West Coast, praising the beauty of the
Prairies, the Rockies, and even the "unique climate of the Far North."
Canadian leisure activities are enthusiastically described with a special place
reserved for hockey. "So you've never skated? You'll learn. Come with us;
you'll have a great time." The Warm Canadian wants the newcomer to share
in the pleasures of life in Canada. When she turns her attention to the foreign
student's homeland, she seeks enlightenment, asking questions about its
geography, social and economic conditions, and other concerns not usually
addressed in travel and tourism brochures. The Warm Canadian understands
that the residents of tropical countries are not exotic flower children who sing
and dance with natural rhythm but are individuals who, like Canadians, face
the problems of earning a living and raising a family.

3   Compared to the Warm Canadian, who exudes a springlike optimism, the
Cool Canadian is like November. Conditions may not be unbearable for the
moment, but they are bound to get much colder before there is any sign of
a thaw. The Cool Canadian's first words on hearing that the foreign student is
from a warm country are, "How could you leave such a lovely climate to come
to a place like this?" Not from him will one hear of Banff, or Niagara Falls, or
anything except how cold and dark and dreary it gets in the winter. It sometimes seems that the Cool Canadian's description of his own country is
designed to encourage foreign students to pack their bags and return home
at once. As for the foreign student's country of origin, the Cool Canadian is
not really interested, although he may declare, "I hear it's beautiful. I'd love
to go there." Beyond that, however, he has no interest in information that
may shake the foundations of his collection of myths, half-truths, and geographic inaccuracies. This type of Canadian, if he does travel to a tropical
country, will ensure that he remains at all times within the safe confines of his
hotel and that he returns to Canada with all his preconceived ideas intact.

4   Foreign students should not be upset by the Cool Canadian; they should
ignore his chilliness. Besides, like a heat wave in March, an unexpected thaw

can occur and create extraordinary warmth. Likewise, a Warm Canadian may become a little frosty sometimes, but, like a cold spell in June, this condition won't last. And when the weather changes, foreign students will find an opportunity to display their own qualities of understanding, tolerance, and acceptance of others as they are.

Reprinted by permission of the author.

1. What are the main points of contrast in "The Canadian Climate"?
2. Which method of contrast has the author of "The Canadian Climate" chosen for the subject, block or point-by-point?
3. Why did the author choose this approach? Would the essay work as well if it were organized the other way? Outline the main points of contrast as they would look in the other format.
4. What other points of contrast between the two kinds of Canadians can you think of?
5. What audience does the author have in mind? How do you think Canadians would respond to this essay? Foreign students?

JUSTICE AND JOURNALISM
Victor Chen

1   "Justice must not only be done, it must be seen to be done." This principle, in part, accounts for the news media's appetite for stories about our justice system. It is the principle that news organizations always cite when their access to information about the courts, criminals, or police is limited, or when they are prevented from distributing that information. Given the media's apparent concern for the public's knowledge about Canadian justice, it is troubling to learn that what we read, hear, and see is often distorted. The reality of our justice system and what we learn about it from our media are, all too often, two different things. Two aspects of our justice system will serve to illustrate this contrast: the incidence of violent crime and the sentencing of criminals.

2   Occurrences of violent crime have declined steadily in Canada over the past decade. While this fact has occasionally been reported, it doesn't sell newspapers or advertising nearly as well as juicy stories about murder, mayhem, assault, or aggression. The news media are in business to attract an audience, and the pressure to sensationalize is relentless. Hence, while murders constitute about 1% of violent crime committed in Canada, in our news media more than 25% of crime stories are about killings. Since virtually all of our information about crime comes to us from newspapers and news broadcasts, is it any wonder that we have the impression that murders are far more common than they really are? Furthermore, violent crime itself represents about 12% of all crime that is dealt with by our police and courts. Yet, in the

media, 50% of the coverage of criminal activity is devoted to violent crime. We have two societies: an imaginary one, created by the news media, that most of us live in, and the real, less violent one that few of us know about.

3   As well as a distorted view of violent crime, the media give us false impressions about proceedings in the criminal courts. Except in a few notable cases, reporters are not assigned to cover an entire trial; instead, they attend the courtroom only for the sensational opening addresses and for the verdict and sentencing. Very little of what goes on for most of the trial—the evidence, the arguments, the painstaking detail, and the finer points of courtroom procedure—ever appears in the news. What effect does this omission have on our understanding of law and order? In a recent study, J. Roberts and A. Doob demonstrate that the public's understanding of the justice system is distorted. Half of the participants in the study read the newspaper accounts of a trial. The other half read the court documents—transcripts of what had actually taken place during the trial. Of those who read the newspapers, the vast majority (over 60%) thought that the sentence handed down by the judge was too lenient. Less than 15% felt the sentence was too harsh. However, of those who read the court proceedings without the slant provided by reporters and editors, the majority felt the punishment was too harsh. Less than 20% believed that a more severe sentence was warranted, while more than 50% thought the sentence given for the crime was too long (508–12). What does this experiment tell us about how Canadians form their often strongly held opinions about the justice system?

4   The contrast between what our news media tell us about our justice system and the reality of what is going on in the police departments and courtrooms of the nation is an indictment of the sensationalist media. Even more important, this contrast is a sobering reminder that our opinions can be based on a superficial understanding of the issues. The news media will not change; the pressures for sensational reporting are too great. Public opinion will, therefore, be based on distorted impressions. We can only hope that our lawmakers will form their opinions and base their decisions not on media reports and not on the popular opinion which those reports create, but on a careful, researched study of the reality behind the headlines.

Work Cited

Roberts, J., and A. Doob. "Sentencing and Public Opinion: Taking False Shadows for True Substances." *Osgoode Hall Law Journal* 27.3 (1989): 491–515.

Reprinted by permission of the author.

1. Which method of contrast has Chen used to organize this essay? Using the information given in the essay, write a point-form outline for an

essay organized according to the alternate method. Which organization do you think is more effective? Why?

2. What purpose—other than contrasting the image and reality of our justice system—does the author of this piece have in mind? Does he achieve his purpose?

3. Statistics do not often make very interesting reading. How has the author tried to make the statistics in this essay readable as well as meaningful? Is he successful?

4. So long as they are not overused, rhetorical questions (questions asked for effect rather than to elicit an answer) can be effective in capturing and holding readers' attention. Identify two rhetorical questions in this essay and rephrase them as statements. Which version—question or statement—has more impact on the reader? Why?

5. Parallelism (see Chapter 28) is often used by writers to reinforce the seriousness of a subject or the weight of an argument. Identify four examples of parallel structure that you think contribute effectively to the solemn tone of this essay.

GENESIS 3:6

Rita Klein-Geltink

1   "I don't know why you told them we'd come," complained my husband as we drove home from one of those excruciatingly boring visits. We'd been in such situations before—the well-intentioned hosts regale you with a full synopsis of their family history while you spend most of the time trying to devise plausible reasons as to why you have to be on your way. "And why didn't you tell them sooner that we had to get going?" he continued. I sighed as I reminded him that he, too, has a tongue in his head and that it was unfair to hold me totally responsible for the fact that the better part of our precious Sunday afternoon had been spent in a way neither of us had really wanted.

2   This pattern of the man's inaction, coupled with blame for an undesired consequence being placed upon the woman, plays itself out frequently. Men have devised a tidy little exercise whereby they absolve themselves from all responsibility: they adopt a helpless expression, turn their palms out slightly, and shrug their shoulders.

3   Rewind the tape, if you will, to the scene in the church parking lot where the invitation to visit over coffee is first extended. The woman reminds us that we haven't been by to visit for three weeks, and why don't we come over now? I try to explain to her that the kids are having friends over—"Bring them all along!" she insists. I tell her that we have company coming later in the afternoon—"You'll be home in plenty of time!" she assures me. "I really don't

want to put you out. . . . " "Nonsense," she says. I glance over my shoulder for support from my husband, and cast him an exasperated look that screams, "Say something!" And what does he do? He looks at me with that dazed expression and simply shrugs his shoulders. I turn back to the woman and with a sweet smile say, "We'd love to come."

4   Who made the decision to accept the invitation? My husband insists that I did, and therefore I am to be held responsible for putting both of us through two hours of weak coffee and family photos.

5   Now rewind the tape back even further, to another couple, to another conversation. The serpent asks the woman about God's instructions concerning the fruit trees in the garden. "Did God really say, 'You must not eat from any tree in the garden'?" The woman responds by recalling that God had given them permission to eat from any tree with the exception of the tree in the middle of the garden. "If we eat from that tree, or even if we touch it, we will die," replies the woman, and she looks at her husband, who nods in agreement. "Nonsense," says the serpent. "You will surely not die, for God knows that when you eat of it your eyes will be opened, and you will be like God, knowing good and evil. Just try it." The woman glances over her shoulder for her husband's reaction and casts him a questioning look, "Should we?" In response, her husband looks at her with that dazed expression and simply shrugs his shoulders. She turns back to the serpent and with an uncertain little smile says, "Okay, I'll try it."

6   Who made the decision to accept the fruit? Many men, and women too, have been led to believe that the woman is to be held solely responsible for the decision. They are convinced that the woman chose this course of action in a hasty moment of weakness and then, having eaten the fruit, went off to find her husband to offer it to him. Somehow they skim over the last sentence of Genesis 3:6: "She also gave some to her husband, *who was with her*, and he ate it" (italics added). He was with her. They both heard the arguments presented by the serpent. They both had ample opportunity to decline the offer. The man's inaction has not absolved him of the responsibility God had entrusted to him. Rather, both the man and the woman must bear the consequences of their action/inaction.

The pattern of man's inaction was established centuries ago. Women would do well to be conscious of his strategy and to insist that he bear his share of the responsibility in decision-making, whether in accepting the unsolicited invitation or eating the forbidden fruit.

Reprinted by permission of the author.

1. The author could have begun this essay with the first sentence of paragraph 2, slightly rephrased: "The pattern of a man's inaction, coupled with blame for an undesired consequence being placed upon a woman,

plays itself out frequently." Why did the author not begin this way? What purposes are served by the first paragraph?

2. In your own words, explain the comparison that is the basis of this essay.

3. Which of the five transitional strategies listed on pages 90–91 has the author used in this essay? Identify one or two examples of each.

4. Identify the points of comparison between the scenes described in paragraphs 3 and 5. Consider the author's style (vocabulary, sentence structure) as well as the content.

5. What is the author's main purpose in this essay? Does the essay achieve its purpose?

FOR MINORITIES, TIMING IS EVERYTHING

Olive Johnson

1   Left-handedness and homosexuality both tend to run in families. As my husband's family and mine have some of each, it is not surprising that one of our children is left-handed and another homosexual. Both my left-handed daughter and my homosexual son turned out to be bright, funny, talented people with loving friends and family. But their experience of growing up in different minority groups was a striking contrast and an interesting illustration of how societal attitudes change as sufficient knowledge accumulates to make old beliefs untenable.

2   By the time my daughter was growing up, left-handedness was no longer regarded as a sign of immorality or mental deficiency. Almost everybody knew "openly" left-handed friends, teachers and relatives and viewed them as normal people who wrote differently. Except for a little awkwardness in learning to write at school, my daughter's hand preference was simply never an issue. If people noticed it at all, they did so with a shrug. Nobody called her nasty names or banned school library books about left-handed families, as school trustees in Surrey, B.C., recently banned books about gay families. Nobody criticized her left-handed "lifestyle" or suggested that she might be an unfit role model for young children. Nobody claimed that she *chose* to be left-handed and should suffer the consequences.

3   My gay son did not choose to be different either, but when he was growing up, homosexuality was still too misunderstood to be accepted as just another variant of human sexuality. Because gay people still felt unsafe revealing their sexual orientation, he was deprived of the opportunity of knowing openly gay teachers, friends and relatives. He grew up hearing crude jokes and nasty names for people like him, and he entered adulthood

knowing that being openly gay could prevent you from getting a job or renting an apartment. It could also get you assaulted.

4   Bigotry has never been reserved for homosexuality, of course. I am old enough to remember the time when bigotry directed toward other minorities in Canada was similar to that which is still sometimes aimed at homosexuals. In my Vancouver childhood, Chinese were regularly called "Chinks" (the boys in my high school wore black denim "Chink pants" tailored for them in Chinatown). Black people were "niggers," prohibited from staying in most Vancouver hotels. Kids in the special class were "retards" or "morons." Jews were suspected of all sorts of crazy things, and physically disabled people were often regarded as mental defectives.

5   Left-handed children were still being punished for writing with their left hand, particularly in the more religious parts of Canada. (When I was a graduate psychology student in Newfoundland doing research on handedness, I discovered that several of my "right-handed" subjects were actually left-handers; at school their left hands had been tied behind their backs by zealous nuns.)

6   The gay children and teachers of my childhood were simply invisible. Two female teachers could live together without raising eyebrows, chiefly because women in those days (especially women *teachers*) were not generally thought of as sexual persons. Two male "bachelors" living together did tend to be suspect, and so gay men brave enough to live together usually kept their living arrangements quiet. "Sissy" boys and "boyish" girls took a lot of teasing, but most people knew too little about homosexuality to draw any conclusions. These boys and girls were expected to grow up and marry people of the opposite sex. Some of them did, divorcing years later to live with one of their own.

7   Many of the teachers and parents of my childhood who tried to convert left-handed children into right-handers probably believed they were helping children avoid the stigma of being left-handed, just as many misguided therapists tried to "cure" patients of their homosexuality to enable them to avoid the stigma of being gay in a heterosexual world.

8   Thanks to advances in our understanding, left-handedness gradually came to be seen as a natural and innate trait. We know now that people do not *choose* to be more skillful with one hand than the other; they simply are. While researchers are still debating the precise mechanisms that determine hand preference, there is general agreement that left- and right-handedness are just two different (and valid) ways of being. Left-handers are a minority in their own right, not "deviants" from normal right-handedness.

9   The same is true for sexual orientation. Although we do not yet clearly understand the mechanisms that determine sexual orientation, all indicators point to the conclusion that it results from interactions between genetic, hormonal and possibly other factors, all beyond the individual's control. Like left-

handedness, sexual orientation is an innate trait, not a choice or "lifestyle." Like left-handedness, homosexuality is a valid alternative sexuality, not a deviance from "normal" heterosexuality.

10   As with other minorities, attitudes toward homosexuality are inevitably becoming more liberal, at least in Canada. A recent poll, commissioned by the B.C. Teachers' Federation, found that almost 70 per cent of B.C. residents think students should be taught in school to accept homosexuals and treat them as they would other people. (Twenty per cent said homosexuality should be discouraged, 9 per cent said they didn't know and 3 per cent refused to answer.) These results indicate that overt bigotry toward homosexuality is increasingly limited to religious extremists. The Surrey school trustees who voted against having gay and lesbian resource materials in schools are probably at about the same stage of cultural evolution as were the Newfoundland nuns who tied children's left hands behind their backs 40 years ago.

11   Even so, I'm grateful that they're further along the path of enlightenment than their predecessors in medieval Europe, who burned many left-handers and homosexuals at the stake. Being born in the late 20th century was a wise move on the part of my son and daughter. In some things, timing is everything.

Johnson, Olive. "For Minorities, Timing Is Everything." *Globe and Mail* 7 July 1997: A14.

1. To develop the main points of this essay, the author uses her own children as examples. Would the essay have been more effective had she supported her argument with less personal examples? Why?
2. Under what points does the author compare the treatment of left-handedness and homosexuality in Canada in the last century?
3. Comparing two groups is not the purpose of this essay; it is the means the author has chosen to accomplish her purpose. What is the main purpose of this piece? How effective do you think the author is in achieving it?
4. What is the topic sentence of paragraph 10? How is the topic developed? Do you agree with the statement the author makes in the fourth sentence of that paragraph? Why?
5. Consider the final paragraph of this essay. What function does it serve, other than to conclude the piece? What is its effect on readers?

Exercise 17.1

List eight to ten characteristics of two people, or jobs, or courses. Examine your lists and choose characteristics of each that would make a basis for a comparison between the two. Then go back over the lists and choose characteristics that would make a basis for contrast.

Exercise 17.2

Write a comparison or contrast essay on one of the following subjects. Be sure to follow the guidelines for proper essay development, from selecting a subject, through managing your main points, to outlining your paper and writing your paragraphs.

Two fast food restaurants
Two magazines with the same target audience (e.g., *Maclean's* and *Time*, *People* and *Us*, *Shift* and *Wired*)
Two approaches to child-rearing
College and university
Two political leaders
Two management styles
Your generation and that of your parents (or grandparents)

Exercise 17.3

Contrast papers often turn persuasive, but they don't have to. When you are presenting a contrast, try not to be influenced by your own opinion. List the arguments on both sides of three of these controversial issues.

Single-sex schools
Gun registration
The use of animals in medical research
Nuclear power
Physician-assisted suicide

Exercise 17.4

For one of the topics you worked on in Exercise 17.3, write an essay contrasting the views held by the two sides. Some research may be necessary to find out exactly what the opposing arguments are and to explain those arguments to your reader.

Exercise 17.5

Construct a comparison essay or a contrast essay, using one of the suggestions given below. Develop a thesis statement that reflects the relationship of the two subjects. Before you begin, write an outline of your thoughts, using either the block or the point-by-point method.

Quebec and TROC (the rest of Canada)

Your spouse and the fantasy you had of a spouse before you were married

Two newspapers' coverage of a news event

Your life now with your life five (or ten or twenty) years ago

Working in an office and working at home

Television advertisements for one of these pairs of consumer products: new cars and beer; home care and personal care products; financial services and travel services, a fast food chain and muffler repairs

18

Cause and Effect

- What are some of the effects of low interest rates?
- What are the major causes of global warming?
- What are the causes of addiction?
- Why is interest in alternative medicine growing so rapidly?
- What are the results of a well-conceived business plan?

These are the kinds of subjects often discussed in **causal analysis**. On some occasions, cause and effect may be combined in one paper or report, but its length and complexity would put it out of the range of our introductory discussions here. In short papers, writers usually concentrate either on causes or on effects.

The most common problem found in student causal analysis is oversimplification. In the absence of solid facts, figures, or evidence, inexperienced writers have a tendency to generalize and to substitute unsupported opinions for reasons. One cause of this problem is choosing a topic that is too big for the length of the paper. For example, one student decided to do an effect paper on Canada's immigration policy, a subject so big and so complicated that he could do nothing more than give vague and unsupported opinions. The result made him seem not only racist but also ignorant and foolish. You can avoid this pitfall by choosing your subject carefully, focusing it into a limited topic, and supporting each main point with lots of evidence.

Tips on Writing Causal Analysis

1. Your thesis statement should clearly indicate whether you are tackling cause or effect, and it should present your main points in order. Consider these examples.

The chief causes of complaint among the workers in this office are low wages, health hazards, and boredom.

The beneficial effects of a long canoe trip include reduced stress and increased fitness.

2. Avoid three common logical fallacies: oversimplification, faulty causal relation, and leaping to a conclusion.
   - An oversimplified analysis is one that ignores the complexities of an issue. If, for example, you claim that "men deliberately keep women down" and base this conclusion on the fact that, on average, the annual salary of women is lower than that of men, you are oversimplifying because the two groups are not identical. To take just one difference, there are more part-time workers among females than among males, and the salaries of part-timers cannot be compared to the earnings of full-time workers. (And even if the two wage groups were identical in all respects except one—annual income—that one difference is not proof of male conspiracy.)
   - Just because one event occurs along with or after another event does not mean that the first *caused* the second. For example: on Tuesday, your little brother swallowed a nickel. On Wednesday, he broke out into a rash. To conclude that the nickel caused the rash is a faulty causal relation. He may be allergic to something; he may have measles. As a writer, you must carefully examine all possible causes before determining that Y is the result of X.
   - Leaping to a conclusion (sometimes called hasty generalization) results when you do not consider enough data before forming a judgment. This is a common error: we commit it every time we form an opinion based on one or two instances. For example, just because two cabinet ministers were dismissed within four months of each other for misusing funds is not proof of the assertion, "the Liberal government is full of crooks."

3. Fully support your statements. You must provide proof of what you say in the form of examples, facts, statistics, quotations, anecdotes, etc. (see Chapter 8). If you begin with the assumption that your reader disagrees with you, you will be more likely to provide adequate support for your points.

The following four essays demonstrate writing that discusses causes and effects. In the first essay, the writer uses examples to explain effects; in the second, facts and statistics are used to identify causes and illustrate effects; in the third, the writer uses facts, examples, statistics, quotation, and paraphrase to develop her causal analysis; and in the fourth, all seven developmental strategies are used to explore both cause and effect.

LIGHTWEIGHT LIT.

Brian Green

1   (1) I really enjoy literary discussions. (2) I love it when people at trendy restaurants smack their lips in appreciation of the latest South American novelist, Egyptian poet, or Armenian essayist. (3) By eavesdropping on these discussions, I can find out what's going on in the world of "great literature" so that when people ask me what I've read lately I can pretend that I, too, am devoted to highbrow literature. (4) I'm ashamed to admit my secret vice, but, because we're friends, I can tell you . . . I *love* "trash." (5) I'm embarrassed about it, and I know that my intellectual friends would ridicule me if they found out. (6) Still, I have very good reasons for enjoying light literature. (7) I find it educates, relaxes, and entertains in a way that more cerebral reading doesn't—at least, not for me.

2   (8) The educational nature of popular or junk literature is often overlooked. (9) From reading countless police novels, I know the workings of the Los Angeles and New York police departments inside out. (10) I have a thorough grounding in the operations of the CIA, the KGB, MI5, and any number of less illustrious spy agencies. (11) I'm eagerly awaiting the first novel about a hero from Canada's CSIS. (12) Science-fiction books have detailed for me the ways of life, war, travel, and even agriculture in outer space. (13) My education even includes the laws of nature in alternative universes: I know about the society of Gor, the politics of Fionavar, and the nature of good and evil in a hundred other worlds.

3   (14) Acquiring all this knowledge may sound tiring, but light novels are actually extremely relaxing. (15) The way I read this kind of literature is slouched in my favourite chair with my feet up and a comforting drink close at hand, and, because I can't do anything else while I read, the overall effect is complete physical relaxation. (16) Also, an absorbing novel will take me away from the concerns and stresses of everyday life, allowing me to escape to a world created by the writer. (17) Because I can have no effect on this world, I can, with a completely clear conscience, let things unfold as they may and assume the relaxing role of observer.

4   (18) Although education and relaxation are important, most of us read light novels to be entertained. (19) Entertainment means different things to different people. (20) Some enjoy being frightened half to death by the books of Stephen King or his colleagues; others get satisfaction from the sugary romance of Harlequin novels; many people find science fiction absorbing and devour the works of Isaac Asimov or Jerry Pournelle. (21) Whatever subject or style appeals to you, there are literally thousands of novels to suit your taste. (22) I'm lucky because—with the exception of popular romance—I can find enjoyment in almost any type of reasonably well-written light novel.

5   (23) None of the novelists I read will ever win the Nobel prize for literature, and few of them will be studied in university literature courses. (24) However,

many writers have become wealthy from selling their fantasies to those millions of readers like me who seek entertainment, relaxation, and education
from the novels they enjoy—even if they have to enjoy them in secret.

1. What is the main topic identified in "Lightweight Lit.," and what are
   its three effects?

   The effects of _____ are _____ ,

   _____ , and _____ .

2. What is the author's role in this essay?
3. Who are the intended readers? Will they be convinced of the causes for
   the author's literary preferences?
4. What purpose is served by the author's supposed embarrassment? How
   does this device affect you as a reader?
5. The author uses specific examples to support the main points. List the
   examples used to illustrate each point.

THE ENEMY IN THE MIRROR

Brian Green

1   Our planet is being destroyed. If the cause of its destruction were some
external force, such as aliens or a rogue comet, then we humans would band
together and fight the threat with every resource at our disposal. We wouldn't
count the cost in lives, effort, or money; we would throw every ounce of our
strength and will into the effort. However, while the threat is just as real as if
it came from space ships bombarding us with poison rays, we are doing little
to save ourselves from destruction because the evil-doers are much closer to
home. We see them daily in our mirrors. Motivated by greed and ignorance,
we are wrecking our own environment with ruthless efficiency.

2   Greed—industrial, commercial, and personal—has motivated us to rape
the earth's resources without giving thought to the consequences. A supplement appeared recently in a Canada-wide chain of newspapers. Printed on
recycled paper, it outlined some of the environmental changes brought about
by human greed. Since the industrial revolution, two-thirds of the world's rain
forest has been cut or burned. The rain forest is (was?) the largest single
source of the earth's oxygen supply. Around the world, we pave over, build
on, or otherwise destroy one hectare of agricultural land every 14 seconds. In
Canada, we fill our rivers with chemicals and sewage, kill our lakes and forests
with industrial pollutants, poison the soil and the water table with toxic waste,
all in the name of industrial growth and the jobs it creates. And Canada is one
of the luckier nations. We are relatively rich in natural resources and, in the
short term, can survive our attacks on the environment.

3   Often linked with greed, ignorance is the other prime motivator in our self-destruction. Ignorant and uncaring, we cling to our "freedom machines." Automobiles are the primary source of air pollution, and there are more than twice as many cars on Canadian roads today as there were 20 years ago. Canadians throw away some 275 000 tonnes of disposable diapers every year. We munch our fast food in its environmentally harmful containers; demand that our paper products be bleached pure white despite the horrific pollution of our rivers that is caused by the bleaching process; recycle glass and plastics and papers reluctantly, if at all; and cheerfully accept—even demand—the plastic packaging, plastic bags, and plastic products our supermarkets peddle.

4   Is there any reason for optimism? There is some evidence that Canadians are becoming more conscious of the environment, and consciousness can only lead to changes for the better. In 2000, an Environics poll revealed that environmental concerns outweighed tax cuts in importance to Canadian voters by a margin of 81% to 14%. In 1988, only one in ten thought the environment was the most important national issue, and the year before that it was one in twenty. A clear majority of Canadians now favour tougher action against polluters, even if it means higher taxes, high prices, and fewer jobs. However, this bit-by-bit heightening of concern is far from the concerted, all-out effort to save the planet that would result if we were threatened by an external force. How very much more difficult it is to mobilize resources and will when the enemy lies within!

1. What is the main problem identified in "The Enemy in the Mirror," and what are its two causes?
2. Look at the concluding paragraph of the essay. How does it affect you as a reader? What is its purpose?
3. Describe the role that the author has assumed in developing this essay. Be as precise as you can.

THE PAY EQUITY DEBACLE
Margaret Wente

1   It sounded like a good idea at the time: equal pay for work of equal value. What could possibly be wrong with that? Isn't an office clerk worth as much as a shipping clerk?

2   Ten years ago, the federal government set out to overhaul its entire pay scheme for all its unionized civil servants. The goal was equality for women. On orders from the Canadian Human Rights Commission, it would get rid of all those nasty gender-biased wage gaps and make the system fairer for everyone.

3   It didn't work out that way. Instead, the pay-equity plan grew into an administrative nightmare that threatened to devour the entire civil service.

Instead of creating equity, it created new inequities. Instead of attracting and retaining talented new people to government, it threatened to turn the civil service into the worst place to work in all of Canada. Fortunately, it proved impossible to implement, and two weeks ago it quietly bit the dust. After 10 years of work and more than $100-million in startup costs, the Treasury Board declared the scheme "unworkable."

4   The idea of pay equity is rooted in the 1980s, when businesses were ordered to stop paying women less than men for doing the same job. The Canadian Human Rights Commission, however, went further. it instructed Ottawa to implement equal pay for work of equal value, which is a different proposition altogether.

5   The civil service employs about 150,000 unionized people—clerks and lawyers, statisticians and veterinarians, translators, computer programmers, biologists, librarians, economists. To implement equal pay for work of equal value, it had to come up with a way to compare apples and oranges and grapes and bananas and pomegranates. Should a vet make more than a statistician? In the real world this question makes no sense. The market decides the value of their work. Under the new scheme, the government would decide.

6   And so it set out to create a master plan—a universal yardstick for measuring the objective "value" of every job. Every job would be ranked according to a points system. A job would receive so many points for the "knowledge" component, so many for the physical component, and so on. People's salaries would be determined not by their occupation or by what private-sector firms were paying down the street, but by their point range.

7   You don't need a PhD in economics to figure out why this approach was doomed from the get-go. All you need is a simple grasp of market forces. "It was an elegant model geared only to a particular piece of legislation which was very distant from the real world," says Bill Krause. He's president of the civil service union that includes economists. His union pointed out that points are worthless if you want to hire a computer programmer and someone down the street happens to be paying more for them.

8   There were other major problems. After the first 40,000 jobs had been rated, nearly all the high-tech jobs scored lower than expected. Computer programmers wound up with the same number of points as clerks and dock-hands, and would have been paid far below market rates. Meantime, people doing essentially the same jobs wound up with different ratings. Thousands of professionals with university degrees discovered they'd be red-circled and might end up making not much more than clerical workers. The clerical workers, on the other hand, would be the best-paid clerks in Canada.

9   Rather than throw the plan out, the planners decided to iron out the wrinkles. All the job descriptions were sent back to be redone. More consultants were brought in. Professional writers were engaged to help the managers

classify the jobs more accurately. None of them, of course, could fix the fundamental flaw, which is that supply and demand are impervious to master plans and point schemes. "Labour market volatility was the one thing this approach couldn't handle," says Bill Krause.

10   The universal yardstick has been described as one of the biggest exercises ever undertaken by the federal bureaucracy. it chewed up colossal amounts of management time. And it was a total failure. . . .

11   In any case, the pay-equity overhaul was devised to fix a problem that [has] largely disappeared. Women are no longer disproportionately segregated into lower-paying ghettos. A gender wage gap still exists. But almost all of it is explained by women's different work patterns—taking time out to have kids, working part-time instead of full-time, working shorter hours.

12   And speaking of economists, I asked Mr. Krause how many in the government are women. He looked it up, and told me it's exactly half.

Wente, Margaret. "The Pay Equity Debacle." *Globe and Mail* 21 May 2002: A19.

1. This piece was written as a newspaper column. In your own words, express the author's thesis.
2. The third and fourth paragraphs summarize the whole article. Why has the author given away the "plot" so early, instead of telling us about the situation chronologically?
3. Newspaper writing is generally aimed at high-school level readers. What features of Wente's style make it accessible to readers?
4. In your own words, explain the difference between "equal pay for equal work" and "equal pay for work of equal value." Why, according to Wente, is the latter idea doomed to fail?
5. In its effort to institute equal pay for work of equal value, which of the three logical fallacies defined on page 209 was the government guilty of?
6. Consider the attention-getter and the memorable statement of this article. Given the author's purpose and target audience, are they effective? Why?

THE TELEPHONE

Anwar F. Accawi

1   When I was growing up in Magdaluna, a small Lebanese village in the terraced, rocky mountains east of Sidon, time didn't mean much to anybody, except maybe to those who were dying, or those waiting to appear in court because they had tampered with the boundary markers on their land. In those days, there was no real need for a calendar or a watch to keep track of the

hours, days, months, and years. We knew what to do and when to do it, just as the Iraqi geese knew when to fly north, driven by the hot wind that flew in from the desert, and the ewes knew when to give birth to wet lambs that stood on long, shaky legs in the chilly March wind and baaed hesitantly, because they were small and cold and did not know where they were or what to do now that they were here. The only timepiece we had need of then was the sun. It rose and set, and the seasons rolled by, and we sowed seed and harvested and ate and played and married our cousins and had babies who got whooping cough and chickenpox. We lived and loved and toiled and died without ever needing to know what year it was, or even the time of day.

2   It wasn't that we had no system for keeping track of time and of the important events in our lives. But ours was a natural—or, rather, a divine—calendar, because it was framed by acts of God. Allah himself set down the milestones with earthquakes and droughts and floods and locusts and pestilences. Simple as our calendar was, it worked just fine for us.

3   Take, for example, the birth date of Teta Im Khalil, the oldest woman in Magdaluna and all the surrounding villages. When I first met her, we had just returned home from Syria at the end of the Big War and were living with Grandma Mariam. Im Khalil came by to welcome my father home and to take a long myopic look at his foreign-born wife, my mother. Im Khalil was so old that the skin of her cheeks looked like my father's grimy tobacco pouch, and when I kissed her (because Grandma insisted that I show her old friend affection), it was like kissing a soft suede glove that had been soaked with sweat and then left in a dark closet for a season. Im Khalil's face got me to wondering how old one had to be to look and taste the way she did. So, as soon as she had hobbled off on her cane, I asked Grandma, "How old is Teta Im Khalil?"

4   Grandma had to think for a moment; then she said, "I've been told that Teta was born shortly after the big snow that caused the roof on the mayor's house to cave in."

5   "And when was that?" I asked.

6   "Oh, about the time we had the big earthquake that cracked the wall in the east room."

7   Well, that was enough for me. You couldn't be more accurate than that, now, could you? Satisfied with her answer, I went back to playing with a ball made from an old sock stuffed with other, much older socks.

8   And that's the way it was in our little village for as far back as anybody could remember: people were born so many years before or after an earthquake or a flood; they got married or died so many years before or after a long drought or a big snow or some other disaster. One of the most unusual of these dates was when Antoinette the seamstress and Saeed the barber (and tooth puller) got married. That was the year of the whirlwind during which fish and oranges fell from the sky. Incredible as it may sound, the story of the

fish and oranges was true, because men—respectable men, like Abu George the blacksmith and Abu Asaad the mule skinner, men who would not lie even to save their own souls—told and retold that story until it was incorporated into Magdaluna's calendar, just like the year of the black moon and the year of the locusts before it. My father, too, confirmed the story for me. He told me that he had been a small boy himself when it rained fish and oranges from heaven. He'd gotten up one morning after a stormy night and walked out into the year to find fish as long as his forearm still flopping here and there among the wet navel oranges.

9   The year of the fish-bearing twister, however, was not the last remarkable year. Many others followed in which strange and wonderful things happened: milestones added by the hand of Allah to Magdaluna's calendar. There was, for instance, the year of the drought, when the heavens were shut for months and the spring from which the entire village got its drinking water slowed to a trickle. The spring was about a mile from the village, in a ravine that opened at one end into a small, flat clearing covered with fine gray dust and hard, marble-sized goat droppings, because every afternoon the goatherds brought their flocks there to water them. In the year of the drought, that little clearing was always packed full of noisy kids with big brown eyes and sticky hands, and their mothers—sinewy, overworked young women with protruding collar-bones and cracked, callused brown heels. The children ran around playing tag or hide-and-seek while the women talked, shooed flies, and awaited their turns to fill up their jars with drinking water to bring home to their napping men and wet babies. There were days when we had to wait from sunup until late afternoon just to fill a small clay jar with precious, cool water.

10   Sometimes, amid the long wait and the heat and the flies and the smell of goat dung, tempers flared, and the younger women, anxious about their babies, argued over whose turn it was to fill up her jar. And sometimes the arguments escalated into full-blow, knock-down-dragout fights; the women would grab each other by the hair and curse and scream and spit and call each other names that made my ears tingle. We little brown boys who went with our mothers to fetch water loved these fights, because we got to see the women's legs and their colored panties as they grappled and rolled around in the dust. Once in a while, we got lucky and saw much more, because some of the women wore nothing at all under their long dresses. God, how I used to look forward to those fights. I remember the rush, the excitement, the sun dancing on the dust clouds as a dress ripped and a young white breast was revealed, then quickly hidden. In my calendar, that year of drought will always be one of the best years of my childhood, because it was then, in a dusty clearing by a trickling mountain spring, I got my first glimpses of the wonders, the mysteries, and the promises hidden beneath the folds of a woman's dress. Fish and oranges from heaven . . . you can get over that.

11   But, in another way, the year of the drought was also one of the worst in my life, because that was the year that Abu Raja, the retired cook who used to entertain us kids by cracking walnuts on his forehead, decided it was time Magdaluna got its own telephone. Every civilized village needed a telephone, he said, and Magdaluna was not going to get anywhere until it had one. A telephone would link us with the outside world. At the time, I was too young to understand the debate, but a few men—like Shukri, the retired Turkish-army drill sergeant, and Abu Hanna the vineyard keeper—did all they could to talk Abu Raja out of having a telephone brought to the village. But they were outshouted and ignored and finally shunned by the other villagers for resisting progress and trying to keep a good thing from coming to Magdaluna.

12   One warm day in early fall, many of the villagers were out in their fields repairing walls or gathering wood for the winter when the shout went out that the telephone company truck had arrived at Abu Raja's *dikkan*, or country store. There were no roads in those days, only footpaths and dry steam beds, so it took the telephone-company truck almost a day to work its way up the rocky terrain from Sidon—about the same time it took to walk. When the truck came into view, Abu George, who had a huge voice, and, before the tele-phone, was Magdaluna's only long-distance communication system, bellowed the news from his front porch. Everybody dropped what they were doing and ran to Abu Raja's house to see what was happening. Some of the more digni-fied villagers, however, like Abu Habeeb and Abu Nazim, who had been to big cities like Beirut and Damascus and had seen things like telephones and telegraphs, did not run the way the rest did; they walked with their canes hanging from the crooks of their arms, as if on a Sunday afternoon stroll.

13   It did not take long for the whole village to assemble at Abu Raja's *dikkan*. Some of the rich villagers, like the widow Farha and the gendarme Abu Nadeem, walked right into the store and stood at the elbows of the two important-looking men from the telephone company, who proceeded with utmost gravity, like priests at Communion, to wire up the telephone. The poorer villagers stood outside and listened carefully to the details relayed to them by the not-so-poor people who stood in the doorway and could see inside.

14   "The bald man is cutting the blue wire," someone said.

15   "He is sticking the wire into the hole in the bottom of the black box," someone else added.

16   "The telephone man with the mustache is connecting two pieces of wire. Now he is twisting the ends together," a third voice chimed in.

17   Because I was small and unaware that I should have stood outside with the other poor folk to give the rich people inside more room (they seemed to need more of it than poor people did), I wriggled my way through the dense

forest of legs to get a first-hand look at the action. I felt like a barefoot Moses, sandals in hand, staring at the burning bush on Mount Sinai. Breathless, I watched as the men in blue, their shirt pockets adorned with fancy lettering in a foreign language, put together a black machine that supposedly would make it possible to talk with uncles, aunts, and cousins who lived more than two days' ride away.

18   It was shortly after sunset when the man with the mustache announced that the telephone was ready to use. He explained that all Abu Raja had to do was lift the receiver, turn the crank on the black box a few times, and wait for an operator to take his call. Abu Raja, who had once lived and worked in Sidon, was impatient with the telephone man for assuming that he was ignorant. He grabbed the receiver and turned the crank forcefully, as if trying to start a Model T Ford. Everybody was impressed that he knew what to do. He even called the operator by her first name: "Centralist." Within moments, Abu Raja was talking with his brother, a concierge in Beirut. He didn't even have to raise his voice or shout to be heard.

19   If I hadn't seen it with my own two eyes and heard it with my own two ears, I would not have believed it—and my friend Kameel didn't. He was away that day watching his father's goats, and when he came back to the village that evening, his cousin Habeeb and I told him about the telephone and how Abu Raja had used it to speak with his brother in Beirut. After he heard our report, Kameel made the sign of the cross, kissed his thumbnail, and warned us that lying was a bad sin and would surely land us in purgatory. Kameel believed in Jesus and Mary, and wanted to be a priest when he grew up. He always crossed himself when Habeeb, who was irreverent, and I, who was Presbyterian, were around, even when we were not bearing bad news.

20   And the telephone, as it turned out, was bad news. With its coming, the face of the village began to change. One of the first effects was the shifting of the village's center. Before the telephone's arrival, the men of the village used to gather regularly at the house of Im Kaleem, a short, middle-aged widow with jet-black hair and a raspy voice that could be heard all over the village, even when she was only whispering. She was a devout Catholic and also the village *shlikki*—whore. The men met at her house to argue about politics and drink coffee and play cards or backgammon. Im Kaleem was not a true prostitute, however, because she did not charge for her services—not even for the coffee and tea (and, occasionally, the strong liquor called arrack) that she served the men. She did not need the money; her son, who was overseas in Africa, sent her money regularly. (I knew this because my father used to read her son's letters to her and take down her replies, as Im Kaleem could not read and write.) Im Kaleem was no slut either—unlike some women in the village—because she loved all the men she entertained, and they loved her, every one of them. In a way, she was married to all the men

in the village. Everybody knew it—the wives knew it; the itinerant Catholic priest knew it; the Presbyterian minister knew it—but nobody objected. Actually, I suspect the women (my mother included) did not mind their husband's visits to Im Kaleem. Oh, they wrung their hands and complained to one another about their men's unfaithfulness, but secretly they were relieved, because Im Kaleem took some of the pressure off them and kept the men out of their hair while they attended to their endless chores. Im Kaleem was also a kind of confessor and troubleshooter, talking sense to those men who were having family problems, especially the younger ones.

21   Before the telephone came to Magdaluna, Im Kaleem's house was bustling at just about any time of day, especially at night, when its windows were brightly lit with three large oil lamps, and the loud voices of the man talking, laughing, and arguing could be heard in the street below—a reassuring, homey sound. Her house was an island of comfort, an oasis for the weary village men, exhausted from having so little to do.

22   But it wasn't long before many of those men—the younger ones especially—started spending more of their days and evenings at Abu Raja's *dikkan*. There, they would eat and drink and talk and play checkers and backgammon, and then lean their chairs back against the wall—the signal that they were ready to toss back and forth, like a ball, the latest rumors going around the village. And they were always looking up from their games and drinks and talk to glance at the phone in the corner, as if expecting it to ring any minute and bring news that would change their lives and deliver them from their aimless existence. In the meantime, they smoked cheap, hand-rolled cigarettes, dug dirt out from under their fingernails with big pocket-knives, and drank lukewarm sodas that they called Kacula, Seffen-Ub, and Bebsi. Sometimes, especially when it was hot, the days dragged on so slowly that the men turned on Abu Saeed, a confirmed bachelor who practically lived in Abu Raja's *dikkan*, and teased him for going around barefoot and unshaven since the Virgin had appeared to him behind the olive press.

23   The telephone was also bad news for me personally. It took away my lucrative business—a source of much-needed income. Before the telephone came to Magdaluna, I used to hang around Im Kaleem's courtyard and play marbles with the other kids, waiting for some man to call down from a window and ask me to run to the store for cigarettes or arrack, or to deliver a message to his wife, such as what he wanted for supper. There was always something in it for me: a ten- or even a twenty-five-piaster piece. On a good day, I ran nine or ten of those errands, which assured a steady supply of marbles that I usually lost to Sami or his cousin Hani, the basket weaver's boy. But as the days went by, fewer and fewer men came to Im Kaleem's, and more and more congregated at Abu Raja's to wait by the telephone. In the evenings, no light fell from her window onto the street below, and the laugher and

noise of the men trailed off and finally stopped. Only Shukri, the retired Turkish-army drill sergeant, remained faithful to Im Kaleem after all the other men had deserted her; he was still seen going into or leaving her house from time to time. Early that winter, Im Kaleem's hair suddenly turned gray, and she got sick and old. Her legs started giving her trouble, making it hard for her to walk. By spring she hardly left her house anymore.

24 At Abu Raja's *dikkan*, the calls did eventually come, as expected, and men and women started leaving the village the way a hailstorm begins: first one, then two, then bunches. The army took them. Jobs in the cities lured them. And ships and airplanes carried them to such faraway places as Australia and Brazil and New Zealand. My friend Kameel, his cousin Habeeb, and their cousins and my cousins all went away to become ditch diggers and mechanics and butcher-shop boys and deli owners who wore dirty aprons sixteen hours a day, all looking for a better life than the one they had left behind. Within a year, only the sick, the old, and the maimed were left in the village. Magdaluna became a skeleton of its former self, desolate and forsaken, like the tombs, a place to get away from.

25 Finally, the telephone took my family away, too. My father got a call from an old army buddy who told him that an oil company in southern Lebanon was hiring interpreters and instructors. My father applied for a job and got it, and we moved to Sidon, where I went to a Presbyterian missionary school and graduated in 1962. Three years later, having won a scholarship, I left Lebanon for the United States. Like the others who left Magdaluna before me, I am still looking for that better life.

Accawi, Anwar F. "The Telephone." *Canadian Content.* Ed. Sarah Norton and Nell Waldman. 4th ed. Toronto: Harcourt, 2000. 236–42.

1. Does this essay focus primarily on cause or on effect? Of what?
2. "The Telephone" is divided into two parts: paragraphs 1 to 10 and 11 to 25. Summarize the content of the two halves of the piece.
3. Explain the irony in paragraph 11, the turning point of the essay.
4. In addition to causal analysis, this essay contains strong elements of description and narration. Identify two paragraphs that you think are particularly effective examples of each.
5. The first effect of the telephone on the village community is told through the story of Im Kaleem, "the village *shlikki*" (paragraphs 20 to 22). What is this consequence, and why do you think the author chooses Im Kaleem's story to communicate it?
6. In paragraph 24, we are told that "the calls did eventually come." What happens then? Where do people go? What happens to Magdaluna itself? Do you think that these effects are all due to the arrival of the telephone in the village?

7. In your own words, describe how the author feels about the changes that swept through his world. Refer to specific details from paragraphs 24 and 25.

Exercise 18.1

Develop each of the following thesis statements by adding three good main points.

1. Obesity, a common problem in North America, is the result of three major causes: _____

_____,

_____, and

_____.

2. The positive effects of professional day care upon preschool children are

_____,

_____, and

_____.

3. Some major effects of the NAFTA agreement on Canada have been

_____,

_____, and

_____.

4. The major causes of air pollution are _____

_____,

_____, and

_____.

5. The fitness craze was prompted by these causes: _____

_____,

_____, and

_____.

6. There are several causes for the increase in numbers of full-time workers returning to college for part-time study: _____

_____,

_____, and

_____.

7. Three common effects of emotional stress are _____

_____,

_____, and

_____.

Exercise 18.2

Begin with the question "What are the causes of _____?" and fill in five career-related topics that you know enough about to identify at least three causes. If possible, work with a partner who shares your career interests.

Exercise 18.3

Repeat Exercise 18.2, using the question "What are the effects of _____?"

Exercise 18.4

Choose one of the topics that you have developed in either Exercise 18.2 or Exercise 18.3 and work that topic into a full essay, taking care to select a subject about which you know enough to support your ideas.

Exercise 18.5

Write a cause essay or an effect essay on one of the following subjects. If you don't know enough to fully support your ideas, be prepared to do some research.

Causes
Adjusting to college was not as easy as I'd thought it would be.
Many people look forward to early retirement.
My first job was a good (or bad) experience.
Vandalism is a symptom of adolescent frustration.
Self-employment is the best option for many college grads.
Many workers have unrealistic expectations of their employers.
Eating disorders are a growing problem among young people.
Homelessness is increasingly widespread in large cities.
Many runaways prefer the street to a dysfunctional home life.

Effects

Technology is making us lazy.

A poor manager can have a devastating influence on morale.

Credit cards can be dangerous.

Music can reduce tension.

Being an only child is a difficult way to grow up.

Poor driving skills are a hazard to everyone.

Caffeine is a harmful substance.

Injuries resulting from overtraining are common among athletes.

Worrying can age you prematurely.

Losing your job can be a positive experience.

19

Argument and Persuasion

How many times have you won an argument? If you're like most of us, not very often. Getting people to understand what you say is hard enough; getting them to agree with you is the most difficult task any writer faces.

In the context of writing, the terms *argument* and *persuasion* have specific meanings, slightly different from their meanings in general conversation. An **argument** is a piece of writing that is intended to convince readers that the writer's opinion about an issue is reasonable and valid. Factual reports, memos, and analyses are not likely to be arguments, although some writing intended primarily to inform may also be intended to influence the reader's thinking: "Pucker Up," "The Enemy in the Mirror," and "Justice and Journalism" are just three examples. **Persuasion** takes an argument one step further: it is intended to change the way readers think or feel about an issue, perhaps even to act in some way that supports the writer's point of view (e.g., buy a product, donate to a charity, vote for a particular candidate). An **issue** is an opinion or belief, something that not all people agree on; it is *controversial*, a word that literally means "having two sides." Drafting, revising, and editing argument and persuasion are much the same as for other kinds of writing. Planning, however, requires a slightly different approach.

Choose Your Issue Carefully

Assuming that you have not been assigned a topic, you will need to choose one. Your choice is even more critical for an argument or a persuasive paper than it is for a factual analysis. You can only argue matters of opinion, not fact. Facts can be interpreted in different ways—that's what an argument is:

an interpretation of a set of facts—but no one can dispute the fact that Canada has ten provinces and three territories. An appropriate subject for your paper is one that can be disputed. Someone has to be able to say, "No. You are not right. That's not what these facts mean."

You cannot argue matters of taste, either. Taste is personal preference: there is no point in arguing that Thai food is better than pizza, or that green is more flattering than blue. Even if you could argue these assertions, they are not significant enough to bother with. Choose your subject carefully. It must pass the 4-S test (see page 26), and it should be one you know and care about. Ideally, it should be one your reader cares about, too.

GO TO WEB

EXERCISE 19.1

Next, consider the scope of your subject. How much time do you have to prepare? How long is your paper? Throughout this book, we have recommended that when you choose a subject, you should limit your focus. This recommendation is even more important when you are preparing an argument than it is when you are proposing to explain something. Even subjects that look narrowly focused can require surprising amounts of development when you are composing an argument for or against them. Avoid large, controversial issues: abortion, for example, or capital punishment, or religious faith. There are two reasons for this caution. First, they are hugely complex issues; and, second, they are issues on which virtually everyone already has an opinion. It is difficult enough to convince readers about an issue on which they have not already formed an opinion; it's practically impossible to get them to change their minds when they hold an entrenched belief.

Consider Your Audience

When you are trying to get readers to agree with you, you must know (or be able to make an educated guess about) what opinions they already hold and how likely they are to disagree with your views. If, for example, you want to convince your readers that music broadcasters should be required to adhere strictly to Canadian content regulations, your approach will differ depending on your readers' level of knowledge, their interest in the subject, even their age. What do they think about the issue? Do they care about it, one way or the other? What beliefs do they hold that would make them inclined to agree or disagree with you? If you know the answers to these questions, you'll know how to approach your subject: what points to argue, which to emphasize, and which to downplay.

Identify Your Purpose

Do you want your readers simply to understand and respect your opinion on an issue? Or do you want to change their thinking or their behaviour in some way? If your primary purpose is to get them to agree with you, your argument will rely on solid evidence and sound, logical reasoning. If your primary purpose is to get them to do something, to act in some way, your argument will need to appeal not only to their sense of what is reasonable, but also to their feelings, loyalties, ambitions, or desires.

State Your Thesis

Before you begin your first draft, write out your opinion in the form of a proposition (opinion statement). You may or may not use this statement in your paper, but you need it in front of you as you identify your reasons for holding the opinion you do, list the evidence you intend to use, and decide on the order of presentation. If you have ever heard a formal debate, you know what a proposition is. It is the statement of opinion that one side argues in favour of and the other side argues against. Here are three examples:

> The federal government should take a leading role in preserving public health care. (thesis of "The Scaremongers," pages 230–31)

> A liberal arts education is a sound investment of time and money. (thesis of "Arts Education Does Pay Off," pages 232–33)

> Our schools discriminate against males. (thesis of "Roll Back the Red Carpet for Boys," pages 234–35)

The test of a satisfactory proposition is that it is arguable—someone could defend the contrary point of view. (A statement that includes the word *should* or *must* is likely to be a proposition.) You could argue that the federal government should encourage privately delivered health care, or that a liberal arts education is a waste of time and money, or that our schools do not pay enough attention to female students.

Once you have a clear statement of a specific opinion, you are ready to identify your reasons for holding it and evidence to support your reasons. It is possible to support an argument entirely from personal experience, but you are more likely to convince your readers if you provide a variety of kinds of evidence (see Chapters 8 and 20).

Identify Your Reasons and Evidence

Readers are not likely to be convinced of anything unless the concept is first clearly explained to them. Whichever purpose you have set for yourself, you will need to provide reasons for believing your opinion. Your reasons, which are your main points, must be significant, distinct, and relevant (see Chapter 3). To support each reason, you need to provide plenty of accurate evidence: facts, concrete details, statistics, events or experiences your readers are familiar with, authorities you can refer to or quote. To engage your readers' hearts as well as their minds, at least some of your evidence should be emotionally "loaded"; that is, it should arouse the readers' compassion, or anger, or sense of justice, or any other feeling that supports your side of the issue.

Decide on an Approach: Direct or Indirect?

If your readers are likely to disagree with your view or are even slightly inclined to oppose it, it is best to build your case with definitions, examples, and other evidence before strongly stating your own opinion. Readers who are confronted early by a statement they disagree with are often not open to argument or persuasion. Instead, they are inclined to read the rest of the paper trying to pick holes in your argument and thinking of rebuttals. This audience would respond best to an indirect, or inductive, approach:

> Before we decide how to vote, we should consider the candidates' records, their platforms, and their characters.

On the other hand, if your readers are sympathetic to your point of view, you can state your opinion up front and then identify your reasons and the evidence that supports those reasons. This is called the direct, or deductive, approach:

> Based on her record, her platform, and her character, Julie Kovac is the candidate who deserves your vote.

For an explanation of inductive and deductive reasoning, together with some of the common logical fallacies that can damage your argument, see "Making the Argument" on the *Essay Essentials* Web site (http://www. essayessentials3e.nelson.com).

Arrange Your Reasons and Evidence

An argument or a persuasive paper can be developed in a variety of ways. It is possible, as you will see in the readings for this chapter, to use a number of different structural patterns to convince your readers. A cause-effect analysis might be an effective way to urge action to lower the carbon monoxide and carbon dioxide emissions that contribute to global warming. You might choose comparison to discuss the efficiency of Canada's regulated airline industry as opposed to the deregulated industry in the United States and to argue in favour of one approach over the other.

Two patterns are specific to argument and persuasion. One is the classic "their side–my side" strategy, which is particularly useful when you are arguing a controversial position that may provoke serious dispute. This pattern involves presenting the "con" (or "against") points of an argument, then refuting them with the "pro" (or "for") side of the argument. For instance, if a writer were to argue that women in the Canadian Armed Forces should participate in combat, she might choose to present the opposing view and then counter each point with well-reasoned arguments of her own. Like a comparison, the "their side–my side" strategy can be presented either in block form or in point-by-point form, depending on how many points there are to discuss. Be sure to arrange your points in the order in which they will be most effective (see the list of possible arrangements discussed in Chapter 3).

If you are a skilled debater, you can often dismiss the opposing side's argument by identifying and exposing flaws in reasoning or evidence. If you are an inexperienced writer, however, you will probably find it easier to use the following techniques:

1. Identify any irrelevant or trivial points.
2. Show that a point covers only part of the issue.
3. Show that a point is valid only some of the time.

4. Show that a point may have immediate advantages, but that its long-term results will be negative.
5. Acknowledge the validity of the opposition's point(s), but provide a better alternative.

Carefully presented, the "their side–my side" pattern impresses readers with its fairness and tends to neutralize opposition.

The second structural pattern specific to argument and persuasion makes use of the familiar thesis statement. Add carefully worded reasons to your proposition, and you have a thesis statement that can appear near the beginning of your paper, in a direct approach, or near the end, if you are treating your subject indirectly. Be sure you have arranged your reasons in the most effective order. Usually, writers present their reasons in climactic order, saving their most compelling reason for the end of the paper.

The keys to good argumentation and persuasion are to think carefully about what you are saying and to present fairly your reasons for believing it—*after* you have analyzed your reader's possible biases or prejudices and degree of commitment to one side or the other. To argue or persuade successfully, not only do you need to be well organized, informative, and thorough, but also you need to be honest and tactful, especially if your readers are not already inclined to agree with you.

Tips on Writing Argument and Persuasion

1. Choose an issue that you know and care about and can present with enthusiasm.
2. Select your reasons and evidence with your audience in mind. You are already convinced; your task is to convince your readers.
3. Decide whether your audience can be approached directly or if they should be approached indirectly—gently and with plenty of evidence before receiving your "pitch."
4. Arrange your argument in whatever structural pattern is most appropriate for your issue and your audience.
5. Remember that there is another side to the issue. You can help your own cause by presenting the opposing viewpoint and refuting it. Present the other side tactfully and fairly. You will only antagonize readers by unfairly stating or belittling the case for the other side. Opinions are as sensitive as toes: tread carefully to avoid causing pain.

The five essays that follow illustrate a variety of approaches to argument and persuasion. Read the essays and answer the questions that follow each one.

THE SCAREMONGERS
Judy Rebick

1   For years we've been fed the line that the public health care system is in crisis. An injection of private money and efficiencies is the cure-all, we're told. But Canadians are not buying it. In an Ipsos-Reid poll published this winter [2001], a large majority of Canadians said that what's needed is improvements inside the system rather than user fees or more privatization.

2   The supporters of private health care won't be pleased by such news. For years they've been trying to scare us to soften us up for health-care profiteers. Let's look at their arguments.

3   *Health-care costs are skyrocketing.* It's true that health-care costs have been rising, but they are still only 10 per cent of GDP. In the United States, they are 14 per cent of GDP. And the only component whose costs are dramatically increasing is already in the private sector: drugs. Pharmaceuticals now account for 16 per cent of all costs, an even greater proportion than physician services. There are a lot of reasons for this increase in costs, but private funding won't solve any of them.

4   *As our population ages, the costs will really increase.* The Canadian Institute for Health Information estimates that the aging of our population will result in an increase in per capita health spending of a little more than 1 per cent annually from 2005 to 2025.

5   *The private sector is more efficient.* Wrong again. A 1997 study in *The New England Journal of Medicine* showed that administration accounts for 34 per cent of costs in profit-making private hospitals in the U.S. compared with 26 per cent in public hospitals. In the United Kingdom, where privatizing experiments similar to those proposed by Alberta premier Ralph Klein have been carried out, costs are greater than before and service is worse.

6   In what was touted to be the great reform of the National Health Service in Britain, doctors were permitted to work in both the public system and a new parallel private system. Private hospitals will reduce the pressure on public hospitals, the purveyors of privatization argued. And the result? Patients have watched as waiting lists have grown enormously in the public system. Private hospitals have wound up costing more as well. In Australia, too, costs have increased with privatization.

7   So why do the premiers of Alberta, Ontario and British Columbia insist on exploring privatization? Blind ideology could be one reason. The other might be the money to be made by privateers, many of whom fund right-wing parties.

8   Our new federal health minister, Anne McLellan, is a little too accommodating to these premiers for my liking. The feds should be taking a leading role in preserving our public system. And it's not that tough. The National Forum on Health, commissioned by the Chrétien government, provided the prescription in 1997. Bring home care and pharmacare into the public system.

Home care saves money by keeping seniors and people with disabilities out of expensive long-term-care facilities and, with even greater savings, out of acute-care hospitals.

9   A study by Health Canada in British Columbia in 2001 compared two regions where home-care services such as housecleaning had been cut with two regions where it was provided. After three years, the health-care costs per person where home care was provided averaged $7,808. Where home care had been cut, costs were $11,903 per person. That's a difference of $4,000 per person with home care. What's more, most people would much rather stay in their homes than live in institutions.

10   Reforming primary care—what you get when you go to your doctor—would also save significant amounts of money. Right now doctors do piece-work. They get paid per service. They have an incentive to see as many patients as possible and focus on specific symptoms rather than on the whole person. Financing health care per patient rather than per service—or organizing family physicians in clinics where other professionals like nurses play a more important role and doctors are on salary—would also cut costs. Nurses could do many of the things that doctors do now, at a much lower cost to the system.

11   But the most important reforms that could be made are to invest more in prevention and in reducing poverty, which is the strongest indicator of poor health, both mental and physical. Unfortunately there's not much profit in that.

Rebick, Judy. "The Scaremongers." *Elm Street* Apr. 2002: 90.

1. What is the author's purpose in this piece? Does she hope to convince readers of her point of view or to persuade them to change their minds or act in some way?

2. Is the target audience for this piece hostile or sympathetic? How do you know?

3. Judy Rebick begins her argument by refuting the points of the opposition. She even italicizes them to make them easy to find. What kinds of evidence does she use to refute them? Is she successful?

4. Rebick is not arguing for more money in the system; she is arguing that the money should be spent differently. What two major changes in health-care spending would she like to see?

5. In paragraph 8, Rebick proposes that home care and pharmacare should be part of the public health system. Does she provide evidence to support both? Is there an error in her argument?

6. Why does Rebick think the federal government is not strongly opposed to privately delivered health care? Does she prove her case? Do you agree with her? Can you think of other reasons why the federal government has not passed regulations outlawing private health care in Canada?

ARTS EDUCATION DOES PAY OFF
Livio Di Matteo

1   Canada's universities—particularly the humanities and social sciences—face a major challenge. The current approach to education emphasizes immediate tangible benefits. This has led to government funding initiatives in science and technology that fail to recognize the importance of a liberal arts education. Yet supporting a humanities and social science education is justified on sound economic grounds, not just on the civic and academic grounds usually used.

2   The humanities and social sciences provide social benefits that private market mechanisms do not count. Just as a vaccination benefits people other than those inoculated by reducing disease transmission, the humanities and social sciences have spill-over benefits by transmitting wisdom to society. The inability to attach a market price to a literate and civil society of educated citizens does not make this type of education valueless.

3   The humanities and social sciences complement scientific and technical training, and provide innovative strategies for meeting future challenges. While science graduates can provide technical solutions to problems, only individuals trained in human science can deal with the economic, ethical, cultural and social implications of these solutions. For example, we are told that advances in genetics are making a vastly extended human lifespan possible in the not-so-distant future. How will this affect the distribution of income and employment, and the quality of life in our society? Is this type of analysis not of economic benefit to society?

4   Market benefits to humanities and social science graduates translate into jobs, as economist Robert Allen of the University of British Columbia recently demonstrated in a study. Prof. Allen found that unemployment rates for humanities and social science graduates did not substantially differ from those of graduates in other fields. Moreover, these graduates' age–income profiles can actually be steeper than those in the sciences or technical programs, where the latest technical knowledge depreciates quickly. Like fine wine, humanities and social science graduates appreciate with age as their skills deepen, generating a steeply rising income over their working life. Some universities, such as Dalhousie, are beginning to [issue transcripts that list] skills such as collaborative work, oral communication, and analytical work to their liberal arts graduates. This communicates what was once obvious, but now has to be marketed: Liberal arts graduates are prized because of their ability to think creatively and laterally, using skills acquired in analysis, synthesis, research and communication.

5   Having reduced their market intervention on the grounds that private forces work best, governments are now replicating that interventionist role in

post-secondary education by targeting funding increases to programs in science and technology. These programs are worthy of funding, but for universities to function according to a private-sector model, governments should provide universities with block increases in funding and allow them to pursue those programs they are best at. Targeted funding distorts resource allocation decisions by inducing universities to expand government-favoured programs. This leaves governments selecting educational winners and losers when the economy's future needs are uncertain.

6   Other issues present themselves, too. What about the long-run cost structure of universities, given that the per-student cost of producing science and engineering graduates is higher than in other fields? Who is responsible if such funding generates a graduate glut in any one discipline? Will government be accountable, or will the buck be passed to the universities for once again "failing" in their role to society?

7   Humanities and social sciences students make up approximately half of university enrolments. If you believe that "voting with your feet" is a test of market demand, this enrolment share should be sending a clear message to educational policy-makers as to how the public values these programs. Humanities and social science students should be entitled to adequate research and teaching facilities, and to professors who conduct leading-edge research. When it comes to resource allocation, why should half of university students be places on a path to second-rate treatment when they are indeed "paying customers"?

8   It is time to restore some balance. The current targeted funding approach ignores the obvious demand for humanities and social science training. Governments can best serve the university system by ensuring adequate general funding and allowing universities, in consultation with government and the public, to make the resource allocation decisions. In neglecting the humanities and social sciences, governments have not fully consulted all constituencies, and their funding decisions implicitly attach a negative value to these disciplines. Canadian society will pay huge economic and cultural costs if such myopic policies are continued.

Di Matteo, Livio. "Arts Education Does Pay Off." *Financial Post* 31 May 1999: 3.

1. Does the author approach his argument directly or indirectly? Where is the thesis statement? Identify the reasons the author cites to support his opinion.
2. Who is the target audience for this essay? How do you know?
3. What is the author's purpose: to win his readers' agreement, or to move them to action? What sort of action could they take to support the author on this issue?
4. Identify the various kinds of evidence the author uses in this essay.

5. The author uses a number of rhetorical questions (questions to which no answer is expected). Are they effective in supporting his argument? Why?

6. In your own words, explain why the author thinks targeted funding is a poor idea. (See paragraphs 5 and 6.)

7. Do you agree with the author? Why or why not?

ROLL BACK THE RED CARPET FOR BOYS
Donna Laframboise

1   Every now and again, in random bits and pieces, we run up against the fact that being male isn't the red-carpet experience much of recent feminism would have us believe. Young males are more likely to be physically abused by their parents, to drop out of school, and to face unemployment than their female counterparts. Between the ages of 15 and 24, they take their own lives five times as often. As adults, males are more likely to be homeless, more prone to alcohol and gambling addictions, twice as likely to be robbed or murdered, nine times more likely to be killed in an occupational accident, and [on average] go to their graves six years earlier than their sisters.

2   Yet, so attached are we to the view that the patriarchy has designed the world for the benefit of males that these truths fail to sink in. Although head-lines would scream and alarm bells would ring if the opposite were the case, inequality isn't an important social issue when males are being shortchanged. Talk about youth suicide, for instance, and you'll be informed that what really deserves attention is not the appalling number of dead male bodies, but the fact that girls say they *attempt* suicide more often than do boys.

3   [Recent] examples of this "who cares, they're only guys" mentality are reports that girls are outperforming boys in school. In 1996, six out of ten high-school honours graduates in Ontario and British Columbia were female. Even though girls were besting boys a decade earlier (in 1986, 53 percent of Ontario honours grads and 57 percent of . . . B.C. [grads] were girls), the 1990s have been replete with media commentary telling us it's girls who merit our concern. In 1994, Myra and David Sadker's book *Failing at Fairness: How Our Schools Cheat Girls* appeared. A year later, Michele Landsberg wrote a column in *The Toronto Star* [headed] "School sexism so routine it's almost invisible." A news story, also in *The Star*, about the higher-than-average Montreal dropout rate implied we should be concerned about this phenom-enon partly because "45 percent of dropouts are young women." Despite being in the majority, the boys weren't worth mentioning.

4   When girls do worse in math and science, when they don't sign up for skilled trades or engineering, it's the system's fault. Their parents aren't encouraging

them; the schools are male-oriented and unwelcoming; the boys are harassing them; and society is sending them traditional role-model messages. But when the boys do poorly, it's their own fault. Even though they're children, the responsibility gets loaded directly onto their meagre shoulders. In a recent *Globe* article, "Where the Boys Aren't: At the Top of the Class," educators tell the media that "too many boys don't seem to be even trying," and blame "a boy culture that celebrates bravado, lassitude, and stupidity." Rather than ask boys for their input, the reporter interviewed girls who criticized the boys' study habits.

5   The fact that masculinity and intellectualism have always been an uneasy fit (football players get dates, bookworms don't) doesn't even make it into the conversation. The idea that boys may be confused about whether or not they should excel, since feminism has drawn a straight line between female oppression and male achievement, isn't discussed. The fact that elementary schools are dominated by female teachers who scold and punish boys more frequently than they do girls, and that boys suffer from more learning disabilities, isn't mentioned. The notion that educators, parents, and governments have spent the past 15 years ignoring boys, so it's little wonder that they themselves have become complacent about their performance, isn't considered.

6   Girls are victims of circumstance and boys are masters of their own fate. Girls are moulded and manipulated by social pressures; boys make conscious choices. Girls get to blame everyone but themselves; everyone gets to blame boys. Wasn't feminism supposed to be about abolishing double standards?

Laframboise, Donna. "Roll Back the Red Carpet for Boys." *Globe and Mail* 7 Mar. 1998: D6.

1. As much as we would like to think we examine an argument solely on the basis of the strength of its reasoning, the weight of its evidence, and the power of its language, sometimes our views are swayed by what we know about the author. Donna Laframboise is a well-known feminist writer. How does her reputation lend credibility to her argument? If this article had been written by a man, would your reaction to it have been different?

2. Why is the article titled "Roll Back the Red Carpet for Boys"? What is "red-carpet treatment"? Summarize the author's argument in a single sentence.

3. Laframboise uses both examples and statistics to support her arguments. Do you find them convincing? Or do you think she has "stacked the deck" in the conclusions she draws? For example, consider the last sentence in paragraph 3. If this sentence were to read "Despite being in the majority, the boys were not mentioned," would the effect on the reader be different? Why?

4. One of the author's main targets is the news media because, in her view, they create perceptions that are inaccurate or distorted. Are her examples convincing?

5. After introducing her case with a number of specific examples of what she considers to be unfair treatment, Laframboise closes her argument with a series of general statements. Do these statements follow logically from the evidence she has provided? Can you think of another conclusion this evidence could be used to support?

TRASHING TALK RADIO
Ellen Smithee

1   Listen to the sounds of democracy in action on our radio airwaves:
"The government is in the pockets of big business."
". . . big labour."
". . . environmentalists."
". . . the Americans."
". . . feminists . . . homosexuals . . . the United Nations . . . Martians . . . ."
"Gun control is a communist/right-wing plot."
"Bring back the rope!"
"Elvis is alive and living on a potato farm in Prince Edward Island."

2   In every radio market in the country, phone-in shows dominate both air time and ratings. Some shows are sources of useful information: listeners may learn about gardening, pet care, solutions to computer problems, health tips, taxes, or investments. The typical host of such a program acts as a mediator, a friendly contact between callers who have questions and guest experts who provide answers. This type of show is the product of thoughtful planning, detailed preparation, and a substantial budget. Guest experts must be found, transported to the studio, and in many cases paid a fee for their appearance. Unfortunately, shows like this are not the norm.

3   The more typical call-in show requires no preparation, no planning, and just enough money to pay the host's salary. This type of show seeks to provide an opportunity for frustrated, angry, or just plain lonely members of the listening audience to call in and vent their anger or advance their opinions on whatever may be the topic of the day. The host's job is to provoke, annoy, goad, cajole, or argue—whatever it takes to keep the callers calling and the audience listening. Many of these programs attract huge audiences, and the damage they do to the community is considerable. They offer no useful information or reasoned debate. Instead, they provide a public forum for spreading confusion, ignorance, bigotry, and paranoia.

4   The hosts of these shows are performers. They are on the air to attract the largest possible audience so their stations can charge advertisers top rates.

Hosts who do not create controversy, who do not encourage outrageous callers, will not hold an audience. For this reason, these "type-two" hosts are constantly pushing the envelope, going to the limit and, in many cases, beyond the limit, of what is acceptable in a democracy and permissible under the law. If a host's assertion that Canada is spending too much money on multicultural programs doesn't provoke enough calls, then up the ante: demand that no one without the ability to speak French or English be granted landed immigrant status. If that red flag doesn't provoke listener action, call for an end to immigration. The host of this type of program knows that all he or she needs to do is keep escalating the rhetoric of the challenge, and eventually the phones will ring. And ring. . . .

5   Talk-show hosts who are criticized and occasionally censured for such programming plead innocence: "But no one could possibly take me seriously! I'm an entertainer, not a news broadcaster! This is *schtick* I'm doing!" It's clear from the calls, however, that listeners do take the hosts' views seriously, and the sad result is that legitimacy is given to the bigotry they broadcast in the name of entertainment. The wide distribution of these programs ensures that ignorance and paranoia are reinforced, that simplistic solutions to complex problems are promoted, and that socially unacceptable behaviour is condoned, even encouraged.

6   Another concern is that these "viewpoint" call-in shows tend to lower the level of debate on important issues. Typically, callers are uneducated, fearful, confused, and inarticulate. The demographics for these shows, supplied by the companies who monitor them for ratings, are revealing. In most regions of Canada, the prime listening audience consists of men eighteen to thirty-five years old with little formal schooling. The proportionate age and gender of the listening audience may vary slightly, depending on the region, the station, and the host, but one characteristic remains constant—a low level of education. These listeners are people who may feel uncomfortable speaking out in forums consisting of informed citizens, but as callers to open-line talk shows they have no hesitation in advancing or supporting the views of people who, like themselves, can't understand what's so difficult about the nation's or the world's problems. In an information-overloaded age, simple solutions to complex problems are welcomed by many. Fear, bigotry, and anger are easy substitutes for thoughtful analysis, a time-consuming process in which too many of us are neither prepared nor willing to engage.

7   To be fair, talk-show callers cannot be held entirely responsible for their lack of information or the shallowness of their opinions. Canada has not yet found a way to ensure that all citizens are educated about local and national concerns, let alone global issues. In a democracy, however (so we are taught), everyone is entitled to a voice. Why should anyone be surprised that

open-line callers take advantage of the only forum that offers them an opportunity to be heard?

8   What is deplorable is the cynicism of the hosts, the station owners and managers, and the advertisers. "Say anything—just get the ratings" is their credo. As far as the owners are concerned, lawsuits and investigations by the CRTC (the licensing body for Canada's publicly owned air waves) or the Broadcast Standards Council (a self-regulatory body set up by the stations themselves to forestall government regulation) are not occupational hazards but badges of honour, proof that the show is doing a good job.

9   But what about the cost to Canada's social, cultural, and political well-being? Consider two recent incidents. That one talk-show host could denigrate French Canadians and another could viciously slander Native Canadians without effective reprimand demonstrates the harm these type-two open-line hosts do to our national psyche. And these are only two examples of the hundreds of ignorant, inflammatory comments that have been documented across the country. Let us not underestimate the danger these shows represent to Canada's public interest. Poisonous bigotry on the public air waves threatens the social tolerance of which we are justly proud and diminishes our nation.

Reprinted by permission of the author.

1. This piece begins with a series of quotations, presented without introduction or explanation. Why do you think the author chose to open her article this way? What effect did the quotations have on you? Were you confused? puzzled? intrigued?

2. The author's approach is direct and forceful—not far removed from the style of the talk-show hosts she criticizes. Is Smithee's angry tone appropriate to her argument? Do you think readers would respond more favourably had she toned down the emotional level of the piece?

3. Draft an outline for this essay. Then answer the following questions. Is the structure clear? Is the argument logically presented? Has the author followed the five tips on writing effective persuasion (see page 229)? Are there any sentences or paragraphs you would delete or move to a different spot?

4. Do you agree that something should be done to curb extremism on Canada's radio stations? What might be the dangers of censorship? Can you suggest a workable solution to the problem?

5. In this chapter, you have learned that there are two main types of persuasive writing: one tries to convince readers to agree with the author, and the other tries to get readers to take action of some sort. Into which of these categories does this piece fit? What is the author's purpose? How successful do you think she has been in achieving her purpose?

THE INCREDIBLE RIGHTNESS OF READING
Dennis York

1   Watching a movie or a television program is a passive experience, as any couch potato can attest. Reading, on the other hand, is active; it requires work. But many of us relish the experience of having our imaginations pressed into the work of creating a story. *The Never Ending Story* illustrates this point. It is the tale of a boy who finds himself responsible for the existence of a world that lies between the covers of a book. Only in the boy's imagination is this world given—or allowed—life.

2   Most of us have known since childhood that books require us to participate in the making of their stories. Long before video games boasted of their interactivity, books depended on readers to make them "work." In a video game, the outcomes are programmed and finite, so one's experience of the game is determined largely by the programmer. Thousands or even millions of other players will experience the same outcome you do. In a book, on the other hand, the outcome—the depth and richness of the story—depends entirely on you. No matter how many others may have read it before you, the experience you create is uniquely yours. When you watch a movie or a television program, you are one of possibly millions of passive onlookers; when you read a book, you are engaged in an intimate, collaborative relationship. Together, you and the author create a world.

3   Some of the satisfaction we find in surfing the Internet comes from choosing the paths our curiosity will follow, paths that often lead to the joy of unexpected discoveries. Ironically, our experience with the Internet may be what has inspired us to surf the stacks of big-box bookstores such as Indigo. The immediate availability of hundreds of thousands of Web sites worldwide has led many of us to be impatient with the limitations of small, independent bookstores, rich as they may be in specific subject areas. I suggest that the attraction of the superstores is a consequence of more than their discounted prices. Many consumers, as a result of their experience on the Net, have come to expect more—much more—from bookstores than they can find in local, independent outlets: 100,000+ books, 2,000+ magazines, and dozens of newspapers from around the world, all available in an environment that offers many of the comforts of home: space, light, comfy chairs, and quiet. In short, today's consumers want what our public libraries used to provide.

4   Ironically, at the same time that big-box bookstores are increasing in popularity, the libraries they are modelled on are in decline. Where Indigo now proudly boasts over 100,000 books on virtually every subject, readings and signings by well-known authors, and a vast collection of periodicals designed to satisfy everyone's interests no matter how arcane, our public libraries have always offered these services and more. And, until recently, libraries charged

their users little or nothing. With respect to the distribution of knowledge in our society, public libraries have been the great equalizers for more than 200 years. But reduced funding means that equal access to information is quickly becoming a thing of the past. As a result of government cutbacks, libraries can acquire fewer resources and are forced to charge fees for their services. No longer can we claim that every Canadian has equal access to information. The future looks even more bleak. A recent news story in the *Ottawa Citizen* reports that the Ottawa Public Library lost $235,000 in provincial grants this year [1998] and expects to lose another $635,000 next year as a result of the province's downloading of responsibility for local services to the municipalities. As a result of these sudden, unpredictable changes to its funding, the public library system of our nation's capital expects a shortfall of $2 million next year.

5   Few would argue that governments, federal and provincial, should cut back on deficit spending, but surely the consequences of government-mandated cuts should be considered, if not debated, before the axe is ordered to fall. In a country where illiteracy is considered a significant handicap and literacy programs are officially endorsed (but seldom funded), a relatively small investment in our public library system would do much to complement the efforts of both the public and the private sectors to ensure the right to basic literacy for all.

6   It's not really a question of whether we can afford this public investment in our nation's welfare. It is really a question of whether we can afford not to invest. Adequately funded libraries are a necessity if we want a citizenry equipped with the most basic requirement for survival: literacy. Forty-seven percent of Canadian adults are regular users of our public library system; students rely on it; and countless others make occasional use of it. But more and higher service fees, reduced hours of operation, dilapidated and overcrowded facilities, and decimated acquisitions budgets are eroding much of the utility, let alone the pleasure, of surfing the libraries' shelves. In the information society, is it not ironic that librarians, of all public servants, are forced to go begging? Much work, not to mention thought and feeling, goes into the creation of a book. Too much will be lost if our books are not imagined into life.

Reprinted by permission of the author.

1. What sort of audience is the writer appealing to? How does he attempt to get his readers "on side" in the first two paragraphs?
2. How would the effect of this essay have been different if the writer had clearly stated his position at the beginning and then proceeded to explain the reasons for his opinion?
3. Does the author appeal primarily to reason or to emotion to prove his point?

4. York uses a number of specific, numerical details in this essay. Are they effective support for his argument? For example, are the dollar figures he provides useful out of context—that is, without information about the city's total budget? How much do readers need to know in order to evaluate a writer's opinion?

5. An argument presents an opinion and tries to convince the reader to share that opinion. Has this writer succeeded in achieving this goal? Why or why not?

Exercise 19.1

Read through the following list of propositions. With a partner, select one that you are both interested in, but do not discuss it. Working individually, write down two or three points both for and against the issue. Then exchange papers and read each other's work. Which points appear on both lists? Why? Can you judge from the points presented whether your partner is for or against the issue?

Canada should increase its level of immigration.
The salaries of professional athletes should be capped.
Music lyrics should be monitored and censored.
Technology is improving the workplace.
Courses in physical education should be required throughout high school.
Smokers should not receive the same medical coverage as nonsmokers.

Exercise 19.2

Most people have firm convictions, yet few are willing to take action to uphold them. Everyone agrees, for example, that a cure for cancer should be found, but not everyone participates in fund-raising events or supports the Cancer Society. With a partner, choose a charitable cause in which you believe and list all the reasons why people should give money to support it. Then list all the reasons people might give for not donating. Decide which of you will take the "pro" side and which the "con," and write a short essay arguing your position. You will know from your discussion whether your partner is sympathetic or hostile, so you will know whether you should approach your subject directly or indirectly. Then exchange papers and critique each other's work.

Exercise 19.3

With a partner, select a *small*, controversial, local issue (one involving your community, college, or profession, for example). Choose sides, and write an argument using the "their side–my side" pattern of organization.

Exercise 19.4

Survey at least 20 students in your college, from different programs and different years, to determine their attitude toward one of the following:

food services
class sizes
professors' teaching ability
required (or general education) courses
tutorial (or counselling) services

When you have enough information, compose an indirect argument that arrives at a conclusion about the issue and makes a recommendation based on the evidence you have gathered.

Exercise 19.5

Choose an issue with which you are familiar and about which you feel strongly. If you don't feel strongly about anything, choose a proposition from the list below. Draft a statement of thesis and outline your reasons and evidence. Then write a persuasive paper, making sure that your points are well supported and that the paper is clearly structured. Assume that your reader is not hostile, but is not enthusiastically supportive, either.

Forty percent of the college curriculum should be devoted to liberal arts (general education) courses.

Marijuana should be available for sale through government-controlled retail outlets.

Grades in college courses should take effort into consideration, not just results.

PART 5

The Research Paper

Introduction

A **research paper** is an essay that presents the results of a writer's investigation of a topic in print, electronic, or multimedia formats. The skills involved—finding, evaluating, and assimilating the ideas of other writers—are essential in any field of study. They will also be useful to you in your career. Much of the writing you do on the job, especially if you are in management, requires you to express in your own words the facts, opinions, and ideas of others.

Writing a research paper follows the same process as other kinds of writing, from planning through drafting to revising. The difference is that instead of relying exclusively on what you already know about a topic, you include source material—facts, data, knowledge, or opinions of other writers—to support your thesis. Chapter 20 explains the different kinds of source material you can choose from and tells you the strengths and weaknesses of each. Chapter 21 shows you how to integrate the information you have found into your paper.

Note that a research paper is *not* simply a collection of what other people have said about a subject. It is your responsibility to shape and control the discussion, to make sure that what you include from your sources is interesting and relevant to your thesis, and to comment on its validity or significance. It is *your* paper, *your* subject, *your* main points; ideas from other writers should be included as support for *your* topic sentences.

One of the challenges of writing a research paper is differentiating between your ideas and those you took from sources. Readers cannot hear the different "speakers," so you have to indicate who said what. To separate your sources from your own ideas, research papers require **documentation**—a system of acknowledging source materials. Chapter 22 shows you how to provide your readers with a guide to the information contained in your paper—a play-by-play of who is "speaking."

Research papers are usually longer than essays, and the planning process is more complex. For these reasons, the time you are given to complete a research assignment is usually longer than the time allowed for an essay. Don't fool yourself into thinking you can put the assignment off for a few weeks. You will need all the time you've been given to find the sources you need, decide what you want to say, and then draft, revise, and polish your paper. Instructors assign research papers so that they can assess not only your research skills but also your writing skills.

Tips on Writing a Research Paper

1. Even though your instructor may be your only reader, think of your potential audience as your fellow students—those taking the course with you, those who took it in recent years, and those who will take it in the near future. This way, you can count on a certain amount of shared knowledge. For a course in economics, for example, you can assume your audience knows what the Phillips Curve relationship is; a definition would be superfluous. For a course in literature, you won't need to inform your readers that Jonathan Swift was an eighteenth-century satirist. Think of your readers as colleagues who want to see what conclusions you have reached and what evidence you have used to support them.

2. Manage your time carefully. Divide the work into a number of tasks, develop a schedule that leaves lots of time for revision, and stick to your schedule.

3. Choose a subject that interests you. Define it as precisely as you can before beginning your research, but be prepared to modify, adapt, and revise it as you research and write your paper.

4. If you cannot find appropriate sources, ask a reference librarian for help.

5. When making notes, *always* record the author, title, publication data, and page numbers of the source.

6. Use your source material to support your own ideas, not the other way around.

7. Document your sources according to whatever style your instructor prefers.

8. Revise, edit, and proofread carefully. If you omit this step, the hours and weeks you have spent on your assignment will be wasted, not rewarded.

20

Researching Your Subject

Your first step in writing a research paper is the same as your first step in any writing task: select a suitable subject, preferably one you are curious about. Whether you are assigned a topic or choose your own, don't rush off to the library or log onto the Internet right away. A little preparation up front will save you a lot of time and possibly much grief later on.

First of all, if you're not sure what your instructor expects, clarify what is required of you. Next, even if your subject is tentative, check it with the 4-S test: is it significant, single, specific—or as specific as possible at this early stage—and supportable (researchable)? If not, refine it by using the techniques discussed in Chapter 2. Finally, consider what approach you might take in presenting your subject. Does it lend itself to a comparison? Process? Cause or effect? If the topic is assigned, often the wording of the assignment will suggest how your instructor wants you to develop it. Deciding up front what kind of paper you are going to write will save you hours of time, both in the library and at your desk.

Exercise 20.1

In the workplace, people rarely have the opportunity to select a research topic without consultation. In some cases, the subject is assigned or approved by a board of directors; in others, a committee is responsible for ensuring that a research project meets the company's needs.

Before you start your own research project, take some time to ensure that your proposed subject is appropriate for the time and space you have been given. The class should be divided into "committees" of four or five people. Each committee should be given four or five pieces of coloured paper, a different colour for each group.

- Each committee identifies chairperson and a note-taker. At the direction of the chair, each member of the committee presents an idea for a research paper. After each presentation, discuss the subject in terms of its significance to the target audience (the whole class, including the instructor). If the committee feels a subject requires revision to be significant, make these revisions as a group. It is important that the committee come to a consensus regarding any revisions.
- Once each subject is agreed upon as significant, record it on a slip of the coloured paper assigned to your committee.
- Repeat this procedure until your committee has identified at least one significant subject for each of its members.
- Toss your committee's subjects into the company's think tank (a container), along with the subjects submitted by the other "committees" in the class.
- Once all of the committees have submitted proposed research subjects that are deemed significant, another "committee" will now have a look at them.
- The chair of each committee now draws out of the think tank four or five proposed research subjects. Be sure to draw a representative sampling of colours from other committees.
- As a committee, discuss each subject that has been drawn from the think tank. Since each has already been approved as significant by another committee, your task is to determine whether each proposed subject is single and specific.
- For each subject, record any revisions that the committee deems necessary and briefly explain why.
- Return the revised subjects to their appropriate committees according to the corresponding coloured paper.
- When every committee has gotten back its original proposed research subjects, each group discusses the suggested revisions until everyone understands them.
- Next, as a committee, discuss whether each proposed subject is supportable. What sorts of research materials would you look for to help you explain and defend each subject?
- If, as a committee, you feel a revised subject is not supportable, discuss and be prepared to present your conclusions to the whole "Board."
- Record the final version of the proposed research subjects on a flip chart, ready to present to a board of directors. (You should have one subject for each member of the committee.)
- Present your committee's proposed research subjects before the Board of Directors (the whole class). Discuss the revisions and decide whether each proposal now meets the criteria of the 4-S test.

When you're sure your subject is appropriate and you've decided, at least tentatively, on the approach you're going to take, you are ready to focus on the kind of information you need to look for in your research. For example, if you've been asked to apply four theories of conflict to a case study, you won't waste time discussing the major schools of conflict theory or their development over the last few decades. You can restrict your investigation to sources that contain information relevant to your specific subject.

Once you have an idea of the kind of information you need in order to develop your topic, it's time to find the best sources you can. But how will you know if what you've found is "good" information?

Selecting Your Sources

Not all sources are created equal. There's no point in wasting time making notes on a source unless the information is relevant, current, and reliable. Evaluating the quality of source material before you use it is a key step in the research process.

To evaluate a print source, first check it over closely. Scan the table of contents, the headings, and chapters or articles to make sure the book or periodical contains information relevant to your topic. ("Periodicals" are publications that are produced at regular "periods," such as daily newspapers or monthly magazines.) Then check to see where the information comes from: its author, the date it was published, and the organization or company that published it. Most traditional print sources—newspapers, magazines, and scholarly journals—have fact-checkers and editorial boards to ensure that the information they publish is reliable.

Print sources are easier to assess for reliability than electronic sources. Anyone can post a Web site without knowing much about the topic. Yet the Internet and the World Wide Web have vastly increased the amount of potential research material, and it is essential to learn how to evaluate it. For example, if you are doing a report on a recent business venture or medical breakthrough, the most current information is going to be online. How do you decide, given the millions of pieces of information out there in cyberspace, what is useful for your specific purpose? Of course, when you use online editions of traditional print sources (e.g., electronic versions of newspapers, magazines, and books), you can assume the same standards of credibility and reliability. The CD-ROM full-text versions of *The Globe and Mail* or the *Financial Times* are no less (and no more) accurate than the printed versions.

With electronic sources that have no hard copy equivalent, the domain name is one place to begin your evaluation. Does the source's URL end with .com (commercial), .gov (government), or .edu (educational institution)?

Sites from these different sources will present data on a topic in different ways. A commercial site will probably attempt to influence consumers as well as to inform them. A .edu suffix suggests the credibility of a recognized college or university, but offbeat student Web pages or the informal musings of faculty members at the institution may share the suffix as well.

Another difference between print and electronic sources is authorship. There is seldom any doubt about who wrote a particular book or article. In online material, however, often no author (or date) is identified. Sometimes the person who compiles ("comp") or maintains ("maint") the Web site is the only one named. For academic research, it's wise to be cautious of "no-name" sources. If you wish to use information from one of these sources, be sure the organization or institution where it originated is reliable. You wouldn't want to be researching the history of discrimination in Canada, for example, and find yourself quoting from the disguised Web site of a hate organization.

Recognizing that much online work is collaborative and that several writers may have contributed to a potential source, it is a good idea to check out the people who are involved in producing it. Powerful online search engines such as Google make checking the author's reliability easier for electronic sources than it is for print sources. Simply key the author's name into the search engine and then evaluate the results to see if he or she is a credible person in the field. Often you'll be able to check the author's biography, credentials, other publications, and business or academic affiliation. If no author's name is given, you can check out the company, organization, or institution in the same way. Cyber-sleuthing is a useful skill to learn!

In the end, however, with both print and electronic sources, you must apply your own critical intelligence. Is the information timely, accurate, and reliable? Is there evidence of any inherent bias? How can you best make use of the findings to support and enhance your own ideas? The answers to these questions are critical to producing a good research paper.

Taking Good Research Notes

Once you've found a useful source, record the information you need. You'll save time and money by taking notes directly from your sources rather than photocopying everything. Most often, you will need a summary of the information. Follow the instructions on summarizing given on pages 258–59. Alternatively, you can paraphrase (see pages 261–64). Sometimes a quotation is appropriate; when this is the case, it's wise to make a copy of your source. Whenever you take notes—in any form—from a source, be sure to record the information you will need about the source itself. For each published source that you use in your paper, you should write down the following information.

For Books

1. Author(s)' or editor(s)' full name
2. Full title and edition number (if any)
3. City of publication
4. Name of publisher
5. Year of publication
6. Page(s) from which you took notes
(You will find all this information on the front and back of the title page.)

For Journal Articles

1. Author(s)' full name
2. Title of the article
3. Name of the journal
4. Volume number of the journal
5. Year of publication
6. Inclusive page numbers of the article
7. Page(s) from which you took notes

For Internet Sources

1. Author(s)' full name
2. Title of the document
3. Title of the database, periodical, or site
4. Name of the editor (if any)
5. Date of publication or last update
6. Name of the institution or organization sponsoring the site (if any)
7. Network address, or URL
8. Date you accessed the source

For Newspaper or Magazine Articles

1. Author(s)' full name
2. Title of the article
3. Title of the newspaper or magazine
4. Date of publication
5. Inclusive page numbers of the article
6. Page(s) from which you took notes

Some researchers record each piece of information on a separate index card. Others write their notes on sheets of paper, being careful to keep their own ideas separate from the ideas and words taken from sources. (Using a highlighter or a different colour of ink will help you to tell at a glance which ideas you have taken from a source.) Use the technology available to help you record, sort, and file your notes. You can record and file information by creating a database, and you can use a photocopier (usually available in the library) to copy relevant pages of sources for later use. Whatever system you use, be sure to keep a separate record for each source and to include the documentation information. If you don't, you'll easily get your sources confused. The result of this confusion could be inaccurate documentation, which could lead your reader to suspect you of plagiarizing.

Avoiding Plagiarism

Plagiarism is presenting someone else's ideas as your own. It's a form of stealing (the word comes from the Latin word *plagiarius*, which means "kidnapper.") There have been famous cases of respected journalists and academics who have been accused of plagiarizing the articles or books they have written. Suspected plagiarists who are found guilty often lose their jobs. Sometimes the accusation alone is enough to compromise an author's reputation and thus prevent him or her from continuing to work as a scholar or writer.

Students who copy essays or parts of essays from source material, download them from the Internet, or pay someone else to write them are cheating. And, in so doing, they commit a serious academic offence. Sometimes, however, academic plagiarism is accidental. It can result from careless note-taking or an incomplete understanding of the conventions of documentation. It is not necessary to identify the sources of common knowledge (e.g., *The solstice occurs twice a year; B.C. is Canada's westernmost province*) or proverbial sayings (e.g., *Love is blind*), but when you are not sure whether to cite a source, it's wise to err on the side of caution and provide documentation. Statistics should always be cited because, as you know, the meaning of numbers tends to change, depending on who is using them and for what purpose.

If, after you have finished your first draft, you are not sure which ideas need documenting and which don't, take your research notes and your outline to your instructor and ask. It's better to ask before submitting a paper than to try to explain a problem afterwards. Asking saves you potential embarrassment as well as time.

Using the Library

The electronic age has transformed the library—traditionally a warehouse of information contained within print sources—into a Learning Resource Centre: a portal to sources of information such as databases, e-books, e-journals, and the Internet, together with the traditional print and audiovisual resources. With new technology, information retrieval is faster, easier, and more efficient than ever before. However, this fact does not make the library any less intimidating to inexperienced users. Many students are overwhelmed by what at first appears to be a vast and confusing array of collections. Using the library becomes a less daunting prospect when you realize that all of its contents are organized and classified in such a way as to make finding information easy, if not simple. First, you need to know the organizational system used by your library. In this section, we will describe the collections found in most academic libraries, give you tips on how to access them, and summarize their strengths and weaknesses as sources. We will also decode some of the terminology used by library staff to describe and arrange collections.

THE ONLINE CATALOGUE (OPAC)

All but the smallest libraries today use automated catalogue systems to access collections. These online catalogues are commonly called OPACs (Online Public Access Catalogues). They may be stand-alone computer terminals within the library or accessible via the library's Web site. OPAC search options usually include title, author, subject, or keyword. How you search the catalogue will depend on what you are looking for and on what you already know.

Along with books, the OPAC may list other resources available in the library, such as periodical titles. If a periodical title is available in full-text format from one of the library's subscription databases, there may be a link to the title and, possibly, the text from the OPAC. Many of today's OPACs are Web-based, allowing the library to link to several useful sources of information. Your library's OPAC should be the first place you check for resources when beginning your research paper.

BOOKS

Book collections are represented in the online catalogue and may be searched in a variety of ways: by author, title, subject, keyword, and sometimes call number.

If you know of a particular book by title, choose that option and enter the **title**—*English Online*, for example. If your search is successful, write down the call number of the book. Alternatively, if you know that Eric Crump wrote a book on using the Internet, but you aren't sure of the title, do an **author** search, using the last name first: Crump, Eric. If you don't know of any books or authors in your field of research, begin by doing a **subject** or **subject keyword** search, such as "Internet." Most systems will respond by identifying relevant holdings and listing instructions to follow at the bottom of the computer screen. One of the biggest advantages of automated systems is that they identify the **status** of the book, letting you know if the book is in or when it is due back. Many systems allow you to place a **hold** on a book that is out. This means that when the book is returned to the library, it will be set aside for a period of time to allow you to go in and pick it up.

In order to find a book on the shelves, you must match the **call number** as it appears on the screen or catalogue card with the number taped on the spine of the book. Every book has a unique call number, and books are arranged on the shelves according to their call numbers. Guide signs are usually posted on the ends of shelving units (sometimes called **stacks**). Most colleges and universities use the **Library of Congress (LC)** system of classification, which uses a letter or combination of letters to begin the call number. The LC system is generally more suitable to academic collections than the Dewey decimal system used by public and smaller libraries.

Strengths	Weaknesses
• Author may be an authority on the subject	• Information cannot be as current as other sources
• Information is usually reliable (if published by a respected publisher)	
• Several aspects of the topic may be covered in the book	

A title keyword search is often the fastest way of retrieving books on your topic. If the library carries a book on your subject of research, chances are the topic will appear somewhere in the title.

PERIODICALS

Your library's collection of **periodicals**—publications that are issued at regular intervals, such as magazines, newspapers, and scholarly or technical journals—may contain useful articles on the subject you are researching.

To locate specific articles, you need to use one or more of the databases and periodical indexes available from your library. Before you begin, read the description of the database to determine if it includes periodicals on your topic. Each database has specific strengths and will allow you to search a subject in a wide variety of periodicals. From the selection offered in your library, you may be able to search databases such as EBSCOhost, ProQuest, LexisNexis, or InfoTrac.[1] These databases are delivered using the Internet, but are paid for by the library; their use is limited by license agreements to students and staff of the institution that pays for them. It may be possible to access them from home, but you will need a log-in or other means of identifying yourself as a student. Check with the library staff at your institution to find out more about access from your Internet service provider.

Databases have been created with users in mind; they have search interfaces that make finding information relatively simple. Once you have found the database you wish to use, you will be presented with a search box similar to those found on Internet search engines. Here you type in a word or phrase that relates to your research topic. For example, if you were researching the art movement *Impressionism*, you would enter this word in the text box. The search mechanism of the database would look for this term, and all articles containing the word *Impressionism* would be displayed

---

[1]Your purchase of *Essay Essentials,* Third Edition, entitles you to free access to InfoTrac.

on the screen. From the list, you would select those you think may be useful to you.

Most databases allow you to e-mail the results of your search. If you are pressed for time, do a quick search, e-mail the results to yourself, and check them later for relevancy. You can always delete them and start over.

Increasingly, full-text articles are included with each new release of these databases. This means you can print or download the text of an article without having to retrieve the actual magazine or journal. If you find a reference to a magazine article for which the full text is not available, be sure to note the title and date of the periodical in which it appeared; then check to see if your library subscribes to this periodical.

Strengths	Weaknesses
• Contain current information • Articles in databases are easy to retrieve • Databases are accessible 24/7	• Some articles may be opinion pieces but presented as factual

ENCYCLOPEDIAS

A useful source of general information on a topic is an encyclopedia; it is often a good place to begin your research. There are many types of encyclopedias, and several are now available online or on CD-ROM. Information is easy to find, usually through a user-friendly search screen, and CD versions of encyclopedias often include sound or video clips to enhance the text. You might begin your search with a general encyclopedia such as *Britannica*, *Colliers*, or the *World Book* and then move on to a specialized encyclopedia related to your subject. Look in the reference collection for a call number area that matches the one in which you found books on your topic (for example, medical encyclopedias are in the R section), or ask the reference librarian if a specialized encyclopedia exists on your subject.

Strengths	Weaknesses
• Provide a good overview of a subject • Often list titles of major books on the subject • Online editions are convenient and easy to use	• Information may be dated; not a good resource for current information

THE INTERNET

The most current information on any topic is likely to be found on the Internet. In fact, because the Net is so popular and so widely used, you may be tempted to think, "Everything I need is on the Net." Unfortunately, this is not so. Furthermore, relying on one source to the exclusion of all others is not a responsible way to gather information for a research paper. Although the Internet has made research easier because it can be used to access legitimate information sources, such as the databases described earlier, keep in mind that anyone can create a Web site and claim to be an expert on any topic.

The Web might be described as a huge library without an index. That is, the contents are not arranged according to any classification system or in an organized, logical fashion. You will need to use a **search engine** to help you find your way through the maze of information. Search engines scan sites on the Web for keywords identified by the researcher, then provide lists of sites that contain the keyword(s). Each search engine uses a different technique. None captures every reference to a topic, and some specialize in particular fields, so you may need to try more than one. Computer magazines regularly provide updated descriptions and evaluations of search engines, or your reference librarian can help you to choose an appropriate one.

FINDING A SEARCH ENGINE

The "start page" of the browser you use may have a list of search engines ready for you to click on, or there may be links to popular search engines from your library's Web site. Otherwise you can reach the engine by typing its **URL** (Universal Resource Locator) into the space provided on the screen. Here are some of the best-known search engines, together with their URLs:

Google Canada	http://www.google.ca/
Yahoo!	http://www.yahoo.com/
Yahoo! Canada	http://ca.yahoo.com/
AltaVista	http://altavista.com
Ask Jeeves	http://askjeeves.com/index.asp

USING A SEARCH ENGINE

Some search engines give you a choice of typing keywords or using a directory (a list of categories). It's a good idea to read the search tips or help screen available for most search engines. Not all search engines work the same way, so what works on one will not necessarily produce results on another.

Some search engines allow the use of Boolean operators: the use of AND, OR, and NOT to narrow your search. Many search engines offer advanced search screens to help you focus your search. Using quotation marks around your keywords also has an effect on the number and quality of the results. For instance, entering the phrase "brain stem research" in quotation marks vastly reduces the number of hits from the number you would get if you entered the phrase without the quotation marks. In this way, you can reduce the amount of time spent visiting Web sites that are not appropriate for your subject.

After you have checked out a site to determine its relevance to your paper, you can download it to a disk, print out all or some of it (be sure to include the source data), use links to other sites, or return to your search engine list and choose another site.

If you are not an experienced Internet user, check the Internet Public Library Web site for useful information about using the Web to find information: http://www.ipl.org

OTHER SOURCES

Most libraries contain other collections that may help you in your research. Don't overlook the possibility of finding useful information in the **audiovisual collection**, which normally includes videotapes, films, audiotapes, DVDs, and slide presentations. **Government publications** are another good source of information. The government, as one of the country's largest publishers, may have produced documents related to your topic. Many of these documents are available on the Internet.

Finally, the library is not the only source of information you can use. Interviews with people familiar with your subject are excellent sources because they provide a personal view, and they ensure that your paper will contain information not found in any other paper the instructor will read. It is perfectly acceptable to e-mail a question or set of questions to an expert in a field of study. **Original research**, such as surveys or questionnaires that you design, distribute, and analyze can also enhance your paper. Doing your own research is time consuming and requires some knowledge of survey design and interpretation, but it has the advantage of being original and current.

A good research paper will contain references to material from a variety of sources. Some instructors require a minimum number of references from several types of sources: books, periodicals, encyclopedias, interviews, etc. Most, but not all, institutions will allow you to use Internet sources, but use them with caution. Be mindful that anyone can place information, reliable or not, on any subject at a Web site. For this reason, it is best to use research gathered from reliable sources such as books, encyclopedias, scholarly journals, and reputable magazines.

As you conduct your research and think about your paper, keep your reader in mind. Every teacher faced with a pile of papers hopes to find some that are not simply a rehash of known facts. Before anything else, teachers are learners; they like nothing better than discovering something new. If you cannot find new information about your subject, be sure to provide an original interpretation of the evidence you find.

21

Summarizing, Paraphrasing, and Quoting

Once you have identified and evaluated your research sources, you must make accurate notes of what you find so that you can integrate the information into your own writing effectively. There are several ways to make notes, but the three most useful methods are **summary**, **paraphrase**, and **direct quotation**. When you summarize or paraphrase, you restate in your own words the idea(s) of another speaker or writer. When you quote, you reproduce the exact words of another speaker or writer. Let's look at these techniques in turn.

Summarizing

When you summarize information, you find the main ideas in an article, essay, report, or other document, and rephrase them. You shorten (condense) the most important idea or ideas in the source material and express your understanding of them in your own words. The purpose of summarizing is to give the reader an overview of the article, report, or chapter. If the reader is interested in the details, he or she will read the original.

It's hard to overstate how valuable the ability to summarize is. Note-taking in college is one form of summarizing. Abstracts of articles, executive summaries of reports, market surveys, legal decisions, research findings, and records (called "minutes") of meetings, to name only a few kinds of formal documents, are all summaries. Thesis statements and topic sentences are essentially summaries; so, often, are conclusions. In committee, group, or teamwork, imagination and creativity are valuable, but the ability to summarize is even more so. There is no communication skill that you will need or use more than summarizing.

As a matter of fact, you summarize for yourself and others in every conversation you have. With friends, you may summarize the plot of a movie you've just seen or what happened in class this morning. When your mother calls, you'll summarize the events of the past week that you want her to know about. But most of us are not very good at summarizing effectively, especially in writing. It is a skill that doesn't come naturally. *You need to practise it.* You'll improve very quickly, however, if you think about what you're doing—that is, if you are conscious rather than unconscious of the times and the circumstances in which you call upon your summarizing skills. The following exercise will get you started.

Exercise 21.1

1. In groups of three or four, choose a movie you have all seen, a course you have all taken, a party or concert you have all attended, or a book you have all read. Then, without discussing your topic first, spend five minutes each writing a one-paragraph summary. After you have written your summary, use a highlighter to accent your main points.

2. Read and compare your summaries. What similarities and differences do you notice? Can you all agree that one summary is both complete and accurate? If not—and the chances are slim that you will be able to agree—spend another five or ten minutes discussing which are the main ideas and which are secondary to a discussion of your topic.

3. Now revise your one-paragraph summary to include all the main ideas and no secondary details.

4. Once again, read and compare each other's paragraphs. Which paragraph summarizes the topic best? What features does this paragraph have that the others lack?

HOW TO WRITE A SUMMARY

The work you summarize can be as short as a paragraph or as long as a book, as the following passage demonstrates:

One of Edward de Bono's books is called *Six Thinking Hats.* [In it] he proposes that you adopt six different mind sets by mentally putting on six different coloured hats. Each hat stands for a certain way of thinking about a problem. By "putting on the hat" and adopting a certain role, we can think more clearly about the issues at hand. Because we're only "playing a role," there is little ego riding on what we say, so we are more free to say what we really want to say. De Bono likens the process of putting on the six hats one at a time to that of printing on a multicoloured map. Each colour is not a complete picture in itself. The map must go through the printing press six times, each time receiving a new colour, until we have the total picture.

Perrin, Timothy. "Positive Invention." *Better Writing for Lawyers.* Toronto: Law Society of Upper Canada, 1990. 51.

Notice that Perrin is careful to tell his readers the source of the ideas he is summarizing: both the author and the book are identified up front.

Before you can summarize anything, you need to *read* it and *understand* it. The material you need to summarize is usually an article, essay, or chapter (or some portion of it). Depending on how much of the piece you need, your summary will range from a few sentences to a paragraph—at most, two.[1] Here's how to proceed:

1. Read through the piece carefully, looking up any words you don't understand. Write their meanings between the lines, above the words they apply to.
2. Now read the article or essay again. Keep rereading it until you have grasped the main ideas and formed a mental picture of their arrangement. Highlight the title, subtitle, and headings (if there are any). The title often identifies the subject of the piece, and a subtitle usually indicates its focus. If the article is long, the writer will often divide it into a number of smaller sections, each with its own heading. These headings usually identify the main points. If there are no headings, pay particular attention to the introduction—you should find an overview of the subject and a statement of the thesis—and the conclusion, which often summarizes the information and points to the significance of the topic.
3. In point form, and in your own words, write out a bare-bones outline of the piece. Your outline should consist of the controlling idea (thesis) of the article and the main ideas, in the order in which they appear. Do not include any supporting details—statistics, specific facts, examples, etc.
4. Working from your outline, draft the summary. In the first sentence, identify the article or essay you are summarizing (by title, enclosed in quotation marks) and the author (by name, if known.) Complete the sentence by stating the author's controlling idea. Here's an example:

---

[1]This restriction applies only to the kind of research paper we are discussing in this part: one prepared for a college course. Other kinds of summary are longer. A précis, for example, is one-third the length of the source document. An abstract, which is a summary of a dissertation, academic paper, or public presentation, can be several paragraphs long.

In his essay "The Canadian Climate," D'Arcy McHale divides Canadians into two types: warm and cool.

Then state, in order, the author's main points. After each sentence in which you identify a main point, include any necessary explanation or clarification of that point. (The author, remember, developed each idea in the supporting details.) Try to resist going back to the article for your explanation. If you have truly understood the article, you should be able to explain each point from memory. If the author's conclusion contains any new information (i.e., is more than a summary and memorable statement), briefly state that information in your conclusion.

5. Revise your draft until it is coherent, concise, and makes sense to someone who is unfamiliar with the original work. It's a good idea to get someone to read through your summary to check it for clarity and completeness.

6. Don't forget to acknowledge your source. (Chapter 22 will show you how.)

The paragraph below summarizes the essay found on pages 198–99. Read it first, before you read the summary that follows.

In his essay "The Canadian Climate," D'Arcy McHale divides Canadians into two types: "warm" and "cool." The first category includes people who are enthusiastic about Canada's scenery, climate, and recreational activities, which they encourage newcomers to enjoy. Warm Canadians are also sincerely interested in learning about what life is like in the visitor's country of origin. In contrast, Cool Canadians are negative about their country and find it hard to believe that anyone from a warm climate would choose to endure the cold, bleak Canadian winters. Cool Canadians are not interested in detailed information about the visitor's country of origin, either; they are comfortable with their stereotypes. Finally, McHale acknowledges that the two types are mixed: each can at times behave like the other. Canadians, like the weather, are unpredictable, and newcomers are encouraged to accept them as they are and for themselves.

This seven-sentence paragraph (140 words) captures the gist of McHale's 600-word essay. Admittedly, it isn't very interesting. It lacks the flavour of the original. Summaries are useful for conveying an outline or a brief overview of someone else's ideas, but by themselves they are not very memorable. Details and specifics are what stick in a reader's mind; these are what your own writing should provide.

A summary should be entirely in your own words. Your ability to identify and interpret the author's meaning is evidence of your understanding of the article or essay. If you must include a short phrase from the source because there is no other way to word it, enclose the quoted material in quotation marks.

When writing a summary, do not

• introduce any ideas not found in the original
• change the proportion or emphasis of the original
• introduce your own opinion of the material

Exercise 21.2

Following the first five steps of the process outlined above, summarize "Ready, Willing . . . and Employable," which appears on pages 61–62. When you have completed your work, exchange papers with a partner. Use the following checklist to critique each other's summary.

	✔	✗	So-So
1. The first sentence gives the title and the author's name.			
2. The essay's thesis is clearly and concisely reworded.			
3. Each main point (topic sentence) is restated in a single sentence.			
4. Each main point is briefly explained.			
5. The summary includes no secondary details that could be eliminated without diminishing the reader's understanding.			
6. The summary is balanced and objective.			
7. The paragraph flows smoothly; there are no obvious errors in sentence structure, grammar, spelling, or punctuation.			

Exercise 21.3

Select an article from a professional journal in your field. Summarize it by following the six steps given on pages 258–59. Assume your reader is a professional in the field.

Choose an article that interests you from one of the regular sections (e.g., business, medicine, education, music, art) of a general news magazine such as *Maclean's*, *Time*, *Newsweek*, or the *Economist*. Summarize the article for a friend who is not an expert in the field and who has not read it. Do not evaluate the article or give your opinion about it. In a paragraph of approximately 150 to 200 words, simply inform your friend of its contents. Don't forget to cite your source!

Paraphrasing

When you paraphrase, you restate someone else's ideas in your own words. Unlike a summary, a paraphrase includes both the main and supporting ideas of your source. The usual purpose of a paraphrase is to express someone else's ideas more clearly and more simply—to translate what may be complex in the original into easily understandable prose. A paraphrase may be longer than the original, it may be about the same length, or it may be shorter. Whatever its length, a good paraphrase satisfies three criteria:

1. It is clear, concise, and easy to understand.
2. It communicates the idea(s) of the original passage.
3. It doesn't contain any idea(s) not found in the original passage.

Occasionally, you may need to clarify technical language or explain an aphorism, a proverb, or other saying that states a principle, offers an insight, or teaches a point. Statements that pack a lot of meaning into few words can be explained only at greater length. For example, one of the principal tenets of modern biology is "ontogeny recapitulates phylogeny." It simply isn't possible to paraphrase this principle in three words. (It means that as an embryo grows, it follows the same pattern of development that the animal did in the evolutionary process.)

Working with a partner or a small group, discuss the meaning of the following expressions. When you are sure you understand them, write a paraphrase of each one.

1. One picture is worth a thousand words.
2. Money talks.
3. More haste, less speed.
4. Birds of a feather flock together.

5. Too many cooks spoil the broth.
6. Nothing ventured, nothing gained.
7. Garbage in, garbage out.

To paraphrase a passage, you need to dig down through your source's words to the underlying ideas and then reword those ideas as clearly and simply as you can. Like summarizing, the ability to paraphrase is not an inborn talent; it takes patience and much practice to perfect it. But the rewards are worth your time and effort. First, paraphrasing improves your reading skill as well as your writing skill. Second, it improves your memory. In order to paraphrase accurately, you must thoroughly understand what you've read—and once you understand something, you're not likely to forget it.

First, let's look at how *not* to paraphrase. Assume we are writing an essay on designing an energy-efficient home, and we want to use the information given in the following paragraph.

The site and how the building relates to it is a critical determinant in the calculation of energy consumption. The most profound effects, and the ones the individual has least control over, are the macro-climatic (regional) factors of degree days, design temperature, wind, hours of bright sunshine, and the total solar insolation. Other factors which can have an enormous effect on the energy consumption of a house are micro-climatic. These include the topography of a site, the sun path, specific wind regime, vegetation, soil, and the placement of other buildings.

Argue, Robert. *The Well-Tempered House: Energy-Efficient Building for Cold Climates.* Toronto: Renewable Energy, 1980. 14.

There are two pieces of information in this paragraph that we want to include in our essay:

1. Some of the factors influencing energy consumption relate to the climate and weather patterns of the region (macro-climatic factors).
2. Some of the factors influencing energy consumption relate to the specific characteristics of the building site (micro-climatic factors).

If we are not careful, or if we don't have much experience with paraphrasing, our paragraph might look something like this:

In *The Well-Tempered House*, Robert Argue explains that a designer must consider two critical determinants in building an energy-efficient home. The most important factors, and the ones the individual has least control over, are the macro-climatic (regional) factors of degree days, design temperature, wind, hours of sunshine, and the total solar insolation. The other significant factors are the micro-climatic ones, which include the topography of the site, the sun path, wind regime, vegetation, soil, and the location of other buildings on or near the site.

This is plagiarism. Although we have indicated the source of the information, we have not indicated that the wording is almost identical to that of the original. Of the total 90 words, 50 come from the source. There are no visual or verbal cues to alert the reader that these are Argue's words, not ours. Let's try again.

In *The Well-Tempered House*, Robert Argue identifies two significant influences the cost-conscious home builder must consider in designing an energy-efficient house. The first and strongest influence is the typical weather of the region. The designer must be familiar with such "macro-climatic factors" as "degree days" (the difference between the indoor comfort temperature and the average daily outdoor temperature), "design temperature" (the lowest temperature to be expected during the heating season), wind, and the total effect of the sun. The other influences are called "micro-climatic factors" and include the site's topography (elevation and slope of the land), sun path, prevailing wind pattern, and the presence or absence of vegetation and nearby buildings.

Although this draft is technically a paraphrase rather than plagiarism, it doesn't demonstrate very much work on our part. We have replaced the source's words with synonyms and added explanations where the original is too technical to be easily understood by a general reader, but our paragraph still follows the original too closely. A paraphrase should not be used to pass off someone else's ideas as your own by changing a few words and sentences. A good paraphrase goes further. It uses source information but rearranges it, rephrases it, and combines it with the writer's own ideas to create something new. Let's try once more:

The cost-conscious home builder must consider a number of factors that will affect the energy consumption of his or her new home. The exterior design of the house should take advantage of the natural slope of the land, the presence of sheltering vegetation, prevailing wind patterns, the path of the sun, and other characteristics of the building site (Argue 14). In addition to sufficient insulation, the interior should feature appropriate heating and cooling devices to keep the family comfortable during the coldest winter days and the hottest summer days. To keep costs down, these devices should take advantage of the natural energy sources available: wind, sun, and seasonal fluctuations in temperature can all be used to harness and conserve energy. With careful planning, a new home can be designed to maximize the advantages of even an apparently unlikely site, minimize the negative effects of temperature and weather, and cost surprisingly little to maintain at a comfortable temperature year-round.

Here we have used paraphrase to incorporate information from a published source into a paragraph whose topic and structure are our own. This is how paraphrase can be used both responsibly and effectively. If you want to take ideas more directly from a source, retaining the original arrangement and some of the wording, use quotations.

Quoting

Of the three methods of introducing ideas from a source into your research paper, direct quotation is the one you should use least. (The exception is the literary essay, in which quotations from the original work are the evidence in your argument.) If you use too many quotations, your paper will be a patchwork of the ideas of others, in their own words, and very little of your own thinking will be communicated to the reader. Remember that the main reason teachers assign research papers is to test your ability to find, digest, and make sense of specific information about a topic. If what you hand in consists of a string of quotations, your paper will satisfy only one of these three capabilities.

In most research papers, the ideas or statistics are the important things, not the wording of an idea or the explanation of a statistic. Occasionally, however, you will find that someone else—an expert in a particular field, a well known author, or a respected public figure—has said what you want to say eloquently, vividly, more memorably than you could ever hope to say it. In such cases, quotations, as long as they are short and not used too frequently, are useful in developing your topic. Carefully woven into your paragraphs, they help convince the reader of the validity of what you have to say. Use quotations in writing the way you use salt in cooking: sparingly. You want to enhance, not overwhelm, the flavour of your creation.

You can quote from two kinds of sources—

- people you know, or have heard speak, or have interviewed
- print, electronic, or recorded materials (e.g., books, articles, CD-ROMs, Web sites, films, tapes)

—and your quotation may be long or short.

BLOCK AND SPOT QUOTATIONS

If the material you are quoting is more than 40 words or four typed lines, it is a long—or **block**—quotation. After you have introduced it, you begin the quoted passage on a new line and indent all lines of the quotation ten spaces or 2.5 cm from the left margin. *Do not put quotation marks around a block quotation.* The ten-space indentation is the reader's visual cue that this portion of the paragraph is someone else's words, not yours. Here's an example:

Committees put a lot of thought into the design of fast foods. As David Bodanis points out with such good humour in *The Secret House*, potato chips are

> an example of total destruction foods. The wild attack on the plastic wrap, the slashing and tearing you have to go through is exactly what the manufacturers wish. For the thing about crisp foods is that they're louder than non-crisp ones. . . . Destructo-packaging sets a favourable mood. . . . Crisp foods have to be loud in the upper register. They have to produce a high-frequency shattering; foods which generate low-frequency rumblings are crunchy, or slurpy but not crisp. . . .

Companies design potato chips to be too large to fit into the mouth, because in order to hear the high-frequency crackling, you need to keep your mouth open. Chips are 80 percent air, and each time we bite one we break open the air-packed cells of the chip, making that noise we call "crispy." Bodanis asks:

> How to get sufficiently rigid cell walls to twang at these squeaking harmonics? Starch them. The starch granules in potatoes are identical to the starch in stiff shirt collars. . . . [In addition to starch,] all chips are soaked in fat. . . . So it's a shrapnel of flying starch and fat that produces the conical air-pressure wave when our determined chip-muncher finally gets to finish her chomp.

Ackerman, Diane. *A Natural History of the Senses.* New York: Random House, 1990. 142–43.

Notice that Ackerman is careful to tell her readers the source of her quotations. To introduce the first one, she gives the author's full name and the title of his book. To introduce the second quotation, which is from the same book, she simply identifies the author by surname. Thus, she doesn't waste words by repeating information, nor does she leave readers wondering where the quotation came from. (The only information missing is the publication data—city, publisher, and date—which is presented in the list of sources. See Chapter 22 for information on how to document your sources.)

A **spot quotation** is a word, a phrase, or a short sentence that is incorporated into one of your own sentences. *Put quotation marks before and after a spot quotation.* The quotation marks are a signal to the reader that these aren't your words; a new voice is speaking. The following paragraph contains several spot quotations.

"You are what you quote," in the words of the American essayist Joseph Epstein, himself a heavy user of quotations and the writer who introduced "quotatious" into my vocabulary. Winston Churchill understood the value of a well-aimed quotation: as a young man he read a few pages of *Bartlett's Familiar Quotations* every day to spruce up his style and compensate for his lack of a university education. [Gradually,] he transformed himself from a quotatious writer into the most quoted politician of the western world. . . . Fowler's *Modern English Usage* warns against quoting simply to demonstrate knowledge: "the discerning reader detects it and is contemptuous," while the undiscerning reader finds it tedious. A few years ago Garry Trudeau made fun of George Will's compulsive quoting by inventing a researcher who served as "quote boy" in Will's office: "'Quote boy! Need something on the banality of contemporary society.' 'Right away, Dr. Will!'" . . . As for me, I say don't judge, because you might get judged, too. That's how the quotation goes, right?

Fulford, Robert. "The Use and Abuse of Quotations." *Globe and Mail* 11 Nov. 1992: C1.

HOW TO MODIFY A QUOTATION

In addition to illustrating how to introduce and format block quotations, the examples given above also show how to modify a quotation to fit your space and suit your purpose. Although *you must quote exactly and never misrepresent or distort your source's intention*, you may, for reasons of conciseness or smoothness, omit or add a word or phrase or even a sentence or two.

- To leave out a word or words, indicate the omission by replacing the word(s) you've omitted with three spaced dots called **ellipses** (. . .). If the omission comes at the end of your sentence, add a fourth dot as the period.
- If you need to add or change a word or words to make the quoted passage more readable within your paragraph, use **square brackets** around your own words, as we did when we added "In addition to starch" in Ackerman's second block quotation from Bodanis. If you have omitted some words from a source, you may need to add a transitional phrase or

change the first letter of a word to a capital: [T]hus. Another reason for changing words in a quoted passage is to keep the verb tenses consistent throughout your paragraph. If you are writing in the present tense and the passage you are quoting is in the past tense, you can change the verbs to present tense (so long as the change doesn't distort the meaning) and put square brackets around them so the reader knows you have made these changes.

Modifying short quotations to make them fit smoothly into your own sentences without altering the source's meaning takes practice. Re-read the paragraph that we have quoted on page 266. Notice that to make Fulford's original slightly shorter and easier to read, we made a couple of minor alterations to the original. The signals to the reader that something has been added or left out are the same as those used in a block quotation: square brackets and ellipses.

HOW TO INTEGRATE QUOTATIONS INTO YOUR WRITING

When you decide to quote source material, you must find a way of introducing the quotation so that it will blend as seamlessly as possible into your writing. Don't simply park someone else's words in the middle of your paragraph; you'll disrupt the flow of thought. If Diane Ackerman were not so skilful a writer, she might have "dumped" quotations into her paragraph instead of integrating them. Contrast the readability of the paragraph below with that of Ackerman's original (on page 265).

Companies design potato chips to be too large to fit into the mouth because, in order to hear the high-frequency crackling, you need to keep your mouth open. Chips are 80 percent air, and each time we bite one, we break open the air-packed cells of the chip, making that crispy noise. "The starch granules in potatoes are identical to the starch in stiff shirt collars." Starch is just one of the ingredients that contribute to the crispiness of potato chips. "All chips are soaked in fat." "So it's a shrapnel of flying starch and fat that produces the conical air pressure wave when our determined chip-muncher finally gets to finish her chomp."

Without transitional phrases, the paragraph lacks coherence and doesn't make sense.

Every quotation should be introduced and integrated into an essay in a way that makes clear the relationship between the quotation and your own argument. There are four ways to integrate a spot quotation.

1. You can introduce it with a phrase such as "According to X," or "Y states" (or *observes*, or *comments*, or *writes*), followed by a comma.

Different verbs suggest different attitudes toward the quoted material. For example, "Fulford *suggests* that writers should not overuse quotations" is more tentative than "Fulford *warns* that writers should not overuse quotations." Other verbs you can use to introduce quotations are *asserts, notes, points out, maintains, shows, reports,* and *claims.* Choose your introductory verbs carefully, and be sure to use a variety of phrases. The repetitive "X says," "Y says," and "Z says," is a sure way to put your reader to sleep.

2. If your introductory words form a complete sentence, use a colon (:) to introduce the quotation.

George Bernard Shaw's poor opinion of teachers is well known: "Those who can, do; those who can't, teach."

Oscar Wilde's opinion of teachers is less famous but even more cynical than Shaw's: "Everybody who is incapable of learning has taken to teaching."

3. If the passage you are quoting is a couple of words, a phrase, or anything less than a complete sentence, do not use any punctuation to introduce it.

Oscar Wilde defined fox hunters as "the unspeakable in full pursuit of the uneatable."

Wilde believed that people "take no interest in a work of art until they are told that the work in question is immoral."

4. If you insert your own words into the middle of a quotation, use commas to separate the source's words from yours.

"It is a truth universally acknowledged," writes Jane Austen at the beginning of *Pride and Prejudice,* "that a single man in possession of a good fortune must be in want of a wife."

In general, periods and commas are placed inside the quotation marks (see the examples above). Unless they are part of the quoted material, colons, semicolons, question marks, exclamation marks, and dashes are placed outside the quotation marks. Use single quotation marks to mark off a quotation within a quotation.

According to John Robert Colombo, "The most widely quoted Canadian aphorism of all time is Marshall McLuhan's 'The medium is the message.'"

Block quotations are normally introduced by a complete sentence fol-lowed by a colon (for example, "X writes as follows:"). Then you copy the quotation, beginning on a new line and indenting ten spaces or 2.5 cm. If your introductory statement is not a complete sentence, use a comma or no punctuation, whichever is appropriate. The passage by Diane Ackerman on page 265 contains examples of both ways to introduce block quotations. Turn to it now. Can you explain why Ackerman has used no punctuation to introduce the first block quotation and a colon to introduce the second one?

Exercise 21.6

For each of the following quotations, make up three different sentences as follows:

 a. Introduce the *complete quotation* with *a phrase followed by a comma*.
 b. Introduce the *complete quotation* with *an independent clause followed by a colon*.
 c. Introduce a *portion of the quotation* with a phrase or statement that requires no punctuation between it and the quotation. Use ellipses and square brackets, if necessary, to signal any changes you make in the original wording.

Example: Education is the ability to listen to almost anything without losing your temper or your self-confidence. (Robert Frost)

 a. According to Robert Frost, "Education is the ability to listen to almost any-thing without losing your temper or your self-confidence." (complete quo-tation introduced by phrase + comma)
 b. Robert Frost had a peculiar notion of higher learning: "Education is the ability to listen to almost anything without losing your temper or your self-confidence." (complete quotation introduced by independent clause + colon)
 c. Robert Frost defined education as "the ability to listen to . . . anything without losing [one's] temper or [one's] self-confidence." (partial quota-tion introduced by phrase requiring no punctuation; changes indicated with ellipses and square brackets)

 1. I find the three major administrative problems on a campus are sex for the students, athletics for the alumni, and parking for the faculty. (Clark Kerr, former president of the University of California)
 2. Education is not a *product*: mark, diploma, job, money—in that order; it is a *process*, a never-ending one. (Bel Kaufman, author of *Up the Down Staircase*)

3. School days, I believe, are the unhappiest in the whole span of human existence. (H. L. Mencken, American humorist)

4. In the first place, God made idiots. This was for practice. Then he made school boards. (Mark Twain)

5. Education makes a people easy to lead, but difficult to drive; easy to govern, but impossible to enslave. (Lord Brougham, founder of the University of London, 1825)

TIPS ON USING QUOTATIONS IN YOUR WRITING

1. **Use quotations sparingly and for a specific purpose**, such as for emphasis or to reinforce an important point. Avoid the temptation to produce a patchwork paper—one that consists of bits and pieces of other people's writing stuck together to look like an original work. Far from impressing your readers, overuse of quotations will give them the impression you have nothing of your own to say.

2. **Be sure every quotation is an accurate reproduction of the original passage.** If you need to change or omit words, indicate those changes with square brackets or ellipses, as appropriate.

3. **Be sure every quotation is relevant.** No matter how interesting or well worded, a quotation that does not clearly and directly relate to your subject does not belong in your essay. An irrelevant quotation will either confuse readers or annoy them (they'll think it's padding), or both.

4. **Make clear the link between the quotation and your controlling idea.** Don't assume readers will automatically see the connection you see between the quotation and your topic sentence. Comment on the quotation so they will be sure to make the connection you intend. If you have used a block quotation, your explanatory comment can sometimes form the conclusion of your paragraph.

5. **Always identify the source of a quotation.** This can be done by mentioning in your paragraph the name of the author and, if appropriate, the title of the source of the quotation. Include the page number(s) in a parenthetical citation. See Chapter 22 for details, and follow the format your instructor prefers.

Exercise 21.7

Read the passages below and answer the questions following each.

1.   Whenever college teachers get together informally, sooner or later the conversation turns to students' excuses. The stories students tell to justify

absences or late assignments are an endless source of amusement among faculty. These stories tend to fall into three broad thematic categories.

Accident, illness, and death are at the top of the list. If the stories were true, such incidents would be tragic, not funny. But how could any instructor be expected to keep a straight face at being told, "I can't take the test Friday because my mother is having a vasectomy"? Or "I need a week's extension because my friend's aunt died"? Or—my personal favourite— "The reason I didn't show up for the final exam was because I have inverse testosterone"?

Problems with pets rank second in the catalogue of student excuses. Animals take precedence over tests: "I can't be at the exam because my cat is having kittens and I'm her coach"; and they are often responsible for a student's having to hand in an assignment late. The age-old excuse "My dog ate my homework" gets no more marks for humour than it does for originality, but occasionally a student puts a creative spin on this old chestnut. Would you believe "My paper is late because my parrot crapped in my computer"?

In third place on the list of students' tales of extenuating circumstances are social commitments of various sorts. "I was being arraigned in Chicago for arms dealing"; "I had to see my fence to pick out a ring for my fiancée"; and "I can't take the exam on Monday because my Mom is getting married on Sunday and I'll be too drunk to drive back to school" are just three examples collected by one college teacher in a single semester.

An enterprising computer programmer could easily compile an "excuse bank" that would allow students to type in the code number of a standard explanation and zap it to their professors. I suspect, however, that there would be little faculty support for such a project. Electronic excuses would lack the humour potential of live ones. Part of the fun comes from watching the student confront you, face to face, shamelessly telling a tale that would make Paul Bunyan blush.

1. Are all the quotations relevant to the subject of this brief essay? Are they sufficiently limited, or could the essay be improved by leaving any out?
2. Underline the specific connections the writer makes between her quotations and her controlling idea.
3. What purpose does the concluding sentence serve? Would the essay be equally effective without it? Why?

2.   U.S. federal drug policy, especially the mandatory minimum sentences for drug offenders enacted by Congress in 1987, has so distressed federal judges that approximately 10 percent of them will not hear drug trials. Judge Jack B. Weinstein of Brooklyn, N.Y., is a case in point. In an April 1993 memo to all the judges in his district, he announced that he would no longer preside over trials of defendants charged with drug crimes:

> One day last week I had to sentence a peasant woman from West Africa [with four dependent children] to forty-six months. . . .

On the same day I sentenced a man to thirty years as a second drug offender—a heavy sentence mandated by the Guidelines and statute. These two cases confirm my sense of frustration about much of the cruelty I have been party to in connection with the "war on drugs" that is being fought by the military, police, and courts rather than by our medical and social institutions.

I myself am unsure how this drug problem should be handled, but I need a rest from the oppressive sense of futility that these cases leave. Accordingly, I have taken my name out of the wheel for drug cases. This resolution leaves me uncomfortable since it shifts the "dirty work" to other judges. At the moment, however, I simply cannot sentence another impoverished person whose destruction can have no discernible effect on the drug trade. I wish I were in a position to propose a solution, but I am not. I'm just a tired old judge who has temporarily filled his quota of remorse-lessness.

The sentencing guidelines that Congress requires judges to follow are so harsh they cause, in Weinstein's words, "overfilling [of] our jails and . . . unneccessary havoc to families, society, and prisons." As a senior judge, Weinstein can choose the cases he hears. But 90 percent of judges are not so fortunate. After they have imposed on a low-level smuggler or a poverty-stricken "mule" a sentence far harsher than those mandated for someone convicted of rape or manslaughter, one wonders how—or if—judges can sleep at night.

"The War on Drugs: A Judge Goes AWOL." *Harper's Magazine* Dec. 1993: 18.

1. This writer uses both block and spot quotations to develop her point. Where does she make clear the connection between the block quotation and her topic?

2. The original passage from which the writer extracted her spot quotation reads as follow: "Most judges today take it for granted, as I do, that the applicable guideline for the defendant before them will represent an excessive sentence. The sentencing guidelines result, in the main, in the cruel imposition of excessive sentences, overfilling our jails and causing unnecessary havoc to families, society, and prisons." Why did the writer modify the quotation the way she did?

3. In tip 4 (see page 270), we advise you not to introduce a quotation and just leave it hanging but to comment on it. Where does this writer comment on the quotations she has used?

Additional Suggestions for Writing

1. Interview someone two generations removed from you (e.g., a grand-parent, an elderly neighbour) about his or her life as a young person. What were the sources of entertainment? Leisure activities? Work? Family responsibilities? Major concerns? Goals? Write an essay in which you tell this person's story, using summary, paraphrase, and quotation to develop your main points.

2. Interview a friend, classmate, or relative on one of the following topics. Then write an essay using summary, paraphrase, and quotation to help tell your reader how your interviewee answered the question.
   a. If you were to live your life over knowing what you know now, what would you do differently?
   b. Explain what being a Canadian (or a parent, or childless, or unem-ployed, or successful, or a member of a particular religious group) means to you.
   c. "Once I was _____; now I am _____."

3. Research a topic of particular interest to you and write an essay using summary, paraphrasing, and quotation to develop your main points.

4. Select a news article or a group of articles dealing with a current issue in the scientific, business, arts, or medical community. In a paragraph of approximately 200 to 300 words, summarize the issue for your instructor, who has just returned from spending six months in the wilderness without access to either print or electronic media.

22

Documenting Your Sources

Documentation is the process of acknowledging source material. When you document a source, you provide information that

1. tells your readers that the ideas they are reading have been borrowed from another writer, and
2. enables your readers to find the source and read the material for themselves.

When acknowledging your sources in a research paper, you need to follow a system of documentation. There are many different systems, but one of the most widely used is that of the Modern Language Association (MLA). The instructions and examples in this chapter are a slightly simplified version of the principles outlined by Joseph Gibaldi in the *MLA Handbook for Writers of Research Papers*, 5th ed. (New York: MLA, 1999. http://www.mla.org). Most instructors in English and the humanities require students to use MLA style. Instructors in the social sciences (psychology, sociology, political science, and economics) usually expect papers to conform to the principles of APA style, based on the *Publication Manual of the American Psychological Association*, 5th ed. (Washington, DC: APA, 2001. http://www.apa.org). You will find instruction and examples of APA style on our Web site (http://www.essayessentials3e.nelson.com). For research papers in the biological sciences, your instructor may require the format outlined in the *CBE* [Council of Biology Editors] *Style Manual: A Guide for Authors, Editors, and Publishers in the Biological Sciences* (http://www.bedfordstmartins.com/online/site8.html/). Many academic institutions publish their own style guides, which are available in college and university libraries and bookstores. Be sure to ask your instructor which documentation style he or she prefers.

Introduction: The Two-Part Principle of Documentation

Documentation styles vary in their details, but all styles require that authors

- identify in a parenthetical reference any information taken from a source, and
- list all sources for the paper on a separate page at the end.

A **parenthetical reference** (called a **reference citation** in APA style) tells the reader that the information preceding the parentheses[1] is borrowed from a source and provides a key to the full identification of that source. For the most part, footnotes are no longer used to document source material; they are used to give additional information that cannot be conveniently worked into the body of your paragraph. (Note the example in this paragraph.)

A **Works Cited** list (called **References** in APA style) is a list of all the sources from which you have borrowed words, ideas, data, or other material in your paper.[2] Preparing and presenting a Works Cited list requires paying close attention to the details of presenting the information required in each entry. The format—including the order of information, capitalization, and punctuation—prescribed by your style guide must be followed *exactly*. This requirement may sound picky, but there is a good reason to abide by it.

Every kind of source you use requires a particular format. If entries are formatted correctly, an experienced reader can tell by glancing at them what kinds of sources you have used: books, journal articles, newspaper articles, Web documents, etc. If you use the wrong style, or leave something out, or scramble the elements in a citation, you will mislead or confuse your reader. Fortunately, technology is available to help you make the task of documenting much less onerous than it once was. Before you begin taking notes, find a reference manager program such as EndNote or ProCite. (See http://www.isiresearchsoft.com for these and other managers.) Some programs offer a 30-day free trial. Different programs have different features, but most will help you keep track of the notes you've taken from various sources, and all will format your Works Cited or References list for you.

---

[1] A punctuation note: *parentheses* means the pair of curvy punctuation marks: ( ). *Brackets* are the pair of square marks that surround altered words or phrases in a quotation: [ ].
[2] Formerly, this list was called a *Bibliography*.

How to Punctuate Titles in MLA Style

Unless you are instructed otherwise, *italicize* titles and subtitles of any work that is published as a whole—e.g., the names of books, plays, periodicals (newspapers, magazines, and journals), films, radio and television programs, compact discs—or underline them if you are using a pen or a typewriter. Put quotation marks around the titles of works published within larger works—e.g., the names of articles, essays, poems, songs, and individual episodes of television or radio programs. Also put quotation marks around the titles of unpublished works, such as lectures and speeches. Use capital letters for the first, the last, and all main words in a title and subtitle even if your source capitalizes only the first word in a title.

Parenthetical References in MLA Style

Every time you include in your paper a quotation, paraphrase, summary, fact, or idea you have borrowed from another writer, you must identify the source in parentheses immediately following the borrowed material. The parenthetical reference tells your reader that what he or she has just read comes from somewhere else, and it points your reader to the complete information about the source in your Works Cited. Parenthetical references should be as short and simple as possible while still fulfilling these two purposes.

The standard practice in MLA style is to provide the surname (last name) of the author of the source material and the page number where the material was taken from. Once your reader has the author's name and page number, he or she can find complete bibliographic information about the source in your Works Cited list at the end of your paper. Of course, electronic sources present a challenge to this author-based citation method because they often lack an identifiable author, and they rarely include page numbers. More on this later.

You need to include a piece of source information only once; don't repeat information unnecessarily. For example, if you've already mentioned the author's name in your paragraph, you only need to give the page reference in the parentheses.

Below is an excerpt from a research paper. The writer uses summary, paraphrase, and quotation, and gives the necessary source information in parentheses immediately following each borrowing. This excerpt also demonstrates how to omit a word or words from a source, using ellipses, and how to add or change a word or words, using square brackets.

The attractive young people who are portrayed in tobacco advertising make it easy for viewers to forget the terrible consequences of tobacco addiction. Cigarette advertisements routinely portray happy, energetic young people engaging in athletic activities under invariably sunny skies. The implication of these ads is that smoking is not a deterrent to an active lifestyle; in fact, it may even be a prerequisite (Cunningham 67).

Full parenthetical citation

It is difficult to overstate the impact of tobacco advertising on young people. As Cunningham points out,

> Few teenagers begin smoking for cigarette's inherent physical qualities. Instead, teens are attracted to smoking for its image attributes, such as the five S's: sophistication, slimness, social acceptability, sexual attractiveness, and status. Marketing gives a cigarette a false "personality." (66)

Block quotation

Abbreviated parenthetical citation

Is it any wonder that young people continue to take up the habit?

In an effort to reverse the trend of teenage tobacco addiction, the federal government sponsors awareness campaigns to demonstrate how the tobacco industry dupes and manipulates young people. According to Robert Sheppard, the industry plays on teenagers' "need [for] something to rebel against . . . [which] is exactly how cigarette manufacturers market their wares" (20). To counteract the image of smoking as symbol of rebellion, government anti-tobacco campaigns present smoking as a symbol of conformity.

Short quotation with
- *words changed*
- *words left out*
- *parenthetical citation*

Yielding to pressure from the government and the community, the tobacco industry has begun to sponsor programs aimed at restricting youth access to tobacco products. In a comprehensive review, however, the Ontario Medical Association (OMA) concludes that these programs are ineffective and makes several recommendations to strengthen youth reduction initiatives (OMA).

Parenthetical citation of paraphrase

The OMA recommends that all parties interested in reducing tobacco use endorse a comprehensive tobacco control program. The Association offers to work with the Canadian Medical Association and other interested parties to ensure that its position statement is published as widely as possible. And finally, the OMA recommends that all tobacco industry-sponsored programs be carefully monitored in the future (OMA).

Parenthetical citation of summary

Study the way the writer of this excerpt has used parenthetical references to identify information sources. The introductory paragraph ends with a paraphrase, which is immediately followed by a parenthetical reference. Because the author's name is not mentioned in the writer's paragraph, it is given in parentheses, together with the number of the page on which the information was found. For more details, the reader would turn to the Works Cited page at the end of the paper, where Cunningham's book would be listed as follows:

```
Cunningham, Rob. Smoke and Mirrors: The Canadian Tobacco
     War. Ottawa: IDRC, 1996.
```

The second paragraph includes a block quotation from the same source. The author's name is given in the statement that introduces the quotation, so the parentheses contain only the page number on which the quotation can be found.

The third paragraph includes a short quotation integrated into the writer's own sentence. The introductory phrase gives the author's name, so the parenthetical reference gives only the page number of the article on which this partial quotation is found. In the Works Cited, this source would be listed as follows:

```
Sheppard, Robert. "Ottawa Butts Up against Big Tobacco."
     Maclean's 6 Dec. 1999: 29-24.
```

In the fourth paragraph, the writer includes both a paraphrase and a summary of information found in an unsigned article posted on the Web site of the Ontario Medical Association. The source document is not paginated, so no page number is given. Complete information about this source would appear in the alphabetical list of Works Cited under the name of the association sponsoring the site:

```
Ontario Medical Association. "More Smoke and Mirrors:
     Tobacco Industry Sponsored Youth Prevention Programs in
     the Context of Comprehensive Tobacco Control Programs
     in Canada." A Position Statement. <http://www.oma.org/
     phealth/smokeandmirrors.htm>. (27 Apr. 2002).
```

EXAMPLES OF PARENTHETICAL REFERENCES: TRADITIONAL PRINT SOURCES

1. If you name the source author in your paragraph, give just the page number in parentheses.

```
Isajiw asserts that the twentieth century "has produced
more refugees and exiles than any other preceding period
since the fall of the Roman Empire" (66).
```

The Works Cited entry for this book is on page 282.

2. If you do not name the source author in your paragraph, give the author's surname and the page number.

```
The effect of "status drop" on the psychological well-
being of immigrants can be substantial: "Especially among
those more highly educated, this experience can cause
feelings of bitterness or hostility. . . ." (Isajiw 97).
```

3. If no author is named in the source, give the first few words of the Works Cited entry.

```
Legislation to reduce the amount of pollution generated by
large-scale vehicles has been on the federal agenda for
some time: "Canada has said it will toughen pollution-
emission rules for all new vehicles, ending a loophole
that allowed less stringent standards for popular sport-
utility vehicles and minivans" ("Canada to Toughen" A6).
```

The Works Cited entry for this source is on page 285.

4. If your source was published in more than one volume, give the volume number before the page reference.

```
Only once in his two-volume work does Erickson suggest
conspiracy (2: 184).
```

The Works Cited entry for this source is on page 283.

5. If you are quoting from a literary classic or the Bible, use Arabic numerals separated by periods to identify act, scene, and lines from a play or a Biblical chapter and verse.

```
In Shakespeare's play, the duke's threat to give "measure
for measure" (5.1.414) echoes the familiar passage in the
Bible (Matthew 7.1-2).
```

EXAMPLES OF PARENTHETICAL REFERENCES: ELECTRONIC SOURCES

Parenthetical references for print sources in MLA style usually include the author's surname and the page number of the source. This principle is problematic for electronic sources since many of them lack one or both of these elements. Give enough information to guide your reader to the source listed in your Works Cited list.

1. If the electronic source lists an author, give the surname in your parenthetical reference.

   ```
   Planespotting is a popular hobby, even an obsession, for
   growing numbers of people who are fascinated with
   aviation: "Some spotters take photographs. Others make
   videotapes. But the majority flock to airports around the
   world, equipped with scanners and notepads, with one goal
   in mind--recording the registration numbers painted on
   airplane tails" (Bourette).
   ```

   This quotation comes from *Shift.com*, an online magazine. The Works Cited entry for this quotation is on page 287.

2. If the electronic source does not list an author, give the document title (or a shortened version of the title) in italics or quotation marks as appropriate, instead of the author's name.

   ```
   New Web sites are available to help students navigate their
   way through the challenging works of William Shakespeare:
       There are some people who don't even attempt to learn
       Shakespeare because they think that Shakespeare is . . .
       only for English scholars. But that's not true!
       Shakespeare can be FUN. That's right--Shakespeare can
       actually be something you want to learn about. ("William
       Shakespeare")
   ```

   This quotation comes from a Web site called *Shakespeare: Chill with Will*. The Works Cited entry for this quotation is on page 287.

3. You do not usually find page numbers or other navigation devices in an electronic source. If there are page, paragraph, or section numbers that could guide your reader to the specific material being quoted, include them. If the author's name is included in the parenthetical reference, put a comma after it and include the section or paragraph numbers. Use the abbreviations *sec.* and *par.*

```
Even Margaret Atwood must endure the editing process before
her books are published:
     Being edited is like falling face down into a threshing
     machine. Every page gets fought over, back and forth,
     like WWI. Unless the editor and the writer both have in
     mind the greater glory of the work, . . . blood will
     flow and the work will suffer. Every comma, every page
     break, may be a ground for slaughter. (sec. 6)
```

This quotation comes from an article posted on Atwood's Web site. The Works Cited entry is found on page 287.

If there are no page, paragraph, or section numbers to identify the quotation, simply give the author's name or the title in parentheses. If your reader wants to locate the information, Web browser search engines can often find it through a key word search.

The Works Cited List

The Works Cited list appears at the end of your essay. It includes detailed bibliographical information for all the sources you have summarized, paraphrased, or quoted in your paper. The information listed in the Works Cited list enables your reader to assess the extent of your research and to find and check every source you used.

Begin the list on a new page and number each page, continuing the page numbers of your paper. (The page number appears in the upper right-hand corner, 1.25 cm from the top and lined up with the right margin.) Centre the heading, Works Cited, an inch from the top of the page. Double-space the entire list, including the title and the first entry. Begin each entry at the left margin. If an entry runs more than one line (and most do), indent the subsequent line or lines five spaces or 1.25 cm. This format is called a "hanging indent"[3] and can be found in most word-processing packages.

Arrange the entries alphabetically, beginning with the first word of the entry, which is often the author's surname. If no author is identified in your source, alphabetize by the first word in the title, ignoring *A*, *An*, and *The*. For example, *The Canadian Oxford Dictionary* would be listed under *C*, for *Canadian*. Separate the main parts of each entry with periods. Do not number your entries.

Below you will find instruction and examples for four different kinds of Works Cited entries: books, periodical articles, audiovisual sources, and electronic sources.

---

[3]Hanging indents help readers locate authors' names in the alphabetical listing. If you have only one source to acknowledge, you do not need to indent the second line. For example, see the source citation for Robert Argue's book on page 262.

BOOKS, ENCYCLOPEDIAS, AND GOVERNMENT PUBLICATIONS

Here is the basic model for a book entry in a Works Cited list.

> Last name of author, First name. *Title of Book*. City of
> publication: Publisher, Year of publication.

Note the spacing, capitalization, and punctuation as well as the order of the information. If several cities are listed, use the first one. Shorten the publisher's name. For example, McGraw-Hill, Inc. is abbreviated to McGraw. If the publisher is a well known university press, use the abbreviation UP: e.g., Oxford UP. The year the book was published is usually found on the back of the title page; if it is not given, use the latest copyright date.

- **Book by one author**

> Isajiw, Wsevolod W. *Understanding Diversity: Ethnicity and
> Race in the Canadian Context*. Toronto: Thompson, 1999.

- **Book by more than one author**

> Ulrich, Karl T., and Steven D. Eppinger. *Product Design and
> Development*. Boston: McGraw, 2000.

> Mooney, Linda A., David Knox, and Caroline Schacht.
> *Understanding Social Problems*. 3rd ed. Belmont, CA:
> Wadsworth/Thomson Learning, 2002.

- **Book edited by someone other than author**

> Barnes, Wendy, ed. *Taking Responsibility: Citizen
> Involvement in the Criminal Justice System*. Toronto:
> Centre of Criminology, U of Toronto, 1995.

- **Book with more than three authors or editors**

> Beebe, Steven A., et al. *Interpersonal Communication:
> Relating to Others*. Scarborough: Allyn and Bacon, 1997.

- **Book with a subtitle**

> Johnson, Spencer. *Who Moved My Cheese? An Amazing Way to
> Deal with Change in Your Work and in Your Life*. New
> York: Putnam, 1998.

- **New edition of an older book**

  Cooperman, Susan H. *Professional Office Procedures*. 3rd ed.
  Upper Saddle River, NJ: Prentice, 2002.

- **Paperback edition of a previously published book**

  Jones, Peter. *Living with Haemophilia*. 1995. Oxford: Oxford
  UP, 1998.

- **Recent edition of a classic text**

  Shakespeare, William. *The Tempest*. Ed. S. Orgel. Oxford:
  Oxford UP, 1994.

- **Work in several volumes**

  Erickson, Edward W., and Leonard Waverman, eds. *The Energy
  Question: An International Failure of Policy*. 2 vols.
  Toronto: U of Toronto P, 1974.

- **Article, essay, story, or poem in a collection**

  Kliewer, Gregory. "Faking My Way through School." *Canadian
  Content*. Ed. Nell Waldman and Sarah Norton. 4th ed.
  Toronto: Harcourt, 2000. 311–12.

- **Encyclopedia reference**

  Driedger, Leo. "Ethnic Identity." *Canadian Encyclopedia*.
  2000 ed.

- **Book published by a corporation (company, commission, or agency)**

  International Joint Commission. *Protection of the Waters of
  the Great Lakes: Final Report to the Governments of
  Canada and the United States*. Ottawa: The Commission,
  2000.

- **Government publication**
  If the author is not named, identify the government first, then the
  agency, then the title, city of publication, publisher, and date.

  Canada. Ministry of Supply and Services Canada. *Shared
  Values: The Canadian Identity*. Ottawa: Supply and
  Services Canada, 1991.

Ontario. Ministry of Training, Colleges and Universities.
*Employment Profile: A Summary of the Employment
Experience of 1999-2000 College Graduates Six Months
after Graduation.* Toronto: Ministry of Training, Colleges
and Universities, 2001.

ARTICLES IN JOURNALS, MAGAZINES, AND NEWSPAPERS

As with a book, information for an article begins with the author's name,
if available, includes the title of the article, and ends with the details of
publication, including the date, and the complete pages of the article. For
a periodical that is published weekly or every two weeks, provide the day,
month, and year, in that order. Abbreviate all months except for May, June,
and July (Jan., Feb., Mar., Apr., Aug., Sept., Oct., Nov., Dec.). If the periodical is published monthly, provide month and year.

Works Cited entries for newspapers include the name as it appears on
the masthead (top front page of the paper) but omit *The* (e.g., *Globe and
Mail*). If the name of the city is not included in a locally published paper,
add the city in square brackets—not underlined—after the name so that
readers will know where it was published; for instance, *Comox Valley Record*
[Campbell River].

Give the complete page span for each article in your Works Cited list. For
example, if an article begins on page 148 and concludes on page 164, put
a colon and the pages after the date: 5 June 2002: 148–64. If the article
begins on page 36, then skips to page 40 and concludes on page 41, give
only the first page and a plus sign: 36+. In a newspaper, the sections are
usually numbered separately, so include the section number as well as the
page number: *National Post* 16 Aug. 2002: S1+.

Note the order, punctuation, and capitalization of the information in
the model below.

Author's last name, First name. "Title of Article." *Title
of Periodical* Volume no. [if any] Issue no. [if any]
Date: pages.

• **Article in a scholarly journal**

Lemire, Judith A. "Preparing Nurse Leaders: A Leadership
Model." *Nursing Leadership Forum* 6.3 (2001): 39–44.

Some scholarly journals publish a number of issues each year; together,
these issues make up an annual volume. Give the volume number (in

this example, 6) right after the periodical title, add a period, and then give the issue number (here, 3) immediately before the date, which is placed in parentheses.

- **Article in a monthly magazine**

    Zengotita, Thomas de. "The Numbing of the American Mind."
        Harper's Apr. 2002: 33–40.

- **Signed article in a newspaper**

    Vallis, Mary. "Non-traditional Roles Linked to Early Death."
        National Post 25 Apr. 2002: A1.

- **Unsigned newspaper article**

    "Canada to Toughen Auto-Emissions Rules." *Wall Street*
        Journal 5 Apr. 2002: A6.

- **A review**

    Caldwell, Rebecca. "A Smudgy Comic Book with No Heroics."
        Rev. of *Fourtyseven*, by Margaret Smith and Nicole
        Manek. *Globe and Mail* 29 Apr. 2002: R5.

AUDIOVISUAL SOURCES

- **Television show**

    Remembering Peter Gzowski. Host Mark Kelley. CBC Newsworld.
        30 Jan. 2002.

- **Radio show**

    "J. K. Rowling Interview." *Hot Type with Evan Solomon.* CBC
        Newsworld. 16 Nov. 2001.

- **Recording**

    Chiarelli, Rita. *Breakfast at Midnight.* NorthernBlues, 2001.

- **Film, videocassette, laser disc, or DVD**

    Casablanca. Dir. Michael Curtiz. Perf. Humphrey Bogart,
        Ingrid Bergman, and Paul Henreid. 1943. Laser disc.
        CBS/Fox Video, 1982.

If you wish to give credit to the contribution of a particular individual, begin with that person's name.

```
Hitchcock, Alfred, dir. Rear Window. Perf. Jimmy Stewart, Grace
     Kelly, and Raymond Burr. 1954. DVD. Universal, 2001.
```

ELECTRONIC SOURCES

Documentation guidelines for electronic publications are still being developed, so you should check with your Resource Centre to see if it provides handouts to help you cite these sources. Works Cited entries should identify the source and provide enough information to enable a reader to locate it—author, title, publication information, and date. Providing all this information is not always possible for materials found on the Web. Include as much information as you can, and remember that the key element in citing an electronic source is its electronic address or URL (uniform resource locator).

Do not use a hyphen to divide a URL over two lines; otherwise, you will make it invalid. Record the URL on a single line, or break it after a slash (/). Because the symbols, letters, and numbers that make up a URL are complex and must be recorded accurately, some recent guidelines suggest that angle brackets be omitted. Be sure to use the format your instructor prefers.

Along with the URL, other essential information includes the date of publication (if it is available) and the date that you, as the researcher, accessed the information. The access date is important because online documents can be altered at any time. (Use the abbreviation conventions provided in the guidelines for periodicals above: e.g., Mar. for March.)

 It's a good idea to download and print online material so that you can verify it if, at a later date, it is revised, unavailable, or inaccessible.

Follow this basic model for online source entries in a Works Cited list:

```
Author's last name, First name [if known]. "Title of Document
     or File." Title of Complete Work or Site. Date of docu-
     ment or of last revision. <URL, including protocol⁴>.
     (Date of access).
```

- **Article from an online database**

```
"Fuel Cells Are Getting Hotter." Business Week 15 Apr. 2002:
     106. InfoTrac. <http://www.infotrac-college.com>. (30
     Apr. 2002).
```

---

[4]"Protocol" refers to a particular set of rules for performing tasks on the Internet, such as http (hypertext transfer protocol), ftp (file transfer protocol), telnet, gopher, and so on.

- ## Article in an online periodical

  Bourette, Susan. "Planespotting." *Shift.com* Mar. 2002:
      20-24. <http://www.shift.com/content/10.1/53/1.html>.
      (8 June 2002).

- ## Government publication

  Canada. Health Canada. *Alcohol and Pregnancy.* Nov. 1998.
      <http://www.hc-sc.gc.ca/pphb-dgspsp/rhs-ssg/factshts/
      alcprg_e.html#top>. (18 Apr. 2002).

- ## Online encyclopedia

  "Art Deco." *Britannica Online.* Encyclopaedia Britannica.
      <http://search.eb.com/eb/article?eu=9778>. (29 Apr. 2002).

- ## Online news service

  Associated Press. "Scientists Study Young Orphaned Killer
      Whale." *CNN.com.* 26 Mar. 2002. <http://www.CNN.com/
      2002/TECH/science/03/260orphan.orca.ap/index.html>.
      (4 Apr. 2002).

- ## Personal or professional Web site

  Atwood, Margaret. "The Rocky Road to Paper Heaven." *Margaret
      Atwood Information Site.* N.d. <http://www.owtoad.com/
      road.html>. (10 June 2002).

  Canadian Electronic Scholarly Network. 1998. Industry Canada.
      <http://www.schoolnet.ca/vp-pv/cesn/e/>. (30 Apr. 2002).

  "William Shakespeare." *Shakespeare: Chill with Will.* N.d.
      <http://library.thinkquest.org/19539/front/htm>. (8
      June 2002).

- ## Personal e-mail communication
  Follow this format:

  Author's surname, First name [or alias]. "Title of Message
      [from subject line]." E-mail to First name and Last name
      of recipient. Date.

  ### Never give the writer's e-mail address.

  Zacharatos, Phil. "The Forest or the Trees?" E-mail to
      Caroline Bouffard. 1 Apr. 2002.

- ## Online posting, listserv, or discussion group

  Ballard, Rex. "Re: Windows vs. Linux." Online posting. 22
      Apr. 2002. <news:comp.os.linux.advocacy>. (2 May 2002).

  Wincapaw, Celeste. "Cyber-Fem: New Perspectives on Midwifery."
      Online posting. 27 Mar. 2000. <http://www.hsph.harvard.
      edu/rt21/talk/frame1.html>. (20 Jan. 2002).

- ## CD-ROMs
  Follow this basic model, including as many elements as are given in the
  source:

  Author's surname, First name. "Title of Article, Song, or
      Poem [if relevant]." *Title of the Publication*. CD-ROM.
      Edition, release, or version [if relevant]. Place of
      publication: Name of publisher, date.

  Darby, Michele L. *Software to Accompany Mosby's Comprehensive
      Review of Dental Hygiene*. CD-ROM. 5th ed. Mosby, 2002.

  Harrel, William. *QuarkXPress 4 in Depth*. CD-ROM.
      Scottsdale, AZ: Coriolis, 1999.

On the following page, you will find a sample Works Cited list to show you
what the final page of your paper should look like.

Works Cited

Harris, Charles E. Interview. *Future Sciences
    Interviews.* Mar. 2002. <http://nanotechnow.com/
    charles-harris-interview032002.htm>. (1 May 2002).

"Nanoscience: The New High Frontier." *Nanotechnology.*
    National Research Council, Canada. <http://www.nrc.ca/
    nanotech/home_e.html>. (1 May 2002).

"Nanotechnology." *AccessScience: The Online Encyclopedia
    of Science and Technology.* (1 May 2002).

Regis, Edward. *Nano: The Emerging Science of
    Nanotechnology: Remaking the World--Molecule by
    Molecule.* Boston: Little, Brown, 1995.

Ross, Rachel. "Atoms on a Roll." *Toronto Star* 18 Feb.
    2002: A5.

Rotman, David. "The Nanotube Computer." *Technology
    Review* Mar. 2002: 36-45.

"What Is Nanotechnology?" *NanoTechnology Magazine*
    11 Oct. 2002. <http://www.nanozine.com/>.
    (13 Oct. 2002).

*Print interview
from Internet*

Web site

*Online
encyclopedia*

Book

Newspaper article

Magazine article

Online magazine

Exercise 22.1

For each of the following quotations, write a short paragraph in which you use and document all or a portion of the quotation.

1. From a book entitled Getting it done: the transforming power of self-discipline by Andrew J. Dubrin, published by Pacesetter Books in Princeton in 1995. This sentence appears on page 182: "Stress usually stems from your interpretation and perception of an event, not from the event itself."

2. From a journal article by Linda A. White that appeared on pages 385 to 405 of Canadian Public Policy, a journal with continuous paging: "If a clear connection exists between the presence of child care and high levels of women's labour market participation, that would provide good reasons for governments and employers to regard child care as part of an active labour market policy." White's article is entitled Child Care, Women's Labour Market Participation and Labour Market Policy Effectiveness in Canada. The quote appears on page 389 of the fourth issue of the 27th volume, published in 2001.

3. From the Code of Ethics for Registered Nurses Web site, found at www.nursingethics.ca/codes: "Nurses value and advocate the dignity and self-respect of human beings."

4. From a newspaper article, Bullying widespread, study finds, written by Darren Yourk that appeared on page A11 of The Globe and Mail on May 7, 2002: "One in 10 students surveyed reported having low self-esteem, while 28 per cent said they had elevated psychological stress."

5. From an interview with Hans Selye, conducted on Jan 1, 1982, shortly before his death, on the topic of his pioneering work on stress and illness: "Stress is the non-specific response of a human body to any demand made upon it."

Exercise 22.2*

Prepare a Works Cited list for the sources you used in Exercise 22.1 above.

23

Formatting a
Research Paper

"You can't tell a book by its cover" is an old saying; however, the appearance of a book often influences your decision to read it or pass it by. Similarly the appearance of your paper makes an impression on your reader. A correctly formatted paper reflects the care and attention to detail that instructors value in students' work.

Ask your instructor if he or she has any special requirements for the format of your research assignment. If so, follow them carefully. Otherwise, follow the guidelines in this chapter to prepare your paper for submission. These guidelines are based on MLA style; you will find instruction on formatting in APA style on our Web site at http://www.essayessentials3e.nelson.com. After the guidelines, you will find two model research papers, both formatted according to the MLA principles of documentation. The first, "Uncertain Future: Potential Dangers of Genetically Modified Crops," is an essay on a topic of general interest. The second, "The Evolution of Moral Balance in Charlotte Brontë's *Jane Eyre*," is an essay on a literary topic. Together, they provide examples of most of the possibilities you are likely to encounter when writing and formatting your own research paper.

Paper

Use a word processor (or type) your final draft on 22×28 cm (8.5×11 inch) white bond paper. Be sure to use a fresh cartridge in your printer (or a good ribbon in your typewriter). If your instructor will accept a handwritten document, make sure it adheres to all of the guidelines that follow, including those regarding ink colour, margins, spacing, etc. Print, type, or write on *one side* of the paper only.

Fasten your paper together with a paper clip or a single staple in the upper left corner. Unless your instructor requests them, don't bother with plastic or paper covers; most teachers find it annoying to disentangle your essay for marking.

Printing/Typing

Choose a standard, easily readable typeface, such as Times New Roman, in a 12-point font. Use black ink (or dark blue, if you are writing by hand).

Spacing and Margins

Unless you are instructed otherwise, double-space throughout your essay, including quotations and the Works Cited list. In a handwritten paper, write on every other line of a ruled sheet of white paper.

Adequate white space on your pages makes your paper more attractive and easier to read. It also allows room for instructors' comments. Leave margins of 2.5 cm at the top, bottom, and both sides of your paper. If you are using a word processor, click on the "justify left" formatting command.

Indent the first line of every paragraph five spaces or 1.25 cm; use the tab default setting in your word-processing program. Indent all lines of a block quotation ten spaces or 2.5 cm from the left margin.

Title Page

Do not prepare a separate title page unless your instructor requires it. Instead, at the top of the left margin of the first page of your essay, on separate lines, type your name, your instructor's name, the course number, and the date. Leave a double space and centre the title of your essay. Capitalize key words (see Chapter 40, page 456), but do not underline, italicize, or put quotation marks around your title (unless it contains the title of another author's work, which you should punctuate in the usual way).

Header and Page Numbers

Number your pages consecutively throughout the paper, including the Works Cited list, in the upper right-hand corner, 1.25 cm from the top and

2.5 cm from the right-hand margin. Type your last name before the page number. Use a word processor to create a running head consisting of your last name, a single space, and the page number—no punctuation or *p*. See the student papers at the end of this chapter for examples.

Copy

Always keep a copy of your paper for your files!

Projecting an Image

As well as presenting your understanding of the topic, a research paper demonstrates your writing skills and your ability to follow specific requirements of documentation and format. Meeting your instructor's submission requirements is as important as any other aspect of the preparation of your paper. This may be the last stage of your writing task, but it is the first impression your reader will have of your work.

The paper that follows is an example of a properly formatted, documented essay. Before writing her paper, Soraya prepared an outline. Notice that she included in her outline the sources she wanted to refer to in each section. This technique saves hours of paper shuffling when you sit down to write.

```
            Uncertain Future: Potential Dangers
                of Genetically Modified Crops
Attention-Getter:  Most people eat genetically modified foods
    every day, but few of stop to consider their potential
    dangers.
Thesis Statement:  Genetically modified crops may have disas-
    trous health, environmental, and sociopolitical effects.
I.   GM foods pose incalculable risks to human health.
     A. GM foods may contain toxic proteins. (Commoner; Mellon)
     B. Despite the testing that goes on during the genetic
        engineering process, allergic reactions to GM foods are
        likely. (Hopkin; Humphrys)
```

    C. The spread of antibiotic resistant bacteria is also a
       possibility. (Hopkin)

II. GM crops may have a catastrophic and unpredictable impact on
     the environment.

    A. Built-in pesticides have benefits, but they kill crea-
       tures other than agricultural pests, destroying the bal-
       ance of ecosystems. (Brown; Suzuki)

    B. Pests develop tolerance to built-in pesticides. (Brown)

    C. The transfer of pollen from genetically modified plants
       to weeds creates superweeds. (Randerson)

III. The social, economic, and political effects of GM crops may
     be harmful or even disastrous.

    A. Biotechnology corporations use patents and "terminator
       technology" to control GM seeds; people become dependent
       on these companies. (Kneen)

    B. GM crops won't feed the world. (Suzuki; Mellon)

Summary: The health, environmental, and sociopolitical effects
     of GM crops may be dreadful.

Memorable Statement: More research needs to be done before we
     can evaluate the impact of GM technology. Right now, the
     risks are largely unknown and unpredictable.

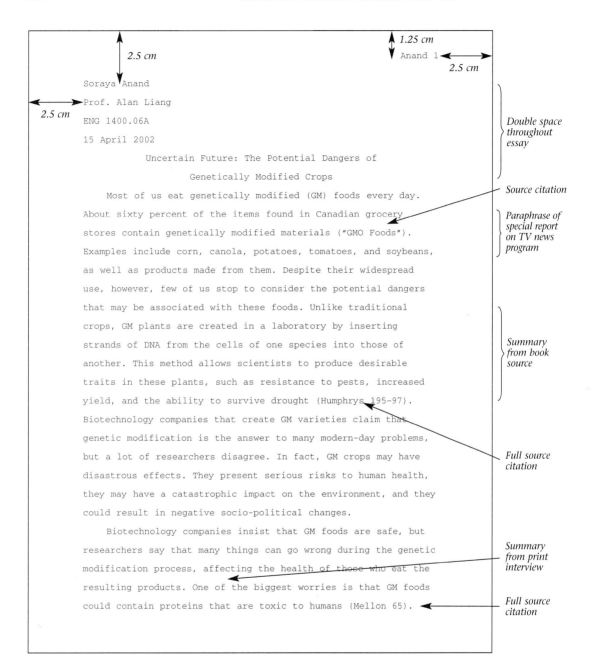

1.25 cm

Anand 1

2.5 cm

2.5 cm

2.5 cm

2.5 cm

Soraya Anand

Prof. Alan Liang

ENG 1400.06A

15 April 2002

Uncertain Future: The Potential Dangers of

Genetically Modified Crops

Most of us eat genetically modified (GM) foods every day. About sixty percent of the items found in Canadian grocery stores contain genetically modified materials ("GMO Foods"). Examples include corn, canola, potatoes, tomatoes, and soybeans, as well as products made from them. Despite their widespread use, however, few of us stop to consider the potential dangers that may be associated with these foods. Unlike traditional crops, GM plants are created in a laboratory by inserting strands of DNA from the cells of one species into those of another. This method allows scientists to produce desirable traits in these plants, such as resistance to pests, increased yield, and the ability to survive drought (Humphrys 195–97). Biotechnology companies that create GM varieties claim that genetic modification is the answer to many modern-day problems, but a lot of researchers disagree. In fact, GM crops may have disastrous effects. They present serious risks to human health, they may have a catastrophic impact on the environment, and they could result in negative socio-political changes.

Biotechnology companies insist that GM foods are safe, but researchers say that many things can go wrong during the genetic modification process, affecting the health of those who eat the resulting products. One of the biggest worries is that GM foods could contain proteins that are toxic to humans (Mellon 65).

Double space throughout essay

Source citation

Paraphrase of special report on TV news program

Summary from book source

Full source citation

Summary from print interview

Full source citation

Anand 2

Quotation from magazine article

Abbreviated citation

Barry Commoner, a senior scientist at City University of New York, points out that recent discoveries prove that the results of DNA transfer are unpredictable. Transferring genes from one organism to another, he says, "might give rise to multiple variants of the intended protein--or even to proteins bearing little structural relationship to the original one" (45).

Summary from article, with full citation

Margaret Mellon notes that "as scientists manipulate systems that they don't completely understand, one of the unexpected effects could be turning on genes for toxins" (65).

Allergic reactions are also a concern (Hopkin 60). In the mid-1990s, scientists tried to genetically improve soybeans with a gene from brazil nuts. The beans caused allergic reactions in people allergic to brazil nuts, so development was stopped (Humphrys 219-20). Supporters of GM technology cite this case as an example of the effectiveness of the testing process, but

Author and title of book source

John Humphrys, the author of *The Great Food Gamble*, says that we may not be so lucky in the future:

10 sp

Block quotation from book

> The brazil nut allergen was well known and could be specifically tested for . . . . In other cases, of course, the allergen might not be known. It is entirely possible that its effects might appear only over a period of time. It might produce a form of allergy of which we have no experience. It might simply not be identified. Far from exonerating the industry, what this little tale tells is that the risks exist. (220-21)

Paraphrase from Web site

The spread of antibiotic resistant bacteria--bacteria that cannot be killed by known antibiotics--is another potential problem. Food engineers often use antibiotic resistant genes

Abbreviated book citation

Full citation for Web site

when designing GM crops (Greenpeace). The possibility that

Anand 3

"resistance genes might somehow jump from GM foods to bacteria in a consumer's gut" is small, but it cannot be ignored (Hopkin 61). If such a jump occurs, antibiotic resistant bacteria could quickly spread, adding to the already serious medical problem of antibiotic resistance.

Genetically modified crops may also harm the environment. Most GM plant varieties are engineered to be resistant to pests such as insects. Supporters of GM crops point out that the farmers who plant them do not have to spray chemical pesticides on their fields, which is good for the environment (Brown 52). Yet there are other consequences as well. Studies indicate that insect-resistant GM crops may kill not only agricultural pests but also other creatures that happen to be exposed to them, such as monarch butterflies and green lacewing caterpillars (Brown 53–54). Long-term effects could be unpredictable but significant enough to affect whole ecosystems. David Suzuki warns readers:

> If we grow fields of crops that are toxic to all organisms except humans, what will that do to beneficial insects, or to the important microorganisms that live in our soils? This could have serious repercussions because depletion of insect numbers, for example, would lead to fewer birds and small mammals, and could have other implications up and down the food chain.

In addition, even the defenders of GM crops are realizing that insect pests will develop a tolerance to built-in insecticides (Brown 54; McHughen 108). When this occurs, entire crops may suddenly fail, causing enormous losses. To prevent this disaster, farmers in the United States and elsewhere are now required to

Paragraph topic developed by paraphrase and block quotation

Block quotation from article on Web site (no page, paragraph, or section numbers given)

Paraphrase of idea found in two sources

Anand 4

set aside a part of their farmland for crops that have not been genetically modified. In these areas, "insects that have acquired some resistance . . . breed with those that have not, diluting the resistance trait" (Brown 57). Many environmentalists question the effectiveness of this strategy. They claim that the areas set aside "are either too small or too poorly designed to keep insect resistance at bay for long" (57). As resistance develops, another form of chemical control will have to be used or food engineers will have to develop new GM crop varieties, causing more environmental devastation.

The transfer of pollen from a genetically modified species to other plants nearby can also lead to environmental damage. The main reason is that many GM crops are designed to be resistant to herbicides--chemical substances that kill plants. As a result, farmers can spray their fields with herbicides to eliminate weeds without damaging their own crops ("Herbicide"). The problem starts when pollen from one of these GM plants is carried to another plant species, such as a weed. The weed obtains the herbicide-resistant gene and can then grow unchecked, since it can no longer be killed by herbicides. It becomes a so-called superweed (Brown 55). According to a study commissioned by English Nature, the advisory body on conservation for the government of the United Kingdom, many superweeds already exist in Canada. Consequently, farmers are often forced to use older, stronger herbicides to kill them (Randerson).

The social, economic, and political implications of GM crops are also worrying. One problem often cited by critics is that a few large corporations control the industry. Because GM seeds can be patented, these companies not only dictate the price of seeds

Short quote integrated into sentence

Summary of encyclopedia article

Summary of online magazine article

Anand 5

but also hold "intellectual property" rights for their products (Humphrys 197–98). Brewster Kneen, the author of *Farmageddon: Food and the Culture of Biotechnology*, explains the results:

> To say the seed is sold . . . is misleading, because in a sense the owners of the technology, the seed companies, do not sell it at all; they rent it out to the farmer for a season. The farmer is not allowed to keep any of the crop for replanting or to share it ~~with a~~ neighbor because the technology [is] owned and patented by one or another major transnational corporation. (107)

Words left out

Word changed

To protect its interests, one company uses what has been called "terminator technology," which makes plants sterile (Robbins). As a result, farmers cannot save seeds from their plants to produce another harvest; they must buy new seeds instead. Kneen argues that as GM crops become more popular, control of the global food supply shifts dangerously. Eventually, he says, corporate ownership of seeds "will end the ability of the majority of the world's people to feed themselves and will make them dependent on corporate seed suppliers" (61).

In light of such practices, many people question what Bill Lambrecht, the author of *Dinner at the New Gene Café*, calls "the grand promise by some of the companies . . . that they will be able to more capably feed the world" with GM crops. Increased productivity will not solve the problem of starvation in developing countries because, as David Suzuki says, "most food shortages are caused by political and social issues, not an overall lack of food production capacity." There is more than enough food in the world, but it doesn't get to those in need (Mellon 64). Drought-tolerant GM crops could potentially benefit people in

Paragraph topic developed by quotations and paraphrase

Anand 6

many countries, but chances are that these people will not be able to afford them (Mellon 64).

The jury is out on GM foods. Scientists, corporations, governments, and the public continue to debate their pros and cons. In the meantime, most of us unknowingly eat products containing genetically modified ingredients every day. As we reach for the corn chips, we should realize that GM crops may have dreadful and unexpected health, environmental, and socio-political consequences. More research and testing need to be done before we can evaluate this technology and its impact on our lives and on the world. Right now, the risks are still largely unknown and unpredictable.

Anand 7

Works Cited

Brown, Kathryn. "Seeds of Concern." *Scientific American*
    Apr. 2001: 52-57.

Commoner, Barry. "Unravelling the DNA Myth: The Spurious
    Foundation of Genetic Engineering." *Harper's* Feb. 2002:
    39-47.

"GMO Foods." *The National*. CBC-TV. Toronto. 23 Aug. 2001.
    Transcript.

Greenpeace. "The Secret Ingredient." <http://www.greenpeace.ca/
    e/resource/publications/gmo/secret_ingredient.pdf>.
    (10 Apr. 2002).

"Herbicide." *The Columbia Encyclopedia*. 2001 ed. <http://
    www.bartleby.com/65/he/herbicid.html>. (10 Apr. 2002).

Hopkin, Karen. "The Risks on the Table." *Scientific American*
    Apr. 2001: 60-61.

Humphrys, John. *The Great Food Gamble*. London: Hodder and
    Stoughton, 2001.

Kneen, Brewster. *Farmageddon: Food and the Culture of
    Biotechnology*. Gabriola Island: New Society Publishers, 1999.

Lambrecht, Bill. Interview. *Canada AM*. CTV. 1 Oct. 2001.
    Transcript.

McHughen, Alan. *Pandora's Picnic Basket: The Potential and
    Hazards of Genetically Modified Foods*. New York: Oxford UP,
    2000.

Mellon, Margaret. Interview. *Scientific American* Apr. 2001: 64-65.

Randerson, James. "Genetically-modified Superweeds 'Not Uncommon.'"
    New Scientist 5 Feb. 2002. <http://www.newscientist.com/
    news/news.jsp?id=ns99991882>. (10 Apr. 2002).

Robbins, John. Interview. *Times-Herald* 13 Jan. 2002: 3.

Anand 8

Suzuki, David. "Genetically Modifying Our Food." Science Matters
    series. 3 Nov. 1999; 10 Nov. 1999. <http://
    www.davidsuzuki.org/Dr_David_Suzuki/Article_Archives/>.
    (10 Apr. 2002).

The following essay won the Sydney Singh Memorial Award at Grant MacEwan College in 2000. This award is given annually to the student who has written the best essay analyzing a work of literature in an English 101 class.

```
                    The Evolution of Moral Balance
                  in Charlotte Brontë's Jane Eyre
Introduction:  Brontë's use of balancing elements contributes to
     the impact of Jane Eyre.
Thesis statement:  Jane is pulled in opposing directions:
     between the values of Helen Burns and those of Bertha
     Mason; between the spirituality of St John Rivers and the
     sensuality of Rochester. Through her struggles with these
     opposing elements, Jane eventually finds a position on the
     moral continuum that satisfies her.
I.   Helen Burns and Bertha Mason represent the externalization
     of "the division of the Victorian female psyche into its
     extreme components of mind and body." (Showalter 68)
     A. Helen is an asexual child, focused on her spirituality
        to the point of physical self-denial.
     B. Bertha is a highly sexual woman, whose excessive indul-
        gence has caused her to lose her reason.
     C. Brontë destroys the two "polar personalities" to make way
        for the integration of Jane's physical and spiritual
        beings. (Showalter 68)
     D. The values represented by Helen and Bertha influence
        Jane's moral development.
     E. The lessons she has learned are most clearly evident
        when she rejects Rochester's proposition.
II.  One of Rochester's arguments for an affair is that nobody
     will be harmed by it because Jane has no family to offend.
     A. Jane initially seems to accept his reasoning. (356)
     B. Helen's indoctrination about the value of one's good con-
        science (81) prevents her from acquiescing.
     C. She cannot live without self-respect. (356)
     D. Bertha's story shows her that if she were to become
        Rochester's mistress, she would share that fate: madness
        and estrangement from Rochester.
```

E. Jane's moral position between the two extremes offered by Bertha and Helen is tested both by Rochester's proposition and by St John's proposal.

III. St John Rivers and Rochester are two characters who balance each other on many levels, from looks to lifestyle. The extremes they represent push her toward middle ground.

A. Description of Rochester: 129–30.

B. Description of St John: 386.

C. Rochester's past: 355.

D. St John's past: 393.

E. Jane is offered contrasting choices: a passionate, illicit affair vs. a pious marriage of convenience.

F. On the surface, the proposals are in contrast, but both would force her to suppress a part of her nature.

G. Both proposals threaten the fulfillment Brontë has in mind for Jane. (Eagleton 33)

H. Jane resists temptation; Brontë saves her for a transformed Rochester.

IV. *Jane Eyre* ends with Jane no longer having to compromise herself in order to be with Rochester.

A. The humbled Rochester is no longer asking Jane to abandon her conscience to live in sin.

B. Rochester and Jane are now a perfect match because he has moved away from his earlier extremes.

C. Rochester's physical mutilation is a "symbolic castration" (Chase, qtd. in Gilbert and Gubar 368), but more than his masculinity, his spirit has been transformed.

D. Humility has taught him wisdom. (495)

E. Their "perfect concord" (500) is made possible by Rochester's movement away from his earlier extreme to become Jane's ideal mate.

F. Their blissful marriage is contrasted with the life and death of St John in India.

G. Brontë pays tribute to St John (417), while still validating Jane's choice.

H. Jane has achieved an ideal moral balance; she can live a full life on earth and still earn the reward of heaven.

Summary: Jane's refusal to reject the demands of either her
    mind or her body is the essence of the novel. She is alter-
    nately taught and tested by Helen Burns and Bertha Mason,
    by St John Rivers and Rochester, and ultimately comes to
    reconcile the two extremes.

Memorable statement: Jane's journey to her own satisfying
    moral code and a life that celebrates it are intensified by
    Brontë's use of balancing elements.

Friedland 1

Jess Friedland

Professor MacDonald

EN101-354X

1 December 2000

The Evolution of Moral Balance in

Charlotte Brontë's *Jane Eyre*

A profusion of balancing elements contribute to the impact of Charlotte Brontë's novel, *Jane Eyre*. Brontë uses these balances to convey the maturation of Jane's value system. The diametrically opposed characters of Helen Burns and Bertha Mason represent the duality of Jane's nature, and ultimately influence her moral choices. The proposals of Rochester and St John Rivers seem antithetical, but display an underlying similarity. Jane is pulled in opposite directions throughout the novel, but her final address to the reader shows that she has found a position on the moral continuum that satisfies her. The balances utilized to demonstrate her journey enhance both our view of Jane's internal struggle and our understanding of her choices.

According to Elaine Showalter, Helen Burns and Bertha Mason represent the externalization of "the division of the Victorian female psyche into its extreme components of mind and body" (68). Brontë's characterizations support this observation. Helen is an unequivocally asexual child, focused solely on her spirituality to the point of physical self-denial. Bertha is an unequivocally sexual woman, who has seemingly lost her mind through excessive indulgence in bodily pleasure. Showalter goes on to say:

> Brontë gives us not one but three faces of Jane, and she
> resolves her heroine's psychic dilemma by literally and
> metaphorically destroying the two polar personalities to
> make way for the full strength and development of the

central consciousness, for the integration of the spirit
and the body. (68)

Jane's rejection of either extreme validates this statement
on a metaphorical level. In the literal sense, however, both
Bertha and Helen influence Jane's morality in more relevant ways
than merely dying. Jane is neither an angel nor a demon, but she
certainly ends up closer to Helen's end of the spectrum than to
Bertha's. Their lessons are most apparent during Jane's rejection
of Rochester's proposition.

One of Rochester's main arguments for an affair is that
nobody will be harmed by it as Jane has no family to offend.
Jane pleads with herself to "tell him you love him and will be
his. Who in the world cares for you? or who will be injured by
what you do?" (Brontë 356; ch. 27). Helen's indoctrination of the
intrinsic value of one's own good conscience prevents her from
acquiescing. "If all the world hated you, and believed you
wicked, while your own conscience approved you, and absolved you
from guilt, you would not be without friends" (Brontë 81; ch. 8).
The opposite must also hold true: if Jane's conscience does not
approve her, Rochester's love will not matter. Jane will be
without her own self-respect. Therefore, she cannot stifle the
"indomitable [. . .] reply--'I care for myself'" (Brontë 356; ch.
27). Bertha's lesson is more subtle, but equally effective. Her
sexual nature has led her to madness and estrangement from
Rochester. Once her story is told to Jane, the implications are
clear. She must reject a life as Rochester's mistress or potentially face similar consequences. Jane's moral position between
the two extremes offered by Bertha and Helen is more a function
of their lives than of their deaths. This moral position is
tested most notably by the aforementioned proposition and by the
proposal of her cousin.

Friedland 3

St John Rivers and Rochester balance each other on many levels, from looks to lifestyle. Again, these extreme options, which are more literally presented to Jane, push her toward middle ground. Jane's first description of Rochester is of "a dark face, with stern features and a heavy brow"; she implies that he is far from being "a handsome, heroic-looking young gentleman" (Brontë 129-30; ch. 12). St John, on the other hand, is "young [. . .] tall, slender," with "a Greek face, very pure in outline: quite a straight, classic nose; quite an Athenian mouth and chin" (Brontë 386; ch. 29). Rochester's past is riddled with "lust for a passion--vice for an occupation" (Brontë 355; ch. 27), whereas St John is called "blameless in his life and habits [. . .] pure-lived, conscientious" (Brontë 393-94; ch. 30). Jane is offered a passionate, illicit affair by one, and a pious marriage of convenience by the other. These proposals are superficially contrary, but if Jane accepted either one, she would be forced to suppress part of her nature.

As Terry Eagleton states in his study of the novel, "Jane [. . .] must refuse Rivers as she has refused Rochester: loveless conventionalism and illicit passion both threaten the kind of fulfilment the novel seeks for her" (33). Fulfillment involves being accepted and loved without moral modification. Jane is sorely tempted, first to turn her back on her conscience for Rochester, and later to turn her back on her heart for St John. Brontë does not allow her to give in to either man at these crucial points, saving her instead for a revised Rochester.

The conclusion of *Jane Eyre* has Jane and Rochester married at last. Jane no longer needs to compromise herself in order to be with him, and his first wife is not the only obstacle that has been removed. The man who insisted that she abandon her conscience to live in sin has changed significantly. Rochester now complements Jane as never before. His mutilation has been

Friedland 4

referred to as a "symbolic castration" by Richard Chase (qtd. in Gilbert and Gubar 368), but it is his spirit rather than his masculinity that seems to have been honed. Rochester has been humbled, and the taste of humility has taught him wisdom. He is able to admit to Jane, "I did wrong: I would have sullied my innocent flower--breathed guilt on its purity" (Brontë 495; ch. 37). During their first engagement, Jane was unsure and often uncomfortable about her place in Rochester's life. In her description of their marriage however, she says that "we are precisely suited in character--perfect concord is the result" (Brontë 500; ch. 38). Such a perfect fit is only made possible by Rochester's movement away from his earlier extreme. He has become a close match for Jane on every level, and therefore becomes her ideal mate.

The final three paragraphs of the novel throw this blissful marriage into sharp contrast with the life and imminent death of St John in India. He is greeting his death at the end of ten years of martyrdom with eagerness, while Jane and Rochester are living life to its fullest. Brontë is giving respectful tribute to St John, but there remains a sense of validation for Jane's choices. St John's reason for clinging solely to his spirituality and rejecting his body is that he will not relinquish his "foundation laid on earth for a mansion in heaven" (Brontë 417; ch. 32). There can be no doubt, however, that Jane will be worthy of heaven upon her death. Jane's moral balance is thus portrayed as ideal; she can live a happy, full life on earth and yet not fear eternal damnation.

Jane's refusal to discount entirely either her mind or her body is the essence of the story. The course by which she comes to reconcile the two is compellingly wrought. She is alternately taught and tested by Helen Burns and Bertha Mason, by St John Rivers and Rochester. Jane's journey to her own satisfying moral code, and a life that celebrates it, are intensified by Brontë's use of balancing elements.

Friedland 5

Works Cited

Brontë, Charlotte. *Jane Eyre*. Harmondsworth, England: Penguin,

1996.

Eagleton, Terry. *"Jane Eyre:* A Marxist Study." *Charlotte*

Brontë's Jane Eyre: *Modern Critical Interpretations*. Ed.

Harold Bloom. New York: Chelsea House Publishers, 1987.

29-45.

Gilbert, Sandra M., and Susan Gubar. *The Madwoman in the Attic*.

New Haven: Yale UP, 1984.

Showalter, Elaine. "Charlotte Brontë: Feminine Heroine." Jane

Eyre: *Contemporary Critical Essays*. New Casebooks. Ed.

Heather Glen. New York: St. Martin's Press, 1997. 68-77.

Reprinted by permission of the author.

PART 6

A Review of the Basics

How to Use This Section

This part of *Essay Essentials* is a workbook designed to improve the correctness of your writing. In Chapters 28 to 42, we look at the errors that give many writers trouble, whether they are writing student papers, professional reports, PowerPoint presentations, or office memoranda. In each chapter, we do three things: explain a point, illustrate it with examples, and provide exercises in the text and on the Web site to help you master the point. The exercises are arranged in sets that get more difficult as you go along. By the end of the last set in each chapter, you should have a good grasp of the skill. You will lose that grasp, however, if you do not practise. To maintain and reinforce your mastery of the skills you've learned, make a conscious effort to apply them every time you write.

You should work your way through this part of the book while you are working on Parts 1 through 5. You may find it helpful to set up a schedule, matching a section of the workbook with a unit of the text. For example, while you are learning how to plan an essay in Part 1, you could set yourself the goal of working through Chapters 24 to 29, on sentence structure; while learning how to write an essay in Part 2, you could work through Chapters 30 to 32, on grammar. You would then cover Chapters 33 to 37, on punctuation, along with Part 3, revising the essay. Finally, as you learn about the different kinds of essays in Part 4, you could cover Chapters 38 through 42, on spelling.

Alternatively, you could go through this workbook section by section, addressing in order the errors your instructor identifies in your writing. Whichever approach you choose, you should make it your goal to complete every chapter of the workbook. If you do so conscientiously, we guarantee that as your papers improve in organization and effectiveness, your writing will also improve in correctness and clarity.

Here's how to proceed in each chapter.

1. Read the explanation. Do this even if you think you understand the point being discussed.
2. Study the highlighted rules and the examples that follow them.
3. Now turn to the exercises. Try at least one set even if you are confident that you understand the principle.
4. *Always check your answers to each set of exercises before going on to the next.* Only if you check your accuracy after every set can you avoid repeating your mistakes and—worse—possibly reinforcing your errors. For those exercises marked with an asterisk (*), you will find the answers in the back of the book. For those on the Web site, the answers are marked automatically, so you will know instantly whether or not you have understood the material.
5. When you find that you've made a mistake, go back to the explanation and examples and study them again. Try making up some examples of your own to illustrate the rule. If you are truly stuck, check with your instructor. You can reinforce your understanding by doing the practice tests that you will find on the student home page of the *Essay Essentials* Web site.

6. At the end of each chapter, there is a mastery test marked with the icon shown in the margin. Your instructor can provide you with the answers for these tests. Use these tests to help track your progress as you master basic writing skills.

On the inside front cover, you will find a Guide to Revision. Use it to check over your papers before you hand them in.

24

Cracking the Sentence Code

There is nothing really mysterious or difficult about sentences; you've been speaking them successfully since you were two. The difficulty arises when you try to write—not sentences, oddly enough, but paragraphs. Almost all college students, if asked to write ten sentences on ten different topics, could do so without an error. But when those same students write paragraphs, then sentence fragments, run-ons, and other sentence faults appear.

The solution to sentence structure problems has two parts.

Be sure every sentence you write
1. sounds correct
         and
2. has both a subject and a verb.

If English is your first language, your ear may be the best instrument with which to test your sentences. If you read a sentence aloud, you may be able to tell by the sound whether it is complete and clear. Sometimes, however, your ear may mislead you, so this chapter will show you, step by step, how to decode your sentences to find their subjects and verbs. When you know how to decode sentences, you can make sure that every sentence you write is complete.

Read these sentences aloud.

Snowboarding is one of the world's newest sports.
Although snowboarding is still a young sport.

The second "sentence" doesn't sound right, does it? It does not make sense on its own and is in fact a sentence fragment.

Testing your sentences by reading them aloud won't work if you read your paragraphs straight through from beginning to end. The trick is to read from end to beginning. That is, read your last sentence aloud and *listen* to it. If it sounds all right, then read aloud the next-to-last sentence, and so on, until you have worked your way back to the first sentence you wrote.

Now, what do you do with the ones that don't sound correct? Before you can fix them, you need to decode each sentence to find out if it has both a subject and a verb. The subject and the verb are the bare essentials of a sentence. Every sentence you write must contain both. There is one exception:

In a **command**, the subject is suggested rather than stated.

Consider these examples.

Sign here. = [You] sign here. (The subject you is implied or understood.)
Charge it. = [You] charge it.
Play ball! = [You] play ball!

Finding Subjects and Verbs[1]

A sentence is about *someone* or *something*. That someone or something is the **subject**. The word (or words) that tells what the subject *is* or *does* is the **verb**. In the following sentences, the subject is underlined once and the verb twice.

Snow falls.
Kim dislikes winter.
We love snowboarding.
Mt. Whistler offers excellent opportunities for winter sports.
In Canada, winter is six months long.
Some people feel the cold severely.

The subject of a sentence is always a **noun** (the name of a person, place, thing, or concept) or a **pronoun** (a word such as *I, you, he, she, it, we*, or *they* used in place of a noun). In the examples above, the subjects include persons (*Kim, we, people*); a place (*Mt. Whistler*); a thing (*snow*); and a concept (*winter*). In one sentence, a pronoun (*we*) is the subject.

[1]If you have forgotten (or have never learned) the parts of speech and the basic sentence patterns, you will find this information on the student page of the *Essay Essentials* Web site, http://www.essayessentials3e.nelson.com

One way to find the **verb** in a sentence is to ask what the sentence says about the subject. There are two kinds of verbs.

- **Action verbs** tell you what the subject is doing. In the examples above, *falls*, *dislikes*, *love*, and *offers* are action verbs.
- **Linking verbs** link or connect a subject to a noun or adjective describing that subject. In the examples above, *is* and *feel* are linking verbs.

    Linking verbs tell you the subject's condition or state of being. (For example, "Tadpoles *become* frogs," "Frogs *feel* slimy.") The most common linking verbs are forms of *to be* (*am, is, are, was, were, have been,* etc.) and verbs such as *look, taste, feel, sound, appear, remain, seem,* and *become*.

Another way to find the verb in a sentence is to put a pronoun (*I, you, he, she, it,* or *they*) in front of the word you think is the verb. If the result makes sense, it is a verb. For example, you could put *it* in front of *falls* in the first sentence listed above: "it falls" makes sense, so you know *falls* is the verb in this sentence. Try this test with the other five example sentences.

    Keep this guideline in mind as you work through the exercises below.

Ask <u>who</u> or <u>what</u> the sentence is about to find the subject.
Then ask what the subject <u>is</u> or <u>is doing</u> to find the verb.

Exercise 24.1*

In each of the following sentences, underline the <u>subject</u> with one line and the <u>verb</u> with two. Answers for exercises in this chapter begin on page 489. If you make even one mistake, go to the Web site and do the exercise listed beside the Web icon that follows this exercise. Be sure you understand this material thoroughly before you go on.

1. Algy met a bear.

2. A bear met Algy.

3. The bear was bulgy.

4. Unfortunately, the bulge was Algy.

5. Grizzlies are famous for their unpredictability.

6. Meeting bears unexpectedly is clearly risky.

7. According to an old myth, bears never run downhill.

8. Take it from me. They do.

9. Females with cubs are especially dangerous.

10. Defending oneself presents a real problem.

GO TO WEB

EXERCISE 24.1

Usually, but not always, the subject comes before the verb in a sentence.

Occasionally, we find the subject after the verb:

- In sentences beginning with *Here* + some form of *to be* or with *There* + some form of *to be*

   Here and *there* are never the subject of a sentence.

   Here <u>are</u> the test <u>results</u>. (Who or what <u>are</u>? <u>Results</u>.)
   There <u>is</u> a <u>fly</u> in my soup. (Who or what <u>is</u>? A <u>fly</u>.)

- In sentences that are deliberately inverted for emphasis

   Finally, at the end of the long, boring joke <u>came</u> the pathetic <u>punch line</u>.
   Out of the stadium and into the pouring rain <u>marched</u> the <u>parade</u>.

- In questions

   <u>Are</u> <u>we</u> there yet?
   <u>Is</u> <u>she</u> the one?

   But notice that in questions beginning with *who, whose, what, where,* or *which,* the subject and verb are in "normal" order: subject followed by verb.

   <u>Who</u> <u>ate</u> my sandwich?   Whose <u>horse</u> <u>came</u> first?
   <u>What</u> <u>caused</u> the accident?   Which <u>car</u> <u>runs</u> best?

Exercise 24.2*

Underline the subject with one line and the verb with two. Watch out for inverted sentences. If you make an error, do the Web exercises that follow.

1. Here is an idea to consider.

2. Lucy Maud Montgomery lived in Ontario before Confederation.

3. Who wants the last piece?

4. Eat slowly.

5. Exercise builds strong bodies and healthy minds.

6. Keep your body fit.

7. Far behind the Liberals and New Democrats trailed the Conservatives, bringing up the rear.

8. Pride goes before a fall.

9. Only in Canada is the lack of national identity a distinctive national characteristic.

10. Irish coffee contains ingredients from all four of the essential food groups: caffeine, fat, sugar, and alcohol.

GO TO WEB

EXERCISES 24.2, 24.3, 24.4

More about Verbs

The verb in a sentence may be a single word, as in the exercises you've just done, or it may be a group of words. When you are considering whether or not a word group is a verb, there are two points you should remember.

1. No verb preceded by *to* is ever the verb of a sentence.[2]
2. **Helping verbs**[3] are often added to main verbs.

---

[2] The form *to* + verb—e.g., *to speak*, *to write*, *to help*—is an infinitive. Infinitives can act as subjects or objects, but they are never verbs.

[3] If you are familiar with technical grammatical terms, you will know these verbs as **auxiliary verbs**.

The list below contains the most common helping verbs.

be (all forms of	can	must/must have
to be can act as	could/could have	ought
helping verbs: e.g.,	do/did	shall/shall have
am, are, is, was, were,	have/had	should/should have
will be, have/had	may/may have	will/will have
been, etc.)	might/might have	would/would have

The complete verb in a sentence consists of the main verb together with any helping verbs.

Here are a few of the forms of the verb *write*. Notice that in questions the subject may come between the helping verb and the main verb.

You <u>may write</u> now.	You <u>ought to write</u> to him.
He certainly <u>can write</u>!	We <u>will have written</u> by then.
We <u>should write</u> home more often.	He <u>had written</u> his apology.
I <u>shall write</u> tomorrow.	I <u>will write</u> to the editor.
He <u>could have written</u> yesterday.	The proposal <u>has been written</u>.
She <u>is writing</u> her memoirs.	Orders <u>should have been written</u>.
<u>Did</u> he <u>write</u> to you?	<u>Could</u> you <u>have written</u> it in French?

One verb form *always* takes a helping verb. Here is the rule.

A verb ending in *-ing* MUST have a helping verb (or verbs) before it.

Here are a few of the forms an *-ing* verb can take:

I <u>am writing</u> the report.
<u>Is</u> she <u>writing</u> the paper for him?
You <u>are writing</u> illegibly.
I <u>was writing</u> neatly.
You <u>will be writing</u> a report.
They <u>must have been writing</u> all night.
<u>Have</u> you <u>been writing</u> on the wall?

Beware of certain words that are often confused with helping verbs.

Words such as *not, only, always, often, sometimes, never, ever,* and *just* are NOT part of the verb.

These words sometimes appear in the middle of a complete verb, but they are modifiers, not verbs. Do not underline them.

> I <u>have</u> just <u>won</u> a one-way ticket to Moose Factory.
> She <u>is</u> always <u>chosen</u> first.
> Most people <u>do</u> not <u>welcome</u> unasked-for advice.

Exercise 24.3*

Underline the subject once and the complete verb twice. Check your answers, and if you made even one mistake, try the Web exercises that follow.

1. He has talked non-stop for three hours.

2. I am not going to drive.

3. Could they return the goods tomorrow?

4. Personal opinion is often presented as fact.

5. Carla should have been filing the letters and memos.

6. Soon he will have been sleeping for 16 hours.

7. Paula's lawsuit should never have been allowed to proceed this far.

8. Have you ever been to the Zanzibar tavern?

9. There has never been a better time to travel to Southeast Asia.

10. How are the club members identified?

GO TO WEB

EXERCISES 24.5, 24.6, 24.7, 24.8

More about Subjects

Often groups of words called **prepositional phrases** come before the subject in a sentence or between the subject and the verb. When you're looking for the subject in a sentence, prepositional phrases can trip you up unless you know the following rule.

> The subject of a sentence is never in a prepositional phrase.

You must be able to identify prepositional phrases so that you will know where *not* to look for the subject. A prepositional phrase is a group of words that begins with a preposition and ends with the name of something or someone (a noun or a pronoun). Often a prepositional phrase will indicate the direction or location of something. Here are some prepositional phrases (the italicized words are prepositions):

about the book	*between* the desks	*near* the wall
above the desk	*by* the book	*of* the typist
according to the book	*concerning* the memo	*on* the desk
after the meeting	*despite* the book	*onto* the floor
against the wall	*down* the hall	*over* a door
along the hall	*except* the staff	*to* the staff
among the books	*for* the manager	*through* the window
among them	*from* the office	*under* the book
around the office	*in* the book	*until* the meeting
before lunch	*in* front of the door	*up* the hall
behind the desk	*inside* the office	*with* a book
below the window	*into* the elevator	*without* the book
beside the book	*like* the book	*without* them

When you're looking for the subject in a sentence, you can make the task easier by crossing out any prepositional phrases. For example,

The keyboard ~~of your computer~~ should be cleaned occasionally.

What <u>should be cleaned</u>? The <u>keyboard</u> (not the computer).

~~In case~~ ~~of an emergency,~~ one ~~of the group~~ should go ~~to the nearest~~ ~~ranger station~~ ~~for help~~.

Who <u>should go</u>? <u>One</u> (not the group).

Exercise 24.4*

In the following sentences, first cross out the prepositional phrase(s), then underline the subject once and the verb twice. Check your answers before going on to the Web exercises that follow.

1. The problem with you is your attitude.

Sentence Structure

2. For many years, we four old friends have been meeting for our vacations.

3. In the state of Florida, it is illegal for single, divorced, or widowed women to parachute on Sunday afternoons.

4. In Kentucky, no woman may appear in a bathing suit on any highway in the state unless escorted by two officers or armed with a club.

5. In my wildest imaginings, I cannot understand the reason for these laws.

6. During a break in the conversation, Darryl's embarrassing comment could be heard in every corner of the room.

7. Without her glasses, Stacey cannot see the blackboard at the front of the room.

8. To the staff and managers of the project, I extend my congratulations for an excellent job.

9. Against all odds, and despite their shortcomings, the Miners made it into the playoffs of the Southern New Brunswick Little League.

10. Walk a mile in my shoes at high noon with your head held high in order to avoid clichés like the plague.

GO TO WEB

EXERCISES 24.9, 24.10

Multiple Subjects and Verbs

So far, you have been working with sentences containing only one complete subject and one complete verb. Sentences can, however, have more than one subject and verb. Multiple subjects are called **compound subjects**; multiple verbs are **compound verbs**. Here is a sentence with a compound subject:

Esquimalt and Oak Bay border the city of Victoria.

This sentence has a compound verb:

She groped and stumbled her way down the dark aisle of the movie theatre.

And this sentence has a compound subject and a compound verb:

The detective and the police sergeant leaped from their car and seized the suspect.

The elements of a compound subject or verb are usually joined by *and* (sometimes by *or*). Compound subjects and verbs may contain more than two elements, as in the following sentences:

Careful planning, organization, and conscientious revision are the keys to good essay writing.

I finished my paper, put the cat outside, took the phone off the hook, and crawled into bed.

Exercise 24.5*

In the following sentences, cross out any prepositional phrases, then underline the subjects once and the verbs twice. Be sure to underline all the elements in a compound subject or verb. Check your answers before continuing.

1. The prime minister and the premiers met at Harrison Lake.

2. They debated and drafted amendments to the employment insurance program.

3. The anesthetist and the surgeon scrubbed for surgery and hurried to the operating room.

4. Blue spruce and hemlock are both native to northern Ontario.

5. I tried and failed once, then tried again and succeeded.

6. My son or my daughter will drive me home.

7. Knock three times and ask for Stan.

8. Our economics instructor and her colleagues went to a conference yesterday.

9. Buy the base model and don't waste your money on the luxury options.

10. Ragweed, goldenrod, and twitch grass formed the essential elements in the bouquet for his English teacher.

GO TO WEB

EXERCISES 24.11, 24.12, 24.13, 24.14

Here's a summary of what you've learned in this chapter. Keep it in front of you as you write the mastery test.

Summary

- The subject is *who* or *what* the sentence is about.
- The verb tells what the subject *is* or *does*.
- The subject normally comes before the verb (exceptions are questions and sentences beginning with *there* or *here*).
- The complete verb = a main verb + any helping verbs.
- By itself, a word ending in *-ing* is not a verb.
- The subject of a sentence is never in a prepositional phrase.
- A sentence can have more than one subject and/or verb.

Exercise 24.6

This challenging exercise will test your subject- and verb-finding ability. In each sentence below, first cross out any prepositional phrases, and then underline each subject with one line and each verb with two lines. Be sure to underline all elements in a multiple subject or verb.

1. The politicians of our time try in vain to change the world but seldom try to change themselves.

2. In the opinion of many Canadians, the word politician is synonymous with "idiot."

3. Hugo went to hockey camp; Sabina spent the summer at her cottage; Walter worked in a children's program; and I stayed home and sulked.

4. Among the many kinds of cheese made in Canada are Camembert, Fontina, and Quark.

5. Shoe companies, video companies, and exercise equipment manufacturers are all profiting from the fitness craze.

6. According to the official course outline, students in this English course must take notes during every class and submit their notes after each class to their instructor for evaluation.

7. On the Lovers' Tour to Lake Louise were two elderly women with walkers, a couple of elderly gentlemen with very young wives, half a dozen middle-aged divorcées, and me.

8. She attended aerobics classes, ran 15 km each week, ate a low-fat diet, practised yoga and tai chi, and last Wednesday was hit by a bus.

9. There, in the old photograph on my grandmother's mantel, my grandfather, in his aviator's uniform, stood at attention beside his biplane and grinned at me from the past.

10. According to its campaign literature, the incoming government will provide jobs for all Canadians, eliminate the national debt, find a cure for cancer, land a Canadian on Mars, and lower taxes, all in its first year of office.

25

Solving Sentence-Fragment Problems

Any group of words that is punctuated as a sentence but that does not have a subject or a complete verb is a **sentence fragment**. Fragments are appropriate in conversation and in some kinds of writing, but normally they are unacceptable in college, technical, and business writing. There are two kinds of fragments you should watch out for: missing piece fragments and dependent clause fragments.

"Missing Piece" Fragments

Sometimes a group of words is punctuated as a sentence but is missing one or more of the essential parts of a sentence: a subject and a verb. Consider these examples.

1. Found it under the pile of clothes on your floor.

   Who or what <u>found</u> it? The sentence doesn't tell you. The subject is missing.

2. Their arguments about housework.

   The sentence doesn't tell you what the arguments <u>were</u> or <u>did</u>. The verb is missing.

3. During my favourite TV show.

   <u>Who</u> or <u>what</u> <u>was</u> or <u>did</u> something? Both subject and verb are missing.

4. The programmers working around the clock to trace the hacker.

> Part of the verb is missing. Remember that a verb ending in *-ing* needs a helping verb to be complete.

Finding fragments like these in your work when you are revising is the hard part. Fixing them is easy. There are two ways to correct sentence fragments. Here's the first one.

> To change a "missing piece" fragment into a complete sentence, add whatever is missing: a subject, a verb, or both.

1. You may need to add a subject:

Your <u>sister</u> found it under the pile of clothes on your floor.

2. You may need to add a verb:

Their arguments <u>were</u> about housework. (linking verb)
Their arguments about housework eventually <u>destroyed</u> their relationship. (action verb)

3. You may need to add both a subject and a verb:

My <u>mother</u> always <u>calls</u> during my favourite TV show.

4. Or you may need to add a helping verb:

The programmers <u>have been</u> working around the clock to trace the hacker.

Don't let the length of a fragment fool you. Students sometimes think that if a string of words is long, it must be a sentence. Not so. No matter how long the string of words, if it doesn't contain both a subject and a verb, it is not a sentence. For example, here's a description of children going from door to door for treats on Halloween:

In twos and threes, dressed in the fashionable Disney costumes of the year, as their parents tarried behind, grownups following after, grownups bantering about the schools, or about movies, about local sports, about their marriages, about the difficulties of long marriages, kids sprinting up the next driveway, kids decked out as demons or superheroes or dinosaurs . . . beating back the restless souls of the dead, in search of sweets.

Moody, Rick. *Demonology*. New York: Little, Brown, 2001. 291.

At 68 words, this "sentence" is long, but it is a fragment. It lacks both a subject and a verb. If you add "The <u>children</u> <u>came</u>" at the beginning of the fragment, you would have a complete sentence.

In the following exercises, decide whether each group of words is a complete sentence or a "missing piece" fragment. Put *S* before each complete sentence and *F* before each fragment. Make each fragment into a complete sentence by adding whatever is missing: the subject, the verb, or both. Then compare your answers with our suggestions. Answers for exercises in this chapter begin on page 491.

Exercise 25.1*

1. _____ Regarding myths and fairy tales.

2. _____ To decide on the basis of rumour, not facts.

3. _____ Trying to be helpful, I offered to check the files.

4. _____ Grading exams all evening after working all day.

5. _____ The party members gathering in the campaign office.

6. _____ We won.

7. _____ Hands over your head.

8. _____ To study without my CD player.

9. _____ Having worked hard all her life.

10. _____ Wanting to please them, she had coffee ready on their arrival.

GO TO WEB

EXERCISES 25.1, 25.2, 25.3, 25.4

Exercise 25.2*

_____ Professional athletes making millions of dollars a year. _____ At the same time, owners of sports franchises growing fantastically rich from the efforts of their employees, the players. _____ The fans being the forgotten people in the struggle for control over major league sports. _____ The people who pay the money that makes both owners and players rich. _____ I have an idea that would protect everyone's interests. _____ Cap the owners' profits. _____ Cap the players' salaries. _____ And, most important, the ticket prices. _____ A fair deal for everyone. _____ Fans should be able to see their teams play for the price of a movie ticket, not the price of a television set.

Dependent Clause Fragments

A group of words containing a subject and a verb is a **clause**. There are two kinds of clauses. An **independent clause** is one that makes complete sense on its own. It can stand alone, as a sentence. A **dependent clause**, as its name suggests, cannot stand alone as a sentence; it depends on another clause to make complete sense.

Dependent clauses are easy to recognize, because they begin with **dependent-clause cues** (subordinating conjunctions). Every time you find one of these words or phrases introducing a clause, that clause is dependent.

Dependent-Clause Cues

after	if	until
although	in order that	what, whatever
as, as if	provided that	when, whenever
as long as	since	where, wherever, whereas
as soon as	so that	whether
because	that	which, whichever
before	though	while
even if, even though	unless	who, whom, whose

Whenever a clause begins with one of these words or phrases, it is dependent.

A dependent clause must be attached to an independent clause. If it stands alone, it is a sentence fragment.

Here is an independent clause:

I am a poor speller.

If we put one of the dependent-clause cues in front of it, it can no longer stand alone:

Because I am a poor speller.

We can correct this kind of fragment by attaching it to an independent clause:

Because I am a poor speller, I have chained my dictionary to my wrist.

Exercise 25.3*

Put an *S* before each clause that is independent and therefore a sentence. Put an *F* before each clause that is dependent and therefore a sentence fragment. Circle the dependent-clause cue in each sentence fragment.

1. _____ Although she practised it constantly.

2. _____ Since the horse stepped on her.

3. _____ As soon as the troops arrived, the fighting stopped.

4. _____ Whichever route the bikers choose.

5. _____ Before Biff bought his Harley.

GO TO WEB

EXERCISES 25.5, 25.6, 25.7, 25.8

Exercise 25.4*

Identify the sentence fragments in the paragraph below by circling the dependent-clause cue in each fragment you find.

Although many companies are experiencing growth, thanks to a healthy economy. Middle managers are not breathing easy. As long as there is a surplus of junior executives. Middle managers will continue to look over their shoulders, never sure when the axe will fall. Whether through early retirement, buyout, or termination. Their positions are being eliminated by cost-conscious firms whose eyes are focused on the bottom line. Because the executive branch of many businesses expanded rapidly during the years of high growth. Now there is a large block of managers who have no prospects of advancement. As one analyst observed, when he examined this block of largely superfluous executives and their chances of rising in the company hierarchy, "You cannot push a rectangle up a triangle."

Most sentence fragments are dependent clauses punctuated as sentences. Fortunately, this is the easiest kind of fragment to recognize and fix. All you need to do is join the dependent clause either to the sentence that comes before it or to the one that comes after it—whichever linkage makes better sense.

One final point: if you join your sentence fragment to the independent clause that follows it, you must separate the two clauses with a comma (see Rule 4, Chapter 33).

Read the following example to yourself; then read it aloud (remember, last sentence first).

> Montreal is a sequence of ghettos. Although I was born and brought up there. My experience of French was a pathetically limited and distorted one.

The second "sentence" sounds incomplete, and the dependent-clause cue at the beginning of it is the clue you need to identify it as a sentence fragment. You could join the fragment to the sentence before it, but then you would get "Montreal is a sequence of ghettos, although I was born and brought up there," which doesn't make sense. Clearly the fragment should be linked to the sentence that follows it, like this:

Montreal is a sequence of ghettos. Although I was born and brought up there, my experience of French was a pathetically limited and distorted one. (Mordecai Richler)

Exercise 25.5*

Turn back to Exercise 25.4 and revise it by joining each dependent clause fragment to an independent clause that precedes or follows it, whichever makes better sense.

GO TO WEB

EXERCISE 25.9

Exercise 25.6*

The following paragraph contains both independent and dependent clauses (fragments), all punctuated as if they were complete sentences. Letting meaning be your guide, join each dependent clause fragment to the independent clause that comes before or after it—whichever makes better sense. Be careful to punctuate correctly between clauses.

In spite of what everyone says about the weak economy and the scarcity of jobs, especially for young people. I have financed my college career with a variety of part-time and seasonal jobs. Right now, for instance, while completing my third year at college. I have not one, or two, but three part-time jobs. I am a short-order cook three nights a week for a local bar and diner. And a telemarketer for a cable company after school. Or whenever I have free time. I'm also a server at a specialty coffee store on weekends. To maintain any kind of social life. While juggling three jobs and the requirements of my third-year program is not exactly easy, but I find it hard to turn down the opportunity for experience. Not to mention cash. I'm willing to put my social life on hold. For a while.

Exercise 25.7

As a final test of your skill in finding and correcting sentence fragments, try this exercise. Make each fragment into a complete sentence.

1. I had never eaten curry, but I decided I liked it. The first time I tasted it.
2. The report identified a serious problem with our system. Our Web site is vulnerable to hackers. Whenever it is being revised or updated.
3. Our family thinks my sister is too young to get married. Since she and her boyfriend want to go to Canada's Wonderland for their honeymoon.
4. It may surprise you to learn that Canadians have made significant contributions to world cuisine. The two best known being baby pablum and frozen peas.
5. Buying a lottery ticket will benefit you about as much as betting that the next U.S. president will come from Moose Jaw. Or that the parrot in the pet store speaks Inuktitut.
6. I dream about spending my retirement sailing, skiing, dining, and dancing. Unfortunately, by that time, probably too old to enjoy any of those activities.
7. I decided to take swimming lessons for two reasons: first, fitness. Second, safety.
8. Learning a new language can be difficult. When you are an adult. It can be done, however.
9. All of us are more aware of the effects of pollution than we were 30 years ago. Because we are continually bombarded with information about the environment. In school, on television, and in newspapers.
10. My second favourite household chore is ironing. My first being hitting my head on the top bunk bed until I faint. (Erma Bombeck)

26

Solving Run-On Problems

Some sentences lack certain elements and thus are fragments. A sentence with too many ideas in it or with inadequate punctuation between clauses is a **run-on**. Run-ons tend to occur when you write in a hurry and are not thinking clearly. If you think about what you want to say and punctuate carefully, you shouldn't have any problems with them.

There are three kinds of run-on sentences: the comma splice, the fused sentence, and the "monster" run on.

Comma Splices and Fused Sentences

As its name suggests, the **comma splice** occurs when two complete sentences (independent clauses) are joined together with only a comma between them. Here's an example:

I stayed up all night, I am exhausted.

A **fused sentence** occurs when two complete sentences are joined together with no punctuation at all:

I stayed up all night I am exhausted.

1. The easiest way to fix a comma splice or a fused sentence is to join the independent clauses with a semicolon.

I stayed up all night; I am exhausted.

To be sure you understand how to use semicolons correctly, read Chapter 35.

> 2. Add an appropriate linking word between the two clauses.

Two types of linking words will work.

1. You can insert one of the following words: *and, but, or, nor, for, so,* or *yet.*[1] These words should be preceded by a comma.

   I stayed up all night, and I am exhausted.

2. You can insert one of the dependent-clause cues listed in Chapter 25, on page 328.

   Because I stayed up all night, I am exhausted.

> 3. Make the independent clauses into separate sentences.

   I stayed up all night. I am exhausted.

All three solutions to the problem require that you use a word or punctuation mark strong enough to come between two independent clauses. A comma by itself is too weak, and so is a dash.

The sentences in the following exercises will give you practice in fixing comma splices and fused sentences. Correct the sentences where necessary and then check your answers, beginning on page 492. (Because there are three ways to fix these errors, your answers may differ somewhat from our suggestions.) If you find that you're confused about when to use a semicolon and when to use a period, be sure to read page 415 before going on.

Exercise 26.1*

1. The fog has lifted, we can go home now.
2. Just let me do the talking, we will get a ticket if you open your mouth.

---

[1]These words are called **coordinating conjunctions** because they are used to join equal (or coordinating) clauses. If you are not sure how to punctuate sentences with coordinating conjunctions, see Chapter 33, Rule 3.

CHAPTER 26: SOLVING RUN-ON PROBLEMS · **335**

Sentence Structure

3. I keep buying lottery tickets, but I have won only once.
4. Hitting a golf ball may look easy, it's not.
5. As long as you smile when you speak, you can say almost anything.
6. Montreal used to be called Ville Ste. Marie, I think, before that it was known as Hochelaga.
7. Students today need summer jobs, tuition and living costs are too much for most families.
8. Bryan will be going to college if he is accepted, his parents are wealthy.
9. My word processor makes writing much easier, but it doesn't seem to spell any better than I do.
10. "I was married by a judge, I should have asked for a jury." (Groucho Marx)

GO TO WEB

EXERCISES 26.1, 26.2

Exercise 26.2*

1. A Canadian who speaks three languages is called multilingual, one who speaks two languages is called bilingual, one who speaks only one language is called an English Canadian.
2. I'm sure the job couldn't have been as bad as he claims, maybe he just didn't try hard enough.
3. Casual meetings are fine for small groups, large groups have to be handled in a different way.
4. I'll be glad to help you just call when you need me, I'll be here all day.
5. In Canada, winter is more than a season it's a bad joke.
6. Perfection is probably impossible to achieve, but that doesn't mean one should stop trying.
7. For students in technology programs, then, the future looks bright, however, a diploma does not guarantee job security.
8. Career opportunities are good for students in technical programs, however most employers are looking for people with experience as well as training.
9. People with high-technology skills are needed in several fields, avionics, computer networking, and environmental technology are three examples.
10. I still believe in a unified Canada, I believe in one nation extending from sea to sea. The Fathers of Confederation were right, a federation of provinces can work.

Monster Run-Ons

In a monster run-on sentence, too many clauses and, often, too many words are crowded together into one sentence. There is no hard-and-fast rule about how many independent clauses you may have in a sentence, but more than two can result in a sentence that is hard to read and even harder to understand.

> There were still a dozen or so guests who remained at the party, not counting the host, but after Raoul and Su Mei left, we decided it was time to go, so we collected our coats and said goodbye to the others, and then, after driving home very cautiously at speeds not exceeding 50 km/h, we sat up drinking coffee until three o'clock in the morning discussing our host's terrible taste in friends.

Clearly, the writer who created this monster got carried away with enthusiasm and just scribbled down everything that came to mind without thinking of the reader's tolerance or patience. If you take your time and remember your readers, you probably won't make this error. If you do find run-on sentences in your writing, however, you can correct them by following two steps.

1. Cut out all unnecessary words.
2. Apply one of the three solutions to comma splice and fused sentence problems: semicolons, linking words, and sentence breaks.

To turn a monster sentence into a correct and civilized one, first read through your sentence and identify any words or phrases that are not essential to its meaning.

> *There were still* a dozen *or so* guests *who* remained at the party, *not counting the host*, but after Raoul and Su Mei left, we decided *it was time* to go, so we collected our coats and said goodbye *to the others*, and then, after driving home *very* cautiously at *speeds not exceeding* 50 km/h, we sat up drinking coffee until three o'clock *in the morning* discussing our host's terrible taste in friends.

Run-on sentences are often made worse by **wordiness** (see Chapter 11 for hints on how to eliminate unnecessary words from your writing). In the example above, the words in italics are unnecessary and should be eliminated. Here's how the sentence reads without them:

A dozen guests remained at the party, but after Raoul and Su Mei left, we decided to go, so we collected our coats and said goodbye, and then, after driving home cautiously at 50 km/h, we sat up drinking coffee until three o'clock discussing our host's terrible taste in friends.

This version is an improvement, but it is not as clear and concise as it could be. Let's move on to step 2 and break the sentences into smaller units.

A dozen guests remained at the party, but after Raoul and Su Mei left, we decided to go. We collected our coats and said goodbye. Then, after driving home cautiously at 50 km/h, we sat up until three o'clock drinking coffee and discussing our host's terrible taste in friends.

This version is both concise and clear.

Exercise 26.3*

In the following exercise, first eliminate all unnecessary words. Then use semicolons, linking words, or sentence breaks to correct what is left. There are several ways to fix these sentences. Just be sure your corrections make sense and are easy to read. The answers provided on page 493 are only suggestions.

1. There are many hilarious examples of newspaper headlines that do not say exactly or clearly what their writers intended, my favourite is from the sports pages and reads, "Grandmother of Eight Makes Hole in One."

2. Other examples of the headline writer's art indicate a pretty impressive ability for stating the obvious, for example, "Smokers Are Productive, but Death Cuts Efficiency" is one classic and another is "Man Is Fatally Slain."

3. If you have trouble getting your child's attention, all you have to do is sit down and get comfortable, pick up a book, or turn on the TV, or just relax, your child will be all over you in no time at all which is why, when young children are home from school or on vacation, parents begin to understand how grossly unappreciated primary school teachers are.

4. I'll bet you didn't know that eyeglasses were invented by the Chinese more or less approximately 800 years ago, which is 500 years before lens grinding in the West was sufficiently refined to permit the making of corrective lenses and we know this because it was Marco Polo who early in the 13th century reported seeing many Chinese wearing eyeglasses during his visit to the Orient in 1275.

5. There is some confusion among modern historians today about the origin of the name "Canada," while some claim it comes from an Iroquois word meaning "village," others think it may derive from the Spanish expression *aquí nada*, which means "there is nothing here," and that the Native peoples may have picked up the term from early Portuguese or Spanish explorers and passed it on to Jacques Cartier, who applied it to the lands he claimed for France.

GO TO WEB

EXERCISE 26.3

Exercise 26.4

As a final test of your ability to identify and correct run-on sentences, find and correct the ten errors in the following paragraphs.

According to a news report, a private girls' school in Victoria was recently faced with an unusual problem, they solved it in a way that can only be described as creative, it is also a good example of effective teaching. Some of the Grade 10 girls, forbidden by their parents to wear lipstick at home, began to apply it at school, in the second-floor washroom. That was the first problem, the second was that after applying the lipstick, they would press their lips to the mirror, leaving dozens of perfect lip prints. Every night, the maintenance crew would remove the prints, the next day the girls would reapply them and finally the principal decided that something had to be done.

She called the girls into the washroom where she met them with one of the maintenance men and he stood by while the principal addressed the girls. She explained that the lip prints on the mirrors were causing a problem for the maintenance crew, they had to clean the mirrors every night instead of doing other work. To demonstrate how difficult the cleaning job was and how much time was wasted on this needless chore, the principal asked the maintenance man to clean one of the mirrors, the girls watched with interest he took out a long-handled squeegee and began scrubbing at the lipstick prints. When he had scrubbed for a while, he turned, dipped his squeegee into one of the toilets, and continued to work on the mirrors and since then, there has not been another set of lip prints left on the washroom mirror.

27

Solving Modifier Problems

Felix was complimented on a great game and a fine job of goaltending *by his mother.*

Snarling furiously and baring his teeth, Maurice crawled through a basement window only to confront an angry watchdog.

When she was a first-year student, the English professor told Mara she would *almost* write all her assignments in class.

These sentences show what can happen to your writing if you aren't sure how to use modifiers. A **modifier** is a word or group of words that adds information about another word in a sentence. In the examples above, the italicized words are modifiers. Used correctly, modifiers describe, explain, or limit another word, making its meaning more precise. Used carelessly, however, modifiers can cause confusion or, even worse, amusement. Few things are more embarrassing than being laughed at when you didn't mean to be funny.

You need to be able to recognize and solve two kinds of modifier problems: **misplaced modifiers** and **dangling modifiers**.

Misplaced Modifiers

Modifiers must be as close as possible to the words they apply to. Usually, readers will assume that a modifier modifies whatever it's next to. It's important to remember this, because, as the following examples show, changing the position of a modifier can change the meaning of your sentence.

Ahmed walked (only) as far as the corner store. (He didn't walk any farther.)

Ahmed (only) walked as far as the corner store. (He didn't jog or run.)

(Only) Ahmed walked as far as the corner store. (No one else went.)

Ahmed walked as far as the (only) corner store. (There were no other corner stores.)

> To make sure a modifier is in the right place, ask yourself "What does it apply to?" and put it beside that word or word group.

When a modifier is not close enough to the word it refers to, it is said to be misplaced. A misplaced modifier can be a single word in the wrong place.

The supervisor told me they needed someone who could use both Word and WordPerfect (badly.)

Is some company really hiring people to do poor work? Or does the company urgently need someone familiar with word processing programs? Obviously, the modifier *badly* belongs next to *needed*.

The supervisor told me they (badly) needed someone who could use both Word and WordPerfect.

> Be especially careful with these words: *almost, nearly, just, only, even, hardly, merely, scarcely.* Put them right before the words they modify.

Misplaced: She (nearly) answered every question.

Correctly placed: She answered (nearly) every question.

Misplaced: After driving all night, we (almost) arrived at 7:00 a.m.

Correctly placed: After driving all night, we arrived at (almost) 7:00 a.m.

A misplaced modifier can also be a group of words in the wrong place.

(Bundled up in down clothing to keep warm,) the dog team waited for the driver.

The modifier, *bundled up in down clothing to keep warm*, is too far away from the word it is supposed to modify, *driver*. In fact, it seems to modify *dog team*, making the sentence ridiculous. We need to rewrite the sentence.

The dog team waited for the driver, (bundled up in down clothing to keep warm.)

Look at this one:

I drove my mother to Saskatoon, where my aunt lives (in a rental car.)

In a rental car applies to *drove* and should be closer to it.

I drove my mother (in a rental car) to Saskatoon, where my aunt lives.

Notice that a modifier need not always go right next to what it modifies; it should, however, be as close as possible to it.

Occasionally, as in the examples above, the modifier is obviously out of place. The writer's intention is clear, and the sentences are easy to correct. But sometimes modifiers are misplaced in such a way that the meaning is not clear, as in the following example:

Raj said (after the game) he wanted to talk to the press.

Did Raj *say* it after the game? Or is he going to *talk to the press* after the game? To avoid confusion, we must move the modifier and, depending on which meaning we want, write either

(After the game,) Raj said he wanted to talk to the press.

or

Raj said he wanted to talk to the press (after the game.)

Now try your hand at relocating modifiers. In Exercises 27.1 and 27.2, rewrite the sentences that contain misplaced modifiers, positioning the modifiers correctly. Check your answers to the first set before continuing. Answers for this chapter begin on page 494.

Exercise 27.1*

1. Trevor left the can of Pet Grrmet out for the dog that he had opened.

2. Our supervisor told us on the first day that no one takes coffee breaks.

3. I enthusiastically recommend this candidate with no experience whatever.

4. Professor Green told us in September he thought our class was a hopeless case.

5. We almost enjoyed the whole movie; only the ending was a disappointment.

6. Leo and Annie found an apartment in a highrise within walking distance of the campus with two bedrooms and a sunken living room.

7. There just are enough pieces to go around.

8. It seems there is almost a game every day during baseball season.

9. A charming, intelligent companion is sought by a vertically challenged but wealthy gentleman who looks good in evening gowns and diamonds.

10. One of us could only go because there was enough money just to buy one ticket.

Exercise 27.2*

1. One finds the best Chinese food in those restaurants where the Chinese eat usually.

2. He caught sight of a canary and several finches using his new binoculars.

3. Juan had played ball professionally before coming to the Blue Jays for several major American teams.

4. The football practices have been organized for players who are not with a team in the summertime as a keep-fit measure.

5. Vancouver is a wonderful city for anyone who likes rain and fog to live in.

6. Some games are less demanding in terms of time and equipment, such as tiddlywinks.

7. The Human Rights Code prohibits discrimination against anyone who is applying for a job on the basis of race, religion, sex, or age.

8. We looked for a birthday present for our boss in a golf store.

9. After dinner, he lit up a huge cigar without getting permission from anyone that smelled like burnt rope.

10. Dr. Neil Paterson, the leader of Canada's Natural Law Party, claimed to be able to eliminate the national debt, achieve world peace, and reduce the number of unemployed using yogic flying.

Dangling Modifiers

A dangling modifier occurs when there is no appropriate word in the sentence for the modifier to apply to. That is, the sentence does not contain a specific word or idea to which the modifier could sensibly refer. With no appropriate word to modify, the modifier seems to apply to whatever it's next to, often with ridiculous results.

(After a good night's sleep,) my teachers were impressed with my unusual alertness.

This sentence seems to say that the teachers had a good night's sleep.

(Trying desperately to finish an essay,) my roommate's stereo made it impossible to concentrate.

The *stereo* was writing an essay?

Dangling modifiers are harder to correct than misplaced ones; you can't simply move danglers to another spot in the sentence. There are, however, two ways in which you can fix them. One way requires that you remember the following rule.

When a modifier comes at the beginning of a sentence, it modifies the subject of the sentence.[1]

---

[1]The rule has exceptions, called adverbial modifiers, but they won't give you any trouble. Example: (Quickly) she did as she was told.

CHAPTER 27: SOLVING MODIFIER PROBLEMS · 345

This rule means that you can avoid dangling modifiers by choosing the subjects of your sentences carefully. All you have to do is make sure the subject is an appropriate one for the modifier to apply to. Using this method, we can rewrite our two examples by changing the subjects.

After a good night's sleep, I impressed my teachers with my unusual alertness.

Trying desperately to finish an essay, I found it impossible to concentrate because of my roommate's stereo.

Another way to correct a dangling modifier is by changing it into a dependent clause.

After I had had a good night's sleep, my teachers were impressed with my unusual alertness.

When I was trying desperately to finish an essay, my roommate's stereo made it impossible to concentrate.

Sometimes a dangling modifier comes at the end of a sentence:

A Neon is the car to buy, looking for power, style, and an affordable price.

Can you correct this sentence? Try it; then look at the suggestions at the foot of the page.

Here is a summary of the steps to follow in solving modifier problems.

1. Ask "What does the modifier apply to?"
2. Be sure there is a word or group of words *in the sentence* for the modifier to apply to.
3. Put the modifier as close as possible to the word or word group it applies to.

Here are two suggestions.
1. Add a subject: Looking for power, style, and an affordable price, I decided a Neon was the car to buy.
2. Change the dangler to a dependent clause: A Neon is the car to buy, because I am looking for power, style, and an affordable price.

Exercise 27.3*

Most of the following sentences contain dangling modifiers. Make corrections by changing the subject of the sentence to one the modifier can appropriately apply to. There is no one right way to correct each sentence; our answers are only suggestions.

1. Driving recklessly and without lights, the police stopped Gina at a road block.

2. My supervisor gave me a lecture about punctuality after being late twice in one week.

3. After criticizing both my work and my atittude, I was fired.

4. Standing a full 2.5 m tall and weighing about 300 kg, Megan decided not to antagonize the bear.

5. After scoring the winning goal in overtime, a huge celebration wound through the city.

6. As a conscientious and dedicated teacher, the workload sometimes seems overwhelming to Nina.

7. In less than a minute after applying the ointment, the pain began to ease.

8. Making her first formal presentation to her colleagues and her supervisor, Henry was probably more nervous than Alison was.

9. When handling hazardous wastes, the procedures to follow are clearly outlined in the safety manual.

10. It was a great moment: after making the speech of a lifetime, the delegates chose Sara to lead the party into the next election.

Exercise 27.4*

Correct the dangling modifiers in Exercise 27.3 by changing them into dependent clauses.

Exercise 27.5*

In the following sentences, correct the misplaced and dangling modifiers in any way you choose. Our answers are only suggestions.

1. Only she was the baker's daughter, but she could loaf all day.

2. Being horribly hung over, the only problem with a free bar is knowing when to quit.

3. Large and purple, the judges were impressed by Sandor's turnips.

4. In a hurry to get to the interview on time, my résumé was left lying on my desk at home.

5. As a college student constantly faced with new assignments, the pressure is sometimes intolerable.

6. Reading *The Globe and Mail*, the provincial premiers plan to meet in Calgary next week.

7. Stopping in Ottawa on a tour with the Barenaked Ladies, the prime minister asked to meet Steven Page.

8. The Canadian Brass receives enthusiastic acclaim for its witty presentation and clarity of tone from Vancouver to St. John's.

9. Rolling on her back, eager to have her tummy scratched, Queen Elizabeth couldn't resist the little Corgi puppy.

10. Sinking lower on the world money markets, the U.S. dollar was a popular choice for investors wanting to get rid of their devalued yen.

GO TO WEB

EXERCISES 27.1, 27.2, 27.3, 27.4

Exercise 27.6

As a final test of your ability to use modifiers, correct the misplaced and dangling modifiers in the sentences below, using any solution you choose.

1. Obviously having drunk too much, I drove poor Tanya to her apartment, made her a pot of coffee, and called her mother.

2. When trying for your Red Cross bronze medal, your examiner will consider speed, endurance, and resuscitation techniques.

3. The Riel Rebellion this month will be featured in *Canadian History* magazine.

4. Trapped under a delicate crystal wine glass on the elegantly set table, his guests observed that most despised of uninvited dinner guests, a cockroach.

5. Not being reliable about arriving on time, I can't hire her to supervise others who are punctual.

6. While they were in my pocket, my children managed to break my glasses by leaping on me from behind.

7. A worm-eating warbler was spotted by Hazel Miller while walking along the branch of a tree and singing.

8. The only used motorcycles we could find had been ridden by bikers that were in pretty bad shape.

9. After travelling to the east coast three times in the past month, our company's planned expansion into Newfoundland has been put on hold, despite my recommendation.

10. "This bus has a seating capacity of 56 passengers with a maximum height of four metres." (Sign on a double-decker bus in Charlottetown)

28

The Parallelism Principle

Brevity, clarity, and force: these are three characteristics of good writing style. **Parallelism** will reinforce these characteristics in everything you write.

When your sentence contains a series of two or more items, they must be grammatically parallel. That is, they must be written in the same grammatical form. Consider this example:

Shefali likes *swimming, surfing,* and *to sail.*

The three items in this series are not parallel. Two end in *-ing*, but the third, *to sail*, is the infinitive form of the verb. To correct the sentence, you must put all the items in the same grammatical form. You have two choices. You can write

Shefali likes *swimming, surfing,* and *sailing.*

Or you can write

Shefali likes *to swim, to surf,* and *to sail.*

Now look at an example with two nonparallel elements:

Most people seek happiness in *long-term relationships* and *work that provides them with satisfaction.*

Again, you could correct this sentence in two ways. You could write "Most people seek happiness *in relationships that are long-term* and *in work that provides them with satisfaction*," but that solution produces a long and clumsy sentence. The shorter version works better: "Most people seek happiness in *long-term relationships* and *satisfying work.*" This version is concise, clear, and forceful.

> Correct faulty parallelism by writing all items in a series in the same grammatical form; that is, all words, or all phrases, or all clauses.

One way to tell whether the items in a series are parallel is to write them out in list form, one below the other. That way, you can see at a glance if all the elements are in the same grammatical form.

Not Parallel	**Parallel**
My brother is *messy,* *rude,* and *an obnoxious person.*	My brother is *messy,* *rude,* and *obnoxious.*
(This list has two adjectives and a noun phrase.)	(This list has three adjectives.)
I support myself by *delivering pizza,* *poker,* and *shooting pool.*	I support myself by *delivering pizza,* *playing poker,* and *shooting pool.*
(This list has two phrases and one single word as objects of the preposition *by.*)	(This list has three phrases as objects of the preposition *by.*)
Jules wants a job that *will interest him,* *will challenge him,* and *pays well.*	Jules wants a job that *will interest him,* *(will) challenge him,* and *(will) pay him well.*
(This series of clauses contains two future tense verbs and one present tense verb.)	(All three subordinate clauses contain future tense verbs.)

As you can see, achieving parallelism is partly a matter of developing an ear for the sound of a correct list. A parallel sentence has a smooth, unbroken rhythm. Practice and the exercises in this chapter will help. Once you have mastered parallelism in your sentences, you will be ready to develop ideas in parallel sequence—in thesis statements, for example—and thus to write clear, well-organized prose. Far from being a frill, parallelism is a fundamental characteristic of good writing.

Correct the sentences where necessary in the following exercises. As you work through these sentences, try to spot parallelism errors from the change in rhythm that the faulty element produces. Then revise the sentence to bring the faulty element into line with the other elements in the series. Check your answers to each set of ten before going on. Answers for this chapter begin on page 496.

Exercise 28.1*

1. This program is easy to understand and using it is not difficult, either.

2. We were told that we would have to leave and to take nothing with us.

3. We organized our findings, wrote the report, and finally our presentation was made.

4. Today's personal computers are fast, high-powered, and compact in size.

5. Elmer's doctor advised that he should be careful with his back and not to strain his mind.

6. The company is looking for an employee who has a car and knowledge of the city would be a help.

7. The workplace-safety committee found the factory to be full of noise, smelly, and dirt everywhere.

8. When I want to get away from it all, there are three solitary pleasures I enjoy: a walk in the country, reading a good book, and fine music.

9. A recent survey of female executives claims that family responsibilities, being excluded from informal networks, and lacking management experience are the major factors keeping them from advancement.

10. If it is to be useful, your report must be organized clearly, written well, and your research should be thorough.

GO TO WEB

EXERCISES 28.1, 28.2

Exercise 28.2*

1. I wanted either a Mother's pizza or I wanted a Big Mac from McDonald's.

2. In my home town, two related crimes prevail: vandalism, and there is a lot of drug trafficking.

3. Bodybuilding has made me what I am today: physically perfect, very prosperous financially, and practically friendless.

4. I'd like to help, but I'm too tired, and my time is already taken up with other things.

5. Bruce claimed that, through repetition and being firm, he had trained his guppy to show loyalty and be obedient.

6. Dogbert understands pretty clearly what he can get away with and what he can't.

7. My sister, who is trying to teach me to play tennis, says that my fore-hand and serve are all right, but to work on strengthening my back-hand.

8. The two factors thought to be most important in a long-lasting marriage are how committed each partner is to the marriage and the willingness to compromise.

9. If there is no heaven, then hell can't exist either.

10. The new budget must deal with several major problems, such as the devalued Canadian dollar and the fact that health costs are rising so rapidly.

GO TO WEB

EXERCISES 28.3, 28.4, 28.5, 28.6

Exercise 28.3*

Make the following lists parallel. In each case, you can make your items parallel with any item in the list, so your answers may differ from ours.

Example:	Wrong:	stick handling	score a goal
	Right:	stick handling	goal scoring
	Also right:	handle the stick	score a goal
1. Wrong:	wine	women	singing
Right:			
2. Wrong:	employers	those working for the employer	
Right:			
3. Wrong:	doing your best	don't give up	
Right:			
4. Wrong:	information	education	entertaining
Right:			
5. Wrong:	individually	as a group	
Right:			
6. Wrong:	privately	in public	
Right:			
7. Wrong:	lying about all morning	to do whatever I please	
Right:			
8. Wrong:	happiness	healthy	wisdom
Right:			
9. Wrong:	insufficient time	too little money	not enough staff
Right:			
10. Wrong:	French is the language of love	English is used in business	profanity sounds best in German
Right:			

Exercise 28.4*

Correct the faulty parallelism in these sentences.

1. Not being able to speak the language causes confusion, is frustrating, and it's embarrassing.

2. Trying your best and success are not always the same thing.

3. The first candidate we interviewed seemed frightened and to be shy, but the second was a composed person and showed confidence.

4. To lick one's fingers and picking one's teeth in a restaurant are one way to get attention.

5. If I could afford it, I'd wear handcrafted shoes and ties made of silk.

6. One executive claims his most valuable business assets are hitting a good backhand and membership at an exclusive golf club.

7. In order to succeed in this economy, small businesses must be creative and show innovation and flexibility.

8. Lowering our profit margin, raising prices, and two management lay-offs will enable us to meet our budget.

9. After an enjoyable dinner, I like to drink a cappuccino, a dark chocolate mint, and, occasionally, a good cigar.

10. In the 1970s, Canada experienced bad management of natural resources, policies regarding national debt were unwise, and demands of workers were inflationary.

Exercise 28.5

As a test of your mastery of parallel structure, correct the six errors in the following paragraph.

The dictionary can be both a useful resource and an educational entertainment. Everyone knows that its three chief functions are to check spelling, for finding out the meanings of words, and what the correct pronunciation is. Few people, however, use the dictionary for discovery as well as learning. There are several methods of using the dictionary as an aid to discovery. One is randomly looking at words, another is to read a page or two thoroughly, and still another is by skimming through words until you find an unfamiliar one. It is by this last method that I discovered the word *steatopygous*, a term I now try to use at least once a day. You can increase your vocabulary significantly by using the dictionary, and of course a large and varied vocabulary can be used to baffle your colleagues, employers will be impressed, and your English teacher will be surprised.

29

Refining by Combining

To reinforce what you've learned about sentence structure, try your voice and your hand (preferably with a pencil in it) at sentence combining. You've rid your writing of fragments; you've cast out comma splices; you're riding herd on run-ons. But you may still find that your sentences, although technically correct, are choppy or repetitious. And you may be bored with conveying the same idea in the same old way. Sentence combining will not only confirm your mastery of sentence structure but also enable you to refine and polish your writing.

What is sentence combining? Sometimes called sentence generating or embedding, **sentence combining** is a technique that enables you to avoid a choppy, monotonous style while at the same time producing correct sentences.

Let's look at two short, technically correct sentences that could be combined:

Our paper carrier collects on Fridays.

Our paper carrier delivers the *Winnipeg Free Press* on Saturdays.

There are several ways of combining these two statements into a single sentence.

1. You can connect them with an appropriate linking word, such as *and, but, or, nor,* or *for.*

Our paper carrier delivers the *Winnipeg Free Press* on Saturdays <u>and</u> collects on Fridays.

2. You can change one of the sentences into a subordinate clause.

Our paper carrier, <u>who delivers the *Winnipeg Free Press* on Saturdays</u>, collects on Fridays.

On Fridays, our paper carrier collects for the *Winnipeg Free Press*, <u>which she delivers on Saturdays</u>.

<u>Although she delivers the *Winnipeg Free Press* on Saturdays</u>, our paper carrier collects on Fridays.

3. You can change one of the sentences into a modifying phrase.

(Having collected her money on Friday,) our paper carrier delivers the *Winnipeg Free Press* on Saturday.

On Fridays, our paper carrier collects for the *Winnipeg Free Press*, (a Saturday paper.)

4. Sometimes it is possible to reduce one of your sentences to a single-word modifier.

On Fridays, our paper carrier collects for the (Saturday) *Winnipeg Free Press*.

In sentence combining, you are free to move parts of the sentence around, change words, add or delete words, or make whatever other changes you find necessary. Anything goes, so long as you don't drastically alter the meaning of the base sentences. Remember that your aim in combining sentences is to create effective sentences—not long ones. Clarity is essential, and brevity has force.

In the following exercises, try your solutions aloud before you write them. You may also want to refer to Chapters 33 and 35 for advice on using the comma and the semicolon, respectively.

Exercise 29.1*

Combine each pair of sentences using the connecting word *and, but, or, nor, for, so,* or *yet*. Suggested answers for the exercises in this chapter begin on page 497.

1. We cannot sell our cottage.
   We will live there instead.

2. There are three solutions given for this problem.
   All of them are correct.

3. The people in our firm work very hard.
   They wouldn't want it any other way.

4. We could spend our day off shopping at the mall.
   We could spend the day fishing.

5. Great leaders do not bully their people.
   They do not deceive them.

6. I will not be able to finish my report by the deadline.
   There are only two hours before the deadline.

7. Jennifer knows that she will probably not get the vice-president's job.
   She wants the experience of applying for it.

8. Finish the estimate.
   Do not begin work until the estimate has been approved.

9. Today has been the worst day of my life.
   My horoscope was right today.

10. The government did not reply to my letter.
    It did not offer me a job.

Exercise 29.2*

Using dependent-clause cues (see Chapter 25, page 328), combine the following sentences into longer, more interesting units.

Hint: Read each set of statements through to the end before you begin to combine them, and try out several variations aloud or in your head before writing down your preferred solution.

1. Leonardo da Vinci was a great artist and inventor.
   He invented scissors, among other things.

2. Cats can produce over 100 vocal sounds.
   Dogs can make only ten vocal sounds.

3. It is said that men don't cry.
   They do cry while assembling furniture.

4. The name Wendy was made up for a book.
   The book was called *Peter Pan*.

5. Ten percent of Canadians are heavy drinkers.
   Thirty-five percent of Canadians abstain from alcohol.

6. Travel broadens the mind.
   Travel flattens the bank account.

7. We are seeking an experienced and innovative director.
   The candidate should be fluent in French.

8. One hundred thousand Vietnam veterans have taken their own lives.
   This is twice the number who were killed in action.

9. An oven is a compact home incinerator.
   Its chief use is the disposal of bulky pieces of meat and poultry.

10. A recipe is a series of step-by-step instructions.
    You can use it to prepare meals.
    The ingredients are in your kitchen.

Exercise 29.3

Combine the following sentences, using the connecting words listed in Exercise 29.1 and the dependent-clause cues listed on page 328.

1. Mario loses a girlfriend.
   He goes shopping for new clothes.

2. Failure breeds fatigue, according to Mortimer Adler.
   There is nothing more energizing than success.

3. We won't have enough stock to fill our orders.
   A shipment arrives today.

4. Friends may come, and friends may go.
   Enemies accumulate.

5. Marriage is for serious people.
   I have not considered it an option.

6. Divorce is an acknowledgement.
   There was not a true commitment in the first place.
   Some people still believe this.

7. In his essay "A Modest Proposal for a Divorce Ceremony," Pierre Berton proposed that Canada institute a formal divorce ceremony.
   The divorce ceremony would be like a formal wedding ceremony.
   All the symbolism would be reversed.

8. The bride, for example, would wear black.
   Immediately after the ceremony, the newly divorced couple would go into the vestry.
   They would scratch their names off the marriage register.

9. Twenty percent of adults in Canada are illiterate.
   Fifty percent of the adults who can read say they never read books.
   This is an astonishing fact.

10. Canada is a relatively rich country.
    Most of us brush up against hunger and homelessness almost daily.
    We encounter men, and less often, women begging.
    They are on downtown street corners.

After you have combined a number of sentences, you can evaluate your work. Read your sentences out loud. How they *sound* is important. Test your work against these six characteristics of successful sentences:

Summary

1. **Meaning:** Have you said what you mean?
2. **Clarity:** Is your sentence clear? Can it be understood on the first reading?
3. **Coherence:** Do the parts of your sentence fit together logically and smoothly?
4. **Emphasis:** Are the most important ideas either at the end or at the beginning of the sentence?
5. **Conciseness:** Is the sentence direct and to the point? Have you cut out all redundant or repetitious words?
6. **Rhythm:** Does the sentence flow smoothly? Are there any interruptions in the development of the key idea(s)? Do the interruptions help to emphasize important points, or do they distract the reader?

If your sentences pass all six tests of successful sentence style, you may be confident that they are both technically correct and pleasing to the ear. No reader could ask for more.

30

Mastering Subject–Verb Agreement

One of the most common grammatical errors is failure to make the subject and verb in a sentence agree with each other. Here is the rule for subject–verb agreement.

> Singular subjects take singular verbs.
> Plural subjects take plural verbs.

Singular and Plural

Here's an example of the singular and plural forms of a regular verb (*write*) in the present tense:

	Singular	**Plural**
First person	I write	we write
Second person	you write	you write
Third person	*she (he, it, one, the student) writes	*they (the students) write

From this example you can figure out what **person** means. We have asterisked the third-person singular form of the verb because it is the only form likely to cause you trouble.[1] Singular verbs regularly end in *s* (*writes*), but singular subjects do not (*student*).

---

[1] All verbs in the present tense have an *-s* form in the third-person singular. The only verb that has an *-s* form in the past tense is *to be*: he (she, it) *was*.

Singular words concern one person or thing:

The <u>phone</u> <u>rings</u>. <u>Alan</u> <u>sleeps</u>.

Plural words (and compound subjects) concern more than one person or thing:

The smoke <u>alarms</u> <u>ring</u>. <u>Jeff and Kendra</u> <u>watch</u> TV.

The rule for subject–verb agreement will cause you no problem as long as you make sure that the word the verb agrees with is really the subject of the sentence. To see how a problem can arise, look at this example:

One of my brothers speak five languages.

The writer of this sentence forgot that the subject of a sentence is never in a prepositional phrase. The verb needs to be changed to agree with the true subject, *One*:

<u>One</u> ~~of my brothers~~ <u>speaks</u> five languages.

If you're careful about identifying the subject of your sentence, you'll have no trouble with subject–verb agreement. To sharpen your subject-finding ability, review Chapter 24, "Cracking the Sentence Code." Then do the following exercises.

Exercise 30.1*

Rewrite each of the following sentences, using the alternative beginning shown. Answers for this chapter begin on page 498.

Example: <u>She</u> <u>wants</u> to make a short documentary.
<u>They</u> <u>want</u> to make a short documentary.

1. He sells used essays to other students.
   They

2. The woman maintains that her boss has been harassing her.
   The women

3. That new guideline affects all the office procedures.
   Those

4. Everyone who shops at Pimrock's receives a free can of tuna.
   All those

5. That girl's father is looking for a rich husband for her.
   Those

GO TO WEB

EXERCISES 30.1, 30.2

So far, so good. You can match up singular subjects with singular verbs and plural subjects with plural verbs. Now let's take a look at a few of the complications that make subject–verb agreement such a disagreeable problem.

Six Special Cases

Some subjects are tricky. They look singular but are actually plural, or they look plural when they're really singular. There are six kinds of these slippery subjects, all of them common, and all of them likely to trip up the unwary writer.

> 1. Compound subjects joined by *or; either . . . or; neither . . . nor;*
>   or *not . . . but*

Most of the compound subjects we've dealt with so far have been joined by *and* and have required plural verbs, so agreement hasn't been a problem. But watch out when the two or more elements of a compound subject are joined by *or . . . either . . . or; neither . . . nor;* or *not . . . but*. In these cases, the verb agrees in number with the nearest subject. That is, if the subject closest to the verb is singular, the verb will be singular; if the subject closest to the verb is plural, the verb must be plural too.

Neither <u>the coach</u> nor <u>the players</u> <u>are</u> ready to give up.

Neither <u>the players</u> nor <u>the coach</u> <u>is</u> ready to give up.

Exercise 30.2*

Circle the correct verb in each of the following sentences.

1. Neither the man nor his previous wives (know knows) who buried the treasure in the orchard.

2. Not the weak dollar but high taxes (is are) Canadians' chief concern.

3. The college has decided that neither final marks nor a diploma (is are) to be issued to students who owe library fines.

4. Either your job performance or your school assignments (is are) going to suffer if you continue your frantic lifestyle.

5. According to the guidebook entitled *Sightseeing in Transylvania*, not sharp stakes but garlic cloves (repel repels) the dreaded vampires.

2. Subjects that look like compound subjects but really aren't

Don't be fooled by phrases beginning with words such as *with, like, together with, in addition to,* or *including*. These prepositional phrases are NOT part of the subject of the sentence. Since they do not affect the verb, you can mentally cross them out.

> Mario's <u>brother</u>, ~~together with three of his buddies~~, <u>is going</u> to the Yukon to look for work.

Obviously four people are looking for work. Nevertheless, the subject (*brother*) is singular, and so the verb must be singular (*is going*).

> All my <u>courses</u>, ~~except economics~~, <u>are</u> easier this term.

If you mentally cross out the phrase *except economics*, you can easily see that the verb (*are*) must be plural to agree with the plural subject (*courses*).

Exercise 30.3*

Circle the correct verb in each of the following sentences.

1. Some Canadians, including the prime minister, (is are) not fluent in either of Canada's official languages.

2. Our city, along with many other North American urban centres, (register registers) a dangerous level of carbon monoxide pollution in the summer months.

3. The Tour de France, like the Olympic Games, (is are) a world-class athletic competition.

4. Daniel's parole officer, together with the police and his wife, (keep keeps) a close eye on him.

5. My English instructor, in addition to my math, biology, and even my learning skills instructor, (put, puts) a lot of pressure on me.

Grammar

3. Words that end in *-one*, *-thing*, or *-body*

When used as subjects, the following words are always singular, and they require the singular form of the verb:

everyone	everything	everybody
anyone	anything	anybody
someone	something	somebody
no one	nothing	nobody

The last part of the word is the tip-off here: every*one*, any*thing*, no*body*. If you focus on this last part, you'll remember to use a singular verb with these subjects. For the most part, these words cause trouble only when modifiers crop up between them and their verbs. For example, no one would write "Everyone are here." The trouble starts when you sandwich a bunch of words in between the subject and the verb. You might, if you weren't on your toes, write this: "Everyone involved in implementing the company's new policies and procedures are here." Obviously, the meaning is plural: several people are present. But the subject (*everyone*) is singular, so the verb must be *is*.

Exercise 30.4*

Circle the correct verb in each of the following sentences.

1. Nobody, according to hundreds of recording artists, (love loves) you when you're down and out.
2. Anyone who ever owned a Volkswagen Beetle (know knows) how much fun driving can be.
3. Everyone who finishes the exam with time to spare (is are) expected to go over it and correct the answers.
4. Everything that could possibly go wrong with our plans (has have) happened.
5. We were offered nothing except possibly the sales positions that (interest interests) us.

4. *Each, either (of), neither (of)*

Used as subjects, they take singular verbs.

<u>Either</u> <u>is</u> acceptable to me.

<u>Each</u> <u>wants</u> desperately to win.

Neither of the stores <u>is</u> open after six o'clock. (Remember, the subject is never in a prepositional phrase.)

Exercise 30.5*

Circle the correct verb in each of the following sentences.

1. Unless we hear from the coach, neither of those two (is are) playing this evening.
2. Each of these courses (involve involves) field placement.
3. When my girlfriend asks if she has lost weight, I know that either of my answers (is are) bound to be wrong.
4. Each of the women (want wants) desperately to win the Ms. Nanaimo bodybuilding competition.
5. Strict discipline is what each of those teachers (believe believes) in.

5. Collective nouns

A **collective noun** is a word that names a group. Some examples are *company, class, committee, team, crowd, band, family, audience, public,* and *jury*. When you are referring to the group acting as a *unit*, use a *singular* verb. When you are referring to the *members* of the group acting *individually*, use a *plural* verb.

The <u>team</u> <u>is</u> sure to win tomorrow's game. (Here *team* refers to the group acting as a whole.)

The <u>team</u> <u>are</u> getting into their uniforms now. (The members of the team are acting individually.)

Exercise 30.6*

Circle the correct verb in each of the following sentences.

1. The whole gang (plan plans) to attend the bikers' rally.
2. The wolf pack (has have) been almost wiped out by local ranchers.
3. By noon on Friday, the whole dorm (has have) left their rooms and headed for the local pubs and coffeehouses.
4. After only two hours' discussion, the committee (was were) able to reach consensus.
5. The majority of Canadians, according to a recent survey, (is are) not so conservative about sex and morality as we had assumed.

Grammar

6. Units of money, time, mass, length, and distance

When used as subjects, they all require singular verbs.

Four kilometres is too far to walk in this weather.

Remember that 2.2 pounds equals a kilogram.

Three weeks is a long time to wait to get your paper back.

Exercise 30.7*

Circle the correct verb in each of the following sentences.

1. No wonder you are suspicious if $70 (was were) what you paid for last night's pizza.
2. Tim told his girlfriend that nine years (seem seems) like a long time to wait.
3. Forty hours of classes (is are) too much in one week.
4. When you are anxiously looking for a gas station, 30 km (is are) a long distance.
5. Ninety cents (seems seem) very little to tip, even for poor service.

In Exercises 30.8 and 30.9, correct the errors in subject–verb agreement. Check your answers to each exercise before going on.

Exercise 30.8*

1. My opinion of the schools are that none of them are any good.

2. Neither of us remember who ran against Gordon Campbell for premier of B.C.

3. Every one of the band's members appeal to my sense of the sublime.

4. My whole family, with the exception of the cat, dislike anchovies on pizza.

5. The applause from a thousand delirious fans were like music to the ears of the skaters.

6. Neither my husband nor my dog understand what I see in cats.

7. Neither age nor illness prevents Uncle Alf from pinching the nurses.

8. Three thousand dollars per term, the students think, are too much to pay for their education.

9. The birth of quintuplets were too much for the parents to cope with.

10. Everything that we agreed to last night seem silly this morning.

Exercise 30.9*

Quebec City, along with Montreal, Toronto, and Vancouver, are among Canada's great gourmet centres. Whereas Toronto is a relative latecomer to this list, neither Quebec City nor Montreal are strangers to those who seeks fine dining. Indeed, travel and food magazines have long affirmed that the inclusion of these two cities in a Quebec vacation are a "must." Montreal is perhaps more international in its offerings, but Quebec City provides exquisite proof that French-Canadian cuisine and hospitality is second to none in the world. Amid the Old World charm of the lower city is to be found some of the quaintest and most enjoyable traditional restaurants; the newer sections of town boasts equally fine dining in more contemporary surroundings. The combination of the wonderful food and the city's fascinating charms are sure to make any visitor return frequently. Either the summer, when the city blooms and outdoor cafés abound, or the winter, when Carnaval turns the streets into hundreds of connecting parties, are wonderful times to visit one of Canada's oldest and most interesting cities.

GO TO WEB

EXERCISES 30.3, 30.4

The box below contains a summary of the rules governing subject–verb agreement. Review them carefully before you try the mastery test for this chapter.

Summary

1. Subjects and verbs must agree: both must be singular, or both must be plural.
2. Subjects joined by *and* are always plural.
3. When subjects are joined by *or; either. . .or; neither. . .nor;* or *not. . .but,* the verb agrees with the subject that is closest to it.
4. The subject is never in a prepositional phrase. Ignore phrases beginning with *as well as, including, in addition to, like, together with,* etc., when deciding whether to use a singular or a plural verb.
5. Pronouns ending in *-one, -thing,* or *-body* require singular verbs.
6. Used as subjects, *each, either,* and *neither* require singular verbs.
7. Collective nouns are usually singular.
8. Units of money, time, mass, length, and distance are always singular.

Exercise 30.10

As a final check of your mastery of subject–verb agreement, correct the following sentences as necessary.

1. In my opinion, neither of the lead singers are any good.

2. The faculty, with the full support of the college administration, treats plagiarism as a serious offence.

3. Either good looks or intelligence run in our family, but never at the same time.

4. No one in accounting, personnel, or sales have ever heard of a policy allowing time off for a bad hair day.

5. Finding my skis after a year away were difficult, but remembering how to use them after all these months are going to be an even greater challenge.

6. The number of layoffs reported in the headlines seems to be increasing monthly.

7. We couldn't help noticing that the orchestra are playing better now that the conductor is sober.

8. With cutbacks at every level of government, it is no longer true that every Canadian who need medical services have access to immediate treatment.

9. Our cafeteria, with its dreary salad bar, greasy chips, and soggy sandwiches, completely take away my appetite.

10. Canada's First Nations population are thought to have come to this continent from Asia thousands of years before the Europeans arrived in North America.

31

Using Verbs Effectively

Now that you've conquered subject–verb agreement, it's time to turn to the three remaining essentials of correct verb use: **form**, **consistency**, and **voice**. These terms may not mean much to you at this point, but don't let them intimidate you. You'll probably discover that you know more about them than you think. You'll also find that using verbs effectively will noticeably improve your writing. Good writers pay especially careful attention to verbs. A verb is to a sentence what an engine is to a car: it's the source of power—but it can also be a source of trouble.

Choosing the Correct Verb Form

Every verb has four forms, called its **principal parts**:

1. The **base** form: used by itself or with *can, may, might, shall, will, could, should, would, must*
2. The **past tense** form: used by itself
3. The **present participle** (the **-ing**) form: used with *am, is, are; was, were; will be; have been*, etc.
4. The past participle form: used with *have, has, had; is, are; was, were*, etc.

Here are some examples:

Base	Past Tense	Present Participle	Past Participle
dance	danced	dancing	danced
learn	learned	learning	learned
play	played	playing	played
seem	seemed	seeming	seemed

To use verbs correctly, you must be familiar with their principal parts. Knowing three facts will help you. First, you won't have trouble with the present participle, the *-ing* form. It is always made up of the base form of the verb + *ing*. Second, your dictionary will give you the principal parts of all **irregular** verbs. Look up the base form, and you'll find the past tense and the present and past participles given beside it, usually in parentheses. For example, if you look up *sing* in your dictionary, you will find *sang* (past tense), *sung* (past participle), and *singing* (present participle) listed immediately after the verb itself. If the past tense and past participle are not given, the verb is **regular**. So, third, you need to know how to form the past tense and the past participle of regular verbs: add *-ed* to the base form. The examples listed above—*dance, learn, play, seem*—are all regular verbs.

Unfortunately, many of the most common English verbs are irregular. Their past tenses and past participles are formed in unpredictable ways. The verbs in the list that follows are used so often that it is worth your time to memorize their principal parts. (We have not included the *-ing* form because, as we have noted above, it never causes any difficulty.)

The Principal Parts of Irregular Verbs

Base	Past Tense	Past Participle
(Use with *can, may, might, shall, will, could, would, should, must*)		(Use with *have, has, had; is, are; was, were*)
awake	awoke/awaked	awaked/awoken
be (am, is)	was/were	been
bear	bore	borne
beat	beat	beaten
become	became	become
begin	began	begun
bid (offer to pay)	bid	bid
bid (say, command)	bid/bade	bid/bidden
bite	bit	bitten
bleed	bled	bled
blow	blew	blown
break	broke	broken
bring	brought (*not* brang)	brought (*not* brung)
broadcast	broadcast	broadcast
build	built	built
burst	burst	burst

Base	Past Tense	Past Participle
(Use with *can, may, might, shall, will, could, would, should, must*)		(Use with *have, has, had; is, are; was, were*)
buy	bought	bought
catch	caught	caught
choose	chose	chosen
come	came	come
cost	cost	cost
cut	cut	cut
deal	dealt	dealt
dig	dug	dug
dive	dived/dove	dived
do	did (*not* done)	done
draw	drew	drawn
dream	dreamed/dreamt	dreamed/dreamt
drink	drank (*not* drunk)	drunk
eat	ate	eaten
fall	fell	fallen
feed	fed	fed
feel	felt	felt
fight	fought	fought
find	found	found
fling	flung	flung
fly	flew	flown
forget	forgot	forgotten/forgot
forgive	forgave	forgiven
freeze	froze	frozen
get	got	got/gotten
give	gave	given
go	went	gone (*not* went)
grow	grew	grown
hang (suspend)	hung	hung
hang (put to death)	hanged	hanged
have	had	had
hear	heard	heard
hide	hid	hidden
hit	hit	hit
hold	held	held
hurt	hurt	hurt

Base	Past Tense	Past Participle
(Use with *can, may, might, shall, will, could, would, should, must*)		(Use with *have, has, had; is, are; was, were*)
keep	kept	kept
know	knew	known
lay (put or place)	laid	laid
lead	led	led
leave	left	left
lend	lent (*not* loaned)	lent (*not* loaned)
lie (recline)	lay	lain (*not* layed)
light	lit/lighted	lit/lighted
lose	lost	lost
mean	meant	meant
meet	met	met
pay	paid	paid
raise (lift up, increase, bring up)	raised	raised
ride	rode	ridden
ring	rang	rung
rise	rose	risen
run	ran	run
say	said	said
see	saw (*not* seen)	seen
sell	sold	sold
set (put or place)	set	set
shake	shook	shaken (*not* shook)
shine	shone	shone
sing	sang	sung
sink	sank	sunk
sit	sat	sat
sleep	slept	slept
slide	slid	slid
speak	spoke	spoken
speed	sped	sped
steal	stole	stolen
stick	stuck	stuck
strike (hit)	struck	struck
strike (affect)	struck	stricken
swear	swore	sworn

Base	Past Tense	Past Participle
(Use with *can, may, might, shall, will, could, would, should, must*)		(Use with *have, has, had; is, are; was, were*)
swim	swam	swum
swing	swung	swung
	(*not* swang)	
take	took	taken
teach	taught	taught
tear	tore	torn
tell	told	told
think	thought	thought
throw	threw	thrown
wake	woke/waked	waked/woken
wear	wore	worn
weave	wove	woven
win	won	won
wind	wound	wound
wring	wrung	wrung
write	wrote	written

Grammar

Exercise 31.1*

Find and correct the verbs in the following sentences. When you have finished, check your answers on page 500.

1. Once I laid down, I found it very hard to get up again.

2. The staff have ate all the sandwiches that were ordered for the board's lunch.

3. Have you ever rode in a Porsche?

4. Having finished his presentation, Greg set down to answer questions.

5. That shirt has laid on the floor for at least a week.

6. The contractor who was eventually chose was the one who submitted the lowest bid.

7. My computer has print the document in a font so small I can't read it.

8. When will I get back the gas money I loaned you last year?

9. After three years of constant use, our copier is practically wore out.

10. I should have knew that all generalizations are false.

GO TO WEB

EXERCISES 31.1, 31.2, 31.3, 31.4

Exercise 31.2

As a final test of your mastery of verb forms, correct the errors in the following sentences.

1. The wind had blew the roof off the house and drove a hole into the side of the barn.

2. The stars shined like diamonds the night I told Emmy-Lou how I feeled about her and gave her the ring that costed me a week's pay.

3. Dan had drove very slowly on the gravel road, but once he reached the highway he speeded away into the darkness.

4. They had all wore yellow ribbons to show they hadn't forgot him.

5. They gypsy fortuneteller had spoke, but she didn't tell us anything that we hadn't knew before.

6. The church bells rung out the news that a great battle had been fought and a great victory had been won.

7. That teached us a lesson that we have keeped all these years.

8. After the band had sang "The Lion Sleeps Tonight" seven times, we realized they had been payed too much, because they only knowed four tunes.

9. The priest has spoke with the condemned man who will be hung in the morning unless the governor gives him a stay of execution.

10. When he slided into third base after he had stole second and the throw had went into centre field, he had tore a big hole in his pants and had to leave the game.

Keeping Your Tenses Consistent

Verbs are time markers. Changes in tense express changes in time: past, present, or future.

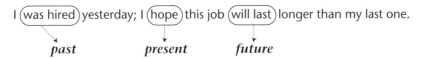

I (was hired) yesterday; I (hope) this job (will last) longer than my last one.

      past   *present*   *future*

Sometimes, as in the sentsence above, it is necessary to use several different tenses in a single sentence to get the meaning across. But most of the time, whether you're writing a sentence or a paragraph, you use one tense throughout. Normally, you choose either the past or the present tense, depending on the nature of your topic. (Few paragraphs are written completely in the future tense.) Here is the rule to follow.

> Don't change tense unless meaning requires it.

Readers like and expect consistency. If you begin a sentence with "I worried and fretted and delayed," your readers will tune in to the past-tense verbs and expect any other verbs in the sentence to be in the past tense too. Therefore, if you finish the sentence with ". . . and then I decide to give it a try," your readers will be jolted abruptly out of one time frame and into another. This sort of jolting is uncomfortable, and readers don't like it.

Shifting tenses is like shifting gears: it should be done smoothly and only when necessary. Avoid causing verbal whiplash: keep your tenses consistent.

Wrong: Monika starts the car and revved the engine.
Right: Monika started the car and revved the engine.
Also right: Monika starts the car and revs the engine.

Wrong: Carrie flounces into the room and sat down. Everyone stares.
Right: Carrie flounced into the room and sat down. Everyone stared.
Also right: Carrie flounces into the room and sits down. Everyone stares.

Exercise 31.3*

In this exercise, most of the sentences contain unnecessary tense shifts. Use the first verb in each sentence as your time marker and change the tense(s) of the other verb(s) in the sentence to agree with it. Answers are on page 500.

Grammar

1. Rolly goes home and kicked his cat.

2. Hank Aaron broke Babe Ruth's record of 714 home runs in a lifetime when he hits number 715 in 1974.

3. Children are quite perceptive and will know when you are lying to them.

4. We had just finished painting the floor when the dog runs through.

5. When Brad Pitt walked into the room, the girls go crazy.

6. You should not go into that building until the police arrive.

7. Tim walked into the room, took one look at Leroy, and smashes him right through the wall.

8. First you will greet the guests; then you show them to their rooms.

9. The largest cheese ever produced took forty-three hours to make and weighs a whopping 15 723 kg.

10. He watches television until he finally went to sleep.

Exercise 31.4*

Correct the 15 faulty tense shifts in this passage.

For some reason, when mistakes or accidents happen in radio or television, they were often hilariously funny. If, in the course of a conversation, someone said, "Here come the Duck and Doochess of Kent," listeners would probably be mildly amused. But many years ago, when an announcer makes that slip on a live radio broadcast, it becomes one of the most famous blunders in radio history. Tapes of the slip will be filed in "bloopers" libraries all over the world. This heightened sense of hilarity is the reason that so many people who work in radio dedicated their creativity to making the on-air announcer laugh while reading the news. To take one example, Lorne Greene's is the deeply serious voice that is heard on the CBC news during World War II. He is the victim of all kinds of pranks aimed at getting him to break up while reading the dark, often tragic, news of the combat overseas.

The pages of his news script are set on fire while he reads. He is even stripped naked as he reads, calmly, and apparently without strain. Lorne Greene will be a true professional. Many other newscasters, however, will have been highly susceptible to falling apart on air at the slightest provocation. And there were always people around a radio station who cannot resist giving them that little push.

GO TO WEB

EXERCISE 31.5

Exercise 31.5

To test and reinforce your mastery of correct verb forms and tense consistency, correct the ten errors in the following paragraph. Use the italicized verb as your time marker.

The art of writing *is* not dead. Thanks to the use of computers in homes and businesses, it will now be more important than ever to be able to write competently. Not everyone agrees with this statement. Many people will continue to think that electronic technology has eliminated the need to learn how to write, but it will be clear that reports of the death of the written word were premature. Computer networking, bulletin boards, e-mail, and electronic forums made it more important than ever to write well. In the past, when letters were written on paper, writers could have checked their messages over before mailing them to ensure that there were no errors or embarrassing miscommunications. Now, however, communication is instantaneous, and any writing faults will be immediately apparent. The exposure of writing flaws, however, is not the only reason electronic communication links require the ability to write clear, unambiguous prose. Paper letters were normally mailed to a few people, at most.

Electronic mail, on the other hand, will often be sent to dozens, even hundreds, of receivers; therefore, the message will need to be carefully composed if all recipients are to understand what the writer intended. In today's world of electronic communication, good writing skills will be more important than ever before.

Choosing between Active and Passive Verbs

Verbs have another quality besides tense (or time). Verbs also have what is called "voice," which means the quality of being either active or passive. In sentences with **active voice** verbs, the "doer" of the action is the grammatical subject of the sentence.

> Active voice: Good parents <u>support</u> their children.
> A car <u>crushed</u> the cat.
> Someone <u>will show</u> a movie in class.

In sentences with **passive voice** verbs, the grammatical subject of the sentence is the "receiver" of the action (that is, the subject is passively acted upon), and the "doer" becomes an object of the preposition *by* or is absent from the sentence entirely, as in the third example below.

> Passive voice: Children <u>are supported</u> by good parents.
> The cat <u>was crushed</u> by a car.
> A movie <u>will be shown</u> in class.

Always use an active verb unless you have a specific reason to choose a passive one.

You probably use the passive voice more often than you think you do. To be a better writer, you need to know the distinction between active and passive, to understand their different effects on the reader, and to use the passive voice only when it is appropriate to your meaning.

There are three good reasons for choosing a passive verb rather than an active one.

1. The person or agent that performed the action is not known.

My books <u>were stolen</u> from my locker this morning.

Giovanna's father <u>was killed</u> in Bosnia.

Unlike the streets of a typical prairie city, which <u>are laid out</u> on a grid, Vancouver's streets <u>are laid out</u> to follow the curves and bends of the harbour and the Fraser River.

2. You want to place the emphasis on the person, place, or object that was acted upon rather than on the subject that performed the action.

Early this morning, the Bank of Montreal at 16th and Granville <u>was robbed</u> by four men wearing nylon stockings over their heads and carrying shotguns.

This sentence focuses the reader's attention on the bank rather than on the robbers. A quite different effect is produced when the sentence is reconstructed in the active voice:

Four men wearing nylon stockings over their heads and carrying shotguns <u>robbed</u> the Bank of Montreal at 16th and Granville early this morning.

3. You are writing a technical or scientific report or a legal document.

Passive verbs are the appropriate choice when the focus is on the facts, methods, or procedures involved rather than on who discovered or performed them. Passive verbs also tend to establish an impersonal tone that is appropriate in these kinds of writing. Contrast the emphasis and tone of the following sentence pairs:

Grammar

Passive: The heat <u>was increased</u> to 200°C and <u>was allowed</u> to remain at that temperature.

Active: My lab partners and I <u>increased</u> the heat to 200°C and <u>allowed</u> it to remain at that temperature.

Passive: Having been found guilty, the accused <u>was sentenced</u> to two years.

Active: The jury <u>found</u> the accused guilty, and the judge <u>sentenced</u> him to two years.

In general, because active verbs are more concise and forceful than passive verbs, they add vigour and impact to your writing. The distinction between active and passive is not something you should worry about during the drafting stage, however. The time to focus on verbs and decide whether active or passive would best serve your purpose is during revision. When you find a passive verb in your draft, think about who is doing what. Ask yourself why the "who" is not the subject of the sentence. If there's a good reason, then use the passive verb. Otherwise, choose an active verb.

Exercise 31.6*

Rewrite the sentences below, changing their verbs from passive to active. Note that you may have to add a word or word group to identify the "doer" of the action of the verb.

Example: Matt's two front teeth <u>were knocked out</u> by Clark's shot.

Clark's shot <u>knocked out</u> Matt's two front teeth.

1. A meeting was called by the department head.
2. The espresso will be made by the server in a few minutes.
3. When it gets cold, the block heater is plugged in overnight.
4. For many years, steroids have been used by professional athletes to improve speech and endurance.
5. The dough must not be kneaded, or your pastry will be tough.
6. *Do-It-Yourself Surgery*, the current best-seller, was written by Dr. Lance Boyles.
7. Four of Paul's buddies were arrested during a routine check of Barry's Bingo Bistro.
8. While our neighbours were vacationing in the Caribbean, their house was broken into by thieves.

9. The latest multimedia technology will be displayed and demonstrated in the graphics lab by technicians from all the leading software firms.
10. The Red Sox and the White Sox have been replaced as the stupidest team names in sports by the Mighty Ducks.

Exercise 31.7*

Rewrite each of the sentences below, changing the verbs from active to passive or vice versa, and then decide which sentence is more effective.

1. Sarah McLachlan won another Juno.
2. Carl spiked the ball after scoring the winning points.
3. City council passed a by-law forbidding smoking in bars and restaurants.
4. Forty-eight hours later, 2 ml of sterile water was added to the culture in the Petri dish.
5. By standing in line all night, Courtenay managed to get four tickets for the concert.
6. The 10 p.m. news revealed the truth behind the famous Doobie Brothers scandal.
7. The judgment was finally announced today, almost a year after the environmental hearings were concluded.
8. After a long debate, the committee finally agreed to endorse Yasmin's fund-raising proposal.
9. A computer program that analyzes speech patterns has been developed by psychologist Dr. Hans Steiner of Stanford University.
10. After years of research among college students, it has been concluded by Dr. Steiner that people who frequently use passive-voice constructions tend to be maladjusted.

Exercise 31.8

Rewrite the following paragraph, changing passive voice verbs to active where appropriate.

(1) After graduation, Claire was hired by a large publishing company to sell humanities textbooks to college professors. (2) Her first call was made at a university with a huge arts faculty. (3) Her company's books were being used by many of the professors, so Claire was not too worried about having to sell aggressively. (4) The popular history text on her list, however, had not been adopted by all faculty in the history department, so that is where her

visit was begun. (5) A list of all the faculty members in the department was provided to Claire by the secretary. (6) Her book was not being used by professors Maheu, Jaffer, and Vacant, so the search for their offices was begun. (7) According to the schedule posted on his door, a class was being taught by Professor Maheu for the next two hours. (8) Professor Jaffer was found by Claire to be receptive and pleasant, but the text was not appropriate for the courses being taught by her. (9) Last, Claire went to find Professor Vacant, and his office was finally located by her. (10) She knocked on the door and was told to come in. (11) When Professor Vacant was asked for by Claire, the woman at one of the desks in the office looked blank. (12) She said there was no person in the history department by that name. (13) The fact that Professor Vacant's name was on the list Claire had been given was politely pointed out by her. (14) The woman at the desk looked at the list and began to laugh. (15) Finally, the joke was understood by Claire. (16) There was no Professor Vacant; the history department had a vacant position.

32

Solving
Pronoun Problems

Look at the following sentences. Can you tell what's wrong with them?

"Dev must choose between you and I," Miranda said.

When you are on a diet, it is a good idea for one to avoid Bagel World.

We had invited everybody to come with their partner, so we were a little surprised when Marcel showed up with his Doberman.

Everyone is expected to do their duty.

Mohammed's nose was badly sunburned, but it has now completely disappeared.

Most of the students that were protesting tuition increases were ones which had been elected to council.

These sentences all contain pronoun errors. After verbs, pronouns are the class of words most likely to cause problems for writers. In this chapter, we will look at the three aspects of pronoun usage that can trip you up if you're not careful: pronoun form, agreement, and consistency. We'll also look at the special problems of usage that can lead to sexist language.

Choosing the Correct Pronoun Form

First you need to be sure you are using the "right" pronouns—that is, the correct pronoun forms—in your sentences. Here are some examples of incorrect pronoun usage:

Her and me can't agree on anything.

The reason for the quarrel is a personal matter between she and I.

How do you know which form of a pronoun to use? The answer depends on the pronoun's place and function in your sentence.

There are two forms of personal pronouns: one is used for subjects, and the other is used for objects. Pronoun errors occur when you confuse the two. In Chapter 24, you learned to identify the subject of a sentence. Keep that information in mind as you learn the following basic rule.

> When a subject or a complement is a pronoun, the pronoun must be in **subject form**. Otherwise, use the **object form**.

Subject Pronouns

Singular	Plural
I	we
you	you
he, she, it, one	they

She and *I* tied for first place. (The pronouns are the subject of the sentence.)

The lucky winners of the all-expenses-paid weekend in Pelvis are *they*. (The pronoun is the complement and refers to the subject of the sentence, *winners*.)

The student who regularly asks for extra help is *he*. (The pronoun is the complement and refers to the subject of the sentence, *student*.)

Object Pronouns

Singular	Plural
me	us
you	you
him, her, it, one	them

Between you and *me,* I think he's cute. (*Me* is not the subject of the sentence; it is one of the objects of the preposition *between.*)

Omar asked *him* and *me* for help. (*Him* and *me* are not the subject of the verb *asked; Omar* is, so the pronouns need to be in the object form.)

Be especially careful when using pronouns in compound subjects or after prepositions. If you can remember the following two tips, you'll be able to eliminate most potential errors.

1. A pronoun that is part of a compound subject is *always* in subject form.
2. A pronoun that follows a preposition is *always* in object form.

Examples:

She and *I* had tickets to U2. (The pronouns are used as a compound subject.)

It is up to *you* and *her* to pay for the damage. (The pronouns follow the preposition *to.*)

Here's a practically foolproof way for native English speakers to figure out which pronoun form you need. (ESL speakers, unfortunately, must rely on applying the rules.) When you have a pair of pronouns to deal with, mentally cross out one at a time. Applying this technique to the first example above, you get "*She* had tickets" and "*I* had tickets," both of which sound right and are correct. In the second sentence, if you try the pronouns separately, you get "It is up to *you*" and "It is up to *her.*" Again, you know by the sound that these are the correct forms. (You would never say "*Her* had tickets," "*Me* had tickets," or "It is up to *she.*") If you deal with paired pronouns one at a time, you are unlikely to choose the wrong form.

Exercise 32.1*

Correct the pronouns in these sentences as necessary. Answers for the exercises in this chapter begin on page 501.

1. No one except you and I would go camping in this weather.
2. Him and I can't figure out this problem set any better than you and her could.
3. George and him fell asleep in class, as usual.
4. Do you want to work with Emma and she?

Grammar

5. We can use the film passes all week, and you and her can use them on the weekend, when Biff and me are going skiing.
6. Thanks to the recommendations provided by your math instructor and I, you and her got the tutorial jobs.
7. As we were going to class, Karl and me heard that there had been an explosion in the lab.
8. If it hadn't been for Hassan and he, the only ones to show up would have been you and I.
9. Quentin and him agreed to split the price of a case with Stan and I.
10. Only two students passed the midterm: Nadia and me.

GO TO WEB

EXERCISES 32.1, 32.2

Choosing the correct pronoun form is more than just a matter of not wanting to appear ignorant or careless. Sometimes the form you use determines the meaning of your sentence. Consider these two sentences:

Stefan is more interested in his new car than *I*.

Stefan is more interested in his new car than *me*.

There's a world of difference between the meaning of the subject form ("Stefan is more interested in his new car than *I* [am]") and the object form ("Stefan is more interested in his new car than [in] *me*").

When using a pronoun after *than, as well as,* or *as,* decide whether you mean to contrast the pronoun with the subject of the sentence. If you do, use the subject form of the pronoun. If not, use the object form.

Biff would rather watch television than I. (*I* is contrasted with the subject, *Biff*.)

Biff would rather watch television than me. (*Me* is contrasted with the object, *television*.)

To test your sentence, try putting a verb after the pronoun. If the sentence makes sense, then the subject form is the form you want.

Biff would rather watch television than I [would].

Exercise 32.2*

Correct the following sentences where necessary.

1. At fourteen, my younger brother is already taller than me.

2. No one likes partying more than him and Anne.

3. Would you like to join Daniel and I for dinner and a movie?

4. Only one person in this firm could manage the department as well as him.

5. At last I have met someone who enjoys grilled liver as much as me!

6. We can skate as well as them, but they are much better at shooting and defending than us.

7. More than me, Serge uses the computer to draft and revise his papers.

Exercise 32.3*

Revise the following paragraph to correct the errors in pronoun form.

(1) My boyfriend and me have different opinions when it comes to food. (2) I like fast food better than him. (3) He likes vegetables better than me. (4) In fact, between you and I, he is a vegetarian, though he would deny it. (5) When we go out with friends, it is difficult for they to know where to take him and I because our tastes are so different. (6) The only type of restaurant where us and them can all have what we like is Italian. (7) There, him and his friends can sample pasta primavera and eggplant parmigiana while my friends and I tuck into spaghetti and meatballs and pepperoni pizza. (8) We are probably not as healthy as they, but they don't seem to enjoy their food as much as us.

Now that you know how to choose the correct form of pronouns within a sentence, let's turn to the problems of using pronouns consistently throughout a sentence and a paragraph.

Grammar

Pronoun–Antecedent Agreement

The name of this pronoun problem may sound difficult, but the idea is simple. Pronouns are words that substitute for or refer to the name of a person, place, or thing mentioned elsewhere in your sentence or your paragraph. The word(s) that a pronoun substitutes for or refers to is called the **antecedent**.

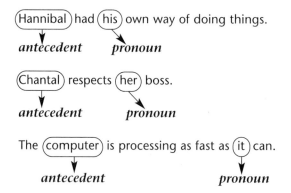

Usually, as in these three examples, the antecedent comes before the pronoun that refers to it. Here is the rule to remember.

A pronoun must agree with its antecedent in
• number (singular or plural)
• person (first, second, or third)
• gender (masculine, feminine, or neuter)

Most of the time, you follow this rule without even realizing that you know it. For example, you would never write

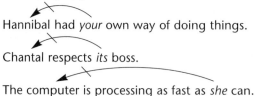

Hannibal had *your* own way of doing things.

Chantal respects *its* boss.

The computer is processing as fast as *she* can.

You know these sentences are incorrect even if you may not know precisely why they are wrong.

There are three kinds of pronoun–antecedent agreement that you do need to learn about. They lead to errors that, unlike the examples above, are not obvious, and you need to know them so you can watch out for them. The rules you need to learn involve **relative pronouns**; indefinite pronouns ending in *-one*, *-body*, or *-thing*; and **vague references**.

1. RELATIVE PRONOUNS

The first potential difficulty with pronoun–antecedent agreement is how to use the relative pronouns—*who/whoever, whom/whomever, which,* and *that.* Relative pronouns can be used for only one purpose: to refer to someone or something specifically mentioned in the sentence or paragraph. Here is the guideline to follow.

> *Who, whom, whoever,* and *whomever* refer to people.
> *That* and *which* refer to everything else.

The student *who* won the Governor General's Academic Medal decided to go to Dalhousie.

For *whom* are you voting: the Liberals or the New Democrats?

The moose *that* I met looked hostile.

Her car, *which* is imported, is smaller than cars *that* are built here.

Tips:

1. Whether you need *who* or *whom, whoever,* or *whomever,* depends on the pronoun's place and function in your sentence. Apply the basic rule of pronoun usage: if the pronoun is acting as, or refers to, the subject, use *who/whoever.* Otherwise, use *whom/whomever.*

   My husband was the idiot *who* entered a contest to win a trip to Moose Factory. (The pronoun refers to the subject of the sentence, *husband.*)

   The trip's promoters were willing to settle for *whomever* they could get. (The pronoun does not refer to the sentence's subject, *promoters;* it is the object of the preposition *for.*)

   An even simpler solution to this problem is to rewrite the sentence so you don't need either *who* or *whom.*

Grammar

My husband entered a contest to win a trip to Moose Factory.

The trip's promoters were willing to settle for anyone they could get.

2. *That* is required more often than *which*. You should use *which* only in a clause that is separated from the rest of the sentence by commas.

The moose *that* I met looked hostile.

The moose, *which* was standing right in front of my car, looked hostile.

Exercise 32.4*

Correct the following sentences where necessary.

1. For two weeks, the pitcher that gave up the winning run had to live in hiding.

2. I am a longtime fan of David Cronenberg, a film director that began his career in Canada.

3. We are often attracted to people which are completely opposite to us.

4. Elmo's grandmother always told him that people that couldn't fly should stay out of airplanes.

5. People that take afternoon naps often pay a penalty: they are also people that suffer from insomnia.

6. The vacuum-cleaner salesperson which came to our door was the sort of person that won't take no for an answer.

7. Holly Cole, which is the star headlining tonight's show, has made two albums which have been nominated for Juno awards.

8. The roast, which had been in the oven for three hours, was dried out by the time the last of the guests that we had invited finally arrived.

9. The math problems which we worked on last night would have baffled anyone that hadn't done all the problem sets.

10. We took our ancient Jeep, that we had bought from a friend that had lost his licence, to a scrap yard who paid us $200 for it.

2. INDEFINITE PRONOUNS: PRONOUNS ENDING IN *-ONE*, *-BODY*, OR *-THING*

The second tricky aspect of pronoun–antecedent agreement involves these pronouns:

anyone	anybody	anything
everyone	everybody	everything
no one	nobody	nothing
someone	somebody	something
each (one)		

In Chapter 30, you learned that when these words are used as subjects they are singular and take singular verbs. So it makes sense that the pronouns that stand for or refer to them must also be singular.

> Antecedents ending in *-one*, *-body*, or *-thing* are singular and must be referred to by singular pronouns: *he, she, it; his, her, its.*

Please put everything back in *its* place.

Anybody can retire comfortably if *he* or *she* begins planning now.

Everyone is expected to do *his* duty.

No one in *his* right mind would claim *he* enjoys living in this climate.

Now take another look at the last two sentences. Until about thirty years ago, the pronouns *he, him,* and *his* were used with singular antecedents and were considered to refer to both men and women. Now, however, many readers are sensitive to gender bias in writing and believe that the masculine pronoun is inappropriate when referring to both sexes. As a writer, you should be aware of this sensitivity. If you want to appeal to the broadest possible audience, you should avoid what may be seen as sexist language.

In speech, it has become acceptable to use plural pronouns with *-one*, *-body*, or *-thing* antecedents. Although these antecedents are grammatically singular and take singular verbs, they are often plural in meaning, and in conversation we find ourselves saying

Everybody clapped *their* hands and cheered.

No one has to stay if *they* don't want to.

Grammar

This usage is acceptable only in speech; it is not acceptable in written English.

Errors in pronoun–antecedent agreement are sometimes made because people are attempting to write non-sexist language—that is, to write without indicating whether the person referred to is male or female. A sentence such as "Everyone is required to do *their* oral presentation" is incorrect, as we have seen, but it does avoid making "everyone" male. It also avoids the awkwardness of "Everyone is expected to do *his* or *her* oral presentation." There are two better ways to solve this problem.

1. Revise the sentence to leave the pronoun out.

An oral presentation is required of everyone.

or

Everyone is required to deliver an oral presentation.

Such creative avoidance of gender-specific or incorrect constructions can be an interesting challenge. The results often sound a little artificial, however. The second method is easier to accomplish.

2. Revise the sentence to make both the antecedent and the pronoun plural.

You are all required to deliver your oral presentations.

or

All students are required to deliver their oral presentations.

Here are two more examples for you to study.

Problem: Each of the workers has his or her assignment.
Revision 1: Each of the workers has an assignment.
Revision 2: All of the workers have their assignments.

Problem: Everyone will enjoy seeing his or her school friends again.
Revision 1: Everyone will enjoy seeing school friends again.
Revision 2: All graduates will enjoy seeing their school friends again.

Exercise 32.5*

In the following sentences, choose the correct word from the pairs in parentheses. Check your answers carefully before continuing.

1. Everyone who enjoys a thrilling match will reserve (his their) seat for today's chess club meeting.
2. Despite the inconvenience, everyone climbed to the fourth floor to hand in (her their) course evaluation.
3. Each of her sons has successfully completed (his their) diploma.
4. Someone with lots of money left (her their) purse in the washroom.
5. Every reporter must decide for (himself themselves) how far (he they) will go in pursuit of a story.

Exercise 32.6*

Rewrite the sentences in Exercise 32.5 to eliminate sexist language.

Exercise 32.7*

Correct the following sentences where necessary, being careful to avoid awkward repetition and sexist language.

1. Virginia claims that every one of her male friends has a room of their own.
2. Almost everyone I know is worried about whether he or she will find a job that will be suitable for him or her.
3. Anybody who applies for a job with this institution can expect to spend a lot of their time in selection committee interviews.
4. Taking a picture of someone when they are not looking can produce interesting results.
5. Nearly every man who can cook will tell you that they enjoy preparing food.

3. VAGUE REFERENCE

Avoiding the third difficulty with pronoun–antecedent agreement depends on your common sense and your ability to think of your readers. If you try to look at your writing from your readers' point of view, it is unlikely that you will break the following rule.

A pronoun must clearly refer to the correct antecedent.

The mistake that occurs when you fail to follow this rule is called a vague reference.

Ari told his brother that he was losing his hair.

Who is going bald? Here's another example:

> The faculty are demanding higher salaries and fewer teaching hours, but the administration does not support them.

What does the administration not favour: higher salaries, fewer classes, or the faculty themselves?

In sentences like these, you can only guess the meaning because you don't know who or what is being referred to by the pronouns. You can make such sentences less confusing by using either more names or other nouns and by using fewer pronouns. For example:

> Ari told his brother Sam that Sam was losing his hair.

> The faculty are demanding higher salaries and fewer teaching hours, but the administration does not support their demands.

Another type of vague reference occurs when there is no antecedent at all in the sentence for the pronoun to refer to.

> I sold my skis last year and can't even remember how to do it anymore. (Do what?)

> Reading is Sophia's passion, but she says she doesn't have a favourite. (A favourite what?)

How would you revise these sentences?

Be sure that every pronoun has a clear antecedent with which it agrees in number, person, and gender. Once you have mastered this principle, you'll have no further trouble with pronoun–antecedent agreement.

Exercise 32.8*

Correct the following sentences where necessary. Some perfectly correct answers of yours may differ from the answers we've given. That's because the references are so vague that the sentences can be understood in more than one way.

1. I know that smoking is bad for me and everyone else, but I can't give them up.

2. If your pet rat won't eat its food, feed it to the kitty.

3. Chuck told Rocco his teeth were falling out.

4. Whenever Stefan and Matt played poker, he stacked the deck.

5. The gorilla was mean and hungry because he had finished it all in the morning.

6. Madonna has transformed herself at least four times in her career, which makes her unique.

7. Dani backed her car into a garbage truck and dented it.

8. Rocco was suspicious of handgun control because he thought everyone should have one for late-night subway rides.

9. Get your ears pierced during this week's special and take home an extra pair free.

10. When Jean and Paul began to argue, he told him that he had never had any respect for him.

Exercise 32.9

To test your understanding of the pronoun problems we have covered so far, try this exercise, which contains all three kinds of pronoun–antecedent agreement errors. Correct the following sentences where necessary.

1. Each of her suitors had their faults, but Denise decided to choose the one that had the most money.

2. Embezzling is what he does best, but he hasn't been able to pull one off lately.

3. Everyone may pick up their exams after Tuesday.

4. Our instructor said that passing grades would be given to those that successfully completed their field placement.

5. Each candidate must submit their portfolio, their résumé, and a neatly folded $50 bill in order to be granted an interview.

6. Parker said to Mila that she had no idea how she felt when Alan broke up with her.

7. Everyone but me said that they would like to work for the company who gave me the job.

8. All of the girls are looked on as a sister here at Camp Kitsch-i-koo-mee.

9. Brad and Jennifer are a couple that don't have to worry where its next dollar is coming from.

10. Before a Canadian votes, it is their responsibility to make themselves familiar with the issues and the candidates.

GO TO WEB

EXERCISES 32.3, 32.4, 32.5, 32.6

Person Agreement

So far, we have focused on using pronouns correctly and clearly within a sentence. Now let's turn to the problem of **person agreement**, which means using pronouns consistently throughout a sentence or a paragraph. There are three categories of person that we use when we write or speak:

	Singular	Plural
First person	I; me	we; us
Second person	you	you
Third person	she, he, it, one; her, him and all pronouns ending in *-one, -thing, -body*	they; them

Here is the rule for person agreement.

Do not mix "persons" unless meaning requires it.

In other words, be consistent. If you begin a sentence using a second-person pronoun, you must use second person all the way through. Look at this sentence:

If *you* wish to succeed, *one* must work hard.

This is the most common error—mixing second-person *you* with third-person *one*.

Here's another example:

One can live happily in Vancouver if *you* have a sturdy umbrella.

We can correct this error by using the second person throughout:

You can live happily in Vancouver if *you* have a sturdy umbrella.

We can also correct it by using the third person throughout:

One can live happily in Vancouver if *one* has a sturdy umbrella.

or

One can live happily in Vancouver if *he* or *she* has a sturdy umbrella.

These last three sentences raise two points of style that you should consider.

1. Don't overuse *one*. Although all three revised sentences are correct, the impression they make on the reader is different. The first sentence, in the second person, sounds the most informal and natural—like something you would say. It's a bit casual for general writing purposes. The second sentence, which uses *one* twice, sounds the most formal—even a little stilted. The third sentence falls between the other two in formality and is the one you'd be most likely to use in writing for school or business. It's grammatically correct and non-sexist, but it raises another potential problem.
2. Don't overuse *he* or *she*. If this construction occurs frequently, the reader cannot help shifting focus from what you're saying to how you're saying it. The best writing is transparent—that is, it doesn't call attention to itself. If your reader becomes distracted by your style, your meaning gets lost. Consider this sentence:

A student can easily pass this course if he or she applies himself or herself to his or her studies.

Awkward, isn't it? Imagine being the unfortunate reader who has to struggle through a whole paragraph filled with this clumsy construction!

Grammar

The solutions to this problem are the same as those for making pronouns ending in *-one*, *-body*, or *-thing* agree with their antecedents. You can either change the whole sentence to the plural—

Students can easily pass this course if they apply themselves to their studies.

—or you can rewrite the sentence without using pronouns:

A student can easily pass this course by applying good study habits.

Exercise 32.10*

In each of the following sentences, select the correct word from the choices given in parentheses. Check your answers before continuing.

1. If you want to make good egg rolls, I advise (them her you) to buy the ready-made wrappings.

2. If you win tonight's lottery, will (one he you) tell (one's his your) friends?

3. Even young children can learn to swim if (one they she) have a good instructor and apply (oneself themselves herself).

4. Every person working in this office should know that (they she) helped to finish an important project.

5. When we toured the House of Commons, (you we he one) didn't see a single MP.

Exercise 32.11*

Correct the following sentences where necessary.

1. After the unfortunate brawl, Biff learned that if a person stomps on police officers, they can expect to end up in jail.

2. Experience is something one doesn't often get until just after you need it.

3. If one leaves garbage at one's campsite, you may well have bears as midnight callers.

4. I knew she wasn't the woman for me when she asked me if Peter Tchaikovsky played for the Canucks.

5. One will always think about the opportunities he's missed, even if you're happy with what you have.

6. Managers who are concerned about downsizing should keep a close eye on your company's income-and-expense statements.

7. You should always wear garlic around the neck if one fears vampires.

8. Any woman who wears garlic won't have to worry about men harassing them, either.

9. Can one really know another person if you have never been to their home?

10. A sure way to lose one's friends is to eat all the ice cream yourself.

Exercise 32.12*

Revise the following passage to make the nouns and pronouns agree in person (first, second, or third) and number (singular or plural). Use the italicized word in the first sentence of each paragraph as your marker.

When *people* see a dreadful occurrence on television, such as a bombing, an earthquake, or a mass slaughter, it does not always affect one. It is one thing for people to see the ravages of war oneself and another thing to see a three-minute newscast of the same battle, neatly edited by the CBC. Even the horrible effects of natural catastrophes that wipe out whole populations are somehow minimized or trivialized when I see them on TV. And though viewers may be horrified by the gaunt faces of starving children on the screen, you can easily escape into your familiar world of Egg McMuffins, Shake'n Bake, and Labatt Blue that is portrayed in commercial messages.

Thus, the impact of television on *us* is a mixed one. It is true that one is shown terrible, sometimes shocking, events that you could not possibly have seen before television. In this way, one's world is drawn together more closely. However, the risk in creating this immediacy is that one may become desensitized and cease to feel or care about one's fellow human beings.

GO TO WEB

EXERCISES 32.7, 32.8

Exercise 32.13

This exercise will test and reinforce your understanding of pronoun form, agreement, and consistency. Revise the following passage, correcting the 15 pronoun errors. (Don't forget to change your verbs when necessary.)

(1) Getting engaged is the worst mistake I ever made. (2) My girlfriend and me should have eloped or just started living together instead of going through the process that has dominated our lives for the past year. (3) Vera wanted a big wedding more than me, but one does what one thinks is necessary, and so I went along with her plans. (4) This meant one had to set the date well in advance so that the photographer, the caterer, and the hall, not to mention your family and friends, could be alerted to keep the day free. (5) Setting the date meant an official engagement, and because Vera wanted one, we went off to the jeweller's. (6) Most of the rings were obviously intended for people much richer than us, but for a mere six weeks' salary, I was able to purchase the smallest one Vera would accept.

(7) Anyone that has gone through this process knows that their whole life is now centred on The Day. (8) One's life is consumed with choosing invitations and menus, with assembling the guest list, with choosing attendants, and with getting fitted for clothes you will probably never wear again. (9) Vera and her parents fretted over the tiniest details. (10) Her mother, Violet, is someone that is so generous she almost smothers you. (11) The salesperson in the bridal salon told her she would look good in a simple dress that cost only as much as a compact car. (12) Vera liked it less

than her mother, but because it reminded her of her own wedding dress, it was the one she had to have. (13) Violet and Murray, her father, ended up making all the decisions that Vera and me should have been making.

33

The Comma

Many writers-in-training tend to sprinkle punctuation like pepper over their pages. Do not use punctuation either to spice up or to decorate your writing. Punctuation marks are functional: they indicate to the reader how the various parts of a sentence relate to one another. By changing the punctuation, you can change the meaning of a sentence. Here are two examples to prove the point.

1. An instructor wrote the following sentence on the board and asked the class to punctuate it: "Woman without her man is nothing."

   The men wrote, "Woman, without her man, is nothing."
   The women wrote, "Woman! Without her, man is nothing."

2. Now it's your turn. Punctuate this sentence: "I think there is only one person to blame myself."

   If you wrote, "I think there is only one person to blame, myself." the reader will understand that you believe only one person—who may or may not be known to you—is to blame.

   If you wrote, "I think there is only one person to blame: myself." the reader will understand that you are personally accepting responsibility for the blame.

The comma is the most frequently used—and misused—punctuation mark in English. Perhaps nothing is so sure a sign of a competent writer as the correct use of commas, so it is very important that you master them. This chapter presents five comma rules that cover most instances in which commas are needed. If you apply these five rules faithfully, your reader will never be confused by missing or misplaced commas in your writing. And if, as occasionally happens, the sentence you are writing is not covered by one of our five rules, remember the first commandment of comma usage: when in doubt, leave it out.

Five Comma Rules

1. Use commas to separate items in a series of three or more.

The required subjects in this program are math, physics, and English.

Drive two blocks north of Main, turn left, go past two traffic signals, and turn right.

Karin went to the movies, Jan and Yasmin went to play pool, and I went to bed.

The comma before the *and* at the end of the list is optional, but we advise you to use it. Occasionally, misunderstandings can occur if it is left out.

Exercise 33.1*

Insert commas where necessary in the following sentences. Answers for exercises in this chapter begin on page 504.

1. Holly held two aces a King a Queen and a Jack in her hand.
2. This food is spicy colourful nourishing and delicious.
3. In Canada, the seasons are spring summer fall winter winter and winter.
4. Just let me have a bath and a haircut before you judge my appearance.
5. Cell phones hand-held computers and DVD players are three popular new technologies.
6. To go winter camping, you need woolen underwear showshoes Arctic boots but very little money.
7. Sleeping through my alarm dozing during sociology napping in the library after lunch and snoozing in front of the TV all are symptoms of my overactive nightlife.
8. Once you have finished your homework taken out the garbage and done the dishes, you can feed the cat clean your room and do your laundry.
9. Don't forget to bring the photo album videotape and souvenirs of your trip to Australia.
10. My doctor and my nutritionist agree that I should eat better exercise more and stop smoking.

2. Use commas to set off any word or phrase that is not essential to the main idea of the sentence.

To find out whether a word, phrase, or clause is essential, try crossing it out. If the main idea remains unchanged and the sentence still makes sense, the crossed-out expression is *non-essential* and should be set off by commas. Study the following four examples.

Writing a good letter of application isn't difficult, ~~if you're careful~~.

The phrase "if you're careful" is not essential to the main idea of the sentence, so it's separated from the rest of the sentence by a comma.

Writing a letter of application ~~that is clear and concise~~ is a challenge.

If you take out "that is clear and concise," you change the meaning of the sentence. Not all letters of application are a challenge to write: only clear and concise ones. Writing vague and wordy letters is easy; anyone can do it. The words "that is clear and concise" are therefore essential to the meaning of the sentence, so they are not set off by commas.

~~One of Canada's best-known novelists~~, Alice Munro spends the summer in Clinton and the winter in Comox.

The phrase "one of Canada's best-known novelists" is not essential to the main idea; it just gives us additional information about Alice Munro. Leaving it out does not change the meaning, so it is set off by a comma.

When non-essential or supplementary information occurs in the middle of the sentence, rather than at the beginning or the end, be sure to put commas both before and after it.

In *Selling Illusions*, ~~published in 1994~~, Neil Bissoondath explains why he thinks Canada's multiculturalism policy has done more harm than good.

The phrase "published in 1994" is a supplementary detail. It is not essential to the meaning of the sentence, so it is set off by commas.

Exercise 33.2*

Insert commas where necessary in the following sentences. Check your answers before going on.

1. Our family doctor like our family dog never comes when we call.
2. This photograph taken when I was only four embarrasses me whenever my parents show it.
3. Mira's boyfriend who looks like an ape is living proof that love is blind.
4. Isn't it strange that the poor who are often bitterly critical of the rich buy lottery tickets?
5. Several premiers and a former political advisor a man now well into his eighties accompanied the prime minister on his trade mission to China.
6. My car made it all the way to Saskatoon without anything falling off or breaking down a piece of good luck that surprised us all.
7. A popular mathematics instructor Professor Lam won the distinguished teaching award again this year.
8. We're going to the shopping mall a weekly ritual we all enjoy.
9. No one who has seen Patrick Roy play can doubt that he is a superstar.
10. Classical music which I call Prozac for the ears can be very soothing in times of stress.

---

3. Put a comma between independent clauses when they are joined by these connecting words:

for	but	so
and	or	
nor	yet	

(You can remember these words easily if you notice that their first letters spell "fanboys.")

I hope I do well in the interview, for I really want this job.

I like José Carreras, but I prefer Placido Domingo.

We shape our tools, and our tools shape us. (Marshall McLuhan)

I knew I was going to be late, so I went back to sleep.

Be sure that the sentence you are punctuating contains two independent clauses rather than one clause with a single subject and a multiple verb.

We <u>loved</u> the book but <u>hated</u> the movie.
(<u>We</u> is the subject, and there are two verbs, <u>loved</u> and <u>hated</u>. Do not put a comma between two or more verbs that share a single subject.)

<u>We</u> both <u>loved</u> the book, but <u>Kim</u> <u>hated</u> the movie.
(This sentence contains two independent clauses—*We* *loved* and *Kim* *hated*—joined by *but*. The comma is required here.)

Exercise 33.3*

Insert commas where they are needed in the following sentences, then check your answers.

1. This has been a perfect day and you have been a perfect host.
2. We have a plan and a budget yet we still don't have the staff we need.
3. Talk shows ran out of things to say years ago but they haven't stopped talking yet.
4. We discovered that we both had an interest in art so we made a date to go to an exhibition at the gallery next Friday.
5. Canadians are proud of their country but don't approve of too much flag waving.
6. Take good notes for there will be an exam on Tuesday.
7. You won't get any sympathy from us nor will we help you explain to your parents.
8. The car swerved wildly and just missed the crossing guard.
9. I have travelled all over the world yet my luggage has visited many more places than I have.
10. Jet lag makes me look haggard and sick but at least I resemble my passport picture.

4. Put a comma after a word or group of words that comes before an independent clause.

Lucas, you aren't paying attention.

No matter how hard I try, I will never forget you.

Exhausted and cranky from staying up all night, I staggered into class.

If that's their idea of a large pizza, we'd better order two.

Until she got her promotion, she was quite friendly.

Exercise 33.4*

Insert commas where they are needed in the following sentences, then check your answers.

1. Unfortunately we'll have to begin all over again.
2. Mr. Dillinger the bank wants to speak with you.
3. In the end the quality of your performance counts more than the effort you put into it.
4. Treading water we waited for the boat to return and rescue us.
5. Even though this photograph is out of focus it does show that Remi did take part in the Polar Bear swim.
6. Finally understanding what she was trying to say I apologized for being so slow.
7. After an evening of watching television I have accomplished as much as if I had been unconscious.
8. Since my doctor recommended that I eat less and exercise more I have been walking around the block during my lunch break.
9. Having munched our way through a large bag of peanuts while watching the game we weren't interested in food at supper time.
10. Whenever a police officer pulls over an optimist the optimist thinks it's to ask for directions.

> 5. Use commas between coordinate adjectives but not between cumulative adjectives.

Coordinate adjectives are those whose order can be changed, and the word *and* can be inserted between them without changing the meaning of the sentence.

Our company is looking for energetic, courteous salespeople.

The adjectives *energetic* and *courteous* could appear in reverse order, and you could put *and* between them: "Our company is looking for courteous and energetic salespeople."

In a series of **cumulative adjectives**, however, each adjective modifies the word that follows it. You cannot change their order, nor can you insert *and* between them.

The bride wore a pale pink silk dress, and the groom wore a navy wool suit.

You cannot say "The bride wore a silk pink pale dress" or "The groom wore a navy and wool suit," so no commas are used with these adjectives.

One final note about commas before you try the review exercises: never place a SINGLE comma between a subject and its verb.

> Wrong: <u>Those</u> who intend to register for hockey, <u>must be</u> at the arena by 8:00 a.m.

> Right: <u>Those</u> who intend to register for hockey <u>must be</u> at the arena by 8:00 a.m.

Two commas, however, between a subject and its verb are correct if the commas set off non-essential material.

> <u>Saied and Mohamed</u>, who intend to register for hockey, <u>have</u> never <u>played</u> before.

Exercise 33.5*

Insert commas where they are needed in the following sentences. Check your answers before continuing.

1. The desk was made of dark brown carved oak.
2. Do you want your portrait in a glossy finish or a matte finish?
3. Bright yellow fabric that repels stains is ideal for rain gear.
4. Toronto in the summer is hot smoggy and humid.
5. Today's paper has an article about a new car made of lightweight durable aluminum.
6. Using the new improved model should increase your productivity.
7. This ergonomic efficient full-function keyboard comes in a variety of pastel shades.
8. We ordered a large nutritious salad for lunch, then indulged ourselves with a whipped-cream topped dessert.
9. Danny bought a cute cuddly pure-bred puppy.
10. Ten months later that cute puppy turned into a vicious man-eating monster.

The rest of the exercises in this chapter require you to apply all five comma rules. Before you start, write out the five rules and keep them in front of you as you work through the exercises. Refer to the rules frequently as you punctuate the sentences. After you've finished each exercise, check your answers and make sure you understand any mistakes you've made.

Exercise 33.6*

1. Pinot noir which is a type of grape grown in California Oregon British Columbia and Ontario produces a delicious red wine.
2. There are I am told people who don't like garlic but you won't find any of them eating at Freddy's.
3. I use e-mail to communicate with my colleagues a fax machine to keep in touch with clients and Canada Post to send greetings to my relatives.
4. Your dogs Mr. Pavlov seem hungry for some reason.
5. According to G.K. Chesterton "If a thing is worth doing it is worth doing badly."
6. Looking for a competent computer technologist we interviewed tested investigated and rejected 30 applicants.
7. How you choose to phrase your resignation is up to you but I expect to have it on my desk by morning.
8. Vinny's sparse grey moth-eaten beard can hardly be described as a fashion statement.
9. Franz wrote the formula on the damp stained linen tablecloth.
10. Canada a country known internationally for beautiful scenery peaceful intentions and violent hockey always places near the top of the United Nations' list of desirable places to live.

Exercise 33.7*

1. Whereas the Super Bowl tradition goes back about four decades the Grey Cup has a history that stretches back to the 19th century.
2. Otherwise Mrs. Lincoln said she had very much enjoyed the play.
3. Our guard dog a Rottweiler caught an intruder and maimed him for life.
4. Unfortunately my Uncle Ladislaw was the intruder and he intends to sue us for every penny we have.
5. The year 1945 marked the end of World War II and the beginning of assistance to war-torn nations.
6. The lovely antique mahogany table was sold for only $300.
7. If there were more people like Gladys global warming would be the least of our worries.
8. We are pleased with your résumé and are offering you an interview this week.
9. Deciding on the midnight blue velvet pants was easy but paying for them was not.
10. Igor asked "May I show you to your quarters or would you prefer to spend the night in the dungeon?"

Punctuation

GO TO WEB

EXERCISES 33.1, 33.2, 33.3

Exercise 33.8

To test your mastery of commas, provide the necessary punctuation for the following paragraph. There are 15 errors.

I sometimes wonder what our ancestors if they were able to observe us now would think of some of the activities we take for granted. I'm sure that rollerblading would seem peculiar to them as would bungee-jumping water skiing and hang gliding. However I suspect that our forebears would find even those strange activities understandable perhaps even enjoyable compared with jogging. The sight of otherwise perfectly reasonable people decked out in brightly coloured fleece underwear doggedly puffing and sweating along every pathway road and trail would I am convinced put The Fear into Great Grandpa and send him scurrying back whence he had come. While running was certainly not foreign to past generations the idea of running slowly with no destination in mind would have been inconceivable. People back then stayed fit from physical labour not from recreational exertion.

34

The Colon

The **colon** functions as an introducer. A colon between a statement and what follows alerts the reader to what is coming. The statement that comes before the colon must be a complete sentence (independent clause). Therefore, a colon should not be used after *is* or *are*.

Incorrect: Two things I cannot stand are: cats and brussels sprouts.

Correct: Two things I cannot stand are cats and brussels sprouts.

The colon can be used to introduce

- a list

The contemporary Canadian fiction course focuses on three authors: Margaret Atwood, Alice Munro, and Carol Shields.

The trees in Stanley Park are all native to British Columbia: red cedar, Douglas fir, arbutus, and dogwood.

- a word or phrase that expands or clarifies the statement that precedes it. The information after the colon often answers the question "What?" or "Who?"

Business and industry face a new problem: Canada's low productivity.

Narcissus peered into the pond, staring at his favourite image: his face.

- a quotation

Lucille Ball once observed that there were three secrets to staying young: "Live honestly, eat slowly, and lie about your age."

Irving Layton is not fond of academics: "There hasn't been a writer of power and originality during the past century who hasn't had to fight his way to acceptance against the educated pipsqueaks hibernating in universities." (Letter to the *Montreal Star*)

The uses of the colon can be summarized as follows.

The colon introduces one of three things: a list, a clarification, or a quotation.

Exercise 34.1*

Put a checkmark next to the sentences that are correctly punctuated. Check your answers before going on. Answers for this chapter begin on page 507.

1. _____ Believe it or not, the country that produces the most films every year is: India.
2. _____ Jordan wants to go home to be comforted by the only person in the world who truly understands him: his mother.
3. _____ I have a hard time choosing between my two favourite teams, which are the Calgary Flames and the Vancouver Canucks.
4. _____ According to Harry, who is several decades out of date, the only important things in life are: sex, drugs, and rock 'n' roll.
5. _____ The company's bankruptcy resulted from the CEO's management style. He relied on: crisis management, seat-of-the-pants planning, and excessive profit-taking.
6. _____ One topic has dominated the health concerns of the world since the late 1980s: AIDS.
7. _____ Two of Canada's highest awards in professional sports are the Stanley Cup and the Grey Cup.
8. _____ All most students ask is that their teachers treat them with: courtesy, fairness, and respect.
9. _____ Of course, there are always a few students who demand what no true professional will provide special treatment.
10. _____ In drafting the budget, we must be careful to avoid the one technique the president has said she will not entertain deficit financing.

Exercise 34.2*

Insert colons in the following sentences where necessary and then check your answers. If you find you've made any mistakes, review the explanation on pages 411–12, study the examples, and be sure you understand why your answers were wrong before going on.

1. I have set myself three goals this year to achieve an 80 percent average, to get a good summer job, and to buy a car.
2. Right after we moved in, we discovered we had a problem termites.
3. Our credit card consultant asked us an interesting question after our bankruptcy "Why don't you cut up your credit cards?"
4. Several Canadian writers are even better known abroad than they are at home Carol Shields, Neil Bissoondath, and Michael Ondaatje are three examples.
5. There are a number of inexpensive activities that will improve physical fitness; swimming, tennis, jogging, even brisk walking.
6. Jocelyn is trying to accomplish two mutually contradictory tasks a significant weight loss and success as a restaurant critic.
7. Several of the animals on the international list of endangered species are native to Canada; the wood bison, the northern kit fox, and the whooping crane.
8. We'll finish the assignment by tomorrow only if we stay up all night and consume vast quantities of pizza and black coffee.
9. The majority of Canada's population is worn out and exhausted at the end of a long, hard winter, but most people are able to console themselves with one comforting thought, spring will arrive sometime in May or June.
10. There are several troublesome implications of biological engineering, but one in particular is frightening to most people the cloning of human beings.

Exercise 34.3*

Correct the incorrectly punctuated sentences in Exercise 34.1.

GO TO WEB

EXERCISES 34.1, 34.2, 34.3, 34.4

Punctuation

Exercise 34.4

To test your mastery of colons, correct any errors in the following sentences.

1. There aren't many people I look up to, but one of them is: Vince Carter.
2. The TV is always asking me challenging questions "It's 11:05. Do you know where your children are?"
3. You have all the qualities of a Doberman: except one, loyalty.
4. For my birthday, my sister gave me: a pair of hand-knit socks (I'm allergic to wool), a box of chocolates (I'm on a diet), and a coffee mug with the Petro-Canada logo on it.
5. One of the symptoms of an approaching nervous breakdown is: the belief that one's work is terribly important. (Bertrand Russell)
6. In spite of his ineptitude, he won a prize; the slow-but-steady-progress award.
7. He wants to apologize to you: but he's afraid you won't talk to him.
8. Several names are not on my list of possible names for our new son: including Rex, Nero, Attila, and Leaf.
9. Studies have shown that in most offices the Internet is used primarily for non-work-related activities; personal e-mail, random surfing, and game playing.
10. I have a meeting this afternoon, but I don't want to go; I know it will be: boring and useless.

35

The Semicolon

The **semicolon** and the colon are often confused and used as if they were interchangeable. They serve very different functions, however. The semicolon is a combination of a period and a comma, and its function reflects its structure. Like a period, the semicolon comes between two independent clauses. Like a comma, the semicolon separates parts of a sentence that are closely related in meaning. Semicolons are needed in four kinds of constructions.

> 1. A semicolon can replace a period; in other words, it can appear between two independent clauses.

You should use a semicolon when the two clauses you are joining are closely related in meaning, or when there is a cause-and-effect relationship between them.

I am too tired; I cannot stay awake any longer.

Montreal is not the city's original name; it was once called Ville Marie.

A period could have been used instead of the semicolon in either of these sentences, but the close connection between the clauses makes a semicolon more effective in communicating the writer's meaning.

Punctuation

Some transitional words and phrases are often put between independent clauses to show a cause-and-effect relationship.

2. When the following words or phrases link two independent clauses, put a semicolon before and a comma after them.

; as a result,	; in contrast,	; on the other hand,
; besides,	; in fact,	; otherwise,
; consequently,	; instead,	; then,
; finally,	; moreover,	; therefore,
; furthermore,	; nevertheless,	; thus,
; however,	; next,	
; in addition,	; on the contrary,	

The forecast called for sun; instead, we got snow.

The monitor went blank; nevertheless, I continued to type.

I'm not offended by dumb blonde jokes because I know I'm not dumb; besides, I also know I'm not blonde. (Dolly Parton)

Note, however, that when the shaded words and phrases are used as non-essential expressions rather than as connecting words, they are separated from the rest of the sentence by commas (see Chapter 33, Rule 2).

Two minutes later, however, he changed his mind.

However hard I try, I just can't seem to master organic chemistry.

3. Use a semicolon after an independent clause that is followed by one of the introductory expressions listed below and a list or example(s).

; also,	; for instance,
; finally,	; namely,
; for example,	; that is,

Canada has produced many internationally acclaimed singers; for example, Celine Dion, Diana Krall, and Nelly Furtado.

I often wonder how to use some punctuation marks; namely, colons and semicolons.

Sometimes semicolons should be used in a list instead of commas.

> 4.   Put semicolons between the items of a complex list.

A complex list is one in which at least one component part already contains commas.

Incorrect: We invited a number of senior managers including Ann Kung, senior vice-president, Lionel Tiger, director of information technology, and Larry Sells, manager of marketing.

Correct: We invited a number of senior managers including Ann Kung, senior vice-president; Lionel Tiger, director of information technology; and Larry Sells, manager of marketing.

Exercise 35.1*

Put a checkmark next to the sentences that are correctly punctuated. Check your answers before continuing. Answers for this chapter begin on page 508.

1. _____ We've eaten all the goodies, it's time to go home.
2. _____ Many doctors claim weather affects our health; in fact, barometric pressure has a direct effect on arthritis.
3. _____ Your instructor would like to see you pass, however, there may be a small fee involved.
4. _____ Molly is going to Chicago, she wants to appear on *Oprah*.
5. _____ Many people dislike hockey; because some of the players act like goons rather than athletes.
6. _____ Orville tried and tried; but he couldn't get the teacher's attention.
7. _____ She presented her report using coloured charts and diagrams; these visual aids woke up even the accountants.
8. _____ First we'll have a cool drink then we'll see if we can find a way to start this car.
9. _____ Rumours of a merger had begun to circulate by five o'clock; so it's no wonder many employees looked nervous on their way home.
10. _____ We knew the party had been a success when Uncle Morty, drunk as usual, tap-danced across the top of the piano, Aunt Madeline, who must weigh at least 80 kg, did her Ally McBeal imitation, and Biff punched out two of his cousins.

Punctuation

Exercise 35.2*

Correct the faulty punctuation in Exercise 35.1.

GO TO WEB

EXERCISES 35.1, 35.2

Exercise 35.3*

Insert commas and semicolons where necessary in these sentences. Then check your answers.

1. Teddy won't stop crying it seems his gerbil is missing.
2. We must organize our finances otherwise we'll be broke before April.
3. We had all hoped you would be able to join us, however, because you have a previous engagement we'll just have to carry on without you.
4. A day without puns is like a day without sunshine, it leaves gloom for improvement.
5. I work on an assembly line; where we believe that if a job is worth doing, it's worth doing 11,000 times a day.
6. It is not very difficult to become wealthy if you're in your early twenties all you need to do is put the price of a pack of cigarettes a day into an RSP each year and you'll be a millionaire by the time you retire.
7. We decided to go to a nearby restaurant for pizza, that is we would have gone but Norm insisted on waiting for Mairi and by the time we got there it was closed.
8. As a dog lover in general and an Afghan owner in particular I have to take a lot of abuse, for example my wife gave me a book rating the intelligence of various breeds of dog and the Afghan ranked seventy-ninth of seventy-nine breeds tested.
9. If you put nonsense into a computer what comes out is nonsense. However once the nonsense has passed through an expensive machine few people seem willing to challenge it.
10. According to a recent *Gourmet Magazine* poll four of the top ten restaurants in the world are in Paris, three those ranking eighth ninth and tenth are in the United States and two are in Tokyo. One is in Thailand.

GO TO WEB

EXERCISE 35.3

Exercise 35.4

Test your mastery of the semicolons and commas by correcting the punctuation in these sentences.

1. Growing old has never really bothered me in fact I consider aging a huge improvement over the alternative.
2. Our marketing campaign is based on sound principles, for example, if you are annoying enough, people will buy just to make you go away.
3. The construction was way behind schedule consequently we lost our performance bonus.
4. Among many products being standardized by the European Community is the condom however a number of nations have complained that the standard size is too small.
5. Failing to stop at the light was; in fact, the least of his offences the police were much more interested in his expired driver's licence.
6. Just as the telephone rang, the fax, which I had anxiously been waiting for, began feeding from the fax machine, all the computers in the office crashed, the paper shredder began to smoke, and the fire alarm went off.
7. I suggest you offer me a 15 percent increase in salary otherwise there will be no reason for me to take on this extra responsibility.
8. A practice that works well in one country may not work in another for example every man in Switzerland is required to own a rifle. The United States might be able to adopt this practice quite comfortably however Canada could not.
9. In politics, if you want anything said, ask a man if you want anything done, ask a woman. (Margaret Thatcher)
10. To use or not to use a semicolon is often a matter of the writer's choice, nevertheless there are some instances in which it is required.

Punctuation

36

Question and Exclamation Marks

The Question Mark

Everyone knows that a question mark follows an interrogative, or asking, sentence, but we all sometimes forget to include it. Let this chapter serve as a reminder not to forget!

> The **question mark** is the end punctuation for all interrogative sentences.

The question mark gives your readers an important clue to the meaning of your sentence. "There's more?" is vastly different in meaning from "There's more!" and that difference is communicated to readers by the punctuation alone.

The only time you don't end a question with a question mark is when the question is part of a statement.

Is anyone there? (question)
I asked if anyone was there. (statement)
Do you understand? (question)
I wonder whether you understand. (statement)

Exercise 36.1*

Supply the correct end punctuation for the following sentences. Then check your answers. Answers for this chapter are on page 509.

1. Do you think that the Canadian dollar will ever rise above the U.S. 70 cents mark

2. The low dollar makes us wonder whether we can afford a trip to Florida

3. I cannot believe that you would question my integrity

4. I wonder if my apartment will ever be the same after their visit

5. What's another word for thesaurus

6. If we can't finish the project on time, will we lose the contract

7. I question the results you got on your survey

8. Did you know there are only 18,000 elephants in all of India

9. We have no answer to why we hired an unqualified, inexperienced person for such a sensitive position

10. If corn oil comes from corn, where does baby oil come from

GO TO WEB

EXERCISES 36.1, 36.2

The Exclamation Mark

In informal or personal writings, the exclamation mark is a useful piece of punctuation for conveying your tone of voice to your readers. There is a distinct difference in tone between these two sentences:

There's a man behind you.

There's a man behind you!

In the first sentence, information is being supplied, perhaps about the line-up at a grocery-store checkout counter. The second sentence might be a shouted warning about a mugger.

Use an **exclamation mark** as end punctuation in sentences requiring extreme emphasis or dramatic effect.

Please note the exclamation mark has "punch" or drama only if you use it sparingly. If you use an exclamation mark after every third sentence, how will your readers know when you really mean to indicate excitement? Note also that exclamation marks are seldom used in academic or professional writing.

Practically any sentence could end with an exclamation mark, but remember that the punctuation changes the meaning of the sentence. Read each of the following sentences with and without an exclamation mark and picture the situation that would call for each reading.

He's gone   Don't touch that button

The room was empty   There she goes again

Exercise 36.2*

Supply the correct end punctuation for each of the following sentences. In many cases, the punctuation you use will depend on how you want the sentence to be read.

1. You must be kidding

2. Turn left Now

3. I can't believe I actually passed

4. Oh, great We're moving to Backwater, Alberta

5. Run It's right behind you

6. I'm freezing Turn the heat up

7. "Workers of the world, unite" (Karl Marx)

8. Finally Someone is coming to take our order

9. For the last time, leave me alone

10. Get lost I can manage perfectly well by myself

GO TO WEB

EXERCISES 36.3, 36.4, 36.5

Exercise 36.3

To test your understanding of where question marks and exclamations should be used, supply correct end punctuation for these sentences.

1. We aren't sure if we're getting paid this week or not

2. Reginald wanted his broker to tell him whether pork bellies would be a good investment

3. What in the world were you thinking of when you had "file not found" tattooed on your arm

4. Arthur asked Guinevere where she was going

5. Would you believe that the heaviest world-champion boxer, Primo Carnera, weighed in at 123 kg in a 1933 fight

6. That's one king-size heavyweight

7. Do you mean to tell me that your lovely necklace is made of shellacked moose-droppings

8. You must be kidding

9. Dr. and Mr. Widget arrived at the reception in their new Rolls-Royce

10. Hooray This chapter is finished

Punctuation

37

Dashes and Parentheses

When you are talking with someone, you use your voice to punctuate: you pause for a short time (commas) or for a longer time (semicolons and periods); you shout (exclamation marks); or you query (question marks). In writing, punctuation substitutes for these vocal markers: it helps you ensure that your writing will make sense to your readers.

One way you can add variety and flexibility to your sentences is by inserting words or phrases that add to but are not essential to the sentence's meaning. That is, the word or phrase could be omitted, and the sentence would still be complete and would still make sense. It might, however, lack grace or interest.

You can use three punctuation marks to add non-essential material to your sentences: commas, dashes, and parentheses. You are already familiar with the first one. Here is your opportunity to master the last two: the **dash**—which looks like this—and **parentheses** (round brackets). (If you are typing, the dash is two hyphens with no space on either side.)

Dashes

Dashes are used to mark a break in thought or an abrupt shift in emphasis.

1. Use a dash to introduce a word, phrase, or clause that summarizes or restates what has just been said.

I still love dried apricots and pickled beets—foods my mother gave me as treats when I was a child.

Perseverance, spirit, and skill—these three qualities ensure a good game.

Atwood, Ondaatje, Laurence, Davies, Clarke, and Richler—for a country with a relatively small population, Canada has produced an extraordinary number of internationally acclaimed novelists.

2. Use a pair of dashes to enclose a series of items separated by commas.

Four of the managers—Olive, Muhsin, Luis, and Neville—are new to the McDonald's franchise at the zoo.

Because they were afraid of the police, my so-called friends—Roman, Shane, and Luba—all betrayed me.

The apartment he showed me would have been fine, had it not been for the tenants—moths, cockroaches, and silverfish—already making it their home.

3. Use a dash or a pair of dashes to set off from the rest of the sentence a climactic or emphatic moment.

I expect—and so does the college—that students at this level should be self-motivated.

Our neighbour—the accused murderer—keeps rabbits in his backyard.

If you really want to go—even though you haven't been invited—I'll take you.

Note that dashes set off material that is not grammatically part of the sentence. If you were to omit the words between the dashes, the sentence would still make sense.

Dashes can be misused if you use them too frequently. Unless you are writing very informally—in a personal letter, for instance—save dashes for the very occasional phrase to which you want to draw emphatic attention.

Exercise 37.1*

Add dashes where they are appropriate. Answers for this chapter begin on page 509.

1. The members of one Aboriginal tribe in England I've forgotten their name painted themselves blue.
2. My purpose in moving from Vancouver to Hope like that of hundreds of people before me was to find affordable housing.
3. We shall have to start without her again!
4. Skiing and skating if you like these sports, you'll love Quebec.
5. Tending to his garden, writing his memoirs, and dining with friends these were the pleasures Arnold looked forward to in retirement.
6. What is missing in his life is obvious rest and relaxation!
7. Zoe should do well in fact, I'm sure she will in the engineering program.
8. Alexei was amazed positively thunderstruck when he learned Uncle Vladimir had won a million dollars.
9. Historians, diarists, and chroniclers these are the recorders of our past.
10. Dashes a kind of silent shout allow you to insert an occasional exclamation into your sentences.

Parentheses

Like dashes, parentheses are used to enclose an interruption in a sentence. The difference between them is a matter of tone: dashes SHOUT—they serve to draw the reader's attention to the material they enclose—but parentheses (which should be used sparingly) "whisper." Parentheses are similar to theatrical asides; they are subordinate to the main action but are not to be missed.

1. Use parentheses around additional information that you wish to include but not emphasize.

Giselle's teaching schedule (she is in class seven hours a day) gives her little time to meet with students individually.

They brought me to their village and presented me to their chief (a woman) and to the tribal councillors.

Note the difference in tone your choice of punctuation makes. Compare the examples above with the following versions.

Giselle's teaching schedule—she is in class seven hours a day—gives her little time to meet with students individually.

They brought me to their village and presented me to their chief—a woman—and to the tribal councillors.

2. Use parentheses to enclose explanatory material that is not part of the main sentence.

"Lightweight Lit." (an essay in Part 4) was written by an English teacher who would have preferred to remain anonymous.

The Malagasy (people of Madagascar) like to eat a kapoaka of rice (enough to fill a condensed-milk can) three times a day.

3. Use parentheses to enclose reference data in a research paper. (See Chapter 22.)

Exercise 37.2*

Add parentheses where they are appropriate.

1. Five of the students I was asked not to name them have volunteered to be peer tutors.
2. The apostrophe is explained in the unit on spelling pages 460–66.
3. Jason complained that being a manager he became one in March was like being a cop.
4. I have enclosed a cheque for one hundred and fifty dollars $150.00.
5. More members of the Canadian Armed Forces died in World War I 1914–18 than in any war before or since.
6. Although Mozart lived a relatively short time he died when he was thirty-six, he composed hundreds of musical masterpieces.
7. As news of her miracle cures spread patients began to come to her from all over the province, the doctor had to move her clinic to a more central location.
8. The new contract provided improved working conditions, a raise in salary 3 percent, and a new dental plan.

Punctuation

9. Ontario and British Columbia now produce world-class wines from their small estate wineries Inniskillin, Hillebrand, Quails' Gate that compete and win internationally.

10. "One of the most important tools for making paper speak in your own voice is punctuation; it plays the role of body language; it helps readers hear you the way you want to be heard" Baker, 48–49.

GO TO WEB

EXERCISE 37.1

Exercise 37.3

Insert dashes and parentheses where appropriate in the following sentences.

1. The function of parentheses see the explanation on page 426 is to set apart material that interrupts the main idea of the sentence and that the writer does not want to emphasize.

2. Dashes, on the other hand I love dashes are used to set off a dramatic or emphatic interruption.

3. When the seasoned liquid tastes hot and pungent remember that some of the pungency will be absorbed by the beans, stir in one-half cup of molasses.

4. This club plays jazz terrific Dixieland nightly from 10 p.m. until 2 a.m.

5. On their first date, Rupert took Freda bowling she hates bowling. I doubt that they will see each other again.

6. Proof of the need to spend on infrastructure as if further proof were needed is the fact that our plant has twice failed fire code inspections.

7. We should we must find a way to cut our expenses by at least 10 percent.

8. Years ago, Victor Borge invented a system of oral punctuation that assigned sounds some of them hilarious to each piece of punctuation, supposedly to give listeners the same benefit readers have in understanding the precise meaning of a message.

9. Obnoxious people Rudolf and Dwight come to mind light up the room when they leave.

10. Canadian hockey broadcaster Foster Hewitt created a sports catchphrase "He shoots! He scores!" during overtime coverage of a hockey match between the New York Rangers and the Toronto Maple Leafs on April 4, 1933. The Rangers won.

38

Three Suggestions for Quick Improvement

Of all the errors you might make in writing, spelling is the one that is noticed by everyone, not just English teachers. Misspellings can cause misunderstandings, as when an English teacher promised his students a course with "a strong *vacational* emphasis." (Those students who weren't misled wondered what he was doing teaching English.)

They can also cause confusion. Take this sentence, for example:

Mouse is a desert with a base of wiped cream.

It takes a few seconds to "translate" the sentence into a definition of *mousse*, a *dessert* made with *whipped* cream.

Most often, though, misspellings are misleading; they spoil the image you want to present. You want to be seen as intelligent, careful, and conscientious. But if your writing is riddled with spelling errors, your reader will think you are careless, uneducated, or even stupid. It is not true, by the way, that intelligence and the ability to spell go hand in hand. It is true, however, that most people think they do. So, to prevent misunderstanding, confusion, and embarrassment, it is essential that you spell correctly.

There are three things you can do to improve your spelling almost instantly.

1. Buy and use a good dictionary.

A dictionary is a writer's best friend. You will need to use it every time you write, so if you don't already own a good dictionary, you need to buy one. For Canadian writers, a good dictionary is one that is Canadian, current, comprehensive (contains at least 75,000 entries), and reliable (published by an established, well-known firm).

Spelling

A convenient reference is the *Gage Canadian Dictionary*, available in an inexpensive paperback edition. It is the dictionary on which we have based the examples and exercises in this chapter. Also recommended are the *Canadian Dictionary of the English Language* (Nelson, 1997), and *The Canadian Oxford Dictionary* (Oxford, 1998). Unfortunately, no comprehensive Canadian dictionary is available on the Internet.

A good dictionary packs a lot of information in a small space. Take a look at the *Gage Canadian Dictionary* entry for the word *graduate*, for example. The circled numbers correspond to the numbers in the list of information dictionary entries provide, which follows the entry.

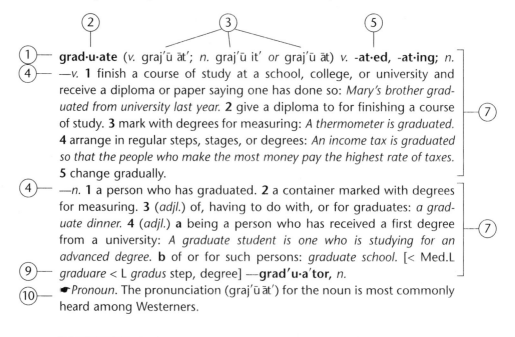

Gage Canadian Dictionary. Toronto: Gage Educational Publishing Company, 1983. 508.

In a dictionary entry, you will find some or all of the following information.

1. **Spelling:** if there are two or more acceptable spellings, the most common one is normally given first
2. **Syllables:** to show you where hyphens can go, if you need to break a word at the end of a line
3. **Pronunciation:** if there is more than one acceptable pronunciation, the most common one is listed first
4. **Grammatical form(s):** e.g., noun (*n.*), verb (*v.*), adverb (*adv.*)

5. Any **irregular forms** of the word, such as the plural form of a noun, or the past tense and past participle of a verb
6. **Usage restrictions:** e.g., slang, informal, archaic, offensive
7. **Definition(s):** the most common meanings are given first, followed by the technical or specialized meanings, together with phrases or sentences illustrating how the word is used
8. **Idioms** using the word
9. **Origins** of the word (etymology)
10. **Other helpful information:** e.g., homonyms (words that sound the same as the entry word); synonyms (words that are similar in meaning to the entry word); antonyms (words opposite in meaning); and special variations in grammar, spelling, pronunciation, and usage

Unless you have already done so (and most people haven't) begin by reading the "Guide to the Dictionary." The information in the Guide may not be very entertaining, but it is essential if you want to understand how to read your dictionary accurately. No two dictionaries are alike. Each sets out its information a little differently from its competitors. Only if you are familiar with your dictionary's symbols, abbreviations, and the format of its entries, will you be able to use it efficiently.

Knowing what is in the Guide will also save you time. For example, you may not need to memorize long lists of irregular plurals. Good dictionaries include irregular plurals in their entries. They also include irregular forms of verbs, adjectives, and adverbs. And if you've forgotten how regular plurals, verbs, adjectives, and adverbs are formed, you'll find that information in the Guide as well.

Exercise 38.1

The following words are tricky to spell because they are not pronounced the way you might expect if you've had no previous experience with them. Look them up in your dictionary and, in the space beside each word, write out its pronunciation (the information given immediately after it in parentheses). Using your dictionary's pronunciation key to help you, practise sounding out each word, one syllable at a time. No answers are given for this exercise.

1. preferable
2. epitome
3. impotent
4. comparable
5. subtle
6. eulogy
7. indict
8. irreparable
9. corps
10. chassis

Spelling

2. Get help!

In addition to your dictionary, there are three other resources you can use to help you turn a misspelled mess into a perfectly spelled document.

- The spellchecker in your word processing program. While far from fool-proof, online spellers are a reliable way to catch most typos and many misspelled words. Get into the habit of spellchecking every document before you print it.
- A hand-held electronic spellchecker. Conveniently pocket-sized and not expensive, these devices contain a large bank of words and can provide the correct spelling if the guess you type in is not too far off. Some checkers even pronounce the word for you. Ask your instructor if you can use this device (with the sound turned off, please) when you are writing in class and during exams.
- A good speller. Some people seem to have been born with the ability to spell. They're usually proud of their talent and pleased to demonstrate it, so don't be afraid to ask. The time to seek their help is at step 3 of the revision process (see pages 131–33).

3. Learn three basic spelling rules.

If you *never* write except with a word processor, and if you *always* use its spellcheck function, you can skip this step and go on to Chapter 39. If, however, like most of us, your job requires you to fill out forms and occasionally to write memos, notes, and messages in longhand, you'd be wise to review these three simple rules.

Ninety percent of English words are spelled the way they sound. Unfortunately, many of the words we use most frequently have irregular spellings, and no rule holds true in all cases. The three rules that follow do hold for most words, however. Mastering them will help you to avoid many common and potentially embarrassing errors.

Before learning the three rules, you need to know the difference between **vowels** and **consonants**. The vowels are *a, e, i, o,* and *u* (and sometimes *y*). All the other letters are consonants.

Rule 1: Dropping the Final *e*

The first spelling rule tells you when to drop the final, silent *e* when adding an ending to a word.

> Drop the final, silent *e* when adding an ending that begins with a vowel.
>
> Keep the final, silent *e* when adding an ending that begins with a consonant.

Keeping the rule in mind, look at these examples.

Endings Beginning with a Vowel

-ing: amuse + ing = amusing
-ed: live + ed = lived
-able: like + able = likable
-ible: force + ible = forcible
-er: use + er = user

Endings Beginning with a Consonant

-ment: amuse + ment = amusement
-ly: live + ly = lively
-ness: like + ness = likeness
-ful: force + ful = forceful
-less: use + less = useless

Exercise 38.2*

Combine each word with the ending to form a new word. Then check your answers. Answers for this chapter begin on page 510.

1. desperate + ly =
2. atone + ment =
3. rare + ly =
4. emerge + ing =
5. positive + ly =

Exercise 38.3*

Add *e* in the blank space wherever it's needed to complete the spelling of these words. If no *e* is needed, leave the space blank.

1. commenc_____ment
2. mov_____able
3. officiat_____ing
4. valu_____ation
5. realiz_____ing

Spelling

EXCEPTIONS TO RULE 1

Three common words do not follow the rule:

argue + ment = argument
nine + th = ninth
true + ly = truly

There is one more exception to Rule 1: after soft *c* (as in *notice*) and soft *g* (as in *outrage*), keep the final, silent *e* when adding an ending beginning with *a* or *o*. Here are two examples:

notice + able = noticeable
outrage + ous = outrageous

GO TO WEB

EXERCISES 38.1, 38.2, 38.3, 38.4

Rule 2: Doubling the Final Consonant

The second rule tells you when to double the final consonant when adding an ending to a word.

When adding an ending that begins with a vowel (e.g., *-able, -ing, -ed,* or *-er*), double the final consonant of the root word if the word

1. ends with a *single* consonant preceded by a *single* vowel and
2. is stressed on the last syllable.

Notice that a word must have *both* characteristics for the rule to apply. Let's look at a few examples:

begin + er	ends with a single consonant (*n*) preceded by a single vowel (*i*) and is stressed on the last syllable (*begín*), so the rule applies, and we double the final consonant:	**beginner**
control + ed	ends with a single consonant (*l*) preceded by a single vowel (*o*) and is stressed on the last syllable (*contról*), so the rule applies:	**controlled**
drop + ing	ends with a single consonant (*p*) preceded by a single vowel (*o*) and is stressed on the last syllable (there is only one: *dróp*), so the rule applies:	**dropping**
appear + ing	ends with a single consonant (*r*) preceded by two vowels (*ea*), so the rule does not apply, and we do not double the final consonant:	**appearing**
turn + ed	ends with *two* consonants (*rn*), so the rule does not apply:	**turned**
open + er	ends with a single consonant (*n*) preceded by a single vowel (*e*) but is not stressed on the last syllable (*ópen*), so the rule does not apply:	**opener**

In words such as *equip, quit,* and *quiz,* the *u* should be considered part of the *q* and not a vowel. These words then follow the rule: *equipping, quitter,* and *quizzed.*

Note: There is a group of words ending in *l, t,* or *s* that, according to our rule, do not need a double consonant before the ending. Some examples are *label, counsel, focus,* and *format.* You will sometimes see this consonant doubled—*labelled, counselled, focussed, formatting*—this spelling is also correct. For these words, it doesn't matter which spelling you choose; what matters is that you use one spelling or the other consistently!

Exercises 38.4 through 38.6 require you to combine each word with the ending to form a new word. Check your answers to each set before going on.

Exercise 38.4*

1. regret + able =
2. admit + ing =
3. bat + ing =
4. beg + ing =
5. entail + ed =

Spelling

Exercise 38.5*

1. forget + ing =
2. confer + ed =
3. refer + ing =
4. strip + ed =
5. recur + ence =

Exercise 38.6*

1. defer + ing =
2. remit + ance =
3. consist + ency =
4. concur + ence =
5. acquit + al =

When it comes to adding *-ence*, three words are especially troublesome. *Prefer*, *refer*, and *confer* all appear to require a double final consonant. But they don't, because when you add *-ence*, the stress shifts to the *first* syllable of the word. So you write:

prefér	preférring	preférred	but	préference
refér	reférring	reférred	but	réference
confér	conférring	conférred	but	cónference

GO TO WEB

EXERCISES 38.5, 38.6, 38.7, 38.8

Rule 3: Words Containing *ie* or *ei*

There are almost a thousand common English words containing *ie* or *ei*, so remembering the rule that governs them is worthwhile. It helps to keep in mind that *ie* occurs roughly twice as often as *ei*.

The old rhyme tells you most of what you need to know to spell these words:

> Write *i* before *e*, except after *c*
> Or when sounded like *ā* as in *neighbour* and *weigh*.

If you remember this rhyme, you'll have no difficulty in spelling words such as *belief, piece, ceiling, receive,* and *freight.*

Unfortunately, the rhyme covers only two of the cases in which we write *e* before *i*: after *c*, and when the syllable is pronounced with a long *ā* sound. So an addition to the rule is necessary.

> If short *ĕ* or long *ī* is the sound that is right,
> Write *e* before *i*, as in *their* or in *height.*

This rule covers words such as *Fahrenheit, seismic, heir,* and *leisure* (pronounce it to rhyme with *pleasure*). *Either* and *neither* can be pronounced "eye-ther" and "nye-ther," so they too require *ei.*

There are, of course, exceptions. This silly sentence contains the most common ones:

A *weird species* of *sheik seized caffeine, codeine,* and *protein.*

Exercise 38.7*

This exercise will help you to pin down *ie* versus *ei*. Fill in the blanks with *ie* or *ei*. Then check your answers.

1. Can we really trust ____ther of them, when we know th____r bel____fs to be so similar?

2. After all, anyone who thinks that we are dec____ved by everything we perc____ve must be a few grams short of a full kilo.

3. If we can't trust our own senses, what conc____vable information is there that we can rec____ve with confidence?

4. Frankly, it would be a great rel____f if n____ther of them ever appeared in my life again.

5. My n____ghbour is so conc____ted, she speaks to no one on our block. The children think she's w____rd.

GO TO WEB

EXERCISES 38.9, 38.10

There are three or four more spelling rules we could explain here, but we won't—for two reasons. First, there are many exceptions to the remaining rules for English spelling. And second, you don't need to memorize more rules if you use your dictionary and a spellchecker.

39

Sound-Alikes, Look-Alikes, and Spoilers

Using a dictionary and a spellchecker, asking a good speller for help, and applying the three spelling rules will make an immediate improvement in your spelling. By following two additional suggestions, you will further increase your spelling accuracy, but the skills involved will take longer to master. First, learn to tell words apart that are often confused because they sound or look alike. Second, learn to spell the words that most people find difficult—words we call spelling spoilers. Don't try to master all of these words at once. Instead, memorize a few each week and review them frequently. In two or three months, you could be one of the people poor spellers turn to for help!

Sound-Alikes and Look-Alikes

Some of your spelling troubles are probably caused by your using words that either sound or look like the words you really want. A computer spellcheck program cannot help you with these words because, if you're like most people, you don't misspell them. What makes the spelling "wrong" is the sense of the sentence in which you've used them. *Hear, our, meat,* and *have* are, as isolated words, correctly spelled. But if you combine them into a "sentence"—*Meat me hear in have an our*—you end up with a tangle of misspellings no computer can unravel.

Careful pronunciation sometimes helps to correct this problem. For example, if you pronounce the words *accept* and *except* differently, you'll be less likely to confuse them in your writing. It is also useful to make up memory aids to help yourself remember the difference between words that sound alike but have very different meanings. (We have also included in this list a few pairs of words that do not look or sound alike but are commonly confused.)

accept **except**	*Accept* means "take." It is always a verb. *Except* means "excluding."
	Everyone *except* Brian *accepted* my explanation.
advice **advise**	The difference in pronunciation makes the difference in meaning clear. *Advise* (rhymes with *wise*) is a verb. *Advice* (rhymes with *nice*) is a noun.
	I *advise* you not to listen to free *advice*.
affect **effect**	*Affect* as a verb means "influence." As a noun, it means "a strong feeling." *Effect* is a noun meaning "result." If you can substitute *result*, then *effect* is the word you need. (Occasionally, *effect* can be a verb—meaning "bring about"—but you probably won't need to use it that way.)
	Learning about the *effects* of caffeine *affected* my coffee-drinking habits.
	Most disturbed people display inappropriate *affect*.
a lot **allot**	*A lot* (often misspelled *alot*) should be avoided. Use *many* or *much* instead. *Allot* means "distribute" or "assign."
	many *much* He still has ~~a lot of~~ problems, but he's coping ~~a lot~~ better.
	The teacher will *allot* the assignments according to the students' interests.
aloud **allowed**	*Aloud* means out loud, not a whisper. *Allowed* means permitted.
	We were not *allowed* to speak *aloud* during the performance.
amount **number**	*Amount* is used with uncountable things; *number* is used with countable things.
	You may have a large *number* of jelly beans in a jar but a small *amount* of candy. (Jelly beans are countable; candy is not.)

are
our

Are is a verb. *Our* shows ownership.

> Marie-Claire Blais and Margaret Atwood *are* two of Canada's best-known writers.
>
> Canada is *our* home and native land.

assure
ensure
insure

Assure means "state with confidence; pledge or promise."

> She *assured* him she would keep his letters always.
>
> The prime minister *assured* the Inuit their concerns would be addressed in the near future.

Ensure means "make certain of something."

> The extra 20 dollars will *ensure* that you get a good seat.
>
> No number of promises can *ensure* that love will last.

Insure means "guarantee against financial loss." We *insure* lives and property.

> Kevin *insured* the book before he sent it airmail.
>
> We have *insured* both our home and our car against fire and theft.

choose
chose

Pronunciation gives the clue here. *Choose* rhymes with *booze* and means "select." *Chose* rhymes with *rose* and means "selected."

> Please *choose* a topic.
>
> I *chose* film-making.

cite
sight
site

To *cite* is to quote or mention. A lawyer *cites* precedents. Writers *cite* their sources in research papers. You might *cite* a comedian for her wit or a politician for his honesty. A *site* is a place.

> You have included only Internet sources in your Works *Cited* list.
>
> The Plains of Abraham is the *site* of a famous battle.
>
> Tiananmen Square is the *site* of the massacre.
>
> Pape and Mortimer is the *site* of our new industrial design centre.

Spelling

A *sight* is something you see.

> With his tattooed forehead and three nose rings, he was a *sight* to behold.

coarse
course

Coarse means "rough, unrefined." (Remember: the word *arse* is co*arse*.) For all other meanings, use *course*.

> That sandpaper is too *coarse*.
> You'll enjoy the photography *course*.
> Of *course* you'll do well.

complement
compliment

A *complement* completes something. A *compliment* is a gift of praise.

> A glass of wine would be the perfect *complement* to the meal.
> Some people are embarrassed by *compliments*.

conscience
conscious

Your *conscience* is your sense of right and wrong. *Conscious* means "aware" or "awake"—able to feel and think.

> After Katy cheated on the test, her *conscience* bothered her.
> Katy was *conscious* of having done wrong.
> The injured man was *unconscious* for an hour.

consul
council
counsel

A *consul* is a government official stationed in another country. A *council* is an assembly or official group. Members of a council are *councillors*. *Counsel* can be used to mean both "advice" and "to advise."

> The Canadian *consul* in Mexico was very helpful.
> The Women's Advisory *Council* meets next month.
> Maria gave me good *counsel*.
> She *counselled* me to hire a lawyer.

continual
continuous

Continual refers to an action that goes on regularly but with interruptions. *Continuous* refers to an action that goes on without interruption.

> The student *continually* tried to interrupt the lecturer, who droned on *continuously*.
> There is a *continuous* flow of traffic during rush hour.

credible
credulous
creditable

Credible means "believable"; *credulous* describes the person who believes an incredible story.

> Nell was fortunate that the police found her story *credible*.
>
> My brother is so *credulous* that we call him Gullible Gus.

Creditable means "worthy of reward or praise."

> After two semesters, Eva has finally begun to produce *creditable* work.

desert
dessert

A *désert* is a dry, barren place. As a verb, *desért* means "leave behind." *Dessért* is the part of the meal you'd probably like a double serving of, so give it a double *s*.

> The tundra is Canada's only *desert* region.
>
> My neighbour *deserted* her husband and children.
>
> *Dessert* is my favourite part of the meal.

dining
dinning

You'll spell *dining* correctly if you remember the phrase "wining and dining." You'll probably never use *dinning*. It means "making a loud noise."

> The children are in the *dining* room.
>
> We are *dining* out tonight.
>
> The noise from the bar was *dinning* in our ears.

disburse
disperse

Disburse means "to pay out money," which is what **bur**sars do. *Disperse* means "to break up"; crowds are sometimes *dispersed* by the police.

> The college's financial-aid officer will *disburse* the students' loans at the end of this week.
>
> The protesters were *dispersed* by the police.

does
dose

Pronunciation provides the clue. *Does* rhymes with *buzz* and is a verb. *Dose* rhymes with *gross* and refers to a quantity of medicine.

> John *does* drive fast, doesn't he?
>
> My grandmother gave me a *dose* of cod liver oil.

Spelling

farther **further**	You'll have no trouble distinguishing between these two if you associate *farther* with *distance* and *further* with *time*. Dana wanted me to walk a little *farther* so we could discuss our relationship *further*.
faze **phase**	*Fazed* usually has a *not* before it; to be *not fazed* means to be not disturbed, or concerned, or taken aback. *Phase* means "stage of development or process." Unfortunately, Theo was not the least bit *fazed* by his disastrous grade report. Since Meiling works full time, she has decided to complete her degree in *phases*.
fewer **less**	*Fewer* is used with countable things, *less* with uncountable things. In May, there are *fewer* students in the college, so there is *less* work for the faculty to do. The *fewer* attempts you make, the *less* your chance of success. With units of money or measurement, however, use *less*: I have *less* than 20 dollars in my wallet. Our house is on a lot that is *less* than four metres wide.
forth **fourth**	*Forth* means "forward" or "onward." *Fourth* contains the number **four**, which gives it its meaning. Please stop pacing back and *forth*. The B.C. Lions lost their *fourth* game in a row.
hear **here**	*Hear* is what you do with your **ear**s. *Here* is used for all other meanings. Now *hear* this! Ray isn't *here*. *Here* is your assignment.
imply **infer**	A speaker or writer *implies*; a listener or reader *infers*. To *imply* is to hint or say something indirectly. To *infer* is to draw a conclusion from what is stated or hinted at.

I *inferred* from his sarcastic remarks that he was not very fond of Sheila.

In her introduction of Rami, Sheila *implied* that she greatly admired him.

it's
its

It's is a shortened form of *it is*. The apostrophe takes the place of the *i* in *is*. If you can substitute *it is*, then *it's* is the form you need. If you can't substitute *it is*, then *its* is the correct word.

It's really not difficult. (*It is* really not difficult.)

The book has lost *its* cover. ("The book has lost *it is* cover" makes no sense, so you need *its*.)

It's is also commonly used as the shortened form of *it has*. In this case, the apostrophe takes the place of the *h* and the *a*.

It's been a good year for us.

later
latter

Later refers to time and has the word **late** in it. *Latter* means "the second of two" and has two *t*s. It is the opposite of *former*.

It is *later* than you think.

You take the former, and I'll take the *latter*.

loose
lose

Pronunciation is the key to these words. *Loose* rhymes with *goose* and means "not tight." *Lose* rhymes with *ooze* and means "misplace" or "be defeated."

A *loose* electrical connection is dangerous.

Some are born to win, some to *lose*.

martial
marshal

Martial refers to warfare or military affairs. *Marshal* has two meanings. As a noun, it refers to a person who has high office, either in the army or (especially in the United States) the police. As a verb, it means to arrange or assemble in order.

She is a *martial* arts enthusiast.

When the troops were *marshalled* on the parade grounds, they were reviewed by the army *marshal*.

Spelling

| miner | A *miner* works in a **mine**. *Minor* means "lesser" or "not |
| minor | important." For example, a *minor* is a person of less than legal age. |

> Liquor can be served to *miners*, but not if they are *minors*.
>
> For me, spelling is a *minor* problem.

| moral | Again, pronunciation provides the clue you need. *Móral* |
| morale | refers to the understanding of what is right and wrong. *Morále* refers to the spirit or mental condition of a person or group. |

> People often have to make *moral* decisions.
>
> The low *morale* of the workers prompted the strike.

| peace | *Peace* is what we want on **Earth**. *Piece* means "a part or por- |
| piece | tion of something," as in "a **piece** of **pie**." |

> Everyone hopes for *peace* in the Middle East.
>
> A *piece* of the puzzle is missing.

| personal | *Personal* means "private." *Personnel* refers to the group of |
| personnel | people working for a particular employer or to the office responsible for maintaining employees' records. |

> The letter was marked "*Personal* and Confidential."
>
> We are fortunate in having qualified *personnel*.
>
> Fatima works in the *Personnel* Office.

| principal | *Principal* means "main." A *principle* is a rule. |
| principle | |

> A *principal* is the main administrator of a school.
>
> Oil is Alberta's *principal* industry.
>
> I make it a *principle* to submit my essays on time.

| quiet | If you pronounce these words carefully, you won't confuse |
| quite | them. *Quiet* has two syllables; *quite* has only one. |

> The librarian asked us to be *quiet*.
>
> We had not *quite* finished our homework.

roll
role

Turning over and over like a wheel is to *roll*; a bun is also a *roll*. An actor playing a part is said to have a *role*.

His *role* called for him to fall to the ground and *roll* into a ditch, all the while munching on a bread *roll*.

simple
simplistic

Simple means uncomplicated, easily understood. Something described as *simplistic* is too simple to be acceptable; essential details or complexities have been overlooked.

This problem is far from *simple*. Your solution to it is *simplistic*.

stationary
stationery

Stationary means "fixed in place." *Stationery* is writing paper.

Sarah Ferguson works out on a *stationary* bicycle.

Please order a new supply of *stationery*.

than
then

Than is used in comparisons. Pronounce it to rhyme with *can*. *Then* refers to time and rhymes with *when*.

Rudi is a better speller *than* I.

He made his decision *then*.

Eva withdrew from the competition; *then* she realized the consequences.

their
there
they're

Their indicates ownership. **There** points out something or indicates place. It includes the word *here*, which also indicates place. *They're* is a shortened form of *they are*. (The apostrophe replaces the *a* in *are*.)

It was *their* fault.

There are two weeks left in the term.

You should look over *there*.

They're late, as usual.

too
two
to

The *too* with an extra *o* in it means "more than enough" or "also." *Two* is the number after one. For all other meanings, use *to*.

He thinks he's been working *too* hard. She thinks so *too*.

There are *two* sides *to* every argument.

The *two* women knew *too* much about each other *to* be friends.

Spelling

weather **whether** **wether**	*Whether* means "which of the two" and is used in all cases when you aren't referring to the climatic conditions outside (*weather*). A *wether* is a castrated ram, so that word's uses are limited.
were **where** **we're**	If you pronounce these three carefully, you won't confuse them. *Were* rhymes with *fur* and is a verb. **Where** is pronounced "hwear," includes the word **here**, and indicates place. *We're* is a shortened form of *we are* and is pronounced "weer."

> You were joking, *weren't* you?
> *Where* did you want to meet?
> *We're* on our way.

who's **whose**	*Who's* is a shortened form of *who is* or *who has*. If you can substitute *who is* or *who has* for the *who's* in your sentence, then you are using the right spelling. Otherwise, use *whose*.

> *Who's* coming to dinner? (*Who is* coming to dinner?)
> *Who's* been sleeping in my bed? (*Who has* been sleeping in my bed?)
> *Whose* calculator is this? ("*Who is* calculator" makes no sense, so you need *whose*.)

woman **women**	Confusing these two is guaranteed to irritate your female readers. *Woman* is the singular form; compare **man**. *Women* is the plural form; compare **men**.

> A *woman's* place is wherever she chooses to be.
> The *women's* movement promotes equality between women and men.

you're **your**	*You're* is a shortened form of *you are*. If you can substitute *you are* for the *you're* in your sentence, then you're using the correct form. If you can't substitute *you are*, use *your*.

> *You're* welcome. (*You are* welcome.)
> Unfortunately, *your* hamburger got burned. ("*You are* hamburger" makes no sense, so *your* is the word you want.)

In Exercises 39.1 and 39.2, choose the correct word from those in parentheses. If you don't know an answer, go back and reread the explanation. Check your answers after each set. Answers for this chapter begin on page 511.

Exercise 39.1*

1. The limited (coarse course) selection will (affect effect) our academic development and subsequent job opportunities.
2. (Are Our) you going to (accept except) the offer?
3. Eat your vegetables; (than then) you can have your (desert dessert).
4. If (your you're) overweight by 20 kg, (loosing losing) the excess will be a long-term proposition.
5. It's (quiet quite) true that they did not get (hear here) until 2:00 a.m.
6. It is usually the saint, not the sinner, (who's whose) (conscience conscious) is troubled.
7. He (assured ensured insured) me he would keep the (amount number) of changes to a minimum.
8. (Its It's) hard to tell the dog from (its it's) owner.
9. To (choose chose) a (coarse course) of action against your lawyer's (advice advise) would be foolish.
10. (Continual Continuous) (dining dinning) out becomes boring after a while.

Exercise 39.2*

1. It is (simple simplistic) to claim that our society's (morals morales) have declined drastically over the last twenty years.
2. After the accident, the (moral morale) of the (miners minors) did not recover for many months, but the owners appeared not to be (fazed phased) by the disaster.
3. The chief librarian did not mean to (infer imply) that (farther further) cuts to services were being considered.
4. The (affect effect) of trying to (disburse disperse) the angry crowd was to cause a riot.
5. (Who's Whose) (principals principles) are so firm that they wouldn't pay (fewer less) taxes if they could get away with it?
6. The (forth fourth) reason Akbar (cited sighted sited) for his absence was the (weather whether wether).
7. It's (your you're) fault that we are (continually continuously) harassed by door-to-door salespeople; your welcoming smile (assures ensures insures) that they'll return again and again.
8. Try to remain (conscience conscious) through today's class because I plan to take my critique of the Young Offenders Act (a lot allot much) (farther further), and this material will be on the test.
9. Ranjan could not (accept except) the fact that the (councillors counsellors) rejected her plan to (faze phase) out parking in the downtown core.

Spelling

10. Canadian (woman's women's) pay, on average, is 30 percent less than that of men; this statistic is a(n) (amount number) that should cause our politicians serious concern.

GO TO WEB

EXERCISES 39.1, 39.2, 39.3, 39.4

Exercise 39.3

Now test your mastery of sound-alikes and look-alikes by correcting the ten errors in the following paragraph.

I would advice anyone who's schedule seems to be full to try the solution I came up with less then three months ago. I pulled the plug on my TV. Overwhelmed with assignments and unable to chose among priorities, I realized I was making the problem worse by sitting for three or four hours a night in front of the tube. I decided I should spend more time on my coarses and less on watching television. To avoid temptation, I put the TV set in the closet. The results have been more dramatic then I thought possible. My apartment is now a haven of piece and quiet, and some of my assignments are actually handed in before their due. Occasionally there is a twinge of regret that I no longer know whose doing what to whom in the latest reality contest, but overall, I'm much happier for choosing to loose the tube.

Spelling Spoilers

Here is a list of words that are frequently misspelled. Have someone dictate the list to you. Circle the ones you misspell and memorize them, a few at a time. Try to learn ten each week. Review your list often, until you have mastered every word. Making up memory aids for especially troublesome words will help you to conquer them. Here are some examples to get you started:

accommodate: It means "make room for," and the word itself makes room for two *c*s and two *m*s.

business: Busi**ness** is no **sin**.

environment: The word *environment*, like the earth, has **iron** in it.

friend: He is a fri**end** to the **end**.

grammar: Poor gram**mar** will **mar** your writing.

absence	explanation	opinion
accommodate	extremely	opportunity
achievement	familiar	paid
acknowledge	February	parallel
across	finally	perform
adolescence	forty	planned
among	friend	possess
answer	gauge	prejudice
argument	government	privilege
beginning	grammar	probably
business	guarantee	procedure
careful	guidance	proceed
category	height	professor
clothes	hoping	psychology
committee	hypocrisy	receive
conscious	immediately	recommend
convenience	independent	relevant
criticism	laboratory	repetition
definitely	liaison	restaurant
dependent	license (*or* licence)	rhythm
desperate	likely	ridiculous
disappear	loneliness	safety
disappoint	lonely	schedule
discipline	maintenance	separate
dissatisfied	marriage	shining
doesn't	mentally	similar
eighth	necessary	somewhat
embarrassed	ninety	speech
environment	ninth	studying
exercise	occasionally	succeed
existence	omission	superintendent

Spelling

supersede	truly	vacuum
surprise	unnecessary	vicious
technique	until	Wednesday
thorough	unusual	writing
tragedy	usually	written

We'd like to make one last suggestion about spelling. Despite all your efforts, you may find there are a few words that you simply cannot remember how to spell correctly. The best solution is to write out a list of these pesky words and tape it on the inside cover of your dictionary or post it close to your computer.

Another, less satisfactory, solution is to try to avoid these words. You could check your dictionary or a thesaurus to find synonyms (different words with the same meanings) for the words you can't spell and use the synonyms instead. The main problem with this solution is that it is even more time-consuming than learning the correct spellings in the first place!

There are, however, occasions when using a synonym will help you convey more accurately the meaning you intend. Two thesauruses are available in inexpensive paperback editions: *Roget's Thesaurus* (buy the one in dictionary form, not the one organized by subject) and the *Collins Paperback Thesaurus in A–Z Form*, which, as its title suggests, is organized alphabetically. Your word processor probably has a built-in thesaurus you can consult, but be careful. You can't just choose any word from the list that pops up when you ask for a synonym for a word you've used too frequently or for one you don't quite feel confident is the word you need.

The information provided by a thesaurus must be used with caution. Inexperienced writers sometimes assume that long, obscure words are sure to impress their readers. In fact, the opposite is usually true. Most readers are irritated, if not confused, by unnecessarily "fancy" language. Why write "The children were enthralled by the antics of the prestidigitator" when what you mean is "The children loved the magician's act"? (For more information on this subject, see Wordiness in Chapter 11.)

40

Capital Letters

Capital letters should be used in a few specific places and nowhere else. Some writers suffer from "capitalitis": they put capital letters on words randomly, regardless of where the words occur in a sentence or whether the words are nouns, verbs, or adjectives.

Not many people have this problem. If you are in the majority who generally use capitals correctly, skip this chapter and go on to something else. If you are puzzled about capital letters, though, or have readers who are puzzled by your use of them, read on.

Capitalize the first letter of a word that fits into one of the six categories listed below:

1. The first word in a sentence, in a direct quotation, or in a sentence from a quoted source

Are you illiterate? Write to us today for free help.

Supermodel Tyra Banks cooed, "I love the confidence makeup gives me."

Writer and broadcaster Lister Sinclair claims that Canadians have one thing in common: "We all hate Toronto."

Exercise 40.1*

Add the seven missing capital letters in the following sentences. Answers for exercises in this chapter begin on page 512.

1. time is nature's way of keeping everything from happening at once.

2. Brad whispered, "there's a light in the Frankenstein house."

3. my parents have a bumper sticker that reads, "money isn't everything, but it sure keeps the kids in touch."

4. Richard Harkness, writing in *The New York Times*, said "a committee is a group of the unwilling, picked from the unfit, to do the unnecessary."

5. in conclusion, I want you to consider the words of Wendell Johnson: "*always* and *never* are two words you should always remember never to use."

2. The names of specific people, places, and things

Names of people (and their titles):

Shania Twain, U.N. Secretary-General Kofi Annan, the Rev. Henry Jones, the Hon. Eugene Forsey, Governor General Adrienne Clarkson

Names of places, regions, and astronomical bodies (but not general geographic directions):

Stanley Park, Lake Superior, Cape Breton Island; Nunavut, the Prairie Provinces, the Badlands; Saturn, Earth, the Moon, the Asteroid Belt; south, north

Names of buildings, institutions, organizations, companies, departments, products, etc.:

the Empress Hotel; McGill University, Red Deer College; the Liberal Party, the Kiwanis Club; Petro-Canada, Radio Shack; the Department of English, the Human Resources Department; Kleenex, Volvo, Labatt

Exercise 40.2[*]

Add capital letters where necessary in the following sentences. There are 30 errors in this exercise.

1. After a brief stay in the maritimes, captain tallman and his crew sailed west up the st. lawrence.

2. The broadcast department of niagara college has ordered six sony cameras for their studios in welland, ontario.

3. Do you find that visa is more popular than American express when you travel to far away places such as mexico, france, or jupiter?

4. Our stay at the seaview hotel overlooking the pacific ocean certainly beat our last vacation at the bates motel, where we faced west, overlooking the city dump.

5. As a member of the alumni association I am trying to raise funds from companies like disney, general motors, corel, and the cbc, where our graduates have positions.

3. Names of major historical events, historical periods, religions, holy texts, and holy days

World War II, the Depression, the Renaissance; Islam, Judaism, Christianity, Buddhism, Hinduism; the Torah, the Koran, the Bible, the Upanishads; Ramadan, Yom Kippur, Easter

Exercise 40.3[*]

Add the 20 capital letters that are missing from the following sentences.

1. The crusades, which were religious wars between muslims and christians, raged through the middle ages.

Spelling

2. The hindu religion recognizes and honours many gods; islam recognizes one god, allah; buddhism recognizes none.

3. The koran, the bible, and the torah agree on many principles.

4. The jewish festival of hanukkah often occurs near the same time that christians are celebrating christmas.

5. After world war I, many jews began to emigrate to Palestine, where they and the muslim population soon came into conflict.

4. The days of the week, months of the year, and specific holidays (but not the seasons)

Wednesday; January; Remembrance Day, Canada Day; spring, autumn

Exercise 40.4*

The following sentences contain both missing and unnecessary capitals. Find and correct the 15 errors.

1. My favourite months are january and february because I love all Winter sports.

2. This monday is valentine's day, when messages of love are exchanged.

3. In the summer, big meals seem too much trouble; however, after thanksgiving, we need lots of food to survive the winter cold.

4. A National Holiday named flag day was once proposed, but it was never officially approved.

5. By thursday, I'll have finished my st. patrick's day costume.

5. The major words in titles of published works (books, magazines, films; essays, poems, songs; works of art; etc.). Do not capitalize minor words (articles, prepositions, conjunctions) in titles unless the word is the first word in the title.

The Colony of Unrequited Dreams   *The Thinker*
Of Mice and Men   "A Tree-Planting Primer"
Maclean's   "In Flanders Fields"
A Room with a View   "If I Had a Million Dollars"

Exercise 40.5*

Add the 30 capital letters that are missing from the following sentences.

1. The review of my book, *the life and times of a chocoholic,* published in *the globe and mail,* was not favourable.

2. Clint eastwood fans will be delighted that the two early movies that made him internationally famous, *a fistful of dollars* and *for a few dollars more,* are now available on DVD.

3. Joseph Conrad's short novel *heart of darkness* became the blockbuster movie *apocalypse now.*

4. Her poem, "a bright and silent place," was published in the april issue of *landscapes* magazine.

5. Botticelli's famous painting, *birth of venus,* inspired my poem "woman on the half shell."

Pay special attention to this next category. It causes everybody trouble.

6. The names of school courses

Marketing 101, Psychology 100, Mathematics 220, English 110

but

a) not the names of school subjects:

marketing, sociology, mathematics

Spelling

b) *unless* the subjects are languages:

English, Spanish, Greek, the study of Chinese history, modern French literature

The names of languages, like the names of countries, are always capitalized.

Exercise 40.6*

Add capital letters where necessary in the following sentences. There are ten errors in this exercise.

1. After studying geography for two years, I began taking courses in ancient greek and modern history.

2. We began our study of sociology with the concept of relationships.

3. By taking Professor Subden's non-credit course, introduction to wine, I qualified to register for oenology 120 the next semester.

4. While math is her strong subject, Laurie has trouble with accounting, english, and conversational french.

5. The prerequisite for theology 210 is introduction to world religions, taught by Professor Singh.

GO TO WEB

EXERCISES 40.1, 40.2

Exercise 40.7

Now try this mastery test to confirm your understanding of the use of capital letters.

1. If today were saturday, I'd have to go home for my Father's Birthday.

2. Failing Sociology is like eating soup with a fork: it's difficult, but you can do it if you really try.

3. July First is canada day, when we celebrate the anniversary of confederation, which occurred in 1867.

4. Although Ms. Lau is a member of the new democratic party, she is quite conservative in her thinking on Economics and social issues.

5. A complex program like microsoft's excel takes up a large amount of computer memory.

6. Trying to learn english as quickly as possible, Wong Bao Lin took two Night School classes a week and listened to audiotapes several hours every day.

7. *The caribe* is the name of the sailboat my french Professor bought for touring the caribbean islands in the Winter.

8. If I drop Math and Accounting, I will be able to concentrate on English and marketing, but it will mean adding a semester to my Program.

9. My German Shepherd's name, Layla, comes from an Eric Clapton song about the former wife of one of the beatles.

10. Biff and George are packing away the essentials, cigarettes, doritos, and Beer, in preparation for the end of the World, which they are convinced will occur on december 31, a.d. 2004.

41

The Apostrophe

We have chosen to deal with apostrophes and hyphens (hyphens are discussed in Chapter 42) in the spelling section because, unlike other punctuation marks, they do not indicate the relationship among the elements of a sentence or a paragraph. Instead, when used correctly, apostrophes and hyphens indicate a relationship between the elements of a word.

Misused apostrophes display a writer's ignorance or carelessness. They also confuse, amuse, and sometimes annoy readers. Sometimes you need an apostrophe so that your reader can understand what you mean. For example, there's a world of difference between these two sentences:

The instructor began class by calling the students' names.

The instructor began class by calling the students names.

In most cases, however, misused apostrophes just amuse or irritate an alert reader:

The movie had it's moments.

He does a days work for every weeks salary.

The Lion's thank you for your contribution.

It isn't difficult to avoid such mistakes. Correctly used, the apostrophe indicates either **contraction** or **possession**. It never makes a singular word plural. Learn the simple rules that govern these uses and you'll have no further trouble with apostrophes.

Contraction

Contraction is the combining of two words into one, as in *they're* or *can't*. Contractions are common in conversational, informal English; however, unless you are quoting someone else's words, you should avoid them in the writing you do for college or work.

The rule about where to put an apostrophe in a contraction is one of those rare rules that has no exception. It *always* holds.

> When two words are combined into one, and one or more letters are left out, the apostrophe goes in the place of the missing letter(s).

Here are some examples.

I am	→ I'm	they are	→ they're
we will	→ we'll	it is	→ it's
she is	→ she's	it has	→ it's
do not	→ don't	who has	→ who's

Exercise 41.1*

Correct these sentences by placing apostrophes where needed. Answers for this chapter begin on page 513.

1. Yes, its a long way from Halifax to Vancouver, but weve been in training for three months.
2. Were taking the train to Antigonish, and were biking to Halifax; then well begin the big trip west.
3. There isnt a dry eye in the theatre when Spielbergs film reaches its climax.
4. Those two havent made it through a meeting since the college adopted its no-smoking policy.
5. Wasnt it Mark Twain who said, "Its easy to stop smoking; Ive done it dozens of times"?

GO TO WEB

EXERCISES 41.1, 41.2

Possession

The apostrophe is also used to show ownership or possession. Here's the rule that applies in most cases.

Add 's to the word that indicates the *owner*.
If the resulting word ends in a double or triple s, delete the last s, leaving the apostrophe in place.[1]

Here are some examples that illustrate the rule.

singer + 's = singer's voice	women + 's = women's voices
band + 's = band's instruments	student + 's = student's report card
players + 's = players's uniforms	students + 's = students's report cards

To form a possessive correctly, you must first identify the word in the sentence that indicates possession and determine whether it is singular or plural. For example, "the managers duties" can have two meanings, depending on where you put the apostrophe:

the manager's duties (the duties belong to one *manager*)
the managers' duties (the duties belong to two or more *managers*)

To solve an apostrophe problem, follow this two-step process:
1. Find the owner word.
2. Apply the possession rule.

Problem: Carmens hair is a mess.
Solution: 1. The word that indicates possession is *Carmen* (singular).
        2. Add 's to *Carmen*.

    Carmen's hair is a mess.

Problem: The technicians strike halted the production.
Solution: 1. The word that indicates possession is *technicians* (plural).
        2. Add 's to *technicians*, then delete the second s, leaving the apostrophe.

    The *technicians'* strike halted the production.

---

[1]Many writers today prefer to keep the final s when it represents a sound that is pronounced, as it is in one-syllable words such as *boss* and *class*, and in some names such as *Harris* and *Brutus*.

Sometimes the meaning of your sentence is determined by where you put the apostrophe.

Problem: The writer was delighted by the critics response to her book.

Now you have two possibilities to choose from, depending on your meaning.

Solution A: 1. The owner word is *critic* (singular).
                2. Add *'s* to *critic*.

The writer was delighted by the *critic's* response to her book.

Solution B: 1. The owner word is *critics* (plural).
                2. Add *'s* to *critics*, then drop the second *s*, leaving the apostrophe.

The writer was delighted by the *critics'* response to her book.

Both solutions are correct, depending on whether the book was reviewed by one critic (A) or by more than one critic (B).

Possession does not have to be literal. It can be used to express the notion of "belonging to" or "associated with." That is, the owner word need not refer to a person or group of people. Ideas or concepts (abstract nouns) can be "owners" too.

> a month's vacation = a vacation of one month
> a year's salary = the salary of one year
> "A Hard Day's Night" = the night that follows a hard day

Note that a few words, called **possessive pronouns**, are already possessive in form, so they don't have apostrophes.[2]

your/yours	our/ours
her/hers	their/theirs
his, its	whose

His music is not like *yours*.

Whose lyrics do you prefer, *theirs* or *ours*?

The dog lost *its* bone.

---

[2]If you add an apostrophe to any of these words, you create an error. There are no such words as *your's, her's, their's,* or *our's.*

Four of these possessive pronouns are often confused with the contractions that sound like them. It's worth taking a moment to learn how to avoid this confusion. When you are trying to decide which spelling to use, expand the contraction into its original two words. Then substitute those words for the contraction in your sentence. If the sentence still makes sense, use the contraction. If it doesn't, use the possessive spelling.

Possessive	Contraction
its = *It* owns something	it's = it is/it has
their = *They* own something	they're = they are
whose = *Who* owns something	who's = who is/who has
your = *You* own something	you're = you are

Error: They're (they are) going to sing they're (they are) latest song.
Revision: They're going to sing *their* latest song.

Exercise 41.2*

Correct the following sentences by adding apostrophes where necessary.

1. A floppy disks quality is measured by its ability to store information without error.
2. Diplomatic ambassadors wives or husbands are often as important to a missions success as the ambassadors themselves.
3. Near Chicoutimi is one of the countrys most beautiful parks, where the skills of canoeists, fishermen, and wildlife photographers can be put to the test on a summers day.
4. The Leafs forward and the Canadiens defenceman were exchanged during the last days trading at the NHL meetings.
5. Janis career got its start when she sang seafarers songs in the yacht clubs dining lounge.

Exercises 41.3 and 41.4 will test and reinforce your understanding of both contraction and possession.

Exercise 41.3*

In each of the sentences below, choose the correct word from those in parentheses. Check your answers before going on.

1. Where (your you're) going, (your you're) biggest problem will be maintaining (your you're) health.

2. (Someones Someone's) got to take responsibility for the large numbers of domestic animals (whose who's) owners have abandoned them.
3. The Ringling (Brothers Brother's Brothers') circus animals were well cared for compared with the animals of (todays today's todays') circuses.
4. Contrary to some (people's peoples) opinions, postal (workers worker's workers') contracts are most often settled by both (sides side's sides') willingness to bend long before a strike is necessary.
5. My (turtles turtle's) legs are shorter than your (turtles turtle's), but I bet (its it's) going to run (its it's) laps faster than (yours your's).

GO TO WEB

EXERCISES 41.3, 41.4

Exercise 41.4

Now test your mastery of apostrophes by correcting the 15 errors in the passage below.

The following advisory for American's heading to Canada was compiled from information provided by the U.S. State Department and the CIA. It is intended as a guide for American traveller's:

Canada is a large foreign country, even bigger than Texas. It has ten states (called provinces) and it's only neighbour is America. Canadas contributions to Western civilization include bacon, hockey players, geese, doughnut's, and the Mountie's red uniform's.

Canadians stand in line without complaining, seldom raise they're voices, and cheer politely when the home or visiting teams players do something worthwhile. Canada has two language's: French and American. Other linguistic oddities include "eh," which can turn any statement into a question, and the pronunciation of *ou* as *uoo*, as in *huoose* or *abuoot*.

The bright color's and funny picture's of Canadian currency may make the unwary tourist think of it as play money, but each blue Canadian five dollar bill is worth about two real dollars. The one- and two-dollar coins, called loonies and toonies, make good souvenir's.

The Canadian government is somewhat left-leaning, providing health care for all and refusing to execute criminal's. Tourists are advised to avoid all political discussion and to remember that politician's in Canada are like politician's anywhere: popular with some people, unpopular with others.

42

The Hyphen

A **hyphen** (-) is required in three distinct writing situations: as part of the correct spelling of a word (e.g., mother-in-law, self-esteem); to divide a word at the end of a line; and to separate or join two or more words or parts of words. There are five rules to follow.

1. Use a hyphen to divide a word at the end of a written or typed line.

Your dictionary shows where words can be divided. Most dictionaries mark the syllables of a word with a dot: syl·lables = syl-lables. Never divide a word of only one or two syllables; reserve the hyphen at the end of a line for words of three or more syllables (e.g., commu-nity). If the word is already hyphenated (e.g., self-reliance, ex-president), break it after the hyphen.

2. Use a hyphen to separate a prefix from the main word when two of the same vowels come together.

Examples: pre-empted, co-operate, re-elected, re-enter

When the two vowels are different, however, no hyphen is required: semiautomatic, realign, preamble

3. Use a hyphen with compound numbers from twenty-one to ninety-nine, with fractions, and with dimensions.

Examples: forty-six, one-eighth, ninety-eight, six-by-eight

Spelling

4. Use a hyphen to join two or more words that serve as an adjective *before* a noun.

Examples: The (first-born) child is often the best loved.

The (best-loved) child is often the first born.

(Word-of-mouth) advertising is very effective.

A good writer has a (well-thumbed, up-to-date) dictionary.

5. Use a hyphen to avoid ambiguity.

Examples: The contractor re-covered the roof with asphalt shingles.

The contractor recovered his money.

The government's plan provided for nursing-home care. (care in a nursing home)

The government's plan provided for nursing home-care. (care at home by nurses)

The prime minister will address small business owners. (Do you really want to say he will talk only to short people?)

The prime minister will address small-business owners. (These people are owners of small businesses.)

Exercise 42.1*

Most of the following sentences require one or more hyphens. Review the rules in the boxes above; then try your hand at correcting these sentences. Answers for this chapter are on page 514.

1. Mei decided to sublet her fifth floor apartment.
2. Anwar claims he is allergic to classical music but addicted to hip hop music.
3. Charest won most of the ethnic vote, which gave him a two thirds majority in a hard fought contest.

4. Hand knit sweaters are usually more expensive than factory produced ones.

5. In 1950, at the age of forty seven, George Orwell died of tuberculosis.

GO TO WEB

EXERCISE 42.1

Exercise 42.2*

In the following sentences, some hyphens are missing, and some are included where they don't belong. Correct the errors in these sentences.

1. For months after Nicolae Ceauçescu was over-thrown, the world was shocked by revelations of the repression suffered by the Rumanian people.

2. Would you re-lay this message to Mr. Chan: the masons would like to relay the bricks this evening?

3. Our next door neighbour teaches in a high-school, but she does not like to be introduced as a high school teacher.

4. A face to face meeting with an anti intellectual always gets my adrenalin going.

5. Because Angela was an attorney at law and had once been an all Canadian athlete, her former coach was not surprised when she became minister-of-recreation.

Exercise 42.3

This last exercise is a mastery test. Insert hyphens where they are needed and delete them where they are not.

1. At twenty one years of age, Trudy began to re-organize her life.

2. Because she is the instructor who is most up to date with trends in the industry, Alysha is the coordinator of our program.

3. Only one third of the team seemed to be reenergized by the twenty-minute break.

4. Vernon wore his hand made three piece suit to his former girlfriend's wedding.

5. Did Natasha enjoy her home stay month with a Canadian family?

6. The space-shuttle will reenter the atmosphere in exactly eighty five seconds.

7. Tim began to recover from his injury after taking an antiinflammatory.

8. Glenn was a big band conductor who played clarinet in some of the best known orchestras of the 40s and 50s.

Spelling

9. Computer generated graphics form ninety nine percent of our business.

10. Trevor was treated for post traumatic stress after his no hope attempt to write the final exam in chemistry.

Appendixes

List of Terms: A Vocabulary of Writing

The following list contains definitions of some common terms referring to syntax and style. For some of the terms, you will find further information in the book or on the *Essay Essentials* Web site (www.essayessentials3e. nelson.com). If a term you are looking for is not listed, check the index or consult your dictionary. For punctuation marks, see Chapters 33 to 42.

abstract, concrete	See **noun**.
active voice	See **voice**.
adjective	A word that modifies (describes) a noun or a pronoun. Adjectives usually answer the questions What kind? How many? Which? The *best* example; *three* strikes; *my morning* class. Nouns, phrases, and clauses can also function as adjectives: *ground* control; *up-to-the-minute* news. See also Parts of Speech on the *Essay Essentials* Web site.
adverb	A word that modifies a verb, adjective, or other adverb. Adverbs usually answer the questions When? How? Where? Why? How much? Nino talks fast (*fast* modifies the verb *talks*); he is a very fast talker (*very* modifies the adjective *fast*); he talks really fast (*really* modifies the adverb *fast*). Adverbs often—but not always—end in *-ly*. A phrase or a clause can also function as an adverb. See also Parts of Speech on the *Essay Essentials* Web site.
agreement	Grammatical correspondence in person and number between a verb and its subject, or in person, number, and gender between a pronoun and its antecedent. See Chapters 30 and 32.
analogy	A comparison between two dissimilar things that share at least one element or characteristic in common. E.g., Time is like a river. Just as the river flows from higher to lower ground, so time flows from the past into the future. Analogies are often used for

stylistic or dramatic effect as well as to explain or illustrate a point.

anecdote
A short account of an event or incident, used to illustrate a point and often intended to entertain. See the first paragraph of Rita Klein-Geltink's "Genesis 3:6" (page 201).

antecedent
From Latin for "coming before; preceding." An antecedent is the word or words that a pronoun refers (usually back) to or stands for. My sister thinks she is always right (*sister* is the antecedent of the pronoun *she*).

article
Often classed as adjectives, the definite article *the* and the indefinite articles *a* and *an* are "determiners" that precede nouns: *the* umpire; *a* baseball bat; *an* orange.

auxiliary
A "helping" verb used with a main verb to form different tenses. The auxiliary verbs are *be, have, do, may, can, ought, must, shall, will* and their various forms.

clause
A group of words containing a subject and a verb. If the group of words can stand by itself as a simple sentence, it is an **independent** (or **main**) **clause**: Great minds think alike. A **dependent** (or **subordinate**) **clause** cannot stand alone as a sentence; it must be linked to a main clause: *Because great minds think alike*, I am sure you will agree with me. See Chapter 25.

cliché
A phrase that has become meaningless through overuse. See Chapter 11.

coherence
The logical and stylistic connection between ideas, sentences, and paragraphs in a piece of writing. See Chapter 9.

collective noun
A noun that names a group; for example, class, faculty, jury, choir. Collective nouns are singular when the group is considered as a unit, plural when the focus is on individual members. The class wants a mid-term break. The class have not yet handed in *their* papers. See **agreement**.

colloquialism
A word or group of words that is appropriate in casual conversation and informal—but not formal—writing. Some common examples are guy, kid, flunk.

comma splice
Two independent clauses joined with a comma: The comma splice is a type of run-on sentence, it is a serious error. See Chapter 26.

complement
A word or phrase that completes the meaning of a verb. Also called a **subjective completion**, a complement is a noun, pronoun, or adjective that follows a linking verb: Jamie is the *manager* (noun complement); The winner was *she* (pronoun complement); Her paper will be *excellent* (adjective complement).

complex sentence	A sentence consisting of one independent clause and one or more subordinate clauses. See also Sentence Structure on the *Essay Essentials* Web site.
compound	Two or more grammatical elements (words, phrases, clauses) joined so that they function as a unit: *Hans, Peter, and Walter* are brothers (compound subject); Hans *works and studies* (compound verb); Peter expects an *A or a B+* (compound object). Also called **multiple** subjects, verbs, objects, or complements.
compound sentence	A sentence consisting of two or more independent clauses. See also Sentence Structure on the *Essay Essentials* Web Site.
compound-complex sentence	A sentence consisting of two or more independent clauses and one or more subordinate clauses. See also Sentence Structure on the *Essay Essentials* Web site.
concrete, abstract	See **noun**.
conjunction	A part of speech. **Coordinating** conjunctions (*and, but, or, nor, for, so, yet*) join equal grammatical elements such as nouns, verbs, phrases, or clauses. **Subordinating** conjunctions are words or phrases that join dependent clauses to main clauses. Some examples are although, because, after, in order that, as soon as. See **dependent clause cues** in Chapter 25. For **correlative** conjunctions, see Parts of Speech on the *Essay Essentials* Web site.
conjunctive adverb	An adverb such as however, therefore, thus, and nevertheless used to indicate a logical relationship between two independent clauses. Conjunctive adverbs are preceded by a semicolon and followed by a comma: Jordan hates math; *therefore*, he is not going to be an engineer.
connotation	The positive or negative meaning associated with a word; for example, *slender* and *skinny* both mean *thin*, but to describe someone as *slender* is a compliment, while to describe someone as *skinny* suggests disapproval.
contraction	The combining of two words into one, spelled with an apostrophe to mark the missing letter or letters: isn't (is not), here's (here is), should've (should have). Contractions are seldom used in formal writing.
dangling modifier	See **modifier**.
declarative sentence	See Sentence Structure on the *Essay Essentials* Web site.
demonstrative	See **pronoun**.
denotation	The specific meaning of a word; the dictionary definition. Compare **connotation**.

dependent clause	See **clause**.
dependent clause cue	A word or phrase that introduces a dependent clause. See Chapter 25.
diction	A writer's choice and use of words. Diction is a feature of style and can be colloquial, informal, or formal. Within the context of a sentence, paragraph, or paper, diction can be appropriate (consistent) or inappropriate (inconsistent).
direct object	See **object**.
ellipsis	The three spaced periods (. . .) used to indicate that a word or words have been omitted from a quoted passage. See Chapter 21.
exclamatory sentence	See Sentence Structure on the *Essay Essentials* Web site.
fragment	A group of words, punctuated like a sentence, that cannot stand alone as a sentence. The word group may be missing a subject, verb, or both subject and verb, or it may be a dependent clause. See Chapter 25.
fused sentence	Two independent clauses with no punctuation between them: The fused sentence is a type of run-on it is a serious error. See Chapter 26.
gender	Nouns and pronouns may be masculine (father, boy, stallion; he, his, him), feminine (mother, girl, mare; she, hers, her); or neuter (laugher, book; it).
gender-biased language	See **sexist language**.
grammar	The description and study of how the elements of language function, by themselves and in relation to one another. See also Grammar on the *Essay Essentials* Web site.
helping verb	See **auxiliary**.
imperative sentence	Also called a **command**. See Sentence Structure on the *Essay Essentials* Web site.
indefinite pronoun	See **pronoun**.
independent clause	See **clause**.
indirect object	See **object**.
infinitive	A verb form usually consisting of *to* + the base form of the verb: to be, to walk, to read, to procrastinate. An infinitive or infinitive phrase can function as a noun, adjective, or adverb, but never as the main verb in a clause. E.g., I offered to help (*to help* functions as a noun, direct object of the verb *offered*).

interrogative sentence	See Sentence Structure on the *Essay Essentials* Web site.
irony	A way of saying one thing while meaning something else, often the opposite of what the words themselves signify. For an extended example of irony, see "A Tree-Planting Primer" (pages 175–80). Situations can also be ironic: In "Pucker Up" (pages 189–91), for example, we learn that a beauty product is made from disgusting materials; in "The Telephone" (pages 214–20), the instrument that was supposed to enhance the life of a village in fact destroys it.
irregular verb	A verb that does not form its past tense and past participle by adding *-ed* or *-d*; for example, write, wrote, written; sing, sang, sung. See Chapter 31.
jargon	Strictly, the specialized technical vocabulary of a particular profession. More broadly, **pretentious language**: wordy, confusing language that is intended to impress the reader. See Chapter 11.
linking verb	See **verb**.
misplaced modifier	See **modifier**.
modifier	A word or group of words that describes, qualifies, or restricts another word, phrase, or clause in a sentence. A modifier can act as an adjective or as an adverb. If a modifier lacks a word in the sentence to refer to, or if the modifier is made to refer grammatically to a word it doesn't actually modify, it is a **dangling modifier**: Standing on the dock, many fish could be seen. A **misplaced modifier** is not placed close enough to the word it is intended to modify: Our team has *nearly* lost half its regular players. See Chapter 27.
noun	A word that names a person, place, thing, idea, quality, action, or event, and that can be made possessive. **Concrete** nouns name things we know through our five senses and can be **proper** (naming a particular person, place, thing, etc.: John, Alberta, July, the *Bluenose*, World War II) or **common** (naming one or more members of a class of things or qualities: boy(s), province(s), month(s), ship(s), war(s)). **Abstract** nouns name ideas or qualities that we know with our minds: truth, excellence, anger. See also Parts of Speech on the *Essay Essentials* Web site.
number	The form of a verb, a noun, or a pronoun may be singular or plural.
object	A noun or noun substitute (pronoun, phrase, or clause) that receives the action expressed by a transitive verb, or that completes a prepositional phrase. Objects of transitive verbs can be **direct** (David wanted a *raise*; Mira promised *to give David a raise*) or **indirect** (Mira gave *David* a raise). The object of a preposition usually follows the preposition (in the *book*, before the *class*),

except in direct questions (*What* are you writing *about*?) and indirect questions (I'm not sure *what* to write *about*).

parallelism   Use of the same form for words, phrases, or clauses that have equal grammatical value and similar function in a sentence or paragraph. Parallel elements match each other in structure as well as meaning: Hot weather makes people *tired*, *cranky*, and *quarrelsome*; *What I said* and *what I meant* are two different things. See Chapter 28.

participle   A verb form regularly ending in *-ing* or *-ed* that can be used as an adjective (the *weeping* willows, a *completed* work) or with an auxiliary as part of a verb phrase (am *succeeding*, have been *rented*). For past participles of irregular verbs, see Chapter 31 or a dictionary.

parts of speech   The nine categories into which traditional grammar classifies words according to their function in a sentence: noun, pronoun, verb, adjective, adverb, conjunction, preposition, article, expletive. See also Parts of Speech on the *Essay Essentials* Web site.

passive voice   See **voice**.

person   A quality of pronouns and verbs that shows whether they refer to someone speaking (**first person:** I, we), to someone being spoken to (**second person:** you), or to someone or something being spoken about (**third person:** he, she, it, they, everyone).

personal pronoun   See **pronoun**.

phrase   A group of meaning-related words lacking a subject and/or a verb; compare **clause**. The different kinds of phrases function as grammatical units (parts of speech) and syntactical elements (subject, verb, object, etc.). For example,

Please order more legal-size file folders. (noun phrase acting as object of verb *order*)

I must have been sleeping when you called. (verb phrase acting as main verb in independent clause)

prefix   One or more letters that can be added to the beginning of a word (1) to make a new word or (2) to change its part of speech.

1. a + sexual = asexual
   contra + diction = contradiction
   mis + spell = misspell
   un + thinkable = unthinkable

2. de + nude (adjective) = denude (verb)
   in + put (verb) = input (noun)
   a + maze (noun) = amaze (verb)

Some prefixes require a hyphen: e.g., *anti*-reform, *all*-Canadian, *mid*-season, *self*-control. See Chapter 42.

preposition　A word that links a noun, pronoun, or phrase (object of the preposition) to some other word(s) in the sentence. Prepositions may be a single word (from, upon, within, to, for) or a phrase (apart from, on account of, in spite of).

prepositional phrase　A group of words consisting of a preposition and its object(s), along with any modifiers. Prepositional phrases usually function as adjectives or adverbs:

Mine is the second office *on the right*. (adjective modifying noun *office*)

Please go *into my office*. (adverb modifying verb *go*)

pretentious language　Wordy, roundabout, or unintelligible language. Also called gobbledygook. Pretentious writing is a kind of jargon characterized by wordiness, long words, vague abstract nouns, and frequent use of the passive voice. See Chapter 11.

principal parts　The forms of a verb from which all its tenses are derived: the **base form** (walk, write, drink), the **present participle** (walking, writing, drinking), the **past tense** (walked, wrote, drank), and the **past participle** (walked, written, drunk). The principal parts of irregular verbs are listed in the dictionary. See Chapter 31.

pronoun　A word that stands for or refers to a noun or another pronoun (its antecedent). There are several kinds of pronouns:

personal:	I, we, you, he, she, it, they (subject forms) me, us, him, her, it, them (object forms)
possessive:	my, our, your, his, her, its, their
demonstrative:	this, these, that, those
relative:	who, which, that, whom, whose
interrogative:	who, whose, whom, which, what
indefinite:	any, some, all, one, everybody, anything, each, either, few, none, several, etc.

See **antecedent**, **number**, **person**, and Chapter 32.

run-on　Two or more independent clauses lacking appropriate punctuation between them. See Chapter 26.

sentence　The basic unit of connected speech and writing. A sentence can assert, question, request, command, or exclaim. See Sentence Structure on the *Essay Essentials* Web site.

sexist language　Writing that calls attention unnecessarily to the sex of the person being written about: actress, waitress, female author. Also, the use of masculine nouns and pronouns to refer to persons of both sexes: A good *salesman* listens to *his* customers. See Chapter 11.

slang　A highly colloquial word or phrase, used by speakers belonging to a particular group; e.g., high school students, music lovers, or sports fans. Slang is not appropriate in academic or professional writing. See Chapter 11.

style
A characteristic of written language; good style, whether formal or informal, is concise, clear, and pleasing.

subject
In a sentence, the person, place, thing, or concept that the sentence is about (see Chapter 24). In a paper, what the essay is about—the topic (see Chapter 2).

subordinate clause
See **clause**.

suffix
One or more letters added to the end of a word (1) to change its meaning, (2) to change its grammatical function, or (3) to change its part of speech.

1. king + dom = kingdom
   tooth + less = toothless
   few + er = fewer

2. love (base form) + s = loves (3rd person singular, present tense)
   student (singular) + s = students (plural)
   eat (base form) + en = eaten (past participle)

3. happy (adjective) + ness = happiness (noun)
   happy (adjective) + ily = happily (adverb)
   hope (noun) + ful = hopeful (adjective)

tense
The quality of a verb that indicates time: past, present, or future. The tense of a verb is indicated by its ending (play*s*, play*ing*, play*ed*) and by any auxiliary verbs associated with it (*will* play, *has* played, *must have* played).

Simple tenses	Perfect tenses
present: ask, asks	has (have) asked
past: asked	has (have) asked
future: will ask	will have asked

The simple and perfect tenses can also be **progressive**: am asking, have been asking, will be asking.

thesis
The point that an essay sets out to prove or explain. See Chapter 4.

tone
A writer's attitude toward his or her subject and intended audience, conveyed through style and ideas. Tone is an emotional quality, and there are as many different kinds of tone as there are emotions: objective, angry, sarcastic, humorous, solemn, anxious, concerned, etc. See Chapter 9.

transition
Any device used to connect ideas within a sentence, a paragraph, or a paper. See Chapter 9.

unity
The quality of oneness in a sentence, paragraph, or essay. A piece of writing should focus on a single topic or thesis; everything in the piece should relate directly to the topic or thesis; there should be no unrelated ideas or digressions.

usage   The customary or conventional way of using words and combinations of words in a language. The incorrect use of words and expressions (called "abusages" in this book) is a sign of non-standard English. See Chapter 11.

verb   A part of speech that indicates one of three states:

action: Ravi stopped the ball. (physical action)
            Nina believed the team would win. (mental action)

occurrence: Father's Day falls on the third Sunday in June.

condition: Minnie felt ill.

Transitive verbs require a direct object: I *hate* chemistry; Minnie *lifts* weights.

Intransitive verbs do not require an object: Please *listen* and *learn*.

Linking verbs require a noun or adjective as their complement: Phil is the *manager* of our department (noun); Phil is *ambitious* (adjective).

The most common linking verb is *be* (*am, is, are, was, were,* etc.) Other linking verbs are *appear, become, feel, grow, look, taste, remain, seem, smell,* and *sound.*

See also **auxiliary** verb and Parts of Speech on the *Essay Essentials* Web site.

voice   A quality of verbs, which may be either **active** or **passive**. With an active voice verb, the subject of the verb is performing the action (I *read* your essay); with a verb in the passive voice, the subject of the sentence is being acted upon (Your essay *was read* by me). See Chapter 31.

Answers for Selected Exercises

Answers for Chapter 1: Your Audience and You (pages 9–25)

Exercise 1.1

1. Audience: Literate readers who are interested in exploring a serious analysis of what is usually treated as a trivial topic.

   Writer's role: To provide information.

   Language: Formal. Sentences vary in length; one is quite long and complex. While there are no technical terms, the writer assumes the reader has a broad general vocabulary and good reading ability. Use of third person point of view contributes to the impersonal tone.

2. Audience: Experts in woodworking.

   Writer's role: To provide information in an accessible way. The writer is not instructing the reader, but outlining the function of the tool and some of its possible applications.

   Language: General level, combining technical vocabulary with an informal tone. Sentences vary in length. Writer addresses reader as "you."

3. Audience: Educated female business owners or high-level managers who are interested in doing business in China.

   Writer's role: To inform Canadian women who have little experience with Chinese business culture that it is very different from the Canadian, and that considerable preparation is needed if one is to be successful in that market.

   Language: Formal. Sentences are long and complex; vocabulary is highly sophisticated and includes a few examples of business jargon: e.g., "principals," "power brokers." Tone is serious.

4. Audience: General readers, probably not just parents of young children as might be suggested by the content.

   Writer's role: To make a point in an amusing, friendly way.

   Language: Informal. Includes contractions and colloquialisms ("kids," "slick operator") and slang ("junkies"), but also a couple of challenging phrases and words (e.g., "disdainfully"). Writer addresses readers as "you," as if speaking directly to them.

5. Audience: English professor.

   Writer's role: To demonstrate that she can write a good research paper.

   Language: Formal. Student assumes reader is familiar with Brontë's novel and presents her findings in sentences of varying lengths. Each conclusion is supported with an appropriate quotation from the text. Paragraph is fairly long (11 sentences), and tone is impersonal.

Answers for Chapter 2: Selecting a Subject (pages 26–30)

Exercise 2.1

1. significant
2. significant
3. revise
4. significant
5. revise
6. significant
7. revise

Exercise 2.2

1. revise
2. revise
3. revise
4. single (the subject is *the accuracy of reporting*, not the two media)
5. single
6. revise
7. revise

Exercise 2.3

1. specific
2. revise
3. specific
4. revise
5. revise
6. revise
7. specific

Exercise 2.4

1. supportable
2. supportable
3. supportable
4. revise
5. revise
6. revise
7. supportable

Exercise 2.5
1. not specific
2. not single
3. not supportable
4. satisfactory
5. not specific

Answers for Chapter 3: Managing the Main Points (pages 31–47)

Exercise 3.5
1. cell (not distinct, overlaps with *telephone*)
2. distance from suppliers and markets (not related)
3. repetitive (not related: repetition is a programming problem, not a characteristic of commercials)
4. procrastination (not distinct, overlaps with *poor study habits*)
5. *find a reliable real estate agent* overlaps with *seek expert advice*; also not necessarily relevant—not all people need an agent
6. *competitors offer better pay* overlaps with *salary lower than industry standard*

Exercise 3.6
1. chronological (5, 1, 4, 3, 2)
2. climactic (2, 1, 3, 4)
3. random
4. climactic (3, 1, 2. This order reflects the amount of time it takes for a smoker to quit using each method and also the amount of agony the smoker will suffer in the process.)
5. random

Answers for Chapter 4: Writing the Thesis Statement (pages 48–57)

Exercise 4.1
1. Students who try to combine a full-time job with a full-time program face problems at school, at work, and at home.
2. To be successful in a broadcasting career, you must be talented, motivated, and hardworking.
3. The ideal notebook computer for business applications is reliable, lightweight, powerful, and flexible.
4. Establishing a local area network would increase efficiency and flexibility in the office.
5. The chairperson's job calls for a responsible and sensitive person, someone who is knowledgeable about company policy, sensitive to personnel issues, and a creative problem solver. It wouldn't hurt if he or she could also walk on water.
6. The business traveller can learn much from the turtle. Carry everything you need with you. Move slowly but with purpose and consistency. Keep your head down until you are sure you know exactly what is going on.
7. Large energy producers and some provincial governments say we cannot afford to live up to the terms of the Kyoto accord, which seeks to reduce the produc-

tion of greenhouse gases. <u>But can we afford not to comply with this interna-tional agreement</u>? <u>Can we afford to compromise the health of Canadians</u> by continuing to pollute? <u>Can we afford to risk the effects of global warming</u> on our environment? <u>Can we afford to fall behind the rest of the world in research and development leading</u> to a solution to the problem of greenhouse gases?

Exercise 4.6 (suggested answers)

1. When choosing between two fast-food restaurants, consider food, atmosphere, service, and price.
2. Urban overcrowding results in traffic jams, air pollution, homelessness, and vio-lence.
3. Successful small businesses are usually those with adequate capital, a marketable product, dedicated personnel, and a workable business plan.

Answers for Chapter 7: Crafting the Topic Sentence (pages 72–76)

Exercise 7.1

1. Canada makes no economic sense.
2. Tobacco was first used by North American Aboriginal peoples, who introduced it . . . to the early European settlers.
3. In reality, taste buds are exceedingly small.
4. Scholarly explanations of humor fall into three major categories.
5. With the huge variety of computers now on the market, the determining factor in a purchase should be the job the machine will be expected to do.

Answers for Chapter 9: Keeping Your Readers with You (pages 86–96)

Exercise 9.1

1. sentence 6
2. sentence 4
3. sentence 5
4. sentence 5
5. sentence 6

Exercise 9.3

1. Therefore, ...
2. Finally, . . . but . . . .
3. Unfortunately, however, ...
4. On the other hand, ...
5. For example, ... In addition, ...

Exercise 9.5

The transitions in this exercise are identified by category. See the list of techniques on pages 90–91.

1. Finally (5), developing the proper attitude is the key to winning tennis. I define winning tennis (1) as playing the game to the best of your ability, hitting

the ball as well as you can, and enjoying the feeling of practised expertise (4). Winning tennis (1) has little to do with defeating an opponent. Naturally (5), if you learn the basics, practise sufficiently, and concentrate (4), you will win many matches, but that is the reward of playing well, not the reason for playing well (4). People who swear and throw their racquets when they lose are very useful: they (3) are the most satisfying players to trounce. But I do not understand why they (3) play a game (2) that causes them such pain. Tennis players who enjoy the feel of a well hit ball and the satisfaction of a long, skillfully played rally are winners, regardless of the score.

2. Travel abroad offers you the best education you can get. For one thing (5), travel (1) is a course in communication skills. In order to function in a foreign language, you must practise every aspect of the communication process (1, 2) from body language to pronunciation. In fact (5), just making yourself understood is a lesson in creativity, a seminar in sign language, and a lab in communication theory (2, 4). Another educational aspect of travel (5) is the history, geography, and culture (4) that you learn about almost unconsciously. Everywhere you go, you encounter memorable evidence of historic events (2) you may dimly recall from school, and you are continually confronted by the practical realities of geography (1) as you try to find your way around. As for culture (1, 5), no book or course of study could provide you with the understanding and appreciation of another society that living in it (3) can. A third way (5) in which travel (1) educates is through teaching you about yourself. Your ability—or inability—to cope with unfamiliar customs, with language difficulties, and with the inevitable problems of finding transportation and accommodation (4) will tell you more than you might want to know about yourself (2). Without the safety net of family and friends, perhaps without even the security of knowing where you'll spend the night, you develop self-reliance or you go home. Either way (5), you learn valuable lessons. While you may not get a diploma from Travel U., you'll learn more about the world, about people, and about yourself (1, 4) than you will in any classroom.

Exercise 9.8 (suggested answer)

For me, watching baseball is painful. It's a dull game because so little happens. The batter swings on about every third pitch, while the fielders appear to do nothing. In a three-hour game, there may be 15 hits, so the players are active for approximately $7\frac{1}{2}$ minutes of an entire afternoon. Even home runs are dull: one man trots around the bases while the other players stand and watch. I admit that most people enjoy baseball, but its appeal escapes me.

Answers for Chapter 11: Choosing the Right Words (pages 109–20)

Exercise 11.4 (suggested answers)

1. When the rain began, we turned on the windshield wipers.
2. Young people often have difficulty communicating with parents and others in authority.
3. The witness lied when she claimed that the accused had confessed in a meeting with her.

4. The results of our study demonstrate that our survey instrument is as valid as any other.

5. Cancelling IMF loans to Pacific Rim countries could affect the relationship between developed and developing nations.

Exercise 11.5 (suggested answers)

1. The well-known producer, Elaine May, often regrets that she cannot go out in public without attracting the attention of fans and photographers.

2. Amy King first joined the company as a salesperson; only ten years later, she was promoted to president.

3. An executive sitting in the first class cabin rang for the flight attendant, a friendly woman who quickly arrived to assist him.

4. The list of ingredients on food packages contains information that may be important to consumers, especially if they are the parents of young children.

5. The typical family is often hard-pressed to find time for family recreation.

Exercise 11.6 (suggested answers)

1. I do not think there is any basis for believing in UFOs.

2. Getting up at 5 a.m. and repeating the same routine daily for three weeks wore me out.

3. Our competitor's products, although inferior to ours, are selling better than ours.

4. My essay is as good as Krystal's and deserves an equivalent mark, but the professor hates me.

5. Nothing suggests that this unusual situation will occur again, so we can proceed with confidence.

6. My sister and I look alike; we both have curly hair and green eyes.

7. A course in English basics is a prerequisite to success in college, business, and the community.

8. "As a new teacher," we told our English instructor, "you should understand that you can't gain our respect if you insist on grammar rules that inhibit our creativity."

9. This trend can probably be reversed if we go back to our design fundamentals and introduce a few manufacturing innovations.

10. We have deleted any unlawful descriptors, such as race, age, gender, religion, and marital status, and now all our personnel documents are practically identical.

Exercise 11.7 (suggested answers)

1. Regardless of what you think, the problem between her and me has nothing to do with you.

2. If you want to be in the office pool, I need $5.00 from you today because there will be no spots left by tomorrow.

3. Because they didn't finish the job themselves the way they should have, we have to work late to get it done.

4. I didn't feel like seeing anybody, so I went home, turned on the TV, and did nothing for the rest of the night.

5. This used to be a good place to work, but now we're supposed to work a full shift every day, or a penalty is deducted from our pay.

6. Many young people today are trying to fight prejudice not only in society but also within themselves.

7. I'm supposed to ask you if the reason for the delay is that it's raining. (*Better:* . . . ask you if the rain is the reason for the delay.)

8. It's irresponsible of us to blame television or any other medium for causing violence.

9. Television is responsible, however, for the fact that many ungrammatical expressions sound all right to us.

10. Between you and me, the reason I didn't speak to anyone about Elmo's cheating on the test is that he would have broken my arm.

Answers for Chapter 12: The Three Steps to Revision (pages 123–38)

Exercise 12.4 (suggested answers)
1. I **expect** a salary **commensurate** with my qualifications and experience.
2. I have **learned** the Microsoft Word and **Excel spreadsheet programs**.
3. I received a **plaque** for being salesperson of the year.
4. Reason for leaving last job: **maternity** leave.
5. You will want me to be a **manager** in no time.
6. I am a perfectionist and rarely **if ever** forget details.
7. Marital status: **single**.
8. In my previous job, I **learned to trust no one**.
9. As **indicated**, I have **more than** five years **experience in** analyzing investments.
10. I was responsible for **running** a Western chain store. (*Better:* I was responsible for managing a Western chain store.)

Exercise 12.5

In comparing cross-country and downhill skiing, I **considered** four factors. On **every one, cross-country** came out ahead. First, Nordic (cross-country) skiing is **less** expensive, both for the equipment and for a **day's** enjoyment of the activity. Second, it is **much** more **convenient**. Unless you happen to live on a ski hill, you have to drive miles to a slope for Alpine **skiing**, whereas cross-country can be done **anywhere**. Third**,** cross-country skiing is better exercise since you are working steadily instead of **standing** around three-**quarters** of the time, waiting for a lift to the top of a hill. **Finally,** you can have more fun exploring new country, away from the crowds. You can enjoy the scenery, and there is no danger of running into other people or being run into by **hotdoggers** or **snowboarders**. . . .

Exercise 12.6

According to a recent survey in *Maclean's* magazine, only 43% of Canadians are satisfied with their jobs. What can you do to ensure that you will not be one of the 57% who are unhappy with the work they do**?** There are three questions to consider when seeing employment that will provide satisfaction as well as a paycheque.

First**,** are you suited to the kind of work you are applying for**?** If you enjoy the outdoors, for example, and like to be active, **you are** not going to be happy with a nine-to-five office job, no matter how much it pays.

Second**,** is the job based in a location compatible with your **preferred** lifestyle**?** No matter how much you like your work, if you go home every night to an **environment** you are miserable in, it will not be long before you start **transferring** your **dissatisfaction** to your job. If you like the amenities and **conveniences** of the city, you probably will not enjoy working in a small town. If, on the other hand, you prefer the quiet and security of small town life, you may find the city a stressful place in which to live.

Finally, is **the company you are applying to** one that you want to work for**?** Do you need the security of generous **benefits**, a good pension plan, and incentives to stay and grow with one company? Or are you an **ambitious** person who is looking for variety, quick advancement, and a high salary**?** If so, you may have to forego security in favour of commissions or cash incentives and be willing to move as quickly and as often as opportunities occur. Some **careful** self-analysis now, before you start out on your career path, will help you **choose** a direction that will put you in the 43% minority of satisfied Canadian workers.

Answers for Chapter 22: Documenting Your Sources (pages 274–90)

Exercise 22.2

Works Cited

Code of Ethics for Registered Nurses. <http://www.nursingethics.ca/codes.html>. (Date of access).

Dubrin, Andrew J. *Getting It Done: The Transforming Power of Self-Discipline.* Princeton, NJ: Pacesetter, 1995.

Selye, Hans. Interview. 1 Jan. 1982.

White, Linda A. "Child Care, Women's Labour Market Participation and Labour Market Policy Effectiveness in Canada." *Canadian Public Policy* 27.4 (2001): 385–405.

Yourk, Darren. "Bullying Widespread, Study Finds." *Globe and Mail* 7 May 2002: A11.

Answers for Chapter 24: Cracking the Sentence Code (pages 313–24)

Exercise 24.1
1. <u>Algy</u> <u>met</u> a bear.
2. A <u>bear</u> <u>met</u> Algy.
3. The <u>bear</u> <u>was</u> bulgy.
4. Unfortunately, the <u>bulge</u> <u>was</u> Algy.
5. <u>Grizzlies</u> <u>are</u> famous for their unpredictability.
6. <u>Meeting</u> bears unexpectedly <u>is</u> clearly risky.
7. According to an old myth, <u>bears</u> never <u>run</u> downhill.
8. (<u>You</u>) <u>Take</u> it from me. <u>They</u> <u>do</u>.
9. <u>Females</u> with cubs <u>are</u> especially dangerous.
10. <u>Defending</u> oneself <u>presents</u> a real problem.

Exercise 24.2

1. Here <u>is</u> an <u>idea</u> to consider.
2. <u>Lucy Maud Montgomery</u> <u>lived</u> in Ontario before Confederation.
3. <u>Who</u> <u>wants</u> the last piece?
4. (<u>You</u>) <u>Eat</u> slowly.
5. <u>Exercise</u> <u>builds</u> strong bodies and healthy minds.
6. (<u>You</u>) <u>Keep</u> your body fit.
7. Far behind the Liberals and New Democrats <u>trailed</u> the <u>Conservatives</u>, bringing up the rear.
8. <u>Pride</u> <u>goes</u> before a fall.
9. Only in Canada <u>is</u> the <u>lack</u> of national identity a distinctive national characteristic.
10. Irish <u>coffee</u> <u>contains</u> ingredients from all four of the essential food groups: caffeine, fat, sugar, and alcohol.

Exercise 24.3

1. <u>He</u> <u>has talked</u> non-stop for three hours.
2. <u>I</u> <u>am</u> not <u>going</u> to drive.
3. <u>Could</u> <u>they</u> <u>return</u> the goods tomorrow?
4. Personal <u>opinion</u> <u>is</u> often presented as fact.
5. <u>Carla</u> <u>should have been filing</u> the letters and memos.
6. Soon <u>he</u> <u>will have been sleeping</u> for 16 hours.
7. Paula's <u>lawsuit</u> <u>should</u> never <u>have been allowed</u> to proceed this far.
8. <u>Have</u> <u>you</u> ever <u>been</u> to the Zanzibar tavern?
9. There <u>has</u> never <u>been</u> a better <u>time</u> to travel to Southeast Asia.
10. How <u>are</u> the club <u>members</u> <u>identified</u>?

Exercise 24.4

1. The <u>problem</u> with you <u>is</u> your attitude.
2. For many years, we four old <u>friends</u> <u>have been meeting</u> for our vacations.
3. In the state of Florida, <u>it</u> <u>is</u> illegal for single, divorced, or widowed women to parachute on Sunday afternoons.
4. In Kentucky, no <u>woman</u> <u>may appear</u> in a bathing suit on any highway in the state unless escorted by two officers or armed with a club.
5. In my wildest imaginings, <u>I</u> <u>cannot</u> <u>understand</u> these laws.
6. During a break in the conversation, Darryl's embarrassing <u>comment</u> <u>could be heard</u> in every corner of the room.
7. Without her glasses, <u>Stacey</u> <u>cannot</u> <u>see</u> the blackboard at the front of the room.
8. To the staff and managers of the project, <u>I</u> <u>extend</u> my congratulations for an excellent job.
9. Against all odds, and despite their shortcomings, the <u>Miners</u> <u>made</u> it into the playoffs of the Southern New Brunswick Little League.
10. [<u>You</u>] <u>Walk</u> a mile in my shoes at high noon with your head held high in order to avoid clichés like the plague.

Exercise 24.5

1. The prime minister and the <u>premiers</u> <u>met</u> at Harrison Lake.
2. <u>They</u> <u>debated</u> and <u>drafted</u> amendments to the employment insurance program.

3. The <u>anesthetist</u> and the <u>surgeon</u> <u>scrubbed</u> ~~for surgery~~ and <u>hurried</u> ~~to the oper-ating room~~.
4. <u>Blue spruce</u> and <u>hemlock</u> <u>are</u> both native ~~to northern Ontario~~.
5. <u>I</u> <u>tried</u> and <u>failed</u> once, then <u>tried</u> again and <u>succeeded</u>.
6. My <u>son</u> or my <u>daughter</u> <u>will drive</u> me home.
7. [You] <u>Knock</u> three times and <u>ask</u> ~~for Stan~~.
8. Our economics <u>instructor</u> and her <u>colleagues</u> <u>went</u> ~~to a conference~~ yesterday.
9. [You] <u>Buy</u> the base model and <u>don't</u> <u>waste</u> your money ~~on the luxury options~~.
10. <u>Ragweed, goldenrod</u>, and <u>twitch grass</u> <u>formed</u> the essential elements ~~in the bou-quet for his English teacher~~.

Answers for Chapter 25: Solving Sentence-Fragment Problems (pages 325–32)

Exercise 25.1 (suggested answers)
We have made the sentence fragments into complete sentences to give you an idea of how the sentences might be formed. Different sentences can be made out of the fragments in this exercise; just be sure each sentence has a subject and a verb.
1. F   <u>He</u> <u>is</u> the expert regarding myths and fairy tales.
2. F   <u>It</u> <u>is</u> silly to decide on the basis of rumour, not facts.
3. S
4. F   <u>Grading</u> exams all evening after working all day <u>exhausts</u> even an enthusi-astic teacher.
5. F   The party <u>members</u> gathering in the campaign office <u>called</u> for a recount.
6. S
7. F   [You] <u>Put</u> your hands over your head.
8. F   <u>It</u> <u>is</u> impossible to study without my CD player.
9. F   Having worked hard all her life, <u>she</u> <u>was</u> happy to retire.
10. S

Exercise 25.2 (suggested answers)
__F__ Professional athletes <u>make</u> millions of dollars a year. __F__ At the same time, owners of sports franchises <u>grow</u> fantastically rich from the efforts of their employees, the players. __F__ The fans <u>are</u> the forgotten people in the struggle for control over major league sports. __F__ They <u>are</u> the people who pay the money that makes both owners and players rich. __S__ I have an idea that would protect everyone's interests. __S__ Cap the owners' profits. __S__ Cap the players' salaries. __F__ And, most important, (you) <u>cap</u> the ticket prices. __F__ This <u>plan</u> <u>would ensure</u> a fair deal for everyone. __S__ Fans should be able to see their teams play for the price of a movie ticket, not the price of a television set.

Exercise 25.3
1. F   Although
2. F   Since
3. S
4. F   Whichever
5. F   Before

Exercise 25.4
1. Although
2. As long as
3. Whether
4. Because
5. As

Exercise 25.5

Although many companies are experiencing growth, thanks to a healthy economy, **m**iddle managers are not breathing easily. As long as there is surplus of junior executives, **m**iddle managers will continue to look over their shoulders, never sure when the axe will fall. Whether through early retirement, buyout, or termination, **t**heir positions are being eliminated by cost-conscious firms whose eyes are focused on the bottom line. Because the executive branch of many businesses expanded rapidly during the years of high growth, **n**ow there is a large block of managers who have no prospects of advancement. As one analyst observed, when he examined this block of largely superfluous executives and their chances of rising in the company hierarchy, "You cannot push a rectangle up a triangle."

Exercise 25.6

In spite of what everyone says about the weak economy and the scarcity of jobs, especially for young people, I have financed my college career with a variety of part-time and seasonal jobs. Right now, for instance, while completing my third year at college, I have not one, or two, but three part-time jobs. I am a short-order cook three nights a week for a local bar and diner, **a**nd a telemarketer for a cable company after school **or** whenever I have free time. I'm also a server at a specialty coffee store on weekends. To maintain any kind of social life **w**hile juggling three jobs and the requirements of my third-year program is not exactly easy, but I find it hard to turn down the opportunity for experience, **n**ot to mention cash. I'm willing to put my social life on hold **f**or a while.

Answers for Chapter 26: Solving Run-On Problems (pages 333–39)

Exercise 26.1
1. The fog has lifted; we can go home now.
2. Just let me do the talking; we will get a ticket if you open your mouth.
3. correct
4. Hitting a golf ball may look easy, **but** it's not.
5. correct
6. Montreal used to be called Ville Ste. Marie, I think. Before that, it was known as Hochelaga.
7. Students today need summer jobs **because** tuition and living costs are too much for most families.
8. Bryan will be going to college if he is accepted; his parents are wealthy.
9. correct
10. "I was married by a judge; I should have asked for a jury."

Exercises 26.2

1. A Canadian who speaks three languages is called multilingual**;** one who speaks two languages is called bilingual**; and** one who speaks only one language is called an English Canadian.
2. I'm sure the job couldn't have been as bad as he claims**;** maybe he just didn't try hard enough. *Or:* I'm sure the job couldn't have been as bad as he claims**.** Maybe he just didn't try hard enough.
3. Casual meetings are fine for small groups**, but** large groups have to be handled in a different way.
4. I'll be glad to help you**.** Just call when you need me**;** I'll be here all day.
5. In Canada, winter is more than a season**. It**'s a bad joke.
6. correct
7. For students in technology programs, then, the future looks bright**;** however, a diploma does not guarantee job security.
8. Career opportunities are good for students in technical programs**;** however, most employers are looking for people with experience as well as training.
9. People with high-technology skills are needed in several fields**;** avionics, computer networking, and environmental technology are three examples.
10. I still believe in a unified Canada**.** I believe in one nation extending from sea to sea. The Fathers of Confederation were right**;** a federation of provinces can work.

Exercise 26.3 (deleted words and phrases are indicated by ***)

1. **While** there are many hilarious examples of newspaper headlines that do not say exactly *** what their writers intended, *** my favourite is from the sports pages. It reads "Grandmother of Eight Makes Hole in One."
2. Other examples of the headline writer's art indicate a**n** *** impressive ability for stating the obvious. *** "Smokers Are Productive, but Death Cuts Efficiency" is one classic. **Another** is "Man Is Fatally Slain."
3. If you have trouble getting your child's attention, all you have to do is sit down and get comfortable. Pick up a book, turn on the TV, or just relax. Your child will be all over you in no time ***. *** When young children are home from school ***, parents begin to understand how grossly unappreciated primary school teachers are.
4. *** Eyeglasses were invented by the Chinese *** approximately 800 years ago, *** 500 years before lens grinding in the West was sufficiently refined to permit the making of corrective lenses. *** It was Marco Polo who *** reported seeing many Chinese wearing eyeglasses during his visit to the Orient in 1275.
5. There is some confusion among modern historians *** about the origin of the name "Canada**.**" While some claim it comes from an Iroquois word meaning "village," others think it may derive from the Spanish expression *aquí nada*, which means "there is nothing here**.**" The Native peoples may have picked up the term from early Portuguese or Spanish explorers and passed it on to Jacques Cartier, who applied it to the lands he claimed for France.

494 · APPENDIX B

Answers for Chapter 27: Solving Modifier Problems (pages 340–48)

Exercise 27.1

1. Trevor left out the can of Pet Grrmet he had opened for the dog.
2. On the first day, our supervisor told us no one takes coffee breaks. (*Or:* Our supervisor told us no one takes coffee breaks on the first day.)
3. With no experience whatever, I enthusiastically recommend this candidate.
4. In September, Professor Green told us he thought our class was a hopeless case. (*Or:* Professor Green told us he thought our class was a hopeless case in September.)
5. We enjoyed almost the whole movie; only the ending was a disappointment.
6. In a highrise within walking distance of the campus, Leo and Annie found an apartment with two bedrooms and a sunken living room.
7. There are just enough pieces to go around.
8. It seems there is a game almost every day during baseball season.
9. A charming, intelligent companion who looks good in evening gowns and diamonds is sought by a vertically challenged but wealthy gentleman.
10. Only one of us could go because there was just enough money to buy one ticket.

Exercise 27.2

1. One usually finds the best Chinese food in those restaurants where the Chinese eat.
2. Using his new binoculars, he caught sight of a canary and several finches.
3. Juan had played ball professionally for several major American teams before coming to the Blue Jays.
4. The football practices have been organized as a keep-fit measure for players who are not with a team in the summertime.
5. Vancouver is a wonderful city to live in for anyone who likes rain and fog.
6. Some games, such as tiddlywinks, are less demanding in terms of time and equipment.
7. The Human Rights Code prohibits discrimination on the basis of race, religion, sex, or age against anyone who is applying for a job.
8. We looked in a golf store for a birthday present for our boss.
9. After dinner, without getting permission from anyone, he lit up a huge cigar that smelled like burnt rope.
10. Using yogic flying, Dr. Neil Paterson, the leader of Canada's Natural Law Party, claimed to be able to eliminate the national debt, achieve world peace, and reduce the number of unemployed.

Exercise 27.3

1. Driving recklessly and without lights, Gina was stopped by the police at a road block.
2. After being late twice in one week, I was lectured by my supervisor about punctuality.
3. After criticizing both my work and my attitude, my supervisor fired me.
4. Standing a full 2.5 m tall and weighing about 300 kg, the bear made it easy for Megan to decide not to antagonize it.

5. After scoring the winning goal in overtime, the team was carried in a huge celebration through the city.
6. As a conscientious and dedicated teacher, Nina finds the workload sometimes overwhelming.
7. In less than a minute after applying the ointment, I found the pain began to ease.
8. Making her first formal presentation to her colleagues and her supervisor, Alison was probably less nervous than Henry was.
9. When handling hazardous wastes, you should follow the procedures outlined in the safety manual.
10. It was a great moment: after making the speech of a lifetime, Sara was chosen by the delegates to lead the party into the next election.

Exercise 27.4

1. Because she had been driving recklessly and without lights, the police stopped Gina at a road block.
2. After I had been late twice in one week, my supervisor gave me a lecture about punctuality.
3. After both my work and my attitude had been criticized, I was fired.
4. Megan decided not to antagonize the bear, which stood a full 2.5 m tall and weighed about 300 kg.
5. After our team had scored the winning goal in overtime, a huge celebration wound through the city.
6. Because Nina is a conscientious and dedicated teacher, the workload sometimes seems overwhelming to her.
7. In less than a minute after I had applied the ointment, the pain began to ease.
8. When Alison made her first formal presentation to her colleagues and her supervisor, Henry was probably more nervous than she was.
9. When you are handling hazardous wastes, follow the procedures outlined in the safety manual.
10. It was a great moment: after Sara had made the speech of a lifetime, the delegates chose her to lead the party into the next election.

Exercise 27.5

1. She was the baker's only daughter, but she could loaf all day. (*Or:* She was only the baker's daughter, but she could loaf all day.)
2. Being horribly hung over, I came to the realization that the only problem with a free bar is knowing when to quit.
3. The judges were impressed by Sandor's plump, purple turnips.
4. In a hurry to get to the interview on time, I left my résumé lying on my desk at home.
5. As a college student constantly faced with new assignments, I find the pressure is sometimes intolerable.
6. In *The Globe and Mail*, I learned that the provincial premiers plan to meet in Calgary next week.
7. The prime minister asked to meet Steven Page when the Barenaked Ladies stopped in Ottawa on tour.

8. The Canadian Brass receives enthusiastic acclaim from Vancouver to St. John's for its witty presentation and clarity of tone.
9. Queen Elizabeth couldn't resist the little Corgi puppy, which was rolling on her back, eager to have her tummy scratched.
10. The U.S. dollar was a popular choice for investors wanting to get rid of their devalued yen, which were sinking lower on the world money markets.

Answers for Chapter 28: The Parallelism Principle (pages 349–54)

Exercise 28.1

1. This program is easy to understand and to use.
2. We were told that we would have to leave and that we could take nothing with us.
3. We organized our findings, wrote the report, and finally made our presentation.
4. Today's personal computers are fast, powerful, and compact.
5. Elmer's doctor advised him not to strain his back or his mind.
6. The company is looking for an employee who has a car and who knows the city.
7. The workplace-safety committee found the factory to be noisy, smelly, and dirty.
8. When I want to get away from it all, there are three solitary pleasures that I enjoy: walking quietly in the country, reading a good book, and listening to fine music. (*Or:* . . . a walk in the country, a good book, and fine music.)
9. A recent survey of female executives claims that responsibility for their families, exclusion from informal networks, and lack of management experience are the major factors keeping them from advancement.
10. If it is to be useful, your report must be clearly organized, well written, and thoroughly researched.

Exercise 28.2

1. I wanted either a Mother's pizza or a McDonald's Big Mac.
2. In my home town, two related crimes prevail: vandalism and drug trafficking.
3. Bodybuilding has made me what I am today: physically perfect, financially prosperous, and practically friendless.
4. I'd like to help, but I'm too tired and too busy.
5. Bruce claimed that, through repetition and firmness, he had trained his guppy to be loyal and obedient.
6. correct
7. My sister, who is trying to teach me to play tennis, says that my forehand and serve are all right but that my backhand needs strengthening.
8. The two factors thought to be most important in a long-lasting marriage are the commitment of each partner to the marriage and the willingness of each partner to compromise.
9. If there is no heaven, then there is no hell.
10. The new budget must deal with several major problems, such as the devalued Canadian dollar and the high rate of unemployment.

Exercise 28.3

1. wine	women	song
2. employers	employees	

3. do your best	don't give up	
4. information	education	entertainment
5. as individuals	as a group	
6. privately	publicly	
7. lying about all morning	doing whatever I please	
8. happy	healthy	wise
9. not enough time	not enough money	not enough staff
10. French is the language of love	English is the language of business	German is the language of profanity

Exercise 28.4

1. Not being able to speak the language is confusing, frustrating, and embarrassing.
2. Trying your best and succeeding are not always the same thing.
3. The first candidate we interviewed seemed frightened and shy, but the second was composed and confident.
4. Licking one's fingers and picking one's teeth in a restaurant are one way to get attention.
5. If I could afford it, I'd wear handcrafted shoes and silk ties.
6. One executive claims his most valuable business assets are a good backhand and membership at an exclusive golf club.
7. In order to succeed in this economy, small businesses must be creative, innovative, and flexible.
8. Lowering our profit margin, raising our prices, and laying off two managers will enable us to meet our budget.
9. After an enjoyable dinner, I like to drink a cappuccino, eat a dark chocolate mint, and, occasionally, smoke a good cigar.
10. In the 1970s, Canada experienced bad management of natural resources, unwise policies regarding national debt, and inflationary demands of workers.

Answers for Chapter 29: Refining by Combining (pages 355–59)

Exercise 29.1

1. We cannot sell our cottage, **so** we will live there instead.
2. There are three solutions given for this problem, **and** all of them are correct.
3. The people in our firm work very hard, **but** they wouldn't want it any other way.
4. We could spend our day off shopping at the mall, **or** we could spend the day fishing.
5. Great leaders do not bully their people, **nor** do they deceive them.
6. I will not be able to finish my report, **for** there are only two hours before the deadline.
7. Jennifer knows that she likely will not get the vice-president's job, **yet** (*or* **but**) she wants the experience of applying for it.
8. Finish the estimate, **but** do not begin work until it has been approved.
9. Today has been the worst day of my life, **so** my horoscope was right.
10. The government did not reply to my letter, **nor** did it offer me a job.

Exercise 29.2 (suggested answers)

1. Leonardo da Vinci was a great artist and inventor **who** invented scissors, among other things.
2. Cats can produce over 100 vocal sounds, **whereas** dogs can make only ten.
3. **Although** it is said that men don't cry, they do while assembling furniture.
4. The name Wendy was made up for a book **that** was called *Peter Pan*.
5. **Although** 10 percent of Canadians are heavy drinkers, 35 percent abstain from alcohol.
6. Travel broadens the mind **even though** it flattens the bank account.
7. We are seeking an experienced and innovative director **who** is fluent in French.
8. One hundred thousand Vietnam veterans have taken their own lives, **which** is twice the number who were killed in action.
9. An oven is a compact home incinerator **whose** chief use is the disposal of bulky pieces of meat and poultry.
10. A recipe is a series of step-by-step instructions **which** you can use to prepare meals **if** the ingredients are in your kitchen.

Answers for Chapter 30: Mastering Subject–Verb Agreement (pages 360–68)

Exercise 30.1

1. They sell used essays to other students.
2. The women maintain that their boss has been harassing them.
3. Those new guidelines affect all the office procedures.
4. All those who shop at Pimrock's receive free cans of tuna.
5. Those girls' fathers are looking for rich husbands for them.

Exercise 30.2

1. know
2. are
3. is
4. are
5. repel

Exercise 30.3

1. are
2. registers
3. is
4. keeps
5. puts

Exercise 30.4

1. loves
2. knows
3. is
4. has
5. interest

Exercise 30.5

1. is
2. involves
3. is
4. wants
5. believes

Exercise 30.6

1. plans
2. has
3. have
4. was
5. are

Exercise 30.7

1. was
2. seems
3. is
4. is
5. seems

Exercise 30.8

1. My <u>opinion</u> of the schools <u>is</u> . . . .
2. <u>Neither</u> of us <u>remembers</u> . . . .
3. Every <u>one</u> of the band's members <u>appeals</u> . . . .
4. My whole <u>family</u>, with the exception of the cat, <u>dislikes</u> . . . .
5. The <u>applause</u> from a thousand delirious fans <u>was</u> . . . .
6. Neither my <u>husband</u> nor my <u>dog</u> <u>understands</u> . . . . .
7. correct
8. <u>Three thousand dollars</u> per term . . . <u>is</u> too much . . . .
9. The <u>birth</u> of quintuplets <u>was</u> . . . .
10. <u>Everything</u> that we agreed to last night <u>seems</u> . . . .

Exercise 30.9

Quebec City, along with Montreal, Toronto, and Vancouver, **is** among Canada's great gourmet centres. Whereas Toronto is a relative latecomer to this list, neither Quebec City nor Montreal **is a stranger** to those who **seek** fine dining. Indeed, travel and food magazines have long affirmed that the inclusion of these two cities in a Quebec vacation **is a** "must." Montreal is perhaps more international in its offerings, but Quebec City provides exquisite proof that French-Canadian cuisine and hospitality **are** second to none in the world. Amid the Old World charm of the lower city **are** to be found some of the quaintest and most enjoyable traditional restaurants; the newer sections of town **boast** equally fine dining in more contemporary surroundings. The combination of the wonderful food and the city's fascinating charms **is** sure to make any visitor return frequently. Either the summer, when the city blooms and outdoor cafés abound, or the winter, when Carnaval turns the streets into hundreds of connecting parties, **is a** wonderful **time** to visit one of Canada's oldest and most interesting cities.

Answers for Chapter 31: Using Verbs Effectively (pages 369–82)

Exercise 31.1

1. lay	6. chosen
2. eaten	7. printed
3. ridden	8. lent
4. sat	9. worn
5. lain	10. known

Exercise 31.3

1. Rolly goes home and **kicks** his cat.
2. Hank Aaron broke Babe Ruth's record of 714 home runs in a lifetime when he **hit** number 715 in 1974.
3. Children are quite perceptive and **know** when you are lying to them.
4. We had just finished painting the floor when the dog **ran** through.
5. When Brad Pitt walked into the room, the girls **went** crazy.
6. correct
7. Tim walked into the room, took one look at Leroy, and **smashed** him right through the wall.
8. First you will greet the guests; then you **will show** them to their rooms.
9. The largest cheese ever produced took forty-three hours to make and **weighed** a whopping 15 723 kg.
10. He watches television until he finally **goes** to sleep.

Exercise 31.4

For some reason, when mistakes or accidents happen in radio or television, they **are** often hilariously funny. If, in the course of a conversation, someone said, "Here come the Duck and Doochess of Kent," listeners would probably be mildly amused. But many years ago, when an announcer **made** that slip on a live radio broadcast, it **became** one of the most famous blunders in radio history. Tapes of the slip **were** filed in "bloopers" libraries all over the world. This heightened sense of hilarity is the reason that so many people who work in radio **dedicate** their creativity to making the on-air announcer laugh while reading the news. To take one example, Lorne Greene's **was** the deeply serious voice that **was** heard on the CBC news during World War II. He **was** the victim of all kinds of pranks aimed at getting him to break up while reading the dark, often tragic, news of the combat overseas. The pages of his news script **were** set on fire while he **read**. He **was** even stripped naked as he **read**, calmly, and apparently without strain. Lorne Greene **was** a true professional. Many other newscasters, however, **have been** highly susceptible to falling apart on air at the slightest provocation. And there **are** always people around a radio station who cannot resist giving them that little push.

Exercise 31.6

1. The department head called a meeting.
2. The server will make expresso in a few minutes.
3. When it gets cold, we plug in the block heater overnight.
4. For many years, professional athletes have used steroids to improve speed and endurance.

5. You must not knead the dough, or your pastry will be tough.
6. Dr. Lance Boyles wrote the current best-seller, *Do-It-Yourself Surgery*.
7. The police arrested four of Paul's buddies during a routine check of Barry's Bingo Bistro.
8. Thieves broke into our neighbours' house while they were vacationing in the Caribbean.
9. Technicians from all the leading software firms will display and demonstrate the latest multimedia technology in the graphics lab.
10. The Mighty Ducks have replaced the Red Sox and the White Sox as the team with stupidest name in sports.

Exercise 31.7

1. Another Juno was won by Sarah McLachlan. (Active is more effective.)
2. The ball was spiked by Carl, after scoring the winning points. (Active is more effective.)
3. A by-law forbidding smoking in bars and restaurants has been passed by city council. (Passive is more effective, because it focusses the readers' attention on the law rather than on who brought the law into being.)
4. Forty-eight hours later, the technician added 2 ml of sterile water to the culture in the Petri dish. (Passive is more effective; it puts the focus on the procedure rather than on the person.)
5. Four tickets for the concert were got by Courtenay after standing in line all night. (Active is more effective.)
6. The truth behind the famous Doobie Brothers scandal was revealed on the 10 p.m. news. (Passive is more effective; what was revealed is of more interest than who revealed it.)
7. The judge finally announced her judgment today, almost a year after the environmental hearings were concluded. (Passive is more effective, for the same reason as in sentence 6.)
8. After a long debate, Yasmin's fund-raising proposal was finally endorsed by the committee. (Passive is more effective, because it focusses attention on the individual proposal rather than on the anonymous committee.)
9. Dr. Hans Steiner, a psychologist at Stanford University, has developed a computer program that analyzes speech patterns. (Passive is more effective, for the same reason as in sentence 6.)
10. After years of research among college students, Dr. Steiner has concluded that people who frequently use passive-voice constructions tend to be maladjusted. (Active is more effective.)

Answers for Chapter 32: Solving Pronoun Problems (pages 383–401)

Exercise 32.1

1. No one except you and **me** . . .
2. **He** and I can't figure out this problem set any better than you and **she** could.
3. George and **he** fell asleep . . .
4. Do you want to work with Emma and **her**?

5. We can use the film passes all week, and you and **she** can use them on the weekend when Biff and **I** are going skiing.
6. Thanks to the recommendations provided by your math instructor and **me**, you and **she** got the tutorial jobs.
7. As we were going to class, Karl and **I** heard . . .
8. If it hadn't been for Hassan and **him** . . .
9. Quentin and **he** agreed to split the price of a case with Stan and **me**.
10. Only two students passed the midterm: Nadia and **I**.

Exercise 32.2

1. At fourteen, my younger brother is already taller than **I** [am].
2. No one likes partying more than **he** and Anne.
3. Would you like to join Daniel and **me** . . . ?
4. Only one person in this firm could manage the department as well as **he** [could].
5. At last I have met someone who enjoys grilled liver as much as **I** [do].
6. We can skate as well as **they**, but they are much better at shooting and defending than **we** [are].
7. More than **I** [do], Serge uses the computer . . . .

Exercise 32.3

1. My boyfriend and **I** . . . .
2. I like fast food better than **he** [does].
3. He likes vegetables better than **I** [do].
4. In fact, between you and **me** . . . .
5. . . . it is difficult for **them** to know where to take him and **me** . . . .
6. The only type of restaurant where **we** and **they** can all have what we like is Italian.
7. There, **he** and his friends . . . .
8. We are probably not as healthy as they, but they don't seem to enjoy their food as much as **we** [do].

Exercise 32.4

1. For two weeks, the pitcher **who** gave up the winning run had to live in hiding.
2. I am a longtime fan of David Cronenberg, a film director **who** began his career in Canada.
3. We are often attracted to people **who** are completely opposite to us.
4. Elmo's grandmother always told him that people **who** couldn't fly should stay out of airplanes.
5. People **who** take afternoon naps often pay a penalty: they are also people **who** suffer from insomnia.
6. The vacuum-cleaner salesperson **who** came to our door was the sort of person **who** won't take no for an answer.
7. Holly Cole, **who** is the star headlining tonight's show, has made two albums **that** have been nominated for Juno awards.
8. The roast, which had been in the oven for three hours, was dried out by the time the last of the guests [**whom**] we had invited finally arrived.

9. The math problems **that** we worked on last night would have baffled anyone **who** hadn't done all the problem sets.
10. We took our ancient Jeep, **which** we had bought from a friend **who** had lost his license, to a scrap yard **that** paid us $200 for it.

Exercise 32.5
1. his
2. her
3. his
4. her
5. himself, he

Exercise 32.6
1. Everyone who enjoys a thrilling match will reserve a seat . . . .
2. . . . everyone climbed to the fourth floor to hand in the course evaluation.
3. Each of her sons has successfully completed his diploma.
4. Someone with lots of money left a purse in the washroom.
5. All reporters must decide for themselves how far they will go . . . .

Exercise 32.7
1. Virginia claims that every one of her male friends has a room of his own.
2. Almost everyone I know is worried about finding a suitable job.
3. Anybody who applies for a job with this institution can expect to spend a lot of time in selection committee interviews.
4. Taking pictures of people when they are not looking can produce interesting results.
5. Nearly every man who can cook will tell you that he enjoys preparing food.

Exercise 32.8
1. I know that smoking is bad for me and everyone else, but I can't give up cigarettes.
2. If your pet rat won't eat its food, feed the pellets to the kitty.
3. Chuck told Ravi that Chuck's teeth were falling out.
4. Whenever Stefan and Matt played poker, Stefan stacked the deck.
5. The gorilla was mean and hungry because he had finished all his food in the morning.
6. Madonna has transformed herself at least four times in her career, an accomplishment that makes her unique.
7. Dani backed her car into a garbage truck and dented her fender.
8. Rocco was suspicious of handgun control because he thought everyone should have a gun for late-night subway rides.
9. Get your ears pierced during this week's special and take home an extra pair of earrings free.
10. When Jean and Paul began to argue, Paul told Jean that he had never had any respect for him.

Exercise 32.10
1. you
2. you, your

3. they, themselves
4. she
5. we

Exercise 32.11

1. After the unfortunate brawl, Biff learned that if a person stomps on police officers, **he** can expect to end up in jail.
2. Experience is something **you don't** often get until just after you need it.
3. If **you leave** garbage at your campsite, you may well have bears as midnight callers.
4. correct
5. **You** will always think about the opportunities **you've** missed, even if you're happy with what you have.
6. Managers who are concerned about downsizing should keep a close eye on **their** company's income-and-expense statements.
7. You should always wear garlic around the neck if **you fear** vampires.
8. Any woman who wears garlic won't have to worry about men harassing **her** either.
9. Can you really know another person if you have never been to **his or her** home?
10. A sure way to lose your friends is to eat all the ice cream yourself.

Exercise 32.12

When people see a dreadful occurrence on television, such as a bombing, an earthquake, or a mass slaughter, it does not always affect **them.** It is one thing for people to see the ravages of war **themselves** and another thing to see a three-minute newscast of the same battle, neatly edited by the CBC. Even the horrible effects of natural catastrophes that wipe out whole populations are somehow minimized or trivialized when **people** see them on TV. And though viewers may be horrified by the gaunt faces of starving children on the screen, **they** can easily escape into **their** familiar world of Egg McMuffins, Shake'n Bake, and Labatt Blue that is portrayed in commercial messages.

Thus, the impact of television on us is a mixed one. It is true that **we are** shown terrible, sometimes shocking events that **we** could not possibly have seen before television. In this way, **our** world is drawn together more closely. However, the risk in creating this immediacy is that **we** may become desensitized and cease to feel or care about **our** fellow human beings.

Answers for Chapter 33: The Comma (pages 402–10)

Exercise 33.1

1. Holly held two aces, a King, a Queen, and a Jack in her hand.
2. This food is spicy, colourful, nourishing, and delicious.
3. In Canada, the seasons are spring, summer, fall, winter, winter, and winter.
4. correct
5. Cell phones, hand-held computers, and DVD players are three popular new technologies.
6. To go winter camping, you need woolen underwear, showshoes, Arctic boots, but very little money.

7. Sleeping through my alarm, dozing during sociology, napping in the library after lunch, and snoozing in front of the TV all are symptoms of my overactive nightlife.

8. Once you have finished your homework, taken out the garbage, and done the dishes, you can feed the cat, clean your room, and do your laundry.

9. Don't forget to bring the photo album, videotape, and souvenirs of your trip to Australia.

10. My doctor and my nutritionist agree that I should eat better, exercise more, and stop smoking.

Exercise 33.2

1. Our family doctor, like our family dog, never comes when we call.

2. This photograph, taken when I was only four, embarrasses me whenever my parents show it.

3. Mira's boyfriend, who looks like an ape, is living proof that love is blind.

4. Isn't it strange that the poor, who are often bitterly critical of the rich, buy lottery tickets?

5. Several premiers and a former political advisor, a man now well into his eighties, accompanied the prime minister on his trade mission to China.

6. My car made it all the way to Saskatoon without anything falling off or breaking down, a piece of good luck that surprised us all.

7. A popular mathematics instructor, Professor Lam won the distinguished teaching award again this year.

8. We're going to the shopping mall, a weekly ritual we all enjoy.

9. correct

10. Classical music, which I call Prozac for the ears, can be very soothing in times of stress.

Exercise 33.3

1. This has been a perfect day, and you have been a perfect host.

2. We have a plan and a budget, yet we still don't have the staff we need.

3. Talk shows ran out of things to say years ago, but they haven't stopped talking yet.

4. We discovered that we both had an interest in art, so we made a date to go to an exhibition at the gallery next Friday.

5. correct

6. Take good notes, for there will be an exam on Tuesday.

7. You won't get any sympathy from us, nor will we help you explain to your parents.

8. correct

9. I have travelled all over the world, yet my luggage has visited many more places than I have.

10. Jet lag makes me look haggard and sick, but at least I resemble my passport picture.

Exercise 33.4

1. Unfortunately, we'll have to begin all over again.

2. Mr. Dillinger, the bank wants to speak with you.

3. In the end, the quality of your performance counts more than the effort you put into it.

4. Treading water, we waited for the boat to return and rescue us.

5. Even though this photograph is out of focus, it shows that Remi did take part in the Polar Bear swim.

6. Finally understanding what she was trying to say, I apologized for being so slow.

7. After an evening of watching television, I have accomplished as much as if I had been unconscious.

8. Since my doctor recommended that I eat less and exercise more, I have been walking around the block during my lunch break.

9. Having munched our way through a large bag of peanuts while watching the game, we weren't interested in food at supper time.

10. Whenever a police officer pulls over an optimist, the optimist thinks it's to ask for directions.

Exercise 33.5

1. correct
2. correct
3. correct
4. Toronto in the summer is hot, smoggy, and humid.
5. Today's paper has an article about a new car made of lightweight, durable aluminum.
6. Using the new, improved model should increase your productivity.
7. This ergonomic, efficient, full-function keyboard comes in a variety of pastel shades.
8. We ordered a large, nutritious salad for lunch, then indulged ourselves with a whipped-cream topped dessert.
9. Danny bought a cute, cuddly, pure-bred puppy.
10. Ten months later that cute puppy turned into a vicious, man-eating monster.

Exercise 33.6

1. Pinot noir, which is a type of grape grown in California, Oregon, British Columbia(,) and Ontario, produces a delicious red wine.

2. There are, I am told, people who don't like garlic, but you won't find any of them eating at Freddy's.

3. I use e-mail to communicate with my colleagues, a fax machine to keep in touch with clients(,) and Canada Post to send greetings to my relatives.

4. Your dogs, Mr. Pavlov, seem hungry for some reason.

5. According to G.K. Chesterton, "If a thing is worth doing, it is worth doing badly."

6. Looking for a competent computer technologist, we interviewed, tested, investigated(,) and rejected 30 applicants.

7. How you choose to phrase your resignation is up to you, but I expect to have it on my desk by morning.

8. Vinny's sparse, grey, moth-eaten beard can hardly be described as a fashion statement.

9. Franz wrote the formula on the damp, stained linen tablecloth.

10. Canada, a country known internationally for beautiful scenery, peaceful intentions(,) and violent hockey, always places near the top of the United Nations' list of desirable places to live.

Exercise 33.7

1. Whereas the Super Bowl tradition goes back about four decades, the Grey Cup has a history that stretches back to the 19th century.
2. Otherwise, Mrs. Lincoln said, she had very much enjoyed the play.
3. Our guard dog, a Rottweiler, caught an intruder and maimed him for life.
4. Unfortunately, my Uncle Ladislaw was the intruder, and he intends to sue us for every penny we have.
5. correct
6. The lovely, antique mahogany table was sold for only $300.
7. If there were more people like Gladys, global warming would be the least of our worries.
8. correct
9. Deciding on the midnight blue velvet pants was easy, but paying for them was not.
10. Igor asked, "May I show you to your quarters, or would you prefer to spend the night in the dungeon?"

Answers for Chapter 34: The Colon (pages 411–14)

Exercise 34.1

1. incorrect	6. correct
2. correct	7. correct
3. correct	8. incorrect
4. incorrect	9. incorrect
5. incorrect	10. incorrect

Exercise 34.2

1. I have set myself three goals this year: to achieve an 80 percent average, to get a good summer job, and to buy a car.
2. Right after we moved in, we discovered we had a problem: termites.
3. Our credit card consultant asked us an interesting question after our bankruptcy: "Why don't you cut up your credit cards?"
4. Several Canadian writers are even better known abroad than they are at home: Carol Shields, Neil Bissoondath, and Michael Ondaatje are three examples.
5. There are a number of inexpensive activities that will improve physical fitness: swimming, tennis, jogging, even brisk walking.
6. Jocelyn is trying to accomplish two mutually contradictory tasks: a significant weight loss and success as a restaurant critic.
7. Several of the animals on the international list of endangered species are native to Canada: the wood bison, the northern kit fox, and the whooping crane.
8. correct
9. The majority of Canada's population is worn out and exhausted at the end of a long, hard winter, but most people are able to console themselves with one comforting thought: spring will arrive sometime in May or June.

10. There are several troublesome implications of biological engineering, but one in particular is frightening to most people: the cloning of human beings.

Exercise 34.3
1. Believe it or not, the country that produces the most films every year is India.
2. correct
3. correct
4. According to Roderick, who is several decades out of date, the only important things in life are sex, drugs, and rock 'n' roll.
5. The company's bankruptcy resulted from the CEO's management style. He relied on crisis management, seat-of-the-pants planning, and excessive profit-taking.
6. correct
7. correct
8. All most students ask is that their teachers treat them with courtesy, fairness, and respect.
9. Of course, there are always a few students who demand what no true professional will provide: special treatment.
10. In drafting the budget, we must be careful to avoid the one technique the president has said she will not entertain: deficit financing.

Answers for Chapter 35: The Semicolon (pages 415–19)

Exercise 35.1
1. incorrect
2. correct
3. incorrect
4. incorrect
5. incorrect
6. incorrect
7. correct
8. incorrect
9. incorrect
10. incorrect

Exercise 35.2
1. We've eaten all the goodies; it's time to go home.
2. correct
3. Your instructor would like to see you pass; however, there may be a small fee involved.
4. Molly is going to Chicago; she wants to appear on *Oprah*.
5. Many people dislike hockey because some of the players act like goons rather than athletes.
6. Orville tried and tried, but he couldn't get the teacher's attention.
7. correct
8. First, we'll have a cool drink; then we'll see if we can find a way to start this car.
9. Rumours of a merger had begun to circulate by five o'clock, so it's no wonder many employees looked nervous on their way home.
10. We knew the party had been a success when Uncle Morty, drunk as usual, tap-danced across the top of the piano; Aunt Madeline, who must weigh at least 80 kg, did her Ally McBeal imitation; and Biff punched out two of his cousins.

Exercise 35.3
1. Teddy won't stop crying; it seems his gerbil is missing.

2. We must organize our finances; otherwise, we'll be broke before April.

3. We had all hoped you would be able to join us; however, because you have a previous engagement, we'll just have to carry on without you.

4. A day without puns is like a day without sunshine; it leaves gloom for improvement.

5. I work on an assembly line where we believe that if a job is worth doing, it's worth doing 11,000 times a day.

6. It is not very difficult to become wealthy if you're in your early twenties; all you need to do is put the price of a pack of cigarettes a day into an RSP each year, and you'll be a millionaire by the time you retire.

7. We decided to go to a nearby restaurant for pizza; that is, we would have gone, but Norm insisted on waiting for Mairi, and by the time we got there, it was closed.

8. As a dog lover in general and an Afghan owner in particular, I have to take a lot of abuse; for example, my wife gave me a book rating the intelligence of various breeds of dog, and the Afghan ranked seventy-ninth out of seventy-nine breeds tested.

9. If you put nonsense into a computer, what comes out is nonsense; however, once the nonsense has passed through an expensive machine, few people seem willing to challenge it.

10. According to a recent *Gourmet Magazine* poll, four of the top ten restaurants in the world are in Paris; three, those ranking eighth, ninth(,) and tenth, are in the United States; and two are in Tokyo. One is in Thailand.

Answers for Chapter 36: Question and Exclamation Marks (pages 420–23)

Exercise 36.1

1. question mark
2. period
3. period
4. period
5. question mark
6. question mark
7. period
8. question mark
9. period
10. question mark

Exercise 36.2

1. exclamation mark
2. exclamation mark, exclamation mark
3. exclamation mark
4. exclamation mark, exclamation mark (or period)
5. exclamation mark and period
6. two exclamation marks (or exclamation mark and period)
7. exclamation mark (inside final quotation mark)
8. exclamation mark, exclamation mark (or exclamation mark and period)
9. exclamation mark
10. exclamation mark, exclamation mark (or exclamation mark and period)

Answers for Chapter 37: Dashes and Parentheses (pages 424–28)

Exercise 37.1

1. The members of one Aboriginal tribe in England—I've forgotten their name—painted themselves blue.

2. My purpose in moving from Vancouver to Hope—like that of hundreds of people before me—was to find affordable housing.
3. We shall have to start without her—again!
4. Skiing and skating—if you like these sports, you'll love Quebec.
5. Tending to his garden, writing his memoirs, and dining with friends—these were the pleasures Arnold looked forward to in retirement.
6. What is missing in his life is obvious—rest and relaxation!
7. Zoe should do well—in fact, I'm sure she will—in the engineering program.
8. Alexei was amazed—positively thunderstruck—when he learned Uncle Vladimir had won a million dollars.
9. Historians, diarists, and chroniclers—these are the recorders of our past.
10. Dashes—a kind of silent shout—allow you to insert an occasional exclamation into your sentences.

Exercise 37.2

1. Five of the students (I was asked not to name them) have volunteered to be peer tutors.
2. The apostrophe is explained in the unit on spelling (pages 460–66).
3. Jason complained that being a manager (he became one in March) was like being a cop.
4. I have enclosed a cheque for one hundred and fifty dollars ($150.00).
5. More members of the Canadian Armed Forces died in World War I (1914–18) than in any war before or since.
6. Although Mozart lived a relatively short time (he died when he was thirty-six), he composed hundreds of musical masterpieces.
7. As news of his "miracle cures" spread (patients began to come to him from all over the province), the country doctor had to move his clinic to a more central location.
8. The new contract provided improved working conditions, a raise in salary (5 percent), and a new dental plan.
9. Ontario and British Columbia now produce world-class wines from three small estate wineries (Inniskillin, Hillebrand, Quail's Gate) that compete and win internationally.
10. "One of the most important tools for making paper speak in your own voice is punctuation; it plays the role of body language; it helps readers hear you the way you want to be heard" (Baker 48–49).

Answers for Chapter 38: Three Suggestions for Quick Improvement (pages 429–38)

Exercise 38.2

1. desperately
2. atonement
3. rarely
4. emerging
5. positively

Exercise 38.3
1. commencement
2. movable
3. officiating
4. valuation
5. realizing

Exercise 38.4
1. regrettable
2. admitting
3. batting
4. begging
5. entailed

Exercise 38.5
1. forgetting
2. conferred
3. referring
4. stripped
5. recurrence

Exercise 38.6
1. deferring
2. remittance
3. consistency
4. concurrence
5. acquittal

Exercise 38.7
1. either, their, beliefs
2. deceived, perceive
3. conceivable, receive
4. relief, neither
5. neighbour, conceited, weird

Answers for Chapter 39: Sound-Alikes, Look-Alikes, and Spoilers (pages 439–52)

Exercise 39.1
1. course, affect
2. Are, accept
3. then, dessert
4. you're, losing
5. quite, here
6. whose, conscience
7. assured, number
8. It's, its
9. choose, course, advice
10. continual, dining

Exercise 39.2
1. simplistic, morals
2. morale, miners, fazed
3. imply, further
4. effect, disperse

5. Whose, principles, less
6. fourth, cited, weather
7. your, continually, ensures

8. conscious, much, further
9. accept, councillors, phase
10. women's, number

Answers for Chapter 40: Capital Letters (pages 453–59)

Exercise 40.1

1. **T**ime is nature's way of keeping everything from happening at once.
2. Brad whispered, "**T**here's a light in the Frankenstein house."
3. **M**y parents have a bumper sticker that reads, "**M**oney isn't everything, but it sure keeps the kids in touch."
4. Richard Harkness, writing in *The New York Times*, said "**A** committee is a group of the unwilling, picked from the unfit, to do the unnecessary."
5. **I**n conclusion, I want you to consider the words of Wendell Johnson: "*A*lways and *never* are two words you should always remember never to use."

Exercise 40.2

1. After a brief stay in the **M**aritimes, **C**aptain **T**allman and his crew sailed west up the **S**t. **L**awrence.
2. The **B**roadcast **D**epartment of **N**iagara **C**ollege has ordered six **S**ony cameras for their studios in **W**elland, **O**ntario.
3. Do you find that **V**isa is more popular than American **E**xpress when you travel to far away places such as **M**exico, **F**rance, or **J**upiter?
4. Our stay at the **S**eaview **H**otel overlooking the **P**acific **O**cean certainly beat our last vacation at the **B**ates **M**otel, where we faced west, overlooking the city dump.
5. As a member of the **A**lumni **A**ssociation I am trying to raise funds from companies like **D**isney, **G**eneral **M**otors, **C**orel, and the **CBC**, where our graduates have positions.

Exercise 40.3

1. The **C**rusades, which were religious wars between **M**uslims and **C**hristians, raged through the **M**iddle **A**ges.
2. The **H**indu religion recognizes and honours many gods; **I**slam recognizes one god, **A**llah; **B**uddhism recognizes none.
3. The **K**oran, the **B**ible, and the **T**orah agree on many principles.
4. The **J**ewish festival of **H**anukkah often occurs near the same time that **C**hristians are celebrating **C**hristmas.
5. After **W**orld **W**ar I, many **J**ews began to emigrate to Palestine, where they and the **M**uslim population soon came into conflict.

Exercise 40.4

1. My favourite months are **J**anuary and **F**ebruary because I love all **w**inter sports.
2. This **M**onday is **V**alentine's **D**ay, when messages of love are exchanged.
3. In the summer, big meals seem too much trouble; however, after **T**hanksgiving, we need lots of food to survive the winter cold.
4. A **n**ational **h**oliday named **F**lag **D**ay was once proposed, but it was never officially approved.

5. By **T**hursday, I'll have finished my **St. P**atrick's **D**ay costume.

Exercise 40.5

1. The review of my book, *The Life and Times of a Chocoholic*, published in *The Globe and Mail*, was not favourable.
2. Clint **E**astwood fans will be delighted that the two early movies that made him internationally famous, *A Fistful of Dollars* and *For a Few Dollars More*, are now available on DVD.
3. Joseph Conrad's short novel *Heart of Darkness* became the blockbuster movie *Apocalypse Now*.
4. Her poem, "**A B**right and **S**ilent **P**lace," was published in the **A**pril issue of *Landscapes* magazine.
5. Botticelli's famous painting, *Birth of Venus*, inspired my poem "**W**oman on the **H**alf **S**hell."

Exercise 40.6

1. After studying geography for two years, I began taking courses in ancient **G**reek and modern history.
2. correct
3. By taking Professor Subden's non-credit course, **I**ntroduction to **W**ine, I qualified to register for **O**enology 120 the next semester.
4. While math is her strong subject, Laurie has trouble with accounting, **E**nglish, and conversational **F**rench.
5. The prerequisite for **T**heology 210 is **I**ntroduction to **W**orld **R**eligions, taught by Professor Singh.

Answers for Chapter 41: The Apostrophe (pages 460–66)

Exercise 41.1

1. Yes, it's a long way from Halifax to Vancouver, but we've been in training for three months.
2. We're taking the train to Antigonish, and we're biking to Halifax; then we'll begin the big trip west.
3. There isn't a dry eye in the theatre when Spielberg's film reaches its climax.
4. Those two haven't made it through a meeting since the college adopted its no-smoking policy.
5. Wasn't it Mark Twain who said, "It's easy to stop smoking; I've done it dozens of times"?

Exercise 41.2

1. A floppy disk's quality is measured by its ability to store information without error.
2. Diplomatic ambassadors' wives or husbands are often as important to a mission's success as the ambassadors themselves.
3. Near Chicoutimi is one of the country's most beautiful parks, where the skills of canoeists, fishermen, and wildlife photographers can be put to the test on a summer's day.

4. The Leafs' forward and the Canadiens' defenceman were exchanged during the last day's trading at the NHL meetings.
5. Janis'(s) career got its start when she sang seafarers' songs in the yacht club's dining lounge.

Exercise 41.3
1. you're, your, your
2. Someone's, whose
3. Brothers', today's
4. people's, workers', sides'
5. turtle's, turtle's, it's, its, yours

Answers for Chapter 42: The Hyphen (pages 467–70)

Exercise 42.1
1. Mei decided to sublet her fifth-floor apartment.
2. Anwar claims he is allergic to classical music but addicted to **hip-hop** music.
3. Charest won most of the ethnic vote, which gave him a **two-thirds** majority in a **hard-fought** contest.
4. **Hand-knit** sweaters are usually more expensive than **factory-produced** ones.
5. In 1950, at the age of **forty-seven**, George Orwell died of tuberculosis.

Exercise 42.2
1. For months after Nicolae Ceauçescu was **overthrown**, the world was shocked by revelations of the repression suffered by the Rumanian people.
2. Would you **relay** this message to Mr. Chan: the masons would like to **re-lay** the bricks this evening.
3. Our **next-door** neighbour teaches in a **high school**, but she does not like to be introduced as a **high-school** teacher.
4. A **face-to-face** meeting with an **anti-intellectual** always gets my adrenalin going.
5. Because Angela was an **attorney-at-law** and had once been an **all-Canadian** athlete, her former coach was not surprised when she became **minister of recreation**.

Index

Credits

This page constitutes an extension of the copyright page. We have made every effort to trace the ownership of all copyrighted material and to secure permission from copyright holders. In the event of any question arising as to the use of any material, we will be pleased to make the necessary correction in future printing. Thanks are due to the following authors, publishers, and agents for permission to use the material indicated.

Page 6: Excerpted from *The Autobiography of Bertrand Russell,* Bertrand Russell, Routledge, Bertrand Russell Peace Foundation. Reprinted by permission.

Pages 18 and 189–91: Excerpted from David Bodanis, *The Secret House: 24 Hours in the Strange and Unexpected World in Which We Spend Our Days and Nights.* Copyright © 1986. Reprinted by permission of International Creative Management, Inc.

Page 19: Excerpted from *Lee Valley Tools Catalogue,* Tenth Anniversary Issue. Copyright © 1987–1988. Reprinted by permission of Lee Valley Tools, Ltd.

Pages 21–22 and 303–10: Jess Friedland, "The Evolution of Moral Balance in Charlotte Brontë's *Jane Eyre.*" Reprinted by permission of the author.

Page 69: Excerpted from Martin Luther King, Jr., "Three Types of Resistance to Oppression," in *Stride Toward Freedom.* Reprinted by arrangement with The Heirs to the Estate of Martin Luther King, Jr., c/o Writers House, Inc. as agent for the proprietor. © 1958 by Martin Luther King, Jr., © renewed 1986 by Coretta Scott King.

Page 70: Excerpted from Barry Callaghan, "Canadian Wry," in *Canadian Content.* Copyright © October 1985.

Page 70: Excerpted from Ravi Shankar, "Studying Music in India," in *My Music, My Life.* Copyright © 1968 by Kinnara School of Indian Music, Inc.

Pages 74, 82–83, and 265: Excerpted from A NATURAL HISTORY OF THE SENSES by Diane Ackerman, copyright © 1990 by Diane Ackerman. Used by permission of Random House, Inc.

Pages 77–78: Excerpted from Thomas Hurka, "Should Morality by a Struggle? Ancient vs. Modern Ideas about Ethics." Copyright © 1994. Reprinted by permission.

Pages 79 and 81: Excerpted from Martin Luther King, Jr., "The Dimensions of a Complete Life," in *The Measure of a Man.* Reprinted by arrangement with The Heirs to the Estate of Martin Luther King, Jr., c/o Writers House, Inc. as agent for the proprietor. © 1958 by Martin Luther King, Jr., © renewed 1986 by Coretta Scott King.

Page 83: Excerpted from Nell Waldman, "Flunking with Style," in *Canadian Content.* Copyright © October 1985.

Page 84: Excerpted from Pierre Berton, "Baked Beans," in *Canadian Content.* Copyright © October 1985.

Pages 143–44: Wade Davis, "The White Darkness." Reprinted by permission of Wade Davis.

Pages 144–46: Witold Rybczynski, "A National Billboard," in *Looking Around: A Journey through Architecture.* Copyright © 1992 by Witold Rybczynski. Reprinted by permission.

Pages 160–65: Carol Geddes, "Growing Up Native," in *Canadian Content,* 4th ed. Copyright © 1990 by Carol Geddes. Reprinted with the permission of the author.

Pages 172–73: Paul Allen, "Forging: The Black Art." Reprinted by permission of the author.